5 95
philosophy

FROM GEORGES SOREL

From Georges Sorel

Essays in Socialism and Philosophy

Edited with an Introduction by
JOHN L. STANLEY
and Translated by
JOHN AND CHARLOTTE STANLEY

New York
OXFORD UNIVERSITY PRESS
1976

Printed in the United States of America

FOREWORD

There are many persons whose suggestions and labors have helped the editor to form this volume. In particular, he wishes to thank Irving Louis Horowitz, whose idea it was, and Robert A. Nisbet for his criticism and encouragement. Donna Beckage and Ruth Burke assisted with the translations of "Necessity and Fatalism in Marxism" and portions of *Reflections on Violence;* Thomas P. Jenkin, Neal Wood, Sally Dufek, and Peter Steinberger contributed valuable ideas.

The editor is grateful to Mr. Alain Hénon of the University of California Press for permission to reprint parts of *The Illusions of Progress.*

All of the other writings herein, including those from the *Reflections on Violence,* have been newly translated for this edition.

A grant from the National Endowment for the Humanities allowed the editor access to materials at the Bibliothèque Nationale, and an intramural grant from the University of California, Riverside, made possible further research as well as clerical assistance.

J.L.S.

Riverside, California
March 1975

Contents

FROM GEORGES SOREL

Editor's Introduction

I ON DESCRIBING SOREL

Several years ago the present writer published an English translation of Georges Sorel's *Les Illusions du progrès*.[1] This was the first of Sorel's major works to be made available in English since T. E. Hulme translated his *Réflexions sur la violence* nearly half a century ago, but it has become apparent that something of a revived interest in Sorel is occurring in Britain and America; several lengthy studies of Sorel have now appeared in influential literary and scholarly journals.[2]

Les Illusions du progrès was published as a history of an idea and may be considered a sourcebook for Sorel's ideas; but, focused as it is on the history of a single concept, though grantedly quite wide-ranging, it cannot do justice to the depth and scope of an author of over a dozen books and many hundreds of articles and reviews ranging from the problems of experimental physics to the sociology of primitive Christianity. In lesser degree, the *Réflexions* presents similar problems. This work, originally published in the same year as the *Illusions*, is concerned with the myth of the general strike; and although some segments contain excellent statements of Sorel's position on philosophical issues, others relate primarily to the questions of socialism current in 1906. Indeed, since in Sorel's other writings we see very little of this particular myth as such, the *Réflexions* may be viewed as a *livre de circonstance* more than many of his other writings. This is not to deny the importance of the work, but to stress that Sorel wrote much else of importance.

This volume attempts to correct whatever imbalance excessive reliance on *Réflexions sur la violence* may have produced, and although I will pay close attention to Sorel's *chef d'œuvre* in this Introduction, the scope of the articles we have translated should prove to most readers that Sorel is more than merely interested in the myth of the general strike and is more than primarily a theorist of "violence."

The selection of articles to translate was a difficult task, and critics may quarrel with some of the choices I have made, though it would be well to keep in mind that Sorel himself did some of the selecting. Many of the articles presented here are those he republished in later collections: much of the *Matériaux d'une théorie du prolétariat* and all of the *Saggi di critica del marxismo* were compendia of works previously published. I have included large portions of these books in the present collection. In addition, I have translated a small section of Sorel's book on Socrates, a discrete article on the ethics of socialism, a large section from *De l'utilité du pragmatisme*, the first chapter of *Les Illusions du progrès* as well as newly translated selections from the *Réflexions*.

I shall pay no little attention to Sorel's writings on Marxist theory. These were, in many respects, ahead of their time, anticipating contemporary viewpoints, even though Sorel did not share in the fashionable emphasis on "alienation" that has permeated Marxist criticism today. But, if this is so, it may be asked, why has comparatively little attention been paid to these studies? Part of the answer may lie in the fact that a peculiarly disturbing quality in Sorel sometimes makes it difficult for contemporary social theorists to deal with him. Sorel is a moralist who sees no reason to separate fact and value in social commentary. This is a characteristic that many critics of sociological and economic writing find difficult to understand and appreciate in a period that has seen the rise of "systems analysis" and mathematical techniques in sociology, political science, psychology and even philosophy. Sorel's moral severity is amplified by an extremely didactic style which leaves the superficial reader with the impression that he is reading political tracts rather than elevated theory—and, as we have said, excessive reliance on the *Réflexions sur la violence* does not help this situation.

More importantly, however, many writers view Sorel as an irrelevant voice of the past or as a reactionary of the worst order. In very recent articles and reviews he has been labeled as a precursor of the modern extreme "right" by excellent writers, who offer little more evidence for Sorel's "Fascism" than his love of Wagner, his detestation of Cartesianism, or his assertion that we must carry socialism in our own hearts. The last postulate was used by one writer to indicate that Sorel stood at the roots of European reaction because Hitler said the same thing.[3] There is a curious lack of logical rigor in many of these criticisms, for they emphasize similarities without mentioning vast disparities between the philosophy of Sorel and that of Fascism.

One of the strongest statements of this position is found in an article by J. L. Talmon entitled "The Legacy of Georges Sorel." Talmon makes the following four assertions: (1) Sorel "comes close to Fascism" because his doctrines are not genuinely socialistic but rather "a Nietzschean repudiation of bourgeois mediocrity" in which "Sorel expects a revaluation of all values and the enthronement of a heroic civilization to come from the proletariat"; (2) Sorel flirted with *Action Française*, the *Cercle Proudhon* and other rightist groups from 1910 to 1914; (3) his followers, especially Georges Valois, had Fascist and Nazi sympathies; (4) Mussolini and the French Fascist Ramon Fernandes gave him credit as their inspiration.[4]

To this I answer:

(1) The relation between Sorel and Nietzsche is not as clear-cut as Talmon implies. Though in his *Réflexions sur la violence* Sorel cites Nietzsche as a thinker who upholds the heroic virtues and hence confirms Talmon's assertion that "the impulse" of both thinkers was the same (or similar), Sorel is not attacking the bourgeois class *per se*— only its degenerate form. He considers it quite incorrect to say that the proletariat constitutes the sole vehicle for the transvaluation of all values. Sorel maintains that the American capitalist is also the repository of the essential virtues. Furthermore, in the *Réflexions* Sorel mocks a comparison of the proletarian with Nietzsche's Superman;[5] the comparison was made by none other than Jean Jaurès, reportedly! In any event, I had thought that the sub-philosophic superstition that Nietzsche was a precursor of the Nazis had been laid to rest. This accusation points to the logical and methodological horrors of a kind of intellectual guilt by association, a philosophic McCarthyism. Sorel phrased it— referring to scholastic formulations, to be sure—that ideas "end by furnishing justification to groups whose existence their authors had not even suspected." Not only is the proposition true with respect to Sorel, but any other view leads to our maintaining that Marx was a Bolshevik.

(2) Sorel's flirtation with rightist groups was temporary, and Pierre Andreu, his biographer, reports that Sorel ended by condemning *L'Indépendance* as "reactionary." Even Talmon admits that Sorel's association with the French right in any direct sense was "reluctant."[6]

(3) Talmon correctly maintains that Georges Valois, a Fascist, though one who became a loyal patriot, was a close follower of Sorel; but he admits that Valois also had mentors not common with Sorel, such as

Auguste Comte, whom Sorel loathed. More important, Talmon ignores the closest follower of Sorel and the nearest equivalent of Frederick Engels to Sorel's Marx: he was not Valois but Eduard Berth. Berth wrote for Marcel Rivière, Sorel's publisher, and Sorel wrote a preface to Berth's *Les Méfaits des intellectuels.* In this book Berth said, in a fore-word to the second edition written, to be sure, after Sorel's death, "The War irretrievably shattered *Maurrasisme*; and this is undoubtedly why a man like Valois cannot remain in the ranks of *Action Française.* Valois actually wanted to instigate a movement similar to Italian Fascism in France; but the conditions of France are not those of Italy; Fascism is an entirely Italian phenomenon, and I do not think of the future of a 'French Fascism.' " Furthermore, Berth stressed, "We must not forget the radical difference which separates *Fascist violence* from *Sorelian violence.* The latter is the true violence, that which tends to destroy the traditional state and institute a *free order.* The former is by definition only a *bourgeois force* tending, on the contrary, to restore the tradi-tional state and consequently to consolidate the bourgeois order...." And again, "Neither Fascism nor Communism has succeeded in restor-ing national or revolutionary values except in a rather regressive re-gime."[7] This he wrote in 1926, four years after Sorel's death. Later, in 1931, in *Du "Capital" aux "Réflexions sur la violence,"* he asserted: "It is thus absolutely vain and ridiculous to want to transform Sorel into 'the spiritual father of Fascism.' . . . One thing ought to be most clear: proletarian violence has nothing in common, according to Sorel, with either Blanquist or Fascist violence; its acts are only comparable to the acts of war of an army on the march."[8] It might be added that confus-ing Sorelianism with Fascism is to make the same mistake as to single out war as the most characteristic trait of Fascism rather than internal state terror, which Sorel abhorred.[9]

(4) Finally, to make much, as does Talmon, of the fact that Sorel was praised by Fascists, and especially Mussolini, ignores Ernst Nolte's research on the question: the closeness of Mussolini to Sorel is over-drawn and "not nearly so close and cordial as was later claimed. There was, of course, a time when he called him 'our master.' But when Sorel made the famous switch to Maurras in 1910 Mussolini broke vitupera-tively with the 'pensioned bookworm' and did not refer to him again until 1914. It was not Sorel but Marx whom he called 'the magnificent philosopher of working class violence.' "[10] So, according to Talmon's logic, it is really Marx who should be considered the precursor of Fascism.

If one were to use political allegiances as a means of evaluating a person's social theory, the best argument to sustain Sorel's "Fascism" would be his brief flirtation with the rightist *Action Française* just prior to World War I; but Sorel's connection with members of this group was very short-lived and was followed by an acceptance of Leninist Communism. Indeed, it might even be asked whether the seemingly quixotic changes in Sorel's political allegiances are the cause for suspicion that we are dealing with a less than serious writer. However, I shall attempt to show in the following pages that there is a strong thread of consistency winding its way through Sorel's writings. Though it would be too much to call his works the components of a grand system, they offer a group of perspectives which make Sorel a very interesting social and political theorist. The more we read Sorel, the less relevant his biography or even his political allegiance of the moment becomes, for Sorel, like Marx, is best regarded not as a propagandist and proponent of "engagement" but as a highly suggestive social theorist, in the grand manner.

As an intellectual Sorel often fools us when we attempt to classify him. Unlike his intellectual predecessor, Pierre-Joseph Proudhon, he did not come from a poor family, nor could he, like Proudhon, be called "working-class." Indeed, one writer attributes Sorel's apparently disturbing beliefs to the "peasant patrist society" of his youth;[11] but there is more to Sorel than that, and it is often hazardous in the history of thought to attempt to connect a man's social background with his ideas. Though it did not in this case, such efforts often lead to a mistaken emphasis on "causation" and an illogical focus on biography and sociology rather than on the ideas themselves; it is a rather elegant equivalent of the *argumentum ad hominem*. If we were to place Sorel in any category, we should call him a provincial petit-bourgeois and a product of the elitist education of the French mandarinate, but his biography does not help us understand him very well.

II   THE DEVELOPMENT OF SOREL'S THOUGHT

Georges Sorel was born in Cherbourg in November 1847, raised by a traditionally pious mother, the daughter of the mayor of Barfleur, and a businessman father of unknown ancestry. Sorel's careful biographer, Pierre Andreu, speculates that the bankruptcy of his father might have made Sorel more disposed to accept socialist ideas because it "separated him from the life of his class";[12] but there is very little to sustain that conclusion. Sorel's youth was the very picture of bourgeois placidity. During summer vacations, he would stay at the seashore at the home of his grandmother with his brother and his cousin Albert Sorel, later to become one of the great French historians and President of the French Senate. Indeed, Georges retained quite conventional political views until long after his formal schooling was completed.

He was educated at the College of Cherbourg, from which he grad-
uated with distinction in 1864. In the same year he came to Paris to
enroll in *l'Ecole Polytechnique,* the summit of French technical and scientific achievement. In 1867 he joined the Bureau of Bridges and High-
ways as an engineer, a dispassionate servant of the Empire (with which
he was then in vague sympathy) and subsequently of the Third Republic. After moving from place to place, in 1879 Sorel finally settled in
Perpignan in the Eastern Pyrenees, where he spent the remaining years
of his short working career. Though his father was not a financial success, his mother seems to have had some money, and shortly after her
death in 1887 he retired on a modest inheritance as well as on his
state pension.

Nothing in this conventional career would have predicted the making
of a revolutionary theorist. Sorel apparently performed his engineering
tasks with efficiency and diligence and, on his retirement, received a
letter of commendation from the Perpignan Municipal Council, and was
made a Chevalier of the Legion of Honor in 1891.

What makes a man think as he does? Edward Shils speculates that
Sorel's engineering career led to his hostility to intellectualism and his
respect for experienced workmen and technocrats over liberal arts
graduates.[13] This could well be true, but it does not explain Sorel's
concern for the "heroic" qualities to be found on the workshop floor.
His focus on heroism is one of the mainstays of his thought, and a
society of engineers does not call to most minds the sublime.

Class analysis certainly does not help us uncover the social basis of
Sorel's thought: to begin with, there are vast ideational differences between Georges Sorel and his cousin Albert despite the similarity in their
backgrounds. To proclaim that Sorel thought as he did because of his
capacity as an "independent intellectual" is only a non-explanation—a
confession of failure on the part of the sociology of knowledge. To be
sure, Sorel was content in his retirement to roam the fields of thought,
the Socrates of the Latin Quarter, living quietly at Boulogne-sur-Seine
near Paris, but he is interesting as an original figure, not as a member
of a certain social group. The broadest and most deterministic theory
of the sociology of knowledge does not tell us why it was Georges Sorel
who chose to concentrate on certain events and ignore others. It tells us
little about the positive and more subtle aspects of his thought beyond
the obvious fact that it was a mixture of unknown proportions of biography, history, literary tradition, class, and perhaps a thousand other
factors.

What, for example, attracted Sorel to his own unique type of "socialism" and thence to the idea of the myth of the general strike? And why
did he encase this theory in a severely Puritanical moralism, when some

men in similar circumstances lived, and justified in their writings, a highly sybaritic life? Andreu speculates that it may have been the influence of his life's companion, Marie-Euphasie David.[14] Practically illiterate and two years his senior, it may have been she who inspired the character of his work by her devotion to the poor, her personal fidelity, compassion and religious severity. Certainly she was close to the model of virtue against which Sorel measures so many of the events and personages of his time. His *Réflexions sur la violence* is dedicated to her memory as "entirely inspired by her spirit," and Sorel implies in a concluding note to the fourth edition of the work that she revealed his genius to him.

Was the disapproval of a society which caused Sorel to live with Marie-Euphasie in a "common-law" relationship even more important in causing him to revile the hypocrisy of bourgeois society? Marie's lowly birth may have prevented formal marriage between her and the graduate of the *Ecole Polytechnique.* Yet Sorel admired many of the characteristics of traditional society expressed in "tribal" conventions. His earlier writings are devoid of "socialist" concepts as such, and a rebellion against bourgeois society does not explain why he selected certain aspects of socialism and rejected others. Andreu lists all of the titles of the books Sorel borrowed from the library at Perpignan, and the works of Marx were not among them. It is evident that he read Proudhon, and indeed *Le Procès de Socrate* is infused with Proudhonian notions rather than specifically Marxist or socialist ones; but this only indicates, finally, that it is intellectual history and the ideas of Proudhon that provided Sorel with the basis of his social thought. Although Marie-Euphasie may have inspired Sorel, it is Proudhon who is cited most frequently in his early writings, and she is never mentioned in his "Confessions." The extent to which his biography "explains" Sorel's gravitation toward particular viewpoints remains so obscure that even Andreu finally throws up his hands. We will never know, he says, why Sorel adopted certain views.[15]

The problems of determining the "causes" of Sorel's thought are further complicated by the changes in perspective that he underwent during his writing career. Indeed, it is possible to outline at least six stages in Sorel's intellectual and political development.

The first stage includes Sorel's writings through 1889 or 1890. His first two books, *Contribution à l'étude profane de la Bible* and *Le Procès de Socrate,* were both published in 1889, two years before his retirement. It appears from these works that Sorel was, with many of his countrymen, caught up in the despair that swept France after the debacle of the Franco-Prussian war. (Perhaps it is for this reason that he found appealing the writings of Ernest Renan pleading for a new heroism.) As we have noted, nothing specifically socialist is found in these early books; they are devoted, rather, to the heroic qualities of ancient civilizations. Yet it is these writings which set the tone of Sorel's work, however much he was later professedly aware of their short-comings. In these two works, Sorel establishes himself as a moralist—a position from which he was never to swerve. He opens the preface to the *Contribution à l'étude profane* by saying that "The Bible is the book which can best serve the instruction of the people, initiate the heroic life, combat the deleterious tendencies of utilitarianism and arrest the propagation of the revolutionary idea."[16] He is also "conservative," if we use the conventional standards of liberalism to evaluate him. No civil libertarian, he argues that Socrates undermined the virtues of the ancient polis; his punishment was ultimately a just one.

It was the qualities of heroism pronounced by Proudhon that stimulated Sorel to view the heroic life as functionally related to productive life, and this emphasis on the importance of production led Sorel to begin an investigation of what he called socialism in 1890. In 1892, he wrote a long article on Proudhon[17] that may be considered to mark the beginning of the second stage of his development, and from 1894 to 1897 Sorel spent most of his time editing and writing for two socialist journals, *Ere Nouvelle* and *Devenir Social*. His purpose, he later said, "was to probe Marxism in depth."[18]

In his examination of socialism, Sorel uncovered the same problems of definition of that word that we find today: he was constantly wrangling with the distinctions among state socialism, economic social-ism and the working-class movement; it was the last that Sorel came to recognize as the "true" socialism, considering the others faulty imperson-ations of Marx's true intentions. As will become apparent in the follow-ing pages, the movement itself was of prime concern to Sorel rather than its economic return. Socialism, to Sorel, had to distinguish itself from mere state redistribution of wealth. For Marx, this was an un-necessary distinction; parliamentary democratic parties in his day did not speak for the working class. With the development of what was called "social democracy," and the active participation of socialist parties in politics, on the other hand, it was increasingly difficult to proclaim democracy a "bourgeois mask." By 1890 or so democracy, socialism, progress, reason and statism all seemed to become increasingly blurred into a dry academicism which obscured the exclusively working-class nature of genuine socialism.

The third stage of Sorel's development was marked by an increasing awareness of the problem of socialist orthodoxy. In 1897 he resigned from *Devenir Social*, disenchanted with its orthodoxy. At that time, the official German Social Democracy as personified in Karl Kautsky had influenced the entire European movement. Academic, deterministic and transfixed by science, its spokesmen appeared to abandon all moral aspiration and to pursue narrow economic ends almost exclusively. Sorel sided with Eduard Bernstein's attacks on official Marxism, insisting that it was not Marx's "predictions" that were important but giving the workers a better life in every sense of the word.[19]

In Sorel's view, Bernstein was attempting to restore moral integrity to Marxism and, because he was closer to understanding reality than Kautsky, to science as well. Thus, for a time Sorel did see some hope in a kind of parliamentary revisionism. "I thought then," he recalled later, "that a temporary coalition established in a quite determined goal and alien to economic considerations between men of groups regarded as fatal enemies by Marxist theorists would not necessarily hurt the autonomy of socialist thought."[20] But even in this period Sorel came to express his desire to see socialism autonomous: in 1898 appeared *L'Avenir socialiste des syndicats*.[21] In it Sorel discusses the self-government of socialist institutions freed from state interference and from the academic Marxists. It would seem that his inclination toward social democracy was tactical, an alliance formed on the rebound from his disenchantment with *Devenir Social*.

Sorel's final breach with political socialism came in about 1901. This year begins the fourth period of Sorel's thought—the period of "socialist autonomy" and disillusionment with politics in general. The precipitating event was the Dreyfus Affair, the facts of which are well known. Alfred Dreyfus, an army captain, was wrongly convicted of espionage; because new evidence was uncovered implicating a Major Esterhazy as the real culprit, the original conviction was placed under a cloud of suspicion. The army failed to exonerate Dreyfus, and Esterhazy was acquitted. By 1898 practically the whole of French society had become polarized on the question—the left staunchly supporting Dreyfus and demanding a reopening of the case, the right defending the increasingly beleaguered army. The rightists acted in such a way as to make it appear that they were attacking the Republic itself rather than the Dreyfusards, or so the partisans of Dreyfus made it appear. The latter saw in the case an ideal opportunity to gain power by "defending the Republic." The many leftist radicals coalesced around the Dreyfus cause in order to excoriate the Army with the same demagogic shrillness of earlier French republican governments in their attacks on the Church, and they assumed power by the same method—or so it seemed to Sorel.

At first Sorel was sympathetic to the Dreyfus cause and its socialist allies. But in June 1899 Millerand, who orchestrated the coalition of Dreyfus factions, was invited into the new government by Premier Waldeck-Rousseau; it was the most leftist government since the Com-

mune of 1870, and Sorel dubbed it "the Dreyfus revolution."[22] When
the government, in July 1901, passed a law limiting the autonomy of the
religious orders, Sorel saw a similarity between the government of his
time and the repressive Jacobinism of earlier times. It seemed apparent
to him by then that the "autonomy" of socialism was being swallowed
by the office-seeking and corruption of what Sorel called "the democratic ocean."[23] He believed that the socialist leader Jean Jaurès was
leading socialism to a kind of Jacobinism and statist dictatorship and
was substituting economic redistribution and confiscation for the demands of the Third Estate in the earlier Revolution. Sorel saw as the
only hope the creation of a non-party, non-parliamentary workers' movement—by approaching the revision of Marxism by a method other than
Bernstein's. It is this that stands at the basis of his attack on French
democracy.

Only by thoroughly freeing itself from statism could socialism effectuate moral reform. The institutions seen by Sorel as best able to
carry out this reform in France were the unions, or "syndicates," and
their corollary organizations known as the *bourses du travail*, or labor
exchanges. The labor exchanges were, roughly speaking, employment
agencies run by the unions independently of parallel state organizations. Together with the unions, the *bourses* established themselves as
virtual "states within states." Only in 1902, with the appearance of
Fernand Pelloutier's book *L'Histoire des bourses du travail*,[24] to which
Sorel had written an introduction, did he, by his own confession, come
to grips with the true differences between what he called "proletarian
socialism and political socialism."[25] In any event, the insights of this
period led to Sorel's greatest productivity. In 1904 he wrote *Le Système
historique de Renan*, and in the following year he joined the board of
the journal *Mouvement Socialiste*, in whose pages in 1906 *Réflexions
sur la violence* and *Les Illusions du progrès* first appeared.

The fifth stage in Sorel's thinking began in about 1907. The May
1906 general strike in which hundreds of thousands of French workers
laid down their tools (and which coincided with the original publication of the last chapters of the *Réflexions*) gave way to a series of long
and bloody specific strikes the following year. They mark the beginning
of a period of disillusionment for Sorel. The general strike had lost
its universal character, its heroism, and had been replaced by bitterness and hostility. By 1908 in Villeneuve-Saint-Georges and Auquonte,
nine strikers had been killed and 69 soldiers and strikers wounded.
Clemenceau had employed the most extreme methods of repression, and
Aristide Briand had used all his subtlety and persuasive powers to
seduce the syndicates into abandoning their old rigor. In 1909, Victor
Griffuelhes was forced out of his post as the militant head of the Gen-

eral Confederation of Labor. With the checking of a number of strikes
by postmen and railwaymen, it appeared that ten years of heroic
struggle had left the working class disoriented and tired. To Sorel union
activity now seemed directed more toward raising salaries than toward
maintaining an independent existence. The proletariat was becoming
bourgeoisified, hence sapped of its moral strength.

In 1909, also, Sorel abandoned *Le Mouvement Socialiste*, though he
never abandoned his desire for an autonomous working-class movement.
It seemed to him that no one but himself, with perhaps a few followers,
was willing to bring to society the moral sensitivity that had originally
attracted him to the socialist movement. From this time we may date
Sorel's period of deepest pessimism and despair—a period that has
been the most controversial of all his stages of thought because it was
the time in which he flirted with what was later known as the "pre-
Fascist" right. At about the time of Sorel's departure from *Le Mouvement Socialiste*, Georges Valois published his *La Monarchie et la classe
ouvrière*, in which he suggested an alliance between syndicalism and
royalism. This idea impressed Sorel and stimulated the beginning of the
enigmatic "Fascist" period of Sorel's writings. In a letter to Benedetto
Croce, Sorel wrote of his distaste for his association with them but also
of his deep admiration for the intelligence of a group of Royalists who
had gathered around the journal *Action Française*. "It seems to me," he
wrote to Maurras, one of the Royalist luminaries, "that your criticism of
contemporary experience well justifies what you have established: 'In
modern France, the traditional monarchy would be the sole institution
able to carry out the immense tasks that the present theorists of the
modern state assign to the government of a great country.'"[26]

But clearly it was not the statist aspects of Maurras's theory which
appealed to the philosopher of syndicalism. As he said to Jean Variot,
"I am not a prophet; I do not know if Maurras will bring back the
king of France and it is not that which interests me. What I am concerned with is that he confronts the dull and reactionary bourgeoisie in
making it ashamed of being defeated and in trying to give a doctrine to
it."[27] Sorel's "monarchy" is, therefore, quite similar to the myth of the
general strike in that it is a pragmatic means of inculcating more heroic
virtues. With the failure of syndicalism, Sorel turned to monarchism in
the hope that it would perform the mission syndicalism had so far failed
to do.

A further insight into the reasons for his temporary flirtation with the
rightists can be found in Sorel's letter to Lanzillo in 1910: "I am scolded
for having hailed the renaissance of patriotism after having said that
the syndicalism I have defended is anti-patriotic, but there are also
certain facts that we must recognize. . . . In order to judge a movement,

it is necessary to place oneself in it and acquire an intelligent sympathy for it; without this one cannot get to the basis of things. . . . It is only this detestable democratic education that prevents us from seeing this."[28]

This peculiarly Gallic statement of *verstehen* did not assuage the constant uneasiness that Sorel felt in the presence of the extreme reactionaries. For one thing, according to Sorel, they did not understand Proudhon any better than did democrats. Their peculiar understanding of virtue was, to him, more statist and more militarist than Proudhon's (at least as Sorel understood Proudhon). For Sorel, as for Proudhon, the state was never an *end* as it was for the royalists, but only a device. At any rate, Sorel confined himself to a single contribution to *Action Française*, an article on Péguy published in 1910.[29]

In the following year Jean Variot established the journal *L'Indépendance* especially for Sorel. Despite the tone of his article entitled "Several Jewish Pretensions,"[30] Sorel was as much disturbed by the character of the new journal as he had been about that of *Action Française*. In the end, Sorel simply was neither a reactionary nor an ultra-nationalist nor even a very good anti-Semite; and by the eve of the first World War, Sorel had ceased writing for *L'Indépendance*.

His final break with the rightists came with the Great War itself. The rightists supported the war in a "sacred union" with the other parties, proving again to Sorel how movements of opposition could be swallowed easily by democracy. For himself, although the warrior ethic appealed to him, World War I increased his despair because of his doubt that anyone would realize its meaning.[31] Rather than an arena for heroism, the war seemed to him bureaucratic carnage designed specifically to bolster the power of the state at the expense of the working classes; the rhetoric of the war was filled with the "creative hatred" and demagoguery that Sorel despised: its soldiers were "mercenaries engaged by the plutocracies of the Entente." When the Entente failed in its attempt to suppress Bolshevism, Sorel was stimulated by the Bolsheviks' success against overwhelming odds. Furthermore, he was under the (quite illusory) impression that Lenin had strengthened the autonomy of the workers through the Soviets. Here at last, it seemed, a vehicle for the rebirth of the great virtues had been discovered.

In his remaining years, from 1918 until his death in 1922, Sorel was sympathetic to the Communist cause, his final articles appearing in Communist journals. "Cursed be the plutocratic democracies which starve Russia!," he wrote. "I am only an old man whose life is at the mercy of slight accidents, but may I, before descending into the tomb, see humiliated the arrogant bourgeois democracies, today cynically triumphant."[32] Had he lived, he would have seen still another apparent repository of virtue wrecked at the hands of political ambition. Alone in a small Paris apartment, Sorel died in October 1922 at the age of seventy-four.

It is an interesting biography, not, as we have said, because of the uneventful course of Sorel's engineering career, but because of the intellectual transmigration that took place after his retirement. It is the variety of "stages," or tendencies, in Sorelian thought that makes succinct interpretation of it so difficult and challenging. What sense can we make of a man who speaks of social revolution one year and of monarchy the next; of independence from the state in one breath and of tradition and community in subsequent utterances? Writers looking for "contradictions" in Sorelian thought will find no resistance from the writer himself, who not only confessed to such changes but flaunted them. In *Matériaux d'une théorie du prolétariat* he said, "I have never hidden variations in my thought and one can do nothing but admit that I have always conducted my research in complete good faith."[33]

Furthermore, Sorel's writing style does not earn him any award. In the *Réflexions* he maintained that the "incorrigible vice" of his prose was due to his continual effort "to escape the constraints of what had previously been constructed for everyone, in order to find what is personal in it. To me, it seems interesting to put in my notebooks only what I have not encountered elsewhere. I willingly avoid the transitions because they are always found among commonplaces."[34] Sorel thought it was better to appeal to a few readers to stimulate personal inquiry: "I do not think that I praise myself needlessly in saying that I have sometimes succeeded in stimulating the spirit of invention in my readers; and it is the spirit of invention which it is above all necessary to provoke in the world. It is better to have obtained this result than to have gained the banal approbation of people who repeat formulas and enslave their thought in scholastic disputes."[35]

The question of Sorel's originality is perplexing partly because of his style and partly because so much of his writing consists in criticism of others. But the careful student will find something fascinating in this writer. Inventiveness is indeed there, and it is this very creativity that makes categorizing Sorel such a challenging undertaking.

In the following section I shall attempt to sketch the intellectual background of Sorel's ideas, for it is here, I think, more than in his biography or his politics, that the basis of his thought can be found.

III   INTELLECTUAL BACKGROUND*

The intellectual influences on Georges Sorel can be divided roughly into three categories: the early influences, notably Renan and Proudhon,

* See Chapter 7, section 2 and Chapter 6, section 1.

who provided him with the moral basis of his thought; the later influences—especially Bergson and William James—who gave him the means by which his ideas could be applied to the contemporary social world at various times; and, as a sort of interstice, Marxism.

The famous "variations" in Sorel's thought are due in large part to the shifting emphasis he places on one of the later influences as opposed to another at various times. Thus, in the *Réflexions sur la violence*, Bergson receives great attention while in the *Utilité du pragmatisme*, the thought of James is emphasized. In the same vein, the use to which Marx is put varies with historical circumstances. In 1898 Sorel is a reformist socialist but after the Dreyfus Revolution, as we have seen, he abandons the political arena altogether. Thus in the earlier period Bernstein's critical revision of Marx leads Sorel to conclusions different from those in the later times when he uses Marx to justify direct action through syndicalism. But it is safe to say that after 1898 and his resignation from *Devenir Social*, Sorel rarely bothers to renounce one position as it is being supplanted by another. Instead, his thought consists of layers or tendencies, sometimes emphasizing one component, sometimes another.

The common thread in this process is provided by the early influences on Sorel's thought which give him a thoroughgoing moral outlook from which he rarely, if ever, strays. This outlook can be described fundamentally as an offshoot of the intellectual tradition of the French *moralistes*, most specifically those who wrote about political and religious matters with an eye to the "decadence" of existing society. But care must be taken not to include all moralists in this stable of Sorelian influences. Only the most severe of them seemed to appeal to Sorel, which is why it is dangerous to look for really close parallels with Rousseau. To be sure, both Rousseau and Sorel saw the importance of a simple society of limited size, of rigid and severe morals; both were "anti-intellectual" and opposed to the idea of progress; both saw virtue resting in a regime of warrior-producers; and, in a way, for both "the heart has its reasons." But Sorel's debt to Rousseau had to be filtered through pessimism and an abhorrence of abstractions: for Sorel, Rousseau's concept of the general will embodies all the worst features of the chicanery and double-talk of philosophic politicians.[36] Sorel notes that Rousseau would have been horrified at the use to which the Jacobins put this idea, but that its very vagueness encouraged this misuse. For these reasons, Sorel approves of Joseph de Maistre's condemnation of Rousseau's abstract man.[37] It might be objected that both Sorel and de Maistre were closer to Rousseau than either was willing to admit; as anti-rationalists both could find comparisons in the ideas of the "father of romanticism." But Sorel rejected the notion of "natural

sympathy," or of sentimentalizing about the downtrodden, to stress that
only effort and sacrifice can bring about social improvement.

We should also note Sorel's expressed preference for classicism as
opposed to romanticism in literature. He lauds Corneille's subordination
of passion to duty.[38] He writes sympathetically of Boileau's satires
against the fashionable partisans of literary "progress" in the seventeenth
century, even though the Romantics attempted to rehabilitate some of
the victims of the satires.[39] But Rousseau, too, had scoffed at the notion
of progress in any field, and it may well be that Sorel is closer to him
than he realized.

In any event, while Sorel obviously shares some of Rousseau's concerns, the latter's positive view of human nature stands in marked contrast to the Augustinian morality that Sorel lauds in the works of Pascal,
of whom he writes with great sympathy. Like Sorel, Pascal had a pessimistic view of human nature, a disdain for the Enlightenment, and he
too was a man of science who believed strongly in the limits of human
rationality. "It is likely," Sorel writes, "that Pascal wrote his *Pensées*
against the Cartesians" who gave the impression of being able to explain
everything in order to please the "aristocratic modes of thought."[40] It
was not reason that Pascal attacked but a rationalism that used pseudo-
mathematical reasoning for answering moral questions. In fact, mathematical reasoning, to Pascal, constituted a very limited area in the whole
field of knowledge. In the face of scientistic *hubris*, Pascal and Sorel
were strongly attracted by the miracle; and while Sorel was not a be-
liever like Pascal, he recognized the importance that mystery plays in
human affairs: there are some things that cannot be answered by science
properly understood.

Sorel's willingness to accept the non-scientific dimension of thought
was not a late development of his thinking. His early appreciation of
the importance of at least the moral function of religion led him to
the works of the religious historian, Ernest Renan (1823–92). The author
of *La Réforme intellectuelle et morale*, *The Life of Jesus*, and *The
History of Christianity*, Renan held the chair of Hebrew at the Sorbonne.
He astounded his contemporaries by placing Christianity in a historical
sweep of grandeur and comprehensiveness that it had not received in
the rationalist works of the eighteenth century. Writing under the
shadow of the disasters of 1870, Renan felt that, since the 1851 coup of
Napoleon III, France had been immersed in an era of the most debased
plutocracy: "Every rebel is, with us, more or less a soldier who has
missed his vocation, a being made for the heroic life. . . . The European
race is a race of masters and soldiers. If you reduce this noble race to
work in a slaves' prison like Negroes or Chinamen, it will rebel."[41]

"Moral values decline," said Renan, "sacrifice has almost disappeared;

one sees the day coming when everything will be syndicalized, when organized egoism will replace love and devotion. There will be strange upheavals. . . . The two things which until now have alone resisted the decline of respect, the army and the Church, will soon be swept away by the general torrent."[42] Sorel was impressed with Renan's "remarkable insight"; at a time when men were optimistic about progressive elements in the Church, Renan was struck by the decay of religious ideas and said, "An immense, moral and *perhaps intellectual* degeneracy will follow the disappearance of religion from the world. We, at the present day, can dispense with religion, because others have it for us . . . but on the day when the majority loses this impulse, the men of spirit themselves will go feebly to the attack."[43]

It was, according to Sorel, the absence of the spirit of sublimity that Renan dreaded. "Man is of value in proportion to the religious sentiment that he brings from his early education and that affects his whole life." But the source of the sublime had dried up. Jesuitical Catholicism was in danger of becoming the accomplice of a servile humanitarian socialism. A general renewal was needed, a new religion: "Tremble! At this moment perhaps the religion of the future is being made . . . without us." Sorel insists that there is nothing incompatible between what Renan says and his own concept of the class war: regeneration in society is brought about, in Renan's words, by "the source of life forces always returning to the surface," that is, by a class which works subterraneously and is separating itself from the modern world as Judaism did from the ancient world.[44]

It is illuminating to examine Sorel's criticisms of Renan in some detail. The problem, as Sorel saw it, was that Renan preached heroism rather than practiced it, that he played the role of the apostle of heroism, but that this was, along with playing the Protestant preacher, only one of a number of roles that he played throughout his career. Nowhere is this role-playing more striking than in a statement in Renan's *Souvenirs*, in which he virtually confesses his role as a preacher of heroism and an avoider of all action: "Teachers have inculcated in me the idea that the man who does not have a noble mission is the blackguard of creation. I have always been instinctively very unjust toward the bourgeoisie. On the other hand, I have a vivid liking for the people, for the poor." But he goes on to proclaim that his dream is to be "lodged, nourished, clothed and warmed, free from having to think about it, by someone who will take the enterprise from me and allow me all my freedom. . . . I will leave life without having possessed anything other than what I consume by use, according to the Franciscan rule."

But, according to Sorel, Renan has been a bit dishonest even here and omitted the real reason for proclaiming the ascetic concept that "values give income without giving anyone any cares." Unlike the chief of an enterprise, the ascetic intellectual can enjoy benefits without having any responsibility. Thus, while he preaches heroism on the one hand, Renan's rebellion against the civilization of Chinese coolies is predicated entirely on an almost Platonic distaste for the material civilization of capitalism; and while Sorel sympathizes with Renan's antagonism to bourgeois materialism, the latter's solution is the opposite of that which Sorel desired. Sorel sought a world of *Homo faber* while Renan wanted a world free from the cares of labor. But the thinker who starts out by condemning the world of coolies must eventually help to create it, according to Sorel; for a world which rejects all material value and speaks only of the "ethereal and the lofty" ideal condemns the world of labor to vassalage and produces an "intellectual feudalism." Bearing this out, in the *Apostles* Renan proclaims that the materialists will be hunted down and whipped, and the scholars will live in the manner of the medieval Franciscan monks. The great souls will form an "alliance against vulgarity. . . . One will assume that possessing things represents inferiority."[45]

Except for Renan's early writings in *La Réforme*, which profoundly moved him, Sorel found Renan to be fundamentally a liberal and a positivist-rationalist who attempted to "please a frivolous public" by *explaining* Christianity to them. In doing so, by giving quasi-scientific "explanations" for religious phenomena, he ended by partly debunking Christianity. But his attempt was not successful, because Renan profoundly misunderstood Christianity. Sorel insists that to probe religious phenomena, one must take them on their own terms and look at their results, rather than their causes (the same perspective he took with the *Action Française*). This approach demands non-scientific methods of speculation, and Renan failed to comprehend adequately the radically different methods of understanding in science and religion. Like Pascal, Sorel calls for a truce between the two.

The thinker who is closest to Sorel is still Pierre-Joseph Proudhon (1809–65). Of all the writers encountered in Sorel's works, it is Proudhon who receives the warmest affection and tribute. Even Marx is more heavily criticized by Sorel, and he considered Marx's criticism of Proudhon in the *Poverty of Philosophy* "unfortunate."[46]

Variously labeled an "anarchist" (he is said to have coined the term) and "mutualist," Proudhon is not any easier to categorize than Sorel, although again Rousseau invites comparison. Sorel and Proudhon share Rousseau's love for classical culture, his egalitarianism, his bias in favor of rural life, his contempt for social decadence, and his contradictions. It is in Proudhon's contradictions that we begin to see the outlines of Sorelian thought: this often confused and complex writer, the author of the phrase "property is theft," was himself a great defender of property; a defender of war and enemy of militarism; an anarchist who upheld the old traditions; a proponent of "progress" who was, toward the end of his life, plunged into despair.

Proudhon, like Sorel, is just now emerging from the over-shadowing of his ideas by Marxism and Social Democracy. His recent obscurity is all the more ironic, for it was Proudhon, not Marx, who dominated the French working-class movement during the early years of its development. The workers of the Paris Commune, for example, were led by men who called themselves "mutualists" and followers of Proudhon.

To understand the context of Sorelian thought, then, it should be useful to discuss Proudhon briefly. This is not simple, for although Proudhon's thought, like Sorel's, is dominated by a few basic concepts— justice, liberty, love, virtue—their expression, also like Sorel's, is complicated by disorder of presentation and by fluidity.

Proudhon starts with a somber view of human nature. Like Hobbes, he views man as seeking the greatest possible good for himself, and, he argues, those who seek to restructure society can ill afford to ignore this trait. "It is ridiculous," he says, "to want to submit the human masses, in the name of their own sovereignty, to laws against which their instincts rebel; on the contrary, it is a sane policy, and it is just and truly revolutionary, to prepare to give them what their egoism seeks and what they want to demand enthusiastically. The egoism of the people in political matters is the first law."[47] Sorel shares this view and argues that this egoism is overcome only in periods of great effort and struggle. Proudhon departs from it in that his thought comes to be dominated by the idea that man is inherently just and justice is not a mere harmony of selfish interests, as liberal philosophers have seen it; rather, it is a balance between egoism and altruism. (Interests are not the same as justice but their existence is not incompatible with it.) Selfish interests are balanced by an individual's recognition of the dignity of his fellow creatures. This recognition is the basis of the equality necessary to justice.

This central idea is apparent in Proudhon's view of property. He says that the opponents of *laissez-faire* are for the most part wrong because their solutions call for a tyrannical kind of state communism that kills the public spirit, the liberty which alone can rule our lives justly. Liberty is as essential to justice as equality, and when tempered by rules it becomes a "collective sovereign force" which thrives only with voluntary social institutions and associations. Thus civil liberty means liberty of property also. Yet Proudhon is aware that the distribution of property tends to be unequal and that this imbalance is reflected in the public force: "Government must be property's creature."[48] Men of property tend to dominate governments and therefore other men. Consequently, Proudhon tended (as did Sorel) to be hostile to government as such, opposing its attempt to dominate everything it touches. Yet Proudhon insists that property is also the preserver of liberty and a "balance" against state power. It is not the creation of law but its counter-weight, produced spontaneously by society and ensuring the limitation of law.

Proudhon asserts that a kind of balance should exist not only between altruism and egoism, property and the state, but in other areas as well: between one economic force and another, between one country and another, and one group and another. It is the totality of the balance of forces in society that Proudhon calls justice. In the political and economic realm he calls this justice "mutualism," a system based on balance and reciprocity. In the realm of punishment it means "an eye for an eye"; in society it means voluntary associations, co-operatives and mutual aid societies rather than the state; it is essentially a form of "anarchism."

To Proudhon, men come together in mutual societies only insofar as this is required by the demands of production, and it is in the economic realm—in productivity—that mutualism is based. The mechanism that he sees as preserving economic justice is *competition*, but here Proudhon gives his thought a twist which places him at odds with the *laissez-faire* theorists. Since poverty is relative and human wants are infinite, the two balance each other. The desire for more goods is the motive of social progress, and this desire is in our nature. Luxury is synonymous with progress; it is, at each moment of social life, the expression of maximum well-being realized by labor, and "it is the right, as it is the destiny, of everyone to attain it." It is the taste of luxury that in our times, lacking religious principles, maintains the social movement and "reveals to the inferior classes their dignity."[49] But the taste for *luxe* is balanced by the existence of poverty. The poverty arising from increasing population requires men to work harder and to create new productive forces. And, unlike Malthus, Proudhon sees poverty as a beneficent social force: "It is celebrated by antiquity and by Christianity. The hero is poor, temperate and surrounded by a large family: the ideal of those revealers of beauty [the poets] . . . [poverty] is not an object of fear for men imbued with the idea of justice."[50]

Proudhon's "idea of justice" is not contingent on social circumstances, nor does it arise like some mechanism from the social order—it is not an "ideology" in the Marxist sense. The idea of justice is as much a part of ourselves and our nature as the emotion of love. In fact, Proudhon sees love as a major force for justice, and a strong family life based on conjugal fidelity as its institutional basis. "For myself," said Proudhon, "the more I think of it, the less I am able to imagine woman outside

the family and marriage. I see nothing between the state of courtesan
and that of homemaker (I say homemaker, not servant). . . . Mankind
is created male and female: from this results the necessity of the ménage
and of property. The two sexes are united: at once from this mystical
union, the most astonishing of all human institutions, is created, by an
irreconcilable marvel, property, the division of the common patrimony
into individual sovereignties."[51]

If marriage based on love is institutionally at the basis of justice, the
same "balance" prevailing in the just society must prevail within the
household itself. The physical distinction between the sexes is transformed into a balance between the force and productivity of men and
the grace and ideals of women. If woman does not personify her qualities by accepting the feminine role, ideal values will be degraded and
the union between idealism and productivity—between justice and
economics—will be shattered. That is, when the male represents the
warrior, the embodiment of productivity and force, organizer of the
city and leader of the social movement, and the female is mother, educator of children and mistress of the household, the union of the ideal
and the real is found in marriage.[52]

Proudhon found it important to conceive an economic realm which
unites the household with production. Agriculture best performs this
function. No enemy of the "idiocy of rural life," as Marx is, Proudhon
proclaims that "when I turn the tracks made by my plow, I am king."[53]
The regime of farming allows woman to remain in the home uncorrupted
by the life of the factory; only when this agrarian virtue is somehow
brought into the new industrial society will justice and honor prevail.
Only then will the same sense of possession and pride that has characterized the peasant be found in the industrial worker. Again justice is
found in a balance: a partnership between peasant and industrial
worker. Unlike Marx, who believed that agrarian life was destined to
disappear, Proudhon believed that it is the peasant who provides the
model of the best human being and that rural life can be preserved.

The idea of balance pervades the whole of Proudhon's thought. The
love and harmony that pervade the household reinforce the self-sus-
taining nature of the ménage. Each household is a kind of independent
unit, a Roman *dominium*, and, as in the *dominium*, the *pater familias*
must be able to defend it. Therefore Proudhon believed that to maintain justice a certain militancy is necessary. Like patriotism, justice is
nothing if it is not armed, for it is not only the enemy within that must
be vanquished but also the one from outside. "To me," he says, "it is
clear that war is linked at a very deep level and in a way we are just
beginning to perceive, with man's sense of religion, justice, beauty and
morality. War is the basis of our history, our life and our whole being.

It is, I repeat, everything. . . . People speak of abolishing war as they might of local taxes or customs duties. They do not see that if man takes away war . . . nothing in his past remains, and not an atom is left on which to build the future. I would ask these inept peacemakers, as I myself was once asked in connection with property, 'What sort of society do you envisage once you have abolished war . . . ? What will become of mankind in this state of permanent *siesta*?' "[54]

As with all his viewpoints, Proudhon considers an institutional basis to cope with the necessity for war. Since mutualism calls for a justice based on reciprocity—an eye for an eye—and since official proceedings often miss the real causes of wrongdoing, groups must be organized to prevent unpunished transgression. The ineptitude of the legislator is universal and he deals with only the least dangerous part of wrongdoing. Voluntary groups known as *justiciers*, or lovers of justice, are seen by Proudhon as necessary to provide the essential balance against state-administered justice. These vigilantes he defines as "juries of honor with the right of pursuit, judgement and execution." The Roman *pater familias* of Proudhon's vision could, like Cincinnatus, leave his home to defend it; he creates an equivalent of the upright Roman soldier-laborer.

These views horrify us today, lending credence to the view that the tradition of Proudhon (and Sorel) is closer to that of the Ku Klux Klan than it is to an enlightened path of social understanding. But we should not condemn Proudhon quite so precipitously. For one thing, he was well aware that modern warfare leads to the most appalling butchery and that the Bonapartist regime under which he lived used militaristic and chauvinistic slogans to sustain its power. Louis Napoleon's empire was a hierarchy upheld by despots and demagogues that bore no similarity to the *polis* of the amateur soldier fighting to preserve freedom in the ancient world. In the modern world, Proudhon saw a balance of power between one country and another as a salvation from militarism. Since sovereignty in the modern sense represents not justice but only one force, or territory, opposed to another, justice is found in the balance between and among those sovereignties.[55]

More importantly, the meaning of Proudhon's *justiciers* anticipates Sorel's thought in another way: Proudhon says that even if the two sides are equal in strength and justice, there is justification for the battle itself—or at least its preparation. "Man first dreamed of glory and immortality as he stood over the body of an enemy he had slain. Our philanthropic souls are horrified by blood that is spilled so freely and by fratricidal carnage. I am afraid this squeamishness may indicate that our virtue is failing in strength. What is so terrible in supporting a great cause in heroic combat, at the risk of killing or being killed, if both sides are equally honorable and their claims equally just? What is there so particularly immoral about it? Death is the crown of life. How could man, who is a thinking, moral, free being, have a more noble end?"[56]

What Proudhon means is that the just and good society is possible only through action, and action is obtained when men are stimulated to fight an enemy. "Action is the principal condition of life, health and strength in an organized being. . . . For there to be action . . . there must be some ground that exists in relation to the acting subject . . . and that resists and opposes the acting self. Action, therefore, is a struggle. To act is to fight."[57] Proudhon is not the first theorist (nor, as we shall see when we read Sorel, the last) to assert that a society in torpor abdicates its self-rule to the parasitic few.

But a serious problem in Proudhon's thought emerges from this, in Sorel's view. If it is acknowledged that competing sovereignties are, as such, only balanced competing forces, can dispassionate judgment, rather than mere force, result from the Proudhonian vigilance committees? What is to prevent the excesses of vigilantism that are now the common experience of humanity? Proudhon seems well aware of this problem when he makes it clear that his "supplemental justice" is to be directed against immoral and ignominious acts rather than strictly criminal ones. This means, however, that vigilantism, which is a very logical anarchist replacement for officers of police, presumes a counterbalancing force—an "official," or state, mechanism to care for problems of greatest need. And the problem of the dispassionate judge remains after Proudhon has dispensed with the state as an objective, dispassionate and interest-free institution. If justice is balance, rather than objectivity and detachment, if the "umpire" of the liberal state is a myth as he implies it is, then the problem of detached *judgment* remains. One possible response is that it is only the balance itself, irrespective as to what is being balanced, that Proudhon regards as justice —that the innate justice in men corresponds to that balance.

It is at this point that Sorel finds Proudhon's thought contradictory. Despite the fact that he links the idea of justice to specific social institutions and an attempt to balance those institutions, Sorel shares Marx's opinion that Proudhon remains a prisoner of subjective and abstract ideals. In some writings Proudhon admits this, as, for example, in his assertion that justice is not merely the attribute of some authority: "Justice is the attribute of man that no *raison d'état* ought to despoil." But since Proudhon makes justice as much an attribute of human nature as of the balance of forces in society, Sorel, echoing Marx's criticism, wonders if Proudhon was "the victim of a strange illusion when he assumed that our nature leads us toward justice. On the contrary, it would seem that law was imposed on man by historical accidents. . . ."[58] Sorel finally perceives a utopian element in Proudhonian concepts. If justice is not a power play and the truly "candid judge" must be above all interest, Sorel says that justice then becomes absolute. "It is an idea that can comprehend relations among men only in the mythical city conceived by reason."[59]

For Sorel, then, the great challenge in Proudhon's writing is to disentangle idealistic and metaphysical remnants from it. Proudhon himself is well aware that justice, as such, is subject to a grave dilemma which Sorel spells out in some detail in his writings. If justice is based on natural law, on some abstract principle of right or of total reason, and if this principle is thought to be known to the legislator, then, in Sorel's opinion, force and repression may be used to enforce it. This leads to the complete disappearance of both tradition and freedom except for the freedom of the philosopher to discover the good. Absolute justice then leads to injustice. What repressive regime, asks Sorel, has not justified itself on the basis that it was the possessor of truth? "The philosophy of natural right is in perfect agreement with that of force [that is, state repression]."[60] Citing Pascal, Sorel says that "Justice is subject to dispute; force is very recognizable and undisputed. Thus we have not been able to give force to justice, because force contradicts justice and is itself just. Thus, not being able to make what is just strong, what is strong we make just."[61] Moreover, according to Sorel, Pascal saw the absurdity of the theory of natural right: if this theory were correct, we would need to find laws which are universally admitted, but actions which we regard as criminal have at other times been regarded as virtuous. "Three degrees nearer the pole reverse all jurisprudence; a meridian decides the truth." And "Truth on one side of the Pyrenees is error on the other. . . . It is said we must go back to the early and fundamental laws of the state, abolished by unjust custom. . . . This is a game that is sure to lose all; nothing will be just on that criterion."[62]

Sorel asks, "Who will know these laws?"[63] No one, and an arbitrary state power will end in making "power" the same as "right." This is the end of all certitude in law and morals and the principle of legitimacy disappears from the law itself. What started out as a standard of conduct which is contrary to the law of brute force, ends by disappearing altogether and justice becomes the interest of the stronger. It is Sorel's intention, then, to replace the theory of natural right, however conceived, by a theory of historical justice with its focus on the productive warrior.

What this means in a practical sense is that the problem of distributive justice, either as regards rotation of offices or distribution of wealth, is made by Sorel into a secondary question and replaced by the idea of virtue in the producers. We can gain some insight into this problem from the *Réflexions sur la violence*: "The Napoleonic soldier's sacrifice of his life in return for the honor of working in an 'eternal' Epic and of living in the glory of France, all the while saying that 'he would always be a poor man'; the extraordinary virtues shown by the Romans who resigned themselves to a frightful inequality and who endured such sacrifices to conquer the world; 'the faith in glory of unequalled value' created by the Greeks and thanks to which 'a selection was made from the teeming throng of humanity, [all showed that] life had a purpose, that there was reward here for those who pursued the good and the beautiful.' "[64]

In other words, men should not work for nothing, but their reward should be epochal and not financial or political. It is not economic inequality nor even human suffering which, for Sorel, constitutes the prime injustice, but the sapping of the incentive for glory and thus victimization by the "pride of a few"[65]—by "historical superiorities,"[66] that is, by repressive force.[67]

Sorel is indebted to Proudhon for (1) the idea of a strong family structure based on the productive household, (2) the warrior ethic and (3) the distrust of state power with the corollary that it is among voluntary associations based on production that one finds the freest institutions. In rejecting the theory of abstract natural right and replacing it with the rather vague formula of "the protest against traditional 'historical superiorities,'" Sorel became obligated to carry out two tasks: he must elaborate his attack on the theory of natural right, and he must replace this notion with a theory of morality better adapted to Proudhonian institutions, that is, based on productive life itself.

As with Proudhon, Sorel looked to Greek and Roman antiquity for answers to the problems of a good society. It was in the early stages of these societies that Sorel discovered both that the origins of virtue are to be found in productivity itself and that the means by which productive methods are transmitted to coming generations is through the epic. It is in later classical antiquity that the doctrine of natural right first appears. It is not surprising that one of Sorel's first works, therefore, was an attack on the principle of natural right as embodied in the teachings of Socrates, perhaps the greatest philosopher of natural right.

In *Le Procès de Socrate*, published in 1889, Sorel attempts to outline the reasons for the decline of Greece and explain how its heroic virtues were altered in such a way as to make this decline inevitable. *Socrate* provides us with the basis of Sorel's ideas on morals that are altered only slightly in his later writings.

IV   THE SUBVERSION OF ANCIENT VIRTUES*

Sorel sees early Athens as the quintessence of the best heroic society— a society based on production—and Socrates as responsible for helping

* See Chapter 1.

to subvert its virtues. Although the trial of Socrates itself was demagogic and badly conducted, its verdict culminated an understandable
reaction to the subversive nature of his teaching.

The writer Sorel uses to elucidate the best qualities of old Athens is
Xenophon, the only source outside Plato and Aristophanes for our
knowledge of Socratic teaching. Himself a student of Socrates but,
unlike Plato, not prone to exaggeration of the value of the Socratic
method, it is Xenophon to whom Sorel turns in discussing Socrates'
trial. It also is Xenophon's portrayal of the farming life of the old
Athenian citizen-warrior that Sorel uses as his model of the good society.

"Old" Athens rested its society on a citizenry of farmers. Sorel sees
Xenophon as virtually positing that it is household management as much
as politics which constitutes the "master science," because only the
household could both provide for the necessities of life and make its
members bold in defense of their freedoms.

In any event, Sorel's exposition of Xenophon's *Oeconomicus*[68] argues
that there is a parallel between home economics and war that makes the
art of the household a school for warriors as well. Sorel insists that in
ancient times the tradition was that anyone could learn military tactics;
that one learned the art of command by habit and by obedience. The
same obtains in the household: the well-ordered household puts everything in its proper place, just as the well-ordered army does; routine
execution of tasks in the home parallels the routine of the marching
phalanx. In both, Sorel asserts, we can combine routine execution of
tasks and a kind of excellence that shows itself in the mass—that is,
anyone can master what is required if he applies himself. As long as
"obedience was the school of command,"[69] no science of military tactics
beyond tradition really existed and the distance between commander
and private was minimal. In the household, wifely obedience was a
"school of command" but a rough equality prevailed between husband
and wife, divided, as they were, only by their differing tasks—a division
of labor.

It is in this Xenophonic picture of ancient society that Sorel finds the
most felicitous combination of productivity, domestic virtue, equality
and heroism—with each of the qualities dependent upon the others. To
disturb either the domestic or the military attributes of the farmer
fighting in defense of the freedom of his city would be to undermine
the best qualities of the old society. Sorel must say that in Xenophon's
Oeconomicus there is nothing that belongs to Socratic teaching. To
Sorel, Socrates, in acting as a spokesman for the life of the mind rather
than for the life of production, was a critical factor in the decline of
Greece.

Here we have a Sorelian outrage. Socrates, the patron saint of intellectuals, is now pronounced guilty, and it is precisely in Socrates' intel-

lectualism that Sorel finds his influence so pernicious. Socrates under-
mines domestic virtues, according to Sorel, by his very contempt for the
physical side of life. By emphasizing the philosophical and the spiritual,
Socrates implies that love of one's fellow human beings is best when it
is on an abstract level. The physically productive family is replaced by
a "moral family." Heterosexual love, in Socrates, is reduced to mere
procreation and deprived of its sentimental functions and marriage
degenerates from a divinely ordained physical union into a mere social
contract.[70] (Sorel takes care to admit that Socrates was perfectly correct
in his day-to-day behavior, however; and since, by his time, many other
Greeks were calling everything into question, Sorel considers the accusation against Socrates to be technically a weak one.)

Sorel builds his case by discussing the strictly military virtues of
antiquity. War, based on the tradition of epic poetry,[71] is the vehicle
for social equality. The same farmer-warriors who produce for survival
also govern themselves and fight to keep the city free—that is, self-
governing. Furthermore, it is in battle that man "discovers his own best
qualities: courage, patience, disregard of death, devotion to glory and
the good of his fellows, in a word: his virtue."[72]

Now if virtue was produced in the old egalitarian phalanx, it was
Socrates' claim to a "science" of military organization that destroyed
the old basis of military command. Socrates "proved" that the old ways
were insufficient for military excellence. The system in which heroism
could emerge from anywhere was called into question.[73]

But, to Sorel, nowhere was the new philosophic teaching more subversive than in the thesis that the good society is best run and best
served by "those who know"—that is, by experts in the field of political
rule itself. The old democratic tradition of ostracizing men of pronounced superiority whose continued political activity would compromise obedience to the laws was now replaced by the belief that
there can be no law contrary to men who are utterly superior. Once
this has taken place and society is divided into classes in terms of knowledge, according to Sorel, "the question of oligarchy is soon posed."[74]
Excellence and democratic equality united in the old farmer-warrior
ethic is now supplanted by the rule of philosophers who, with Socrates
at their head, maintain that the only legitimate rule of the city belongs
to scholars. "How nice it would be," intones Sorel sarcastically, "if the
assembly had dialecticians instead of old sailors!" Is not the right to
rule of "those who know natural law superior to a purely formal
legality"?[75]

Were not social conditions ripe for the transformations described
by Sorel? Sorel does not deny that conditions enabled Socrates more
easily to corrupt society, but he also never denies the efficacy of ideas

themselves, and he says one cannot exonerate Socrates unless one can attribute no importance to them.[76]

Socrates' following came from the class of urban elitists who, Sorel claims, were responsible for taking power and authority away from the farmer-warriors. In short, Sorel argues that Socrates' constituency was the same as that of the Sophist school. Now Sorel admits that Socrates differed from the Sophists both in refusing payment and in rejecting demagogic rhetorical techniques. But like the Sophists, Socrates pretended to a science of politics for which there was a ready-made following eager and able to put it to their own uses. Socrates' superiority over his sophistic rivals made him the chief ideologue of the new urban oligarchy, an oligarchy consisting in a class of shopkeepers and wealthy bourgeois who were unacquainted with the life of production and who subverted the old democracy.[77]

Sorel admits that the new followers of Socrates perverted Socratic teaching, but he considers Socrates' failure here not to be one of commission but one of omission. Far from questioning the sincerity of Socrates' intentions, Sorel says that the philosopher's failure was his inability to perceive that his teaching, though powerful, was not strong enough: that men could not remain pure, and that men who study philosophy could not help but become arrogant, partly because they came to feel they possessed a special "science," a special knowledge of political things.

Sorel uses Xenophon's own examples of Critias and Alcibiades to support the contention that Socrates' teaching was inherently corrupting. These two men were students of Socrates, but they stayed around Socrates only long enough to absorb certain lessons from him.[78] Their failure to remain in the Socratic stable constitutes, for Sorel, an example of the original sin of politics: the separation of theory from practice by separating men of thought from men of production. Critias and Alcibiades, upright only as long as they remained within the circle of Socrates, typified the new men of action, the true political professionals, who either divided Greece or enslaved it.

Clearly there is a problem here in terms of the concept of political action. Socrates, according to Sorel, had insisted that the savants perform the mission of action—that they were born to act and not merely to "cross their arms and laugh."[79] This injunction brings into play two different moral qualities which must be harmonized: the virtue involved with activity, which is *prudence*, and the virtue involved with thought, which is *knowledge* or *science*. Socratic political philosophy distinguishes prudence from science, but Critias and Alcibiades were corrupted after they left Socrates. Philosophy had imposed *temperance* on them, but this quality is not a science in the ordinary sense of the word.[80] It is a

kind of virtue which requires continuous teaching, as in the case of
the Franciscan monks.[81] Hence, Socratic temperance consists in detach-
ing the self from the world, as is reflected in Socrates' asceticism. In
"putting the body out to pasture," only the intellect can be relied upon
to be temperate, and the body must be supervised continuously. But
the Franciscans voluntarily take an oath of separation from the work-
aday world, a self-denial in need of continuous reinforcement, while
Alcibiades left his exemplar and went out into the world of politics.
Self-denial on essentially secular grounds, without continuous religious
reinforcement, is the more difficult; under such circumstances, Franciscans might well become corrupt too. Sorel sums up his understanding
of this problem when he says, "Men of science do not interfere in active
politics. It is remarkable enough that they are all the more timid as
they are all the more firm and radical in their doctrines. In general,
men who resort to violence are the most theoretically weak. Our revolutionary assemblies are the best example of this."[82]

To summarize, instead of the single-class state of farmer-soldiers that
existed in pre-Socratic times, the Greece of Socrates is a three-class state,
of farmers, professional politicians and professional intellectuals. The
politicians use the intellectuals as their professional ideologues, while
the latter are incapable of practical action. In Sorel's view this leads to
the corruption of both. The professional politicians become more arbitrary while the philosophers who have no practical ties become more
utopian and less tolerant of opposed opinion. By reducing all political
problems to formulae, the philosophers tend to place everything in rigid
molds and the result is the loss not only of the old virtues, but of freedom itself.[83] Politics does not conform to the concepts; thus practical
politicians can only use utopias in an improper way while the intellectuals can do nothing to stop them: men of intellect become divorced
from men of politics as the old farmer-soldier class that united the two
in heroic myths is shunted aside. Without access to the "science" of the
men of intellect, the old Athenian warriors no longer find it possible to
be "good" citizens. For them, good citizenship had meant a virile education based on mythology. When Socrates replaced this with study,
he replaced the souls of free men with the minds of savants.[84] Production became irrelevant and politics lost its moral roots. As a consequence
of the separation of thought from action, then, Socrates' attempt at
moral reconstruction of the city only sped his own death, after which
the proliferation of Sophistic philosophy continued.

The productive farmer-warrior class that Aristotle, Xenophon, Jeffer-
son and Proudhon all thought necessary to democracy is replaced in the
course of the Socratic teaching by a class of political consumers—the

urban oligarchs—whose chief "virtues" are found in the leisure necessary for political activity. The wealthiest of these oligarchs, despising
labor, yet relying on slavery far more than the old farmers did, must
become the great moving agents of moral corruption; for, to Sorel, one
of the primary "laws of nature" is that when one gives up laboring in
order to acquire power, moral corruption sets in.

As with Proudhon, it is this "moral corruption" which concerns Sorel.
Socrates, Sorel is careful to say, was a staunch advocate of obedience
to the law, but he insisted that the task of the philosopher is to search
for the just law, an absolute law of nature. Hence, the whole Socratic
tradition places great importance on the distinction between the just
man and the just citizen. The just man is just only insofar as he conforms to natural law, whereas the just citizen conforms to the laws of
his own society. Pure justice must be placed in the context of absolute
and unvarying rules whose quintessence is the Platonic utopia. This
justice is phrased in terms of absolute laws, and adherence to these
higher laws becomes the ultimate virtue.

It is perhaps right in one respect that Sorel should choose Xenophon
to emphasize this point. In the *Cyropaedia*, Xenophon emphasizes the
distinction between justice and conventional obedience to law when
Cyrus' "teacher in justice" thrashes him for approving of exchanging
coats with another little boy on the grounds that the coats fit better
after the exchange.[85] What is naturally fitting is not the same as what
belongs to one by dint of the positive law. Xenophon also compares
war to creative activity, which neither Plato nor Aristotle does.[86] But
Xenophon surely falls short of being an ideal source. It is curious that
he insists on the importance of Cyrus' mastering the military arts. Here
is outlined a science of military excellence and a military division of
labor alien to Sorel's notion of the old ideas in which tradition governs
military practice. That Xenophon should have been a student of Socrates
while remaining an "old Athenian" likely to divest the Socratic teaching
of Platonic "exaggerations" (and there no doubt were some) does not
alter the fact that here, too, a division of labor between statesmen and
producers, leaders and led, is implied. We ask further how Sorel can
hail the equalitarianism of the battlefield and justify division of labor in
the household. It is even more eccentric to uphold Xenophon as the
more accurate reporter of Socratic teaching while proclaiming the
Oeconomicus as un-Socratic. Indeed, is the teaching of Xenophon really
incompatible with that of Socrates or even of Plato's *Laws* which extols
the farmer class? Sorel is really being unfair to Socrates who was compelled by circumstances to fight the Sophists on their own philosophic
ground. To proclaim the virtue of the old farmer-warrior class in an

urbanized society already corrupted by Sophistic philosophy would
have been ineffective if methods other than those of Socrates had been
used.

Le Procès de Socrate was an unsatisfactory work, by Sorel's later admission. He was too harsh on Socrates; but the standards by which
Socrates was judged became a permanent basis for his later writings,
and all of Sorel's numerous transformations occurred *around* these standards, without changing the basic criteria themselves. The task which
Sorel sets for himself—and it is a task that largely dominates his writing
from 1889 until his dying breath—is the *task of the moral reconstruction
of socialism* along what we might call "anti-Socratic" lines: that is, to rid
the socialist movement of its domination by a class of intellectuals who
are separated from the life of work and who impose on Marxist doctrine
the abstractions of justice, devoid of concrete historical relations, and the
calculations of party advantage similar to those shown by Alcibiades when
out of the reach of Socrates.

In this attempt, Sorel would have the socialist movement concerned
more with the virtue of its members, and less with the distribution of
goods in society; more with proletarian action and less with the well-
being of a class of intellectuals and political professionals who know
even less about productive life than the capitalist ruling class they pretend to replace; more with the productive process itself and with class
struggle itself than with their respective final outcomes.

V SOCIALISM AND PROGRESS*

After Sorel completed his 1892 study of Proudhon, he began writing articles on socialist theory. Some of the best of these he wrote immediately
after his departure from *Devenir Social* in 1897. From that year until
about 1903, when, presumably, he was concentrating on his book on
Renan, Sorel produced extremely interesting work on Marxism, the best of
which is published in an Italian collection, *Saggi di critica del Marxismo*.
(After dealing with Renan, he returned to the task as a central concern
in a number of writings.)

The basic endeavor of these critical articles was to undertake a
thoroughgoing recomposition of Marxism under principles that were in
keeping with the spirit of its founder. The inspiration of many of Sorel's
ideas on Marx was the Italian socialist Antonio Labriola, whose *Essays
in the Materialist Conception of History* Sorel proclaimed a "landmark
in the history of socialism" in his preface to the French translation.
Labriola emphasized the tentative nature of Marx's teaching but stressed

---

* See Chapters 2 through 5.

its theory of action. The metaphysical basis of Marx had yet to be probed. From this emphasis, Sorel was impelled to observe that the master apparently feared nothing so much as the idea of excessive rigidity; Marx was extremely prudent and did not attempt to make any theory final. That Sorel saw fit to approach Marxism from an entirely fresh perspective dominated by the moral concerns of Proudhon did not make for an easy task. Marx's bitter criticism of Proudhon in the *Poverty of Philosophy*, published in 1845, required some rather radical surgery, even though Sorel had already jettisoned Proudhon's theory of justice as Marx had. Marx saw in Proudhon's notion of "justice as balance" a failure to resolve the inherent contradictions of the bourgeois order. While Proudhon looked to continued social plurality as fostering man's natural inclination to justice, Marx wished to resolve the differences between classes by overcoming social conflict and hence doing away with the human misery produced by the capitalist division of labor. Sorel, accepting from Proudhon the idea that good morals are a function of a balance of competing forces in society, insisted that there is no natural inclination to balance or to justice.

It was Marxian *praxis* derived from the idea that man knows what he makes that Sorel grafted onto the notion of balanced conflict. For Sorel, morality was inseparable from conscious human activity but this consciousness makes for pessimism; the solution to the problem of the division of labor as Sorel saw it, the unification of the man of intellect with laboring life, does not lessen the probability of continued struggle with the forces of nature itself. "The more scientific our production becomes, the better we understand that our destiny is to struggle without a truce and thus to annihilate the dreams of paradisiacal happiness which the old socialists had taken for legitimate anticipation. Everything allows for the assumption that work will be constantly intensified. Again we can recognize that this pessimism tends to reinforce the sentiment of reality, because we will never take for illusions the sensations engendered by strongly disciplined labor."[87]

Sorel argues that two tendencies in Marx's own thought implicitly contain some of the utopianism of the old socialists. First, the theory of surplus value infuses Marxism with a theory of distributive justice notwithstanding Marx's hostility to such a concept. Second, Marx's theory of history leads him unnecessarily toward an anticipation of a resolution to class conflict, a resolution which, in Sorel's eyes would be bound to end in decadence.

In the eyes of some socialists Marxism is associated with the ethics of distribution; that is, it postulates that a just society is one in which wealth and the means of production are distributed in relation to the contribution made to society by the laboring class on the basis of the need of each man. A genuine theory of Marxist justice is concerned, among other things, with economics. For this reason, Sorel regards Marx's labor theory of value and its corollary theory of "surplus value" as part of the theory of justice of the "orthodox" Marxists. But he also regards these theories as contradictory to the dynamic aspects of Marxian class struggle in that they impose a rigid carcass of abstractions on the just distribution of wealth in society.[88] Now by the term "surplus value" Marx means the amount of labor time expended in production that is "unpaid" (and hence to Sorel by implication, unjust). The worker, in short, does not receive the full value of his labor in his wages, the remainder going to the capitalist. Without this theory of "surplus value" one cannot establish, with any sureness or on any scientific basis, the validity of capitalist "greed" or the "injustice" of capitalism in a strictly economic way. Yet, according to Sorel, the theory is extremely weak, for it implies an ability to define what a "normal" work day is and what "extra profit" is. To do so would require the same degree of arbitrariness that is found in theories of natural law. If the deprivation of the "full" price of one's labor is somehow established, it can be termed "unjust" only in the most abstract sense; that is, one must affirm a sort of "natural right" to the full product of one's labor.[89] Sorel goes so far as to say that this harks back to medieval notions of the "just price"—in this case, the price of labor itself.[90] Further, if "labor time" is the basis for the scientific measurement of exploitation, is it really more important than instrumental differences of function, talent or virtue? Marx's theory assumes a kind of "normal state" in which all industries and all laborers are of a uniform type, according to Sorel.[91] By reducing other economic factors to "labor", Marx has made labor into a metaphysical concept—a force often hidden beneath appearances.

Now if the natural right to one's labor were to become enshrined in the socialist parthenon, the "statist," "reactionary" and idealist components of socialism—its utopianism—would overtake its ethical ones. Laws would be passed limiting profits and the autonomy of the producers would be limited by the sovereign authority of "those who know" the laws of political economy and who work toward running industry through committees made up of an elite of intellectuals, politicians and office-holders. In short, Marx's economics are "uneconomic" in that they lead to the separation of the producer from the thinker.

Sorel's criticism of the theory of justice held by the followers of Marx, therefore, is that it "Socratizes" socialism, as it were; that is, that utopian thinking, which is specifically rejected by Marx himself as ultimately reactionary, is built into the very fabric of the Marxist theory of value. This Marxist utopianism is reactionary because its abstractions fail to change and adapt to the exigencies of constant economic transformations; it is "fixed" so that what is *avant-garde* at one time later becomes out of touch with historic development and hence requires the state apparatus to enforce it. To Sorel it is statist because utopias are products of the intellect and of theorists who, "after having observed and discussed the facts, try to establish a model with which existing societies can be compared. . . . It is a composition . . . offering close enough analogies with real institutions so that the jurist can discuss it; it is a construction which can be broken down into parts and of which certain parts have been set up in such a way as . . . to be included in pending legislation."[92] Utopias, according to Sorel, can be transformed easily into legislation for reforms, losing their oppositionist character. Since utopias can be adapted to the present system, many utopians, after sufficient experience, come to be prudent and clever statesmen.

For Sorel it is essential, if Marxism is to be salvaged, that its theory emphasize the "spirit of revolt" as opposed to this utopian element. Empirically, it means that Marxism be not a dogma but an open-ended means of inquiry. Ethically, it means abandoning the ethics of distribution and the hope of a communist society: "It is of small import," he says, "whether communism arrives sooner or later or whether it ought to be preceded by more or less numerous stages: what is essential is that we can account for our own conduct."[93]

The same reasons that impelled Sorel to oppose the Marxian theory of value caused him to take a fresh look at Marx's historical viewpoint. If utopias are ends and fixed states (however adaptable), socialists must be wary of attaching an end, or teleology, to history. For Marx, history is a constantly unfolding process. In "La Necessità e il fatalismo nel Marxismo" and "Y'a-t-il de l'utopie dans le Marxisme?" Sorel attempts to disabuse Marxism of this teleology by establishing that Marx himself had given up the theory of final communism (that is, utopianism) by the time the *Critique of the Gotha Program* was written in 1876.[94]

Sorel notes that the utopian teleology of the followers of Marx depends heavily upon a deterministic theory of history whereby the revolution of the proletarians and ultimate communism are considered inevitable. In order to free Marxism from the utopianism of its official spokesmen, it becomes necessary, in Sorel's view, to rid Marxism once and for all of its fixation on historical inevitability. The device that Sorel chooses for this task, in the *Saggi di critica del marxismo*, is an exegesis on Marx's own texts: by examining Marx's writings in detail, Sorel attempts to prove that Marx did not always look upon history as some kind of abstract force governing our lives in a predetermined or fatalistic way, like so many of Tolstoy's generals.

It is true that Sorel's own position with regard to Marx's determinism was ambiguous, at times seeming contradictory. In *Les Illusions du*

progrès, he had asserted the opposite view, that "Marx's Hegelian leanings led him to admit, without being generally aware of it, that history
advances . . . under the influence of the force of the mysterious *Weltgeist*," or world spirit. "The same Hegelian biases inspired in Marx the
idea of a technological development in modern production resulting in
the disappearance of small enterprises which would be crushed by industrial giants," the end of rural life as we know it, etc.[95] Marx also was
transfixed by the development of history in the form of great historical
periods or epochs—feudalism, capitalism, socialism—in which entire
periods are treated as historical wholes and perceived *en bloc*. Clearly
this deterministic character in Marx is seen in the *Communist Manifesto*,
wherein the socialist revolution is looked upon as inevitable, and also in
the penultimate chapter of *Capital* in which Marx says that capitalism
will be destroyed in its own contradictions "with the inexorability of a
law of nature."[96]

In *Saggi di critica del marxismo*, however, Sorel takes the perspective
on Marx's determinism more commonly associated with his name as a
Marxist critic. He attempts to explain—and sometimes explain away—the
deterministic passages in the works of the father of scientific socialism.

The first of the three points Sorel makes is that Marx differed from
Hegel in being an empirical theorist whereas Hegel did not base his
political theory on observations of the contemporary social order. Marx
was inspired to write of the imminent demise of the capitalist order not
because of historical fate but because he observed the proximity of upheaval in the period preceding 1848, the year the *Communist Manifesto*
was published. This prediction, says Sorel, concerned a revolutionary
event extremely close at hand that did occur—though in quite a different form from the one anticipated by Marx. (Furthermore, Sorel comments that the political pressures of the other members of the League
of Communists forced Marx to take a more daring position than he
otherwise might have.)

Sorel's second point is a more dubious one. By the time Marx had
published *Capital* in 1867, the "apocalyptic" Marx predicting imminent
revolution had all but disappeared, according to Sorel. A more prudent
Marx had replaced the one dominated by revolutionary instinct. The
penultimate chapter of *Capital*, in which Marx predicts the inevitable
demise of capitalism was "a fragment which, like so many other old sections, was introduced into *Capital* and which Marx thought worth preserving because it presented the schema of the class struggle in a very
lively manner."[97]

In contrast with such highly speculative and unprovable assertions,
the third argument made by Sorel has the most appeal and plausibility.
Sorel distinguishes between two kinds of determinisms. The first kind is

found in the fatalism in which spontaneous and necessary natural forces dominate events, "the natural law" that seemed to be sweeping capitalism away through the forces of historical contradictions, and which *seemed* to be the perspective of the end of *Capital.* The other determinism is one in which technological and social accidents merely "average out" to form historical tendencies so that, for example, life insurance companies can arrive at probabilities on longevity. Marx, according to Sorel, is characteristically closer to this second kind of determinism.

In Sorel's view, the "later" Marx of *Capital* usually meant by *necessity* a blind unconscious force arising from a multitude of daily actions. Thus Marx "does not refer to the order in which industrial processes succeed one another" following some Hegelian world spirit. On the contrary, Sorel says, Marx really stresses the importance of technological and historical accidents in the day-to-day decisions of industrialists.[98] These innovations, such as new inventions, do not "cause" other social phenomena in some simplistic way. Sorel says that Marx was concerned above all with "the reciprocal dependence of social phenomena" which are due to "an infinity of causes." These causes, obscure and often extremely difficult to analyze, average out in what he calls "sets," or groups of phenomena whose development is "necessary" only insofar as they do not reveal "the free reaching out to an end chosen by the will for reasons consistent with the result." Social phenomena thus have meaning or intelligibility in a historical sense only in the same way that the law of chance produces average results capable of being regularized.[99] As an example, Sorel offers the law of supply and demand, in which a host of individual decisions on the part of buyers and sellers determines the price of a commodity. Since it is economics, of all the social sciences, that is most capable of mathematical understanding, it is not surprising to Sorel that Marx placed economic phenomena at the base of the social structure. The economy is subject to great change and wide variations, and economic laws are little more than appearances of general trends that might not apply to any one particular instance. Sorel notes that the actuarial tables of insurance companies speak of average life spans but cannot predict the longevity of any one individual. To Sorel, Marx's alleged determinism or fatalism need not be any more "deterministic" than these tables or than the price-system theory of the *laissez-faire* economists.[100]

We may ask ourselves why Sorel undermined the value of his argument by sometimes contradicting himself and asserting that Marx had "Hegelian" leanings. The answer is found in the ambiguity of Marx's own position. Because the founder of modern socialism did not bother to make Sorel's distinction between the two kinds of determinism, it was easy for his followers to assume that the "average" tendencies or results of Marxian theory bespoke the rigid determinism that is apparent in the final chapters of *Capital*. The result was that they took the extrapolation of the events of 1848, by which Marx predicted the proletarian revolution, as an iron law. By reducing the observation of infinitely complex phenomena to a simple historical tendency, later Marxists subsumed all human activities under a single entity known as "history." Sorel, instead, attempted to separate the "soft" determinism of Marx, which deals with social averages, from the Hegelian or fatalistic side, a side particularly detrimental to the empirical aspects of Marxian social science. That is why he could argue, in a seemingly contradictory way, that Marx is both dominated by Hegelian fatalism and a "soft" determinist. Sorel implies that Marx's own vagueness prevented any strict delineation of these two trends of thought.

It was the necessity for this and other distinctions within the body of Marxist thought that led Sorel to approach social phenomena from the perspective of the part rather than the whole. With such modern thinkers as Sir Karl Popper, he maintains that it is impossible to do what Marx attempted, that is to "take in" an entire period; the historical tendencies of an epoch cannot be examined except by means of pluralistic and piecemeal perspectives. In Sorel's view, Marx at his best did this; at his most obscure and confused, he was guilty of looking at the world from the point of view of what Popper calls "holism,"[101] and what Sorel calls a "unity," the idea that the world can be understood from a total perspective.

Methodologically, Sorel attempts to deal with the problem of holism by using what he calls *diremption:* "the examination of certain parts without taking into account all their connections with the whole, to determine in some way the nature of their activity by isolating them."[102] This method in Sorel's hands results in a fragmentation of Marxism; by taking certain of Marx's precepts such as the theory of ideology with far greater seriousness than others such as the labor theory of value, Marxism no longer need be a complete system—a *Weltanschauung*—for understanding the world, and Sorel can do with its ideas, including the idea of Marxism itself, the same thing that he can do with other social phenomena.

Nowhere is Sorel better at treating Marx "diremptively" than in *Les Illusions du Progrès*. In this work, Sorel uses Marx's ideological method —of unmasking the real or material basis of ideas—against the Hegelian or more deterministic side of Marxism itself. According to Sorel, the holistic or "historicist" Marx is indebted to the idea of progress which caused so much furor in the seventeenth century and became encased permanently in most socialist and social democratic doctrine. It is Sorel's intent to uncover the true reasons for the rise of the idea of progress by using Marx's own historical-analytic methods.

Sorel shows why he focuses on this specific idea for intensive analysis by pointing out that the concept of progress is an aristocratic one aped by the bourgeoisie at a time when fear of sin, respect for chastity, and pessimism had all but disappeared. "Such a society could not abandon itself to happiness without justifying its conduct; it had to prove that it had the right not to follow the old maxims. For if society was not able to give this proof, was it not liable to be compared to the son who is in such a hurry to enjoy the paternal inheritance that he devours all resources for the future?" Further, "The doctrine of progress . . . pleased the old aristocratic society; it will always be pleasing, too, to the politicians elevated to power by democracy, who, menaced by possible downfall, wish to make their friends profit from all the advantages to be reaped from the state."[103] In other words, Sorel argues, the ideology of progress serves the victors of an epoch—the dominant class that inherits power—by making it appear that this class is destined to govern and that its domination is necessary for the continued "progress" of the state. And by uniting all aspects of experience into a coherent historical whole, the idea of progress, inspired by Cartesianism, appears to explain all aspects of life and reinforces a false sense of unity in society. Basic to this holism is the notion of continuity wherein the old regime, liberal democracy and social democracy all appear as manifestations of progress through the growing power of the modern state. Put slightly differently, by legitimizing each revolutionary strengthening of the state, the idea of progress is essentially a conservative force in society and really legitimizes the status quo: *plus ça change, plus c'est la même chose*.

These realities make up one of the main reasons that Sorel is so scornful of the parliamentary socialists and what he calls "democracy" in the modern sense (which he distinguishes from the early *polis*). By losing its will to fight "against the system," by being devoid of its quality of opposition, parliamentary socialism becomes swallowed in the "democratic ocean." By losing its quality of opposition, social democracy becomes a new aristocracy. In calling itself "progressive," it reveals only its own smugness and aids in obscuring the truth that contemporary decadence is not part of the natural order of things.

Saying that "nothing is more aristocratic than democracy," Sorel tries to show that, with the idea of progress, the real change in society that is acted on or, to use Sorel's expression, "forced" by revolutionary agitation, is limited. Class struggle and revolutionary *praxis* are replaced by a kind of social quietism that saps Marxism of its moral energy while the

practitioners of social democracy fold their arms and wait for the "progress of history" to deliver the world to them on a silver platter.

The reason for using the diremptive method on Marxism itself is now
more apparent: the idea of progress presented by Marx as part of dialectical history is particularly detrimental to Marx's writings because it
tends to obscure the ethical component of Marxism. Sorel cites Engels,
who insisted that "Marx never founded his socialist idea on the consideration of injustice that the regime of profit represents; he founded it
solely on the necessary ruin which under our very eyes every day increasingly devours the capitalist mode of production."[104] By diremption,
Sorel can reject Engels's deterministic or "progressive" Marxism; he can
accept the Marx of social action while rejecting parts of the economic
and historical theorist.

Basically, Sorel considers Marxism a method for intepreting, acting on
and understanding events that "leads us to scientific ground." Sorel summarizes the useful part of Marxist doctrine as follows: "one should never
speculate about law, political institutions, the ideologies of art, religion
or philosophy without having a clear picture of the economic life of the
people under consideration in all its reality, with the historical division
of classes, with the development of technical processes and with the
natural conditions of productivity. This connection, thus established between the infrastructure of a society and its superstructure, illuminates
the entities included in the latter and often leads into areas which allow
us to interpret its history. In every type of question, each historian ought
to develop his own ingeniousness so as to show how the most interesting
parts of the social structure relate to one another at a given time: no
general rule can be established to guide such an inquiry."[105] There are
no means of defining or determining social culture or defining interdependence in a general way—only indications of movements.

In Sorel's view, Marx made a contribution to social science because,
at his best, he *rejected* fatality in politics. As Sorel puts it: whoever calls
for "experimentation, social mechanism and human action," as Marx did,
also calls for "movements which can be produced or not produced and
hence exclude all appearance of fatality."[106] In speaking of the necessary progress toward socialism, socialists were returning to the old progressive superstitions of the utopians against whom Marx had fought.
Such reactionary socialists replaced history by a dead succession of
forms engendered by causes independent of human action. But Marx
was essentially an advocate of action rather than a quietist. As Sorel
points out, capitalism for Marx may have been subject to its own laws of
development, but this internal necessity did not extend to the organization of the workers' movement. Nothing obliges or necessitates the
worker to act. On this, Sorel takes his cue from the address to the Inter-

national Workingmen's Association in which Marx says that it is necessary for the workers to organize themselves. Further, Marx has given us several methodological postulates for the organization of the workers' movement. Admitting that they are vague, Sorel stresses that these postulates could force the advance of events, accompanied by strong wills and guided by rich creative imaginations. What is important is that these postulates are guides to *action,* around which the moral content of Sorel's imagination revolves, and it is these postulates of action, taken from the *Critique of Political Economy,* for which the socialist movement owes such a great debt to Marx's pragmatism:

1. Social formations do not disappear before their productive forces can no longer develop.

2. New social relations do not replace the old ones before their material conditions have ripened in the womb of the old society.

3. Tasks do not really exist for mankind unless their material solutions already exist.[107]

The final inference is that these guides to action distinguish Marx from his utopian predecessors. It is left to Marx to act as a kind of roadmarker for those who desire to promote revolutionary action.

VI   THE MYTH OF THE GENERAL STRIKE*

Now, it must be understood that Sorel himself is a progressive of sorts. Like Marx, he admires the achievements of capitalist industry and he does not wish society to revert to the "days of grass," or the *polis.* More than Proudhon, he seems to be looking forward to the possibilities of the new proletarian world. It is not progress as such that Sorel rejects but the reification of progress into a deterministic abstraction. The new heroism possible in the industrial world can come about only through willful action and devotion to duty.

The problem for Sorel, then, is to become truly progressive, and the way to do this is not to talk about progress so much as to act. Sorel's challenge is to reap the benefits of the idea of *certainty* that the notion of the dialectic gives, without accepting the dialectic itself and without falling heir to the quietism of the social democrats who have elevated the inevitability of the revolution into an excuse for inaction.

To do this, Sorel places the class struggle at the center of his thought, for it is only through struggle and action that the proletarians can achieve their goals. But what are the goals? Sorel has largely eliminated economic justice from his desired condition; remaining are those Proudhonian warlike virtues whose sublime qualities make the proletariat ripe for trans-

* See Chapters 6 and 7.

forming European civilization into a civilization fit for heroes. Sorel finds Eduard Bernstein very helpful here, for he had said, "The movement is everything." Sorel embraces this notion and insists that it is the movement itself and the psychological preparation for action—an "anticipation"—that constitute the most important quality of the modern socialist movement. That is why Sorel seems hesitant at times to see the conflict between the bourgeoisie and the proletariat resolved. To do so might be to see the revolution end in the same lax morality and terroristic despotism that were repeated in so many revolutions—especially that of 1789.

Replacing the holism or historicism of the Marxists, then, Sorel gives us a Proudhonian balance between two strong forces—each certain of victory, each determined to triumph. The virile American capitalist should replace the decadent European one (in this instance virtue resides in the ruling class!) and the proletarian should replace the heroic soldier of the Persian wars in the industrial equivalent of war.[108]

Sorel's notion of heroism is, as we have seen, rooted in the process of labor, and it is in the *Réflexions sur la violence* that he links this doctrine most firmly to the class struggle. Sorel does this by focusing on the creative act itself, not only in production but throughout society as well. Just as Marx does, Sorel starts with Giambattista Vico's assertion that "man knows only what he makes."[109] In Sorel's view, *praxis* means both constant improvement in the workshop and in production and constant psychological preparation for the social battle that is "bound" to come. Sorel attempts to depict the interaction between the psychological and the material dimensions of the revolutionary mentality, and the world of fabrication supplies the common denominator of this interconnection. Thus artists, warriors, inventors and producers all possess three characteristics in common.

Sorel first stresses that the experiences found in all these areas are creative: industry, like war, needs its epics, and epics help lead people, whether proletarians or soldiers, into heroic acts of great individuality and originality. The corollary of this individuality is an intense dislike for reproducing accepted types. The avoidance of routine allows each producer to be an inventor who "wears himself out in pursuing the accomplishment of ends which practical people most often declare absurd."[110] The true artists and the true inventors create new things and in doing so anticipate higher and higher forms of achievement. Similarly, the soldier in the wars of liberty "considers himself an important person who has something very important to do in the battle, instead of regarding himself as only a cog in a military machine. . . . Battles, therefore, can no longer be put in the framework of chess games in which man is . . . a pawn; they become compilations of heroic exploits."[111]

Discipline from above is, according to Sorel, relatively unnecessary precisely because of so much individual strength.

In the second place, art, war and industry are seen as alike in that they must be experienced directly. The creative process cannot be analyzed completely any more than one can "see" the Mona Lisa or the Parthenon merely by having it described. Sorel points out that as a result of this the planning of creative actions in advance is virtually impossible. Indeed, before Napolean, war plans as such, he says, never really existed because war cannot be charted. It is not the generals who run wars, it is the soldiers on the line. Similarly, economic life cannot be planned by university graduates, civil servants or politicians, but can be the province only of the producers themselves acting in the capacity of producers. All these activities, only when taken seriously and in this way, can produce a transformation that is really "new."

Finally, the creative processes in art, war and industry "live especially on mysteries, shadows and indeterminate nuances," and production is "the most mysterious aspect of human activity."[112] Thus, the class war does not allow us to depict sentiments and attitudes in a precise way. If one rejects mystery, he reduces all human experience to the common denominator of a superficial rationalism which places many very different matters on the same level through the love of logical simplicity.

Now, the economic epic, the myth of the general strike that Sorel envisages has the twofold function of stirring up war-like feelings and inducing a love for creative and productive work. Fundamentally, it is creative: just as the artist who communicates through symbolic signs wishes to create a fully unified ensemble, so the "social poetry" of the general strike may vary with each individual. Sorel depicts the revolution as based on deeply personal as well as social experience. Invoking Bergson's doctrine of memory, he asks us to consider the "inner states" and what happens during a creative moment. There are, Sorel stresses, "two different selves": the social or "spatial" being and the inner self. We reach our inner states as living things that are in constant flux through "deep introspection"—moments when we "grasp ourselves" that are quite rare, though it is only during these rare moments that we are truly free.[113] Despite the difficulty of achieving it, the myth relies on this experience. What we must do is carry ourselves back in thought to those moments in our own lives when we made serious decisions, moments unique of their kind, never to be repeated. Such "new" decisions break the bond of reason that encloses us in the "circle of the given." For example, one does not learn swimming from textbooks but by being thrust into the new milieu and adapting to it. At such moments we are dominated by an overwhelming emotion characterized by inner turmoil—a psychological *movement*.

It is of the utmost importance that the myth is mysterious. The picture the proletarian has in mind is of some sort of catastrophe which "defies description."[114] To analyze it would be to break it down into its component parts and hence to decompose it. Here is Sorel's description of the myth of the general strike: "an organization of images capable of evoking, *as a whole and solely by intuition* prior to any deliberate analysis, the mass of sentiments which correspond to the various manifestations of the war entered into by socialism against modern society."[115]

Furthermore, whether the content of the myth in its mystery actually materializes in fact is as irrelevant to Sorel as whether the second coming actually occurs amidst the movements of messianic Christianity. "Any discussion on the manner of applying them materially . . . is devoid of sense. *It is only the myth as a whole that counts.*"[116] Thus Sorel finds it easy to say that "no progress of knowledge, no rational induction will ever make the mystery which envelops socialism disappear."[117] It is the beginning, or epic, stages of a revolution in which new doctrines are presented in shades of mystery—incomplete, paradoxical and symbolic—that finally end in being dissolved into the "ensemble of our knowledge."[118]

In 1906 Sorel insisted that the chapter of *Capital* in which Marx asserts the inevitability of the social revolution is based on a myth. Thus he concludes that "the diverse terms that Marx used to depict the preparation for decisive combat should not be taken as materially established, direct and determined in time. It is the ensemble [of images] alone which should impress us, and this ensemble is perfectly clear."[119]

Here, then, Sorel reconciles his criticism of Marxism as a science of predictive history, on the one hand, with his recognition of the necessity for a feeling of certainty on the other, acknowledging both the reality of pluralism and the "need" for men to think holistically. If the integrative and holistic character of thought is viewed in a certain way, it produces spontaneous action rather than quietism. Although we must reject predictive and fatalistic historicism, we can yet reap its benefits by the simple device of not thinking about the future society in a *utopian* way. Some sort of vision of the future is needed, for "we are not able to act without leaving the present, without thinking about the future, which always seems condemned to escape our reason." And "experience proves that some *constructions of a future, undetermined in time,* can possess great effectiveness and have very few disadvantages when they are of a certain nature; this occurs when it is a question of myths, in which are found the strongest inclinations of a people, a party or a class, tendencies which present themselves to the mind with the insistence of instincts in all of life's circumstances, giving an appearance of complete reality to hopes of imminent action on which the reform of the will is based."[120]

Science cannot calculate the future the way an astronomer calculates the phases of the moon. Though the myth of the general strike must deny the accuracy of historical predictions, the device allows the workers to feel that their cause is "assured of triumph," to reject belief in utopia and yet have some picture of the future. Such feelings or visions of future triumph Sorel calls myths; primitive Christianity, the Reformation, the French Revolution and, of course, Marx's catastrophic revolution itself are examples of myths.

How can the general strike myth inculcate conviction and still view historical science with suspicion? Sorel says that the myth must depict the great epic as occurring in the near future, for it is in the nature of epic to deal with the future and not the past. Myths are, therefore, not descriptions of things but "expressions of the will."[121] He takes as a prime example of the phenomenon the French Revolution, which appeared to many as a series of glorious wars unexplained by reason or any law of historical progress; it was "the epic of the wars which had filled the French soul with an enthusiasm analogous to that provoked by religions" and which rendered all criticism impossible.[122] When the masses are deeply moved in such a way, they are thrown into "an entirely epic state of mind" in which the "drama" of the general strike becomes a phenomenon of war. As such a "state of mind" the myth becomes a psychological surrogate for the law of historical development. That the cause of the people is "assured of triumph" is not inconsistent with their failures in a science of historical prediction, for they no longer search for unity in the imminent developments of man that seem to give order and appearance to history, but in psychological developments hidden under them. It is what takes place in our own minds—our own souls —that is important and that is where the myth is. Nowhere is the essential nature of the myth more succinctly stated than in Sorel's assertion that it is not the "socialism of things" with which he is concerned but the "socialism of socialists."[123] If the socialist movement is everything and the economic goals secondary, it is no wonder that Sorel's socialism is the socialism in our hearts. "A moral catastrophe *replaces* a socioeconomic one."[124]

Réflexions sur la violence has often been cited to present Sorel as a blood-and-iron proponent of "Fascist" militarism. However, Sorel defines *violence* specifically as a rebellion against the existing order, while *force* is the might of the state used to maintain the existing order. Sorel was not a proponent of force *per se*, but of the *psychological preparation* in the hearts of those who would *resist* it. He does not seek carnage but insists that, if the myth is followed, the violence against the existing order will take place with a "minimum amount of brutality." The last thing that Sorel desires is what he calls "creative hatred" of the kind used by demagogues—a hatred that creates such brutality. Indeed, it might be said that Sorel wants to have his revolutionary cake and eat it too—to have a revolution that would *avoid* the brutality and bestiality of 1793—and he hits upon the myth of the general strike as a "virtuous" means to do this.

If we can make any comparisons of "Sorelianism" with existing theories, it is not with Fascism but with Albert Camus's ideas on rebellion and revolution. Camus, who owed much to Sorel, distinguishes rebellion, an act of refusal to existing repression, from revolution, which attacks the existing order with both a plan for future organization and a theory of historical destiny. It is with rebellion that the myth of the general strike can be compared because it is "unplanned" and non-utopian and does not rely on the repressive force of the state. Furthermore, to Camus, because of its very nature, rebellion possesses built-in limits to its own force. By a simple act of refusal it is negative at the same time that it establishes limits to force and power. (There are crucial differences between the thinking of Sorel and that of Camus: Camus has no myth, and he rather inconsistently rejects the notion of violence, whereas it would be too much to call Sorel a proponent of passive resistance.)

The subjective quality of the myth of the general strike appears to be missing from Marx's revolutionary theory. Sorel, like Marx, insists that ideas and beliefs do not arise *in vacuo* but only in the "efflux" of material activity. But an "ideology" to Marx is not *simply* a political idea but a rationalization, justification or "reflection," conscious or unconscious, for a particular group or groups in society, a product of historical development. Only the idea which accurately depicts historical reality is properly "scientific" and hence immune from the charge of being an "ideology"—an idol of the mind—characterized by "phantoms" or "false consciousness."[125] In other words, the material reasons for the existence of ideologies are not in strict accord with material reality. Religion is ideological in that there are good historic reasons for its existence, but it is nevertheless a false depiction of reality.[126] For Marx, socialism must be reduced to a science. And even Sorel is at pains to emphasize the basically empirical nature of Marxism as well as the superfluity of its Hegelian overtones, noting that the rationalistic heritage of Marx caused him to view ideas either as "scientific" or as "false consciousness."

The notion of ideology is a double-edged sword, for it is both a concept and a method. Part of political activity for Marx is raising proletarian consciousness to the level of a scientific understanding of the world. Scientific socialism implies the uncovering and sweeping aside of

the phantoms and myths (ideologies) that get in the way of this understanding; this unmasking is what we might call the "ideological method."
If man "understands only what he makes," then, through increasing
social action, work and politics, he becomes more cognizant of the
actual relations governing the world around him, that is, the productive
world. The myth of the general strike, according to Sorel, retains the
qualities of "making" and of creating, and with Marx it unifies theory
and practice in a revolutionary act. But Sorel insists that his "theory"
need not be scientific in *Marx's* understanding of that word: the myth of
the general strike need not imply any such radical unmasking of false
ideas as is implied in the Marxian notion of ideology. Certainly Sorel can
agree with Marx that false, "ideological" views should be torn from the
face of one's opponent in order to uncover the "real" motives for his
action, but he would confine this unmasking process or ideological method
to *rationalist* prejudices such as the idea of progress. Sorel argues that
although "ideologies have only been translations of . . . myths within
abstract forms,"[127] it is rationalist and abstract ideas that are easily
amenable to decomposition and hence to the method of rational dissec-
tion that the Marxist concept of ideology calls for in its unmasking
process. Thus he very cleverly turns the theory of ideology back against
Marx in the last chapter of *Les Illusions du progrès*, stressing the vast
difference between rationalist eighteenth-century ideas and the non-
rational ideas that impel men to action. The latter mythic concepts are
immune to ideological unmasking precisely because it is their nature not
to "come apart under fire," as it were. Their primary characteristic is that
they can only be taken *en bloc* and are hence "secure from refutation."

The best illustrations of the essential differences between Marx and
Sorel are found in two subject areas: art and religion. To begin with, for
Marx, the epic cannot be revived once artistic production has begun, for
the epic is characteristic of a certain primitive stage in historical development. In a world of progressive science, the termination of art and
myth is foreseen as possible: "Greek art presupposes Greek mythology—
Egyptian mythology could never have become the foundation of the
matrix of Greek art, but there had to be *some* mythology. . . . The undeveloped social conditions under which the art arose and under which
alone it can appear can never return."[128] Marx seems to mean that the
myth as a genre can never reappear but only be enjoyed by artistic consumers. Sorel's myth of the general strike would effectively deny this by
not accepting Marx's opposition of science and myth. How else can he
arrive at the rather curious assertion that "In accepting the idea of the
general strike all the while knowing it is a myth, we are operating
exactly like a modern physicist . . ."?[129]

Even more directly opposed to the Marxist point of view on questions of ideology is Sorel's parallel between certain of the mysterious elements of socialism and those of religion. Although Sorel is careful to insist that socialism and religion are not the same thing, he notes, as with the general strike myth, that the mythic or mysterious element in religion has not been attenuated by rationalist liberalism, Protestantism or the assaults of socialism; on the contrary, the more Protestantism degenerates into skeptical Unitarianism, the more mystical Catholicism becomes.[130] Furthermore, Sorel does not foresee any necessary decline of religious enthusiasm in history. Religion is a permanent aspect of the human condition not to be "unmasked" by any progressive de-mythification imposed on the world by Marx's ideological method. Certain aspects of religion, like the myth of the general strike, will remain secure from attack.

This Sorelian approach to religion is nowhere better demonstrated than in the treatment given Ernest Renan. Sorel attacks Renan, not for his religiosity, as Marx might have, but because Renan naïvely attempts to unmask Christianity while sympathizing with it. For example, Sorel notes Renan's assertion that legends are necessary to keep the Church alive; Renan says that these legends are not "true" because they partake of the supernatural and the future will no longer believe in the supernatural: "The supernatural is not true, and everything that is not true is condemned to die. . . . Thus neither Judaism nor Christianity will be eternal."[131] What is truly contradictory about Renan, according to Sorel, is that he participates, in an ambiguous way, in the debunking process: stylistically by making the life of Jesus into a novel (thus making the life itself seem to be only a story) and "scientifically" by tracing the miracles of the Gospels back to everyday events (for example, the Star of the East was a meteorite). This leads Renan into a trap. He must explain the miracles and yet avoid calling them pious frauds—thus *explaining* the glory of heroes and at the same time *preserving* their glory.

By recounting the story of Christianity as a novelist would and insisting on scientific probity at the same time, Renan misses the point. One cannot, according to Sorel, probe fruitfully the origins of Christianity without engaging in highly "unscientific forms of speculation." Science is a misleading procedure when applied to religion. Renan fails to appreciate the radically different bases of analysis of religion on the one hand and science on the other. There must be a truce between theology and science because "There is a mystery in theology which science cannot probe and is unable to deny."[132] Nor can history be written to prove or disprove the Christian *idea* any more than Christianity can depart from its domain and methods and try to prevent historical studies from clarifying *events* in its domain.

It is useless to try to discover what facts were able to give birth to the illusion of a miracle; rather, "the question is of knowing if this belief has produced something in the history of Christianity."[133] The important factor in any religious study is not trying to discover why its adherents believe in a certain thing but why they consider that belief *important*. This Renan fails to do, simply because he is facing backwards. By looking behind a movement, in trying to uncover its origins, the continuity between one movement and another is emphasized. But in tracing Christianity back to its Judaic roots, Renan fails to uncover what was genuinely new in the movement. This concept of the new beginning is feared precisely because it must appeal to miracles and to feats of overwhelming strength. But, Sorel says, "I do not see why it astonishes us more than the creations of cultural causes which by and large escape all determinism, or those of great inventions which remain so deeply mysterious. . . ."[134]

Furthermore, Sorel finds Renan wrong in his conclusions about the end of religion; it is precisely the rationalist prejudice in Renan that leads him to extrapolate this end. But the one important characteristic of Christianity that so impresses Sorel is the ability it has exhibited to renew itself through many transformations.

We can see here, I think, the radical conclusions that Sorel draws from the consequences of both holism and the idea of progress. By refusing to look at history as a logical development of sequential stages and by rejecting the notion of inherent "contradiction," Sorel sees no need for looking at a necessary resolution of these contradictions. Since history is not logical, contradictions are only conflicts which need not be resolved and which produce unpredictable and often unscientific forms of thought. Sometimes (though by no means always) "irrational" thoughts like the myth of the general strike constitute the "true" consciousness of men engaged in everyday activities; and rationalistic and pseudo-scientific ideas like progress, on which Marx relies in part, constitute false consciousness.

It is perhaps boringly fashionable to say that Sorel "stands Marx on his head," but with respect to his theory of myths it is useful to say it. And since it is possible to attribute the differences between Sorel and Marx to Sorel's "Bergsonianism," it is to this problem that we should now turn.

VII   BERGSONIANISM*

Besides William James, Henri Bergson is one of the two important "later" influences on Sorel's thinking, though we must be careful to note that Sorel derived much of his understanding of class struggle and of social

---

* See Chapter 8, section 2.

myths from other sources.[135] Although Sorel had read some Bergson by
1894, it was not until about 1900, when he heard Bergson's lectures at
the *Collège de France,* that the full power of Bergson impressed itself
on Sorel. Primarily, Bergson helped Sorel express the theory of the
myth;[136] and for that reason Bergson's ideas deserve some exposition here.

Bergson distinguishes two basic concepts: time and space. *Space* is
the realm of geometric forms and measurement, the sphere of rational
calculation and of science. *Time* cannot be grasped entirely by the same
intellectual faculties as grasp the spatial object. Basic to the concept of
time is what Bergson calls *duration.* Duration makes it possible to look
at the world in time and this means to look at things that are in a
state of flux, of *becoming.* As Bergson expresses it in *Evolution créatrice,*
the intellect cannot perceive this motion or duration: "When we say
'The child becomes a man,' . . . [t]he reality, which is the *transition*
from childhood to manhood, has slipped between our fingers. We have
only the imaginary stops 'child' and 'man,' and we are very near to saying that one of these stops . . . is . . . at all points of the course."[137] The
world does not stand still, it rushes by in constant turmoil. And there is
"more in a movement than in the successive positions attributed to the
moving object," more than a series of discrete frames, as on a motion
picture film, "more in a becoming than in the forms passed through in
turn, more in the evolution of form than the forms assumed one after
another."[138]

Bergson reifies change into a reality that is more real than the immediate "stops" through which change passes. Movement itself is more
genuine than the snapshots taken in an attempt to depict it. For Bergson, as for Sorel, movement is everything, and for this reason Bergson is
helpful to Sorel in stressing the underlying historicity of social movements while rejecting their hidden reasons. (As we shall see, however,
Bergson sees more unity in movement than Sorel does.)

Now Bergson is a philosopher of life or of the life force—the *élan
vital*—which he depicts as movement. "Life in general is mobility itself;
particular manifestations of life accept this mobility reluctantly, and
constantly lag behind. It is always going ahead; they want to mark time.
. . . It might be said that life tends toward the utmost possible action,
but that each species prefers to contribute the slightest possible effort.
Regarded in what constitutes its true essence, namely, as a transition
from species to species, life is a continually growing action."[139]

This living entity, life as a manifestation of movement, must be appre-
hended by a set of faculties that go far beyond the intellect. "When the
intellect undertakes the study of life, it necessarily treats the living like
the inert, applying the same [geometrical] forms to this new object,
carrying over into this new field the same old habits that have succeeded

so well in the old." Thus if we leave biological and psychological facts to the intellect alone, to positive science, the philosophy based on intellect will "*a priori* accept the doctrine of the simple unity of knowledge and of the abstract unity of nature. The moment it does so, its fate is sealed. The philosopher no longer has any choice except between a metaphysical dogmatism and a metaphysical skepticism."[140] The dogmatism will impose an artificial unity on all things, while the skepticism adds nothing to our knowledge. But if knowledge and understanding of life require us to go beyond the bounds of intellect, the duty of philosophy must be "to intervene here actively, to examine the living without any reservation as to practical utility, by freeing itself from the forms and habits that are strictly intellectual." We should begin this procedure by separating the living from the inert; the inert "enters naturally into the frames of the intellect, but . . . the living is adapted to these frames only artificially, so that we must adopt a special attitude toward it and examine it with other eyes than those of positive science."[141]

Consequently, philosophy is brought to renounce what Bergson calls the "factitious unity which the understanding imposes on nature from outside" and instead "introduces us into that more vast something out of which our understanding is cut, and from which it has detached itself. . . . Into this reality we shall get back more and more completely, in proportion as we compel ourselves to transcend pure intelligence."[142]

Bergson would assign this role of transcendence to the animal instinct, an instinct that is the opposite of intelligence, were it not that instinct is incapable of reflecting on itself and cannot really be a means of understanding. Therefore he discusses *intuition* as performing the function of higher understanding. Intuition is "instinct that has become disinterested, self-conscious, capable of reflecting upon its object and of enlarging it indefinitely." It is intuition that makes us realize that neither mechanical causality nor teleological finality can give us an adequate interpretation of the living process. "By the sympathetic communication which it establishes between us and the rest of the living, by the expansion of our consciousness which it brings about, it introduces us into life's own domain, which is reciprocal interpenetration, endlessly continued creation."[143]

Thus Bergson anticipates the possibility of using intuition to replace the factitious unity of the sciences with a "true inward and living unity." For although it is the tendency of life to bifurcate, to create in the form of a sheaf, by its very growth, divergent directions, nature preserves the different tendencies in the course of their adaptation to its environment. Bergson therefore does not abandon nature and life force to chaos or what he terms "the idea of disorder" or to ignorance but rather would alternate the order of the *inert* and the *automatic* with that of the *vital* and the *willed*.[144] *Disorder* really means the absence of one of these two *orders* and the presence of the other. Even the idea of random selection, chance or accident "merely objectifies the state of mind of one who, expecting one of the two kinds of order, finds himself confronted with the other."[145] If we realize that each of the two types of order is contingent on the other, knowledge is possible. And this knowledge makes us aware of a kind of unity or totality on a transrational level.

Action clearly does not mean disorder; it implies an expanding and changing unity on the order of the willed rather than the geometric (automatic). It is the only kind of unity which allows for creativity. "It is of the essence of reasoning to shut us up in the circle of the given. But action breaks the circle. If we had never seen a man swim, we might say that swimming is an impossible thing. . . . Reasoning, in fact, always nails us down to the solid ground. But if, quite simply, I throw myself into the water . . . I may keep myself up enough at first by merely struggling, and gradually adapt myself to the new environment."[146] It is precisely through such intuited situations which transcend the intellect that "we feel ourselves most intimately within our own life. It is into pure duration that we then plunge, a duration in which the past, always moving on, is swelling unceasingly with a present that is absolutely new." During such moments in the unpredictable aspects of living "we feel the spring of our will strained to its utmost limit. We must, by a strong recoil of our personality on itself, gather up our past which is slipping away, in order to thrust it, compact and undivided, into a present which it will create by entering. Rare indeed are the moments when we are self-possessed to this extent: it is then that our actions are truly free."[147]

It is in these rare moments of Bergson's inner freedom that Sorel believes the working class will attempt to "force" history in response to the myth of the general strike; that is, when the will recoils like a spring to gather up all the memories of experience and coordinate them into a complete and inner coherence. The concept also explains why the myth need never take place as an actual historical event, for the "recoil" may be subjective and focus primarily on men's own conduct as opposed to "externality." In any event, the recoil is immensely creative. The more we succeed in making ourselves conscious of our progress in this act of the recoil of the will, a recoil that allows us to transcend mere intellect, "the more we feel the different parts of our being enter into each other, and our whole personality concentrates itself in a point, or rather a sharp edge, pressed against the future and cutting it unceasingly." If we relax, on the other hand, and allow ourselves to float into passivity, the self is at once scattered, and our past is "broken up into a thousand recollections made external to one another. They give up interpenetrating in the degree that they become fixed." Our personality thus veers away from time and "descends in the direction of space. It coasts. . . ."[148]

 With respect to the positive role Bergson assigns to the intellect, Sorel sees him, like Marx, as stressing the notion of *Homo faber* or man the tool-maker. It is in this function that the rational intellect has scope: "Intelligence, considered in what seems to be its original feature, is the faculty of manufacturing artifical objects, especially tools to make tools, and of indefinitely varying the manufacture."[149] But Sorel criticizes Bergson on this ground. Bergson admits that animals such as insects also fabricate things whereas he considers it essential to determine "in what circumstances the intelligence in manifesting itself ought to establish an absolute demarcation between men and animals." In his zeal to separate the living from the inert, Bergson is led to obscure the difference between men and animals, a confusion Sorel attributes to failure to recognize that "there is a specifically human intelligence which corresponds to the economics of production and there is a zoological intelligence destined to remain mysterious; common sense distinguishes zoological intelligence more or less vaguely in actions where intelligence functions with the instinct; the aesthetic and religious philosophy of life is called to speculate on it."[150] Sorel distinguishes between the objects of intelligence, between the "natural nature" of life itself and of natural phenomena such as planetary movements on the one hand, and the "artificial nature" of human fabrication and experimentation on the other. It is only in the second realm, because of man's ability to impose his will on the heretofore unorganized realm of nature, that man can know what he makes.

 In order to understand this central criticism, we must realize that although Sorel accepts Bergson's distinction between the living and the inert, he does so only for pragmatic reasons; he does *not* accept the metaphysical assumptions that underly Bergson's conception. According to Bergson, the division between living and inert means that the intellect must focus primarily on the geometric or spatial realm, which is the realm of passivity. Bergson contrasts the intellectual realm of geometric thought with that of the vital, the willing. According to Sorel, Bergson's version of the idea that "the more consciousness is intellectualized, the more it is spatialized" is ideally suited to a kind of fabrication in which there is no willing element, that is, to the extreme division of labor at that specific stage of the capitalist era which allowed men operating with increasingly perfected machines to "coast" into automatism as they performed increasingly repetitive and minute tasks. Since mechanism is the realm of spatiality, and since the task of the intellect is, to Bergson, to bind like space to like space, as machinery is perfected "the more easily man can suit his movements to those of a machine." Furthermore, the more easily a worker can do this, the more likely he is to "coast" away from vitality and spirituality toward automatism, the more likely it is that he will become "more insensitive to the insinuations of liberty." As the only free realm, the realm of vitality, disappears from labor, free citizens will become serfs.[151] According to the logic of this position, the mechanistic world of the modern workshop is antithetical to the transrational world of the living and the vital. But this is what Sorel denies.

To Sorel Bergsonianism is an offshoot of an outmoded nineteenth-century view of industry in which the division of labor, with its attendant alienation, boredom and fatigue, was carried to the extremes which Marx described in *Capital*. It is important to understand that Sorel views modern industry as having gone beyond this extreme division of labor and having entered a new stage in which because of rapid technical progress, "qualities of observation, comparison and decision are needed. . . . While in the past the worker would have drifted into automatism, he now thinks about the running of machines, as he recalls the lessons of his professional master."[152] The most modern factories interchange among themselves the workers who operate different machines so as to break the monotony of work. The *alienation* of Marx, with its roots in the division of labor based on specialization, is seen by Sorel to have been passed by in the new pattern: Marx's desire for the transcendance of alienation has already been realized. A romantic view of modern industry replaces Marx's dismal view of wage slavery.

But precisely because creativity does exist in modern production, according to Sorel, the feeling of tension common to any creative enterprise returns; breaking the workers' habits formed under the old system requires good supervision, training and inventiveness. "Only an intelligent apprenticeship, begun early, can give the majority of men confidence in their capacities to adapt to various tasks." Only in this emphasis does Sorel accept the Bergsonian view that men tend to coast when entering the realm of rationalized and mechanized industry. He rejects Bergson's arbitrary separation between spatiality and will and instead distinguishes between abstract and concrete reason. Concrete reason, when related to machines, means that men will have to show more exertion instead of less. Attached to Sorel's romanticism of the role of the worker on the workshop floor is a *Sturm und Drang* view that increasing struggle and effort are necessary to overcome the resistance of nature. Men will be subject to labor indefinitely in the modern machine era precisely because in it, more than in any other age, nature must be dominated. The artificial nature of human artifice will wage incessant war on "natural nature"; the doctrine that the realm of machines compels "relaxation," which Bergson sees as inevitable, can and will be overcome, according to Sorel.[153]

We may ask what the foregoing criticism does to the idea of the myth of the general strike expressed, in 1906, in such strongly Bergsonian terms. Should we not, and can we not, be satisfied with Marxist rationalism, with practical experience? The answer is negative but that it is most likely that Sorel's reliance on Bergson has always been somewhat overstated. As evidence of this, it is not the thought of Bergson that Sorel uses as his final framework of analysis on moral questions but rather pragmatism as reflected in William James's writings. By the time he published *De l'utilité du pragmatisme* in the penultimate year of his life, Sorel could better articulate his criticism of Bergson. Of his earlier judgments he said, "I did not always come to satisfactory conclusions because at this time I had not dreamed of using pragmatism in this criticism."[154] Once Sorel did use pragmatic criteria to judge Bergson, the possibility of his relying on Bergson in social criticism became more remote.

Sorel's pragmatic criticisms of Bergson are found in several areas. First of all, the idea of *duration* associated with life force for Bergson is not merely instrumental as it is for Sorel. Bergson reifies duration into a kind of objective reality rather than a convenient product of the imagination; Sorel phrases it that Bergson "seemed to believe that the precepts of biological philosophy contain more of reality than the laws discovered by physicists in the course of their experiments"[155] instead of understanding that they are merely products of the imagination that have a pragmatic use. By stressing the intuitive nature of knowing, Bergson rules out the conceptual *utility* of the concept of duration that is important to Sorel.

Second, Sorel notes that to use Bergson extensively is to fall into the "vice of parallelism." By stressing the life force, Bergsonianism leads to explanations rooted in biological analogies rather than in clearly explained social facts.[156] Sorel distrusts the analogies which see society as some kind of organism, and he rejects Darwinism in particular to explain the development of society.

Third, Sorel is a methodological as well as an epistemological pluralist, while Bergson is subject to holism. The notion of *diremptions* he had used to understand Marx, Sorel also applies to Bergson. Bergson's holism is reflected in his notion of the *integral experience* and his concept of the *élan vital* that unify into one the whole of human experience. Furthermore, for Bergson, "Sociology and biology formed two . . . concordant series such that the causes suitable for explaining one explain the other." To Sorel each explanation should be rooted in solid but discrete historical reality. But Bergson, he points out, cannot so classify a hypothesis because his distinction between instinct and reason and their respective objects, the vital and the inert, is the kind of speculation that "we cannot control by means of historical proofs."[157]

Fourth, as with other holistic theories such as Platonism, Bergsonianism introduces us to a metaphysical hierarchy. Bergson argues, for example, that *disorder* has no genuine existence and that the term itself only objectifies "the deception of a mind which finds before it an order different from what it needs."[158] Disorder in a room is a kind of order but it is not willed. Sorel insists that disorder is the natural state of humankind surmounted only with great difficulty; that it is to fall victim to the ideology of the nineteenth century to find some hidden cunning or higher order in apparent disorder. In fact, Bergson commits the primal Socratic sin of postulating unity and reality to that which is not real.

In short, though he denies rationalist metaphysics, through his metaphysical holism Bergson readmits it through the back door. His reality is integral, unified and hierarchical, while Sorel's (as is James's) is fragmented, chaotic and pluralistic.

The question remains as to how Sorel can extol the catastrophe of the general strike which confronts the capitalist order by citing the *integral experience* of the proletarian class. One could answer simply that the general strike is a myth, but a more basic clue is found in the essentially pragmatic character of both the general strike and Sorel's general outlook. Sorel insists that even though the general strike is a myth, this myth has certain *practical* consequences. This perspective bears centrally on the fact that, in the final stage of Sorel's career, it is pragmatism, not Bergsonianism, that provides him with the standards he considers appropriate for evaluating social theory.

VIII PRAGMATISM*

William James and Henri Bergson are often linked in philosophical writings, as they are in Sorel's. James accepts the nonrational component of activity from Bergson. Reading Bergson, James says, "made me bold." Similarly, James insists on the importance of *becoming* or on process as opposed to fixed states and static forms.

But while James gains from Bergson both a critique of intellectualism and appreciation of *duration,* there are large differences in what they believe. For James, experience is everything while for Bergson experience, though proclaimed to be supreme, is often viewed through metaphysical lenses. As a consequence, James sees the world as a highly disordered place: a "blooming, buzzing confusion" that cannot be sub-

---

* See Chapter 8, section 1.

sumed under a giant *one*. While the "integral experience" abolishes "otherness" for Bergson, for James the meaning of any proposition can always be brought down to some particular consequence in our future practical experience, and no metaphysically unifying source such as the *élan vital* is needed.

In the same way, James denies that duration is an independent part of reality and in so doing rejects the hierarchy of experience which places duration and life force on a higher plane than empirical experience. Intuitive knowledge for Bergson cannot be used scientifically, for this would give it a quality of rationality, enabling it to invent truth, and would be a contradiction in terms. But James denies the inherent distinction between intuition and reason, between non-reason and science. This emphasis of James's is his most radical: to assert that non-rational and rational experience are equally important in our everyday lives is to strip traditional empiricism of its rationalistic bent and accept *any* experience as data. The distinction between reason and non-reason, or science and intuition, is only a difference of degree.

It is on this matter that Sorel comments on James in a most relevant way. Both James and Sorel are open to charges of being radically subjectivistic, and in *De l'utilité du pragmatisme* Sorel seems to anticipate this criticism by going to some lengths to discuss the problem in James. James, he says, opens himself to subjectivism when he asserts that religious belief has a certain subjective validity if it "assures mental peace."[159] But this cannot be the only standard; pragmatism, according to Sorel, "ought to be taken pragmatically."[160] If we ask why this strand of James's thought should be considered less respectable than Sorel's acceptance of the mysterious quality in socialist and religious thought, Sorel insists that James fell prey to the bland acceptance of religion inherent in Yankee Protestantism; in many competing sects a common core of theology obscured theological differences.[161] Thus all types of spiritual experience seemed the same to James whereas they do not to Sorel.

And just as James unifies spiritual experience, he does the same for what we call *science* in accepting the most naïve versions of it laid down by European theorists. But, Sorel claims, this monolithic science is antithetical to subjectivism; the Americans "would have scarcely admitted that one could find subjectivism in a reasoned description of procedures which had led to the wondrous discoveries of the laboratories."[162] The comment was true especially at a time when it was no longer fashionable for scientists to call forth subjective hypotheses to explain matters. Sorel insists that we must not confuse subjectivism with metaphysical pluralism. Science has wide variations, and its methods vary according to the object of study.

A basic question raised in the context of Sorel's pragmatism is
whether it provides a satisfactory bridge between the pseudo-holism of
the myth of the general strike which, in Bergsonian fashion, should be
accepted *en bloc,* and Sorel's scientific pluralism. It is interesting that in
De l'utilité du pragmatisme Sorel never mentions the myth. Nevertheless, it is apparent in *Réflexions sur la violence* that Sorel judges the
efficacy of the mythic element (if not Bergson's ideas) primarily by
pragmatic criteria. For example: myths "do not prevent a man from
learning to profit from all the observations he makes in the course of his
life and . . . they are no obstacle to the fulfillment of his normal business."[163] English and American sectarians were in no way hindered from
the normal pursuit of their daily occupations, and in their day-to-day
business they were extremely practical. Pragmatism is seen clearly, too,
in Sorel's repeated assertions of the irrelevance of the fulfillment of
myths—that the myth alone is important. Even assuming that the revolutionaries are wholly deluded, they realize great strength in accepting
it: "Even if the only result of the myth is to render the socialist conception more *heroic*, it already would on that account alone be looked upon
as having incalculable value."[164]

What Sorel does with his pragmatism is to bring the Marxist theory
of ideology to its logical conclusion. If, as Marx says in speaking of
ideology, we can never interpret the history of our times in the same
way that actors think of it, if "men make history" but in ways not anticipated by them, and if Sorel is right in saying that "scientific socialism"
is unable to bridge these gaps, then we must, with Sorel, accept, as
any pragmatist will accept, "a heterogeneity between the ends realized
and the ends given."[165] But this should not trouble us any more than a
scientist, an artist or a soldier is disturbed if he is unable to predict the
consequences of his activities. The myth is as much a part of reality as
the machine because the myth moves men to action; that is, it has practical and perceivable consequences. It is a force in the world, and people
act on the present with it. Since to be scientific is to know what forces
exist in the world and how to utilize them by reasoning from experience,
we can now understand better why Sorel says "In accepting the idea of
the general strike, all the while knowing it is a myth, we are operating
exactly like a modern physicist who has full confidence in his science,
all the while knowing the future will consider it antiquated."[166] Knowledge is derived again from the act of *making*, not of predicting.

The difference between Marx and Sorel is the difference between
Marx's view of *praxis* and pragmatism. Bertrand Russell has said that
Marx is really a pragmatist; but other writers have maintained that
because of its pluralism and its acceptance of the irrational, pragmatism
does not have the same cataclysmic vision that Marxism does—that it is

even conservative.[167] Sorel attempts to confound the second assertion, but certainly the pragmatism of his endeavor makes great departures from the Marxist tradition.

One may wonder why Sorel was hesitant to discuss the myth of the general strike after the failure of the workers' revolts in 1909. If he said little about the myth after that, his own pragmatism might be said to be at work. Furthermore, it would be a mistake to attribute complete consistency to Sorel, for he was the last to claim this for himself. The Bergsonian pragmatic myth does not always square so easily with scientific pluralism, and pragmatism's bland acceptance of the religious experience might open it to anything. In James's terms, in a truly pragmatic world all things are acceptable if they can be said to satisfy someone's inner needs; but as a discriminating test for truth, this fails. In short, one might conclude that Sorel has not dodged the question of subjectivism on this issue satisfactorily.

In the later essay "On the Origin of Truth," Sorel seems to anticipate the difficulty readers have had in understanding his shift from emphasizing psychological aspects of the myth of the general strike to discussing the relativistic social pluralism which looks upon established institutions somewhat more sympathetically. In this essay, a chapter of *De l'utilité du pragmatisme,* there is a complete absence of any reference to the myth of the general strike, and the tone throughout is quite new. (It should be emphasized that Sorel never denounced the myth, and in 1920 he wrote an appendix to the *Réflexions* dedicated to Lenin: to his dying breath, he waved the flag of revolution.) It does lend credence to Marxist assertions that the difference between Marxist *praxis* and pragmatism is one of radicalism and conservatism. For whatever Sorel's personal radicalism, the tone of the essay on the pragmatic understanding of truth is a perfect representation of why he cannot be pigeon-holed into any convenient political category. In this work, Sorel leads us to understand that any social institution can be justified if it satisfies certain pragmatic criteria—if it "works." What is common to this essay and his earlier "radical" writings such as the *Réflexions* is their emphasis on certain criteria for the fulfillment of moral ideals. In *Pragmatisme*, for example, Sorel expresses his satisfaction at finding a good test for the difficult unification of moral criteria with productive life.

"On the Origin of Truth" may be seen as a final expression of Sorel's social perspective. In it the ancient rather than the modern version of aristocracy is preferred. Excellence rather than birth or wealth *per se* is offered as the measure of a man; when wealth is the criteria, it should reflect, as Sorel says it does in America, the fulfillment of productive tasks which can be accomplished only through the possession of certain moral qualities—heroic characteristics typical of the great American

financial barons. To understand this combination of equality with exclusiveness, Sorel's notion of the *Cité* is important. In a *Cité* a certain
equality exists, but, in ancient fashion, it is an equality among equals
whose membership is restricted to those directly able to carry out
prescribed tasks. In Aristotle's terms, it is an equality among equals.
Sorel distinguishes himself from the modern elitist, who emphasizes
administrative ability or what he calls *capacité,* by singling out those
who, like the medieval craftsmen of the *Cité esthétique,* worked with a
purpose not entirely understood by the men who used their cathedrals
and other constructions. When these builders began to cultivate the
patronage of artistic consumers, the moral vitality—the integrity—of
the *Cité esthétique* degenerated. In this delicate balance of a certain
kind of aristocracy with a specifically delineated genre of equality, Sorel
discovers the pragmatic criteria for moral excellence which had been
sketched in a somewhat different way in earlier essays (certainly he had
anticipated the values of the *Cité esthétique* in the *Réflexions*). When
aristocracy degenerates into oligarchy, he concludes, when American
millionaires come to lack the public perspective of heads of boards of
trustees and seek only to feather their nests, then they will become a
decomposed elite similar to that governing France in his time.

In the same vein, when an elite is concerned more with the tastes of
the consumer and less with the integrity of production, or when the
man of action becomes an *administrateur* catering to the needs and
traditions of *étatisme,* justifying his superior position on the grounds of
ability, the same phenomenon occurs: the self-enclosed integrity of the
group gives way to a watery and muddled *democracy*—a democracy
which in reality becomes more hierarchical and elitist, more divorced
from reality, than the aristocracy it pretends to replace. Sorel would
prefer the honest exclusiveness of a close-knit creative minority to the
democratic pretentions of a statist oligarchy living from the labor of
others. That is why, even in 1898, he could say that "it does not seem
like a very good idea for the proportion of syndicalists to become very
high in a trade." The continuity between Sorel's final statement of social
theory and his early writings is fairly obvious.

What is more problematic is how in his last work, Sorel can uphold
the *noblesse oblige* of American millionaires serving on boards of
trustees after extolling them for their war-like virtues in the *Réflexions
sur la violence.* Is the notion of a *Cité morale*—an aristocracy of public
service with roots squarely in the business world—compatible with the
virtues of class warfare? Surely the sympathetic picture of America
which Sorel owes to Paul de Rousiers is partly due to a comparative
absence of class struggle—unless perhaps the class struggle has not received enough attention on the part of American historians. But one

wonders at times whether Sorel is not oscillating in a rather arbitrary way between the ideals of social unity and the virtues of social conflict.

It is this difficulty, I think, which makes the thought of Sorel somewhat open to question when applied in modern situations. For example, how would Sorel have interpreted the phenomenal productivity of Japanese workmen cheering the incoming work shifts on to higher levels of achievement? All of Sorel's productive virtues are there, and the pragmatic test of success is fulfilled, but such a system as the Japanese is characterized by extraordinary social cohesion, by what would seem to be a relative absence of class struggle. Conversely, the British working class has a high degree of class consciousness, but it might be questioned whether members live up to Sorel's standard of productivity, inventiveness and heroic self-sacrifice. In short, what kind of struggle constitutes the functional prerequisite to greatness (if any) if nobility of spirit and heroism on the workshop floor exist anyway?

In reading his essay, "On the Origin of Truth," one is confirmed in the impression derived from previous works that Sorel would—pragmatically—scrap social conflict if greatness could be achieved without it, if "struggle" could be interpreted as necessary only to achieve dominance over the materials with which we work. A similar thesis is reflected in Sorel's mildly ambiguous view of the state in the *Réflexions*. At one point it is condemned; at others, Lenin is the "greatest Russian statesman since Peter the Great" (neither being a known anarchist).[168] Part of the resolution to this ambiguity is that the state is usually condemned in modernity because of its failures, not because of its successes. Still, for Sorel the failures or successes are measured by moral criteria. The essay is quite consistent with his other works in one principal way: Sorel did not want men to be virtuous in order to effectuate the social revolution; he wanted social action for the purpose of making men more noble. He is entirely consistent in all his writings when he argues that the state will not produce virtue, only virtue will produce a great society.

Perhaps a further problem exists here, however. How are greatness and nobility and morality to be judged in the first place? The circular question of whether people are great because they are moral or moral because they are triumphant and great is inherent in Sorel's endeavor to tie ethics and productivity together. His attempt to answer the problem through pragmatic criteria underscores the difficulty of applying Sorelian ethics to any dissident group. For example, what are the criteria for success in a group like the Black Muslims? Can we use Sorelian criteria for an understanding of this group without trivializing Sorel? My own inclination is to say yes, since Sorel himself applied his criteria to a working class that, at the time, failed to live up to his standards—that

is, failed to become "great" by his definition. It would be useful to compare the remedy for working-class drunkenness described in Sorel's
essay *The Socialist Future of the Syndicates* with the Muslims' success
in combating drug addiction and crime among blacks today. In both
cases, active organizational struggles by creative minorities produced a
totally new climate of opinion—a new psychology—that had results far
more fruitful than had been obtained by traditional methods.[169]

But whether or not his ideas can be applied to any one group in
society, Sorel can, as I stated at the outset of this essay, tell us something about the nature of social understanding in general. It was Sorel's
belief that most social science is a failure. Whether he would have
judged modern sociology and political science in the same way that he
judged the endeavors of his contemporaries is problematical. We do
know that in order to understand a social movement, one must comprehend the kinds of myths and images—the psychology—that have impelled the movement to a special position above the diverse groups in
society. What is sought is the special quality that makes a movement
exceptional and great beyond its numbers. This force might be said to
be what in politics is called civic responsibility or public spirit; and it is
apparent that modern social science has failed to take sufficient account
of this quality, precisely because it cannot be evaluated and measured
by rational criteria. The question-begging nature of this shortcoming is
one of the matters to which we might speak directly. For Sorel teaches
us that Marxism cannot be looked upon solely from the perspective of
the economic self-interest of the proletariat if it is to survive as a force
and, conversely, that we cannot rely on a road paved with good intentions and good wishes in order to bring about moral transformation. The
delicate combination of psychological and economic impulses which
produces an effective social force is studied by Sorel but not sufficiently
analyzed by modern social science and certainly not by contemporary
political science.

Our failure is understandable if not pardonable. In studying society
from the academy, we become, to an extent, detached from it. Anyone
writing from the ivory tower is at a loss really to "sympathize" with a
movement in the Sorelian sense, unless he departs from the academy at
times and joins the movement directly. We can only understand that it
is necessary to do so.

IX   CONCLUSION

Part of the irony of Georges Sorel's writings is that he is in the same
position as the academician. And none of his writing is more poignant
than his review of a mythical tale told by the writer Lucien Jean of the

voyager arriving among peasants and preaching the necessity of a cult of heroism. "Men generally lack happiness and beauty" because they use up their life "in superfluous efforts without definite end and for derisory causes," the traveler says. To which the peasants respond by going about their business, proclaiming his cult useless because "The exultation which you offer us we find in everything around us," in the life and needs of the working world itself.[170] Sorel lauds the insights of this fable, but it illuminates his own dilemma. This prophet of heroism and practicality was not heeded by the practical heroes who had no time for his books, while the intellectuals, who, of course, constituted his audience, could not accept the strictures he placed on their ability to understand. Aside from a group of like-minded partisans, Sorel really had in the final analysis, a rather small audience. In any event, the maxim that "man knows only what he makes" was followed less by Sorel than by workers' leaders. When asked if he read Sorel, Victor Griffuellhes, secretary general of the Confederation of Syndicates, responded, "I read Dumas."

Certainly Sorel is not the first to emphasize the non-rational elements in politics or the interest basis of ideology; but he is one of the foremost writers of this century to write extensively on the great importance of moral contingency in social movements and the uniqueness of these contingencies. Very few writers today, particularly in the social sciences, write in these ways; and few, to my knowledge, would maintain with Sorel that the fundamental question in a movement for social change is not the politics of development but a psychology of revolution that lies squarely in the sociology of virtue.

J.L.S.

Riverside, California
September 1975

CHAPTER 1

from
The Trial
of Socrates

THE GREEK OLIGARCHY[1]

I   Patriotism of the old democrats. Ancient equality. Influence of the Sophists. Division of classes according to learning. Duties of the privileged. Obligation to revolt.

II   The influence of philosophers on revolutions. The oligarchical principle of revolutionaries. The secret political societies. The end of democracy.

III   Pride of the ancient democrats. Conservative character of Homer. Scorn of the new men for Homer.

I

. . . The Athenians of olden times were quite superior to our envious, ignorant and gluttonous bourgeoisie. The Jacobin type did not exist in early Athens. Citizens were not merchants, demanding a guarantee for their trade, protection of their industry and soliciting government favors. They were soldiers whose existence was tied to the greatness of the city. The least weakness would put the state in peril.

We have said that the chief aim of ancient education was the preparation for war: this education was not very complex, and consequently it was accessible to all citizens. Curtius evaluated this ancient Athenian in-

62

struction very well.[2] "This intellectual culture, so simple in appearance and so unified, nonetheless involved the whole man, all the more profoundly and energetically as these young minds, not being distracted by multiple tasks, could more freely profit from what was offered to them as spiritual nourishment. And, on the whole, look what was given to an Athenian child! The Homeric epic, with its magnificent portrayal of the world, which inspires heroic feelings and the passion for lofty deeds; liturgical hymns, with their rich treasure of sacred legends originating in the temples . . . finally, the elegy in its infinite diversity . . . which expressed with striking clarity everything that a brave citizen of Athens should know and attempt! . . . As the young man had happily grown up assimilating the best of the intellectual richness of the people, participation in public life became for him a superior school in which he perfected himself and demonstrated his ability. Each new progress in poetry was at the same time an extension of popular education."

Here we stop, while regretting that we cannot quote this admirable passage in its entirety.

The men of antiquity did not understand equality in the same way as modern philosophers, or at least as most French writers. Aristotle strongly upheld the principle of equality, but with the reservation that this condition is limited to persons who are capable of being made equal.[3] In his ideal republic, he very strictly maintains the principle of class, and today his constitution would appear to many to be not a little feudal.

Fouillée reproaches the Athenians for forming a false democracy and for not giving political equality to the inhabitants of their empire.[4] One could not be more completely mistaken about the conditions of Hellenic life. Without a doubt such a decree would have resulted in the complete ruination of Greece. The cities, which had accepted the domination of the Persians, and which had long since demonstrated their political impotence, were deservedly transformed into dependency.

The Athenians had proved that they alone had the necessary power to resist the Persians and to conclude great wars successfully. It was necessary and just that leadership devolved on them. Similarly, in the Peripatetic city, power belongs to the warriors who defend the country, govern it and offer sacrifices to the gods! The rest of the inhabitants work to support them.

This privileged position developed in the Athenian plebians a pride which at first glance appears quite misplaced and which comprises the most remarkable trait of the people of this period.

We must not forget that equality is usually an idle word. In order to realize it, and in order for it to be legitimate, one is led to do as Aristotle did—limit it to a small caste. We have seen that in Athens, ancient education had the effect of bringing the citizens very near to this idea of Peripatetic democracy.

The development of Sophist schools completely changed this situation. The question of what bases the existing political inequality rested upon does not seem to have been very carefully examined; rather the Sophists sought to determine on what bases democratic equality could be founded, and it was soon concluded to be absurd in fact and in law.

The ancient uniformity of culture completely disappeared. Society was divided into two distinct categories. The poor generally remained faithful to the old system; few of their children could go near the new schools. The innovators could only ridicule those who were indoctrinated in the old ideas, who mainly admired the old poetic fables and were not up to date on the "correct" ideas.[5]

This aristocracy of intelligence and oratory is often attacked by Aristophanes. The urban Greeks were endowed with such a lively intelligence and such a free spirit that city men were not long in proving to be very superior to country folk. The old soldiers of the Marathon complained of being exposed to ruinous trials, incapable as they were of being able to present their arguments with the finesse of the city dwellers.[6] From the lowly ranks of the urban plebes arose the skillful orators who governed the city.

The Sophists taught the art of debate: the danger of their doctrine was that it did not propose a *moral end* but only success. To succeed by demagogic flattery in a democratic society, by the most refined flattery in the court of a tyrant—such was the aim of the students of the Sophists. They were thus completely indifferent to the principles of different governments. They learned how to manage under all sorts of conditions.[7]

From this point of view, Socrates was quite different from the Sophists, because he sought to convince of the truth, but we also know that his disciples did not always follow him in all his teaching. He had marvelous facility in debate. No Sophist could be compared to him either for his dialectical finesse or for the penetrating grace of his language. All witnesses agree that he was irresistible. We need only have a superficial idea of Hellenic culture in order to recognize that his conversation was extraordinarily compelling.

Xenophon tells us that Critias and Alcibiades attached themselves to Socrates in order to become skillful politicians. It is probable that more than one disciple followed their example. We have already pointed out that this opportunism seems to have been shown in a passage of Aristophanes' *Clouds*. For many students Socrates was the most admirable of professors and the most convincing of Sophists.

When a society is divided into distinct classes in terms of knowledge,

the question of oligarchy is soon posed. We have just said that demagogic rule became a sort of oligarchy of the small shopkeepers and
artisans of Athens—proud and cunning, liars and braggarts—who directed the business of the city to their own profit and to the detriment
of the countryside. . . .

The metaphysical ideas on which Socratism is based lead to further
developing the consequences of this doctrine. We have said that according to Anaxagorism our intelligence produces ideas through participation
in a divine soul. This favor is not entirely natural. By exercise, study and
dialectic it can be increased considerably. We have said that Socrates
was marked by an exceptional sign, but he claimed that equivalent
privilege could be acquired by pious and wise men.

Here we have then the city divided into two categories of citizens.
Those who participate in a very notable way in the divine intellect, who
enjoy a kind of grace, are evidently capable of discovering the truth.
Better than others, they can analyze phenomena and formulate the
natural laws which the divinity has written into nature.[8]

The customary turn of events does not tend to put the government of
cities in the hands of these excellent men who are favored by the gods.
Usually those who possess the power of thought and will necessary to
the administration of states are set aside.

Here we are raised to a new dialectical level. In alienating scholars,
democracy committed an "error" which can be measured by economic
disorder. In alienating privileged people, it commits a "crime" against
divinity. It reverses every law of Providence; it places itself outside the
law.

Those who are prevented from action nevertheless have a mission to
accomplish, for the favors of the gods cannot be considered as merely
creating *rights*. Genius and talent have, above all, duties to fulfill. They
are not allowed to cross their arms and laugh at the stupidities of fools.
They are born for action; they must act.

Socrates asks Charmides:[9] "If someone were capable of winning
laurels in the games, of thus bringing glory to himself and to his homeland, and if, however, he refused to fight, how would you judge such
a man?" "He would clearly be an effeminate coward."

When malevolence and ignorance conspire to prevent the "divine
decree" from being put into practice, the following questions are raised:
Can a government based on the domination of the uneducated over the
educated or the bad over the good call itself legitimate?[10] When the
Good has been formulated and defined, is not a government which is
opposed to the realization of the Good a social ulcer that must be cured
by *sword and fire*? Is not right superior to a purely formal legality? Are
not the good obliged to sacrifice their lives in order to combat evil and

reestablish the divine order, when obstacles exist to its peaceful realization?

This list of questions could easily be lengthened; ordinarily, philosophers dislike taking questions to their logical conclusion and refuse to answer them in a manner consistent with their declared principles. But there is no lack of fervent spirits ready to draw all of the consequences from a doctrine.

II

Revolutions are most often explained in terms of economics. We do not wish to deny the importance of this explanatory factor, but it appears to us to be completely inadequate. Certainly the great crisis of the French Revolution would be mysterious if one did not keep well in mind the appetites of the lower third estate and the agrarian movements. Taine has studied the question from this point of view in an authoritative way. He has given us a definitive psychological description of the men of that time.

Before this admirable work, "revolutionary ideas" were about all that were discussed, and everything was reduced to a sort of crisis of metaphysics. All our histories were deceptive because the authors were incapable of defining these ideas. We do not believe that the study of ideas should be neglected. No constitution can be realized, no important movement can arise in society without an idea. We are thus led to demand from the philosophers an account of their doctrines.

Xenophon tells us that Critias had long been at odds with Socrates. That proves that the philosopher did not directly participate in the revolution. It is even probable that no prominent disciples of Socrates were among the leaders.

All the historians[11] agree on the harmful influence of the Sophists, although none of them participated much in politics. From their abstention one must not draw the conclusion that they were not implicated in Athens' troubles.

Rarely do men of science enter active political life. It is worth noting that usually the more bold and radical they are in their doctrines, the more timid they are in practice. In general, men who resort to violence are quite feeble theorists. We have the example of our revolutionary assemblies as proof of this. Taine has acquainted us with fraudulent "great men" who directed the great European upheaval.

One can go even further and say that the philosophers of the eighteenth century would have protested against their disciples if they had lived long enough to see them in action. Rousseau would have tried in vain to prove to his admirers that they were applying his ideas badly.

They would have replied that a book is made to be read and criticized, that it was regrettable for the author to explain himself so badly. If he had been too recalcitrant, he would have been proscribed like Condorcet.[12] Thus Xenophon's argument does not prove much in favor of his master, Socrates, whom, however, we must be careful not to confuse with the oligarchs.

When the vices of democracy had been brought to light, the need for creating something more scientific was felt. It does not seem that the oligarchs ever had very set ideas on the plan of a constitution. Their ideas had only been seen to work during a revolutionary period. One of the traits of revolutions is to create dictatorial powers in the hands of small groups. We have seen this very well in France in 1793. The majority of a country cannot, in general, easily accept great upheavals founded on absolute theories. A society develops historically and the masses cling to their traditions. Innovators can succeed only by boldness. They are a minority, but if they have faith, they can at times triumph by profiting from favorable opportunities.

Today we know that the Jacobins were few in number. Almost everywhere, the Montagnards were elected only by weak minorities or by fraud. Having attained power, they had nothing more urgent to do than to govern without disturbing the majority. They proved to be more violent the more they were isolated. They were perfectly logical. They alone possessed the revolutionary Idea. Right does not reside in numbers.

In Athens, to return to the old aristocracy was unthinkable; such a restoration would have been impossible. The rich classes were largely won over to the innovations. The youth was full of contempt for the heroic era and for the customs of the time of the Golden Age that Aristophanes longed for so ardently.

In his history Curtius has given curious details on the formation of the oligarchic clubs. He has explained very well the fatal influence of the secret societies on politics of this period. We can only refer to his book.

These societies often served to facilitate debauchery, and it appears that they almost always celebrated some illicit cult.[13] The historian points out a new trait of the secret clubs.[14] "As family ties were loosened these artificial attachments became more frequent. They even imposed on their members, up to a certain point, the obligation of breaking natural ties." Often homosexual love was practiced by the members of the secret societies.

When Aristophanes portrayed the Socratics as animated by a monastic spirit in the Pythagorean way, it is likely that he meant to denounce these new loyalties that were so disastrous for the family and the City.

The restoration of Thrasybulus did not put an end to the transforma-

tion of Athenian society, because the power of the philosophers continued to make itself felt with an ever increasing force. There were no
more soldiers and sailors, but only skeptical and witty shopkeepers. In
a few more years Athens would fall to the level of the Italian republic.

Demosthenes in vain deployed the marvelous resources of his genius
to arouse his fellow citizens. He was admired, but more as a prodigious
artist than a politician. He was not a man of his time. It was Aeschines
who represented progress. Raised on the new doctrines, this rhetorician
was the favorite of the plutocrats while his adversary was wasting his
time trying to revive the ancient spirit of the City.

Aeschines was performing his profession of lawyer; we perhaps have
no right to hold philosophy accountable for his betrayals. But Phocian,
the wise and upright general, was a Socratic. Why did he not uphold
Demosthenes? Why did he go so far as to defend Aeschines in the
scandalous affair of the Embassy?

Curtius perfectly recognized the Platonic influence. In spite of his
admiration for Socrates' disciple, he said,[15] "We must nevertheless agree
that it was impossible to draw lessons from the Academy about solid
principles in order to resolve political questions of the time. . . . The
idealist politics of the Platonists was undoubtedly capable of inflaming
minds; but the Platonists were unable to take a firm stand amidst the
battles of the time and were still less able to cure the ills of this present."

Isocrates was also a Socratic. He was one of Philip's most fervent
admirers. Disillusioned after the battle of Chaeronea in 338 B.C., it is
said that he let himself die of hunger.

Philosophy had completed its work. Athenian democracy succumbed
but it left behind an important monument to its grandeur and its genius
in the work of Demosthenes.

III

Of all governments the worst is the one in which wealth and "talent"
share power. The prejudice of the majority of our historians against the
aristocracy has closed their eyes to the wrongs of constitutional plutocracies.[16]

Under this system, pride of race no longer exists. One must succeed
and once the lid is off, few worry about the means employed. Success
justifies everything and there is no moral ideal—that is the English idea.
The flaw in this government rests on the application of the principle of
exchange. Men do not matter; there are only monetary values. The
predominance of economic ideas thus has the effect not only of obscuring the moral law, but also of corrupting political principles.

Athenian oligarchs came from all social classes. They opened their ranks to all capable and intelligent men. Modern commentators have often been shocked at the way in which Aristophanes treats Euripides. At every turn he reproaches him for being the son of an herb peddler. These criticisms seem in bad taste today.

Demosthenes belonged entirely to the popular party; however, he did not hesitate to reproach Aeschines for his humble origins. In our day, on the contrary, the orator would be given credit for raising himself to a position so far above that of his parents by means of his intelligence and talent. Athenian democracy did not see things in this light. For people of that time it seemed impossible that someone could become a good citizen without having received a manly education. In their opinion nothing could replace this preparation for public life. Study could make a scholar out of a freed slave, but it could not give him the soul of a free man.

We know the important position occupied by Homer in ancient education. This poet was not admired as an artist, but as an excellent teacher. Curtius says quite rightly:[17] "It is through Homer that the Hellenists truly reveal themselves. . . . Thus Homer was like the center of the national conscience, the distinctive symbol of Greece as opposed to the barbarians."

The work of Homer strongly tied the present to the past. The customs of the royal epoch were celebrated with enthusiasm by the poet, who did not foresee that his work, after having charmed the sons of the old Achaean heroes, would become the book of Greek democrats *par excellence*. This epic, so long surviving the circumstances of its creation, imparted to the Greek spirit a conservative complexion.

Aeschylus is hardly less conservative; but, living in a revolutionary period, he pleads the cause of the old customs. His plays are almost all written with the aim of producing a conviction in the mind of the spectators. They are religious, political, and philosophical works.

The principle of finality in art is the rule of aesthetics for Aristophanes: In *The Frogs*, the character representing Aeschylus proves his superiority by establishing that he has formed good citizens, while Euripides maintains that his readers have become subtle and amiable people. We have said that, according to Aristophanes, the new men scorned the old poets. It seems quite certain that the Socratic philosophers shared this viewpoint.

In the *Gorgias*, Socrates says that tragedy is a form of popular rhetoric intended to flatter without edifying.[18] We might think that this senseless statement belongs to Plato himself. One could not be more unjust toward the most marvelous product of Greek civilization.

Fouillée says that Socrates was always reputed to be an enemy of poets;[19] but it could be countered that this tradition originates from the

Platonic dialogues. It is thus useful to see if there are any similar opinions in the works of Xenophon: In his *Banquet*,[20] Niceratus boasts of
knowing all of Homer: "My father, wanting me to become a good man,
compelled me to learn all of Homer's works. . . ." Antisthenes says, "Are
you unaware that every rhapsodist knows these two poems by heart? . . .
Do you know any more inept breed than the rhapsodists?"

Antisthenes has hardly done more than exaggerate Socrates' ideas.
The philosopher, moved by the brutality with which the Cynic spoke
and wanting to console the young man, speaks: "It is evident that they
do not understand the meaning of the verses, unlike you, who have given
a lot of money to Stesimbrotes, Anaxamander and several others, in order
to know the best passage." Then, so as not to prolong the discussion of
this subject, he addresses Critobulus and asks him of what he is proud.

The thought of Socrates is not in doubt. In order to make it clearer
he stresses the price paid to the masters, and we know of his contempt
for the lessons of paid teachers.

In the following chapter each one develops the reasons for his prefer-
ences and Niceratus is asked to justify his admiration for Homer. The
author has him present childish arguments. Niceratus[21] declares that
anything can be found in Homer, and as proof he cites verses of the
Iliad which teach that one should lean forward in a chariot race when
approaching the finish line, and that onion seasons wine well.

Xenophon obviously wants to prove that the supposed practical lessons, drawn from Homer and so praised by the ancients, really do not
amount to much. Antisthenes, always ready to attack, says to Niceratus:
"Do you also know the art of ruling?" The young man cites a verse in
which Homer celebrates Agamemnon as a good prince and brave fighter.
The Cynic makes it clearly understood that Homeric ways are too
ancient to be able to draw practical lessons from the poem, which is
now valuable only as an artistic work.[22]

There were many reasons for the new men abandoning the study of
the old poems. The way in which religious questions are presented
offended them. The Anaxagoreans found the excessively naïve anthro-
pomorphism of Homer absurd. For them, divinity was alien to the world.
Socratic providence was like the counterpart of the ancient gods—
entirely concerned with the passions. The aristocratic temperament, conserver of the old poets, displeased the philosophers, who admitted no
superior qualities other than those of talent and knowledge. . . .

CHAPTER 2

The Socialist Future of the Syndicates[1]

I *New ways of posing the question of the syndicates according to the doctrine of historical materialism.*

II *Difficulties for modern socialism presented by the political problem. Economic bases of the political hierarchy: manual work and intellectual work. Illusion of the supposed superiority of the latter.*

III *Observations of Karl Kautsky on the intelligentsia. Disaster of the intellectuals after a proletarian revolution. The worker against the authority of those outside his profession.*

IV *Formation of the working class according to Marx's schema. Esprit de corps. Importance of strike funds in trade unions. Cooperation: its juridical role.*

V *Moral authority of selected bodies. Governing the working class by its syndicate. Gradual shrinking of the state to the benefit of the trade organs.*

VI *Durkheim's ideas on the moral utility of corporations. Moral influence of English trade unions. Conclusion.*

I

Contemporary socialist writers are far from agreeing on the future of professional syndicates. According to some, syndicates must play a very secondary role and serve as a base for an electoral organization. According to others, the syndicates are called upon to lead the major battle against capitalist society by means of uncompromising strikes. These two theses have been rather improperly designated "political system" and "economic system." I do not want to enter into the argument. I only want to call attention to several theoretical points of view and show that Marx's historical materialism greatly illuminates these problems. Later, when the French public has the complete works of Marx and Engels at its disposal, I plan to treat the theory of the revolutionary proletariat extensively.

First of all, it is necessary to be careful not to confuse Marx's theories with the programs of the parties that quote the author of *Capital* as their authority. "Marxism is and remains a doctrine," says Professor Antonio Labriola. "The parties cannot draw their name nor their reason for being from a doctrine."[2] Even in Germany, from the Congress of Gotha to the Congress of Erfurt, from 1876 to 1892, the Social Democracy wrote into its program proposals whose error Marx had pointed out.[3] Neither should one believe that all the fruits of Marx's labor can be summarized in a few sentences gathered from his works, connected in a dogmatic formula and commented on as the evangelical texts are by theologians. For a long time, Italian socialists have been liberated from any literal restraints: the editors of *Critica Sociale* write easily that Marx's work needs to be completed, that the historical laws of *Capital* can no longer be applied in every instance nowadays. "The moment has come," one of the frequent contributors to this organ of "scientific socialism" recently wrote, "to submit these fundamental principles of socialism to examination. The *Devenir Social* of France contributes rather well to this task of renewal and discussion, as it were, to the tasks set for our scientific equipment. . . . Is it not the mission of Latin peoples to modify, develop and illuminate the content of German thought without altering the substance?"[4] I believe that for the question at hand it suffices to remain faithful to Marx's spirit.

In Marx's doctrine perhaps the most characteristic point, the one that best justifies the name of historical materialism, is this: the development of each system provides the material conditions to execute effective and lasting changes in social relations, in the midst of which the system appears stabilized. We know with what energy the Marxist school insisted on the impossibility of attempting the social revolution so long as capitalism was not sufficiently developed. It is because of this thesis that the school could be accused of fatalism, because it markedly limits the power of will, even when the material force is in the service of an intelligent will.[5]

It seems that too often Marx's thought is not sufficiently probed: all of his disciples say that the revolution can only be the work of the proletariat and that the proletariat is the product of big industry. But they do not see clearly enough that Marx also believed that the working classes would have to acquire juridical and political ability before being capable of victory.

The history of Christianity has often been compared to the history of modern socialism; there is much truth in this comparison, at least in certain respects. If the Church had been merely a school of philosophy preaching a pure morality, it would undoubtedly have disappeared like so many other groups. The Church was a society working to develop new juridical relationships among its members and governing itself according to a new constitution. The day the Edict of Milan proclaimed tolerance, the Emperor gave his blessings to the existence of a hierarchy stronger than the imperial hierarchy and instituted a state within a state. The barbarian invasion did not consist of simple destruction. Today it is generally agreed that the Germans brought juridical systems which were already developed enough to have an influence on institutions, notably on familial organization. Finally, the French Revolution gives us a very clear example of this juridical continuity. What is most striking is not so much its great noisy turmoil, but the preservation of a system which was long developing in the bosom of the bourgeoisie.

It is not a sufficient response to the opponents of socialism, when they ask what the proletarian revolution will be, to ask rhetorically: "On the eve of 1784 could anyone have said what society would be?" Scientific and mechanical prediction is not in any way the province of any social science; for it is not a matter of calculating what will become of particular customs. It is a matter of knowing whether or not the *preparation is sufficient* for the struggle not to end in a destruction of civilization. Paul Deschanel pronounced an incontestable truth when, in his speech to the Chamber of Deputies on July 10, 1897, he said that in 1789 the bourgeoisie had carried out this work of preparation. We should know where the proletariat stands and determine the means that it is using at the present time to prepare itself.

The utopians sought to create a perfect society. The problem is changed; "research no longer relates to what *society should be*, but to what *the proletariat can do*, in the current class struggle."[6] We will now ask what the consequences of syndicalist organization are, as it is now practiced, and consider them from the perspective of preparation.

II

Sociologists confront socialists with the evidence of all known revolutions and ask how one can accept a hypothesis which is based on no historical example. Marx knew the answer very well for he wrote: "All social movements until now have been carried out by minorities for the benefit of minorities."[7]

This empirical law is easily explained when we recall what state ownership has been in modern history. Moreover, the state has played a substantial role in the formation of present industry: "The emerging bourgeoisie could not do without the constant intervention of the state."[8] The thinking of bourgeois socialists is dominated by the statist prejudices of the bourgeoisie.

In a recent book, the most gifted sociologist of the universities, Emile Durkheim, proposes that the organization of corporations and professional federations be subject to the "general action of the state."[9] In the conclusions of his speeches of June 19 and 26 and July 3, 1897, on agriculture, Jaurès proved to be less favorable to associations than the professor from Bordeaux. He declared that henceforth one can form a rather exact idea of what the socialist world will be: "We know that in the property of tomorrow, in the society of tomorrow, the four essential forces which are beginning to form and appear today will combine and function. The first force is the individual—the right of the individual to develop freely without any other limit except to prevent him from exploiting others in any way. . . . There is another element . . . the emerging syndicates, reactionary today, socialist tomorrow, but in any case . . . the first units, in certain respects, of a more collective organization of labor. Then above these agricultural or worker syndicates, or professional groupings by trade, there is the town which, in certain respects and in spite of the division of labor among the diverse parts of the territory, is the first complete unit—richer than the professional organizations, which include only an exclusive and limited element. And finally, above the town, there is the nation, the central organism of unity and perpetuity."[10] It will be noticed that in replacing professional federations by the commune as a middle ground between the local corporations and the state, Jaurès markedly increases the economic power of the state.

I will not stop to discuss in detail this idea which I do not understand clearly, so much is this language devoid of any precision. Besides, is all this really new? Are they not old theories dressed up in beautiful new clothing? The unification of trade associations in the commune seems to be a pure replica of medieval history. If the word "nation" is changed to "kingdom," this becomes a traditional conservative idea. I simply want to call attention to the difficulty which the most intelligent people have in delineating a plan that is independent of traditional political forms.[11] Not only does Jaurès not exclude the state, but he makes it the regulator and master of industrial life!

We are told in response that the future state will be entirely different from that of today; but all we hear are promises of this wonderful change without any other guarantee. Very often we hear the eighteenth-century principle according to which the government would become simply an administrator. My, how advanced! An abstract principle, like the one here, is devoid of any precise meaning as long as it is not fulfilled by revealing its principal motives. We know that economists of the last century greatly admired China: "This imbecilic and barbarous government," said Tocqueville, "seems to them to be the most perfect model for all the nations of the world to emulate."[12] The Saint-Simonians, who spoke much about the "administration of things," often praised Austria; and it was the Austria governed by Metternich! Michel Chevalier in 1840 rated China above France.[13] The true meaning of this famous administrative principle is thus perfectly clear.

In a knowledgeable and perspicacious article, Georges Platon wrote: "*Revolutionary dictatorship of the proletariat!* It is well said. But as Shakespeare said, words are female and only acts are male. . . . In as much as it figures as a passive subject in the very precise economic relations of production, the proletariat emerges as a perfectly distinct notion. The moment it becomes a question of coming to action, of exchanging the passive role which it had in political economy for a politically active role, we see the clear idea gradually becoming blurred. It is imperative that the proletariat organize itself in order to exercise its dictatorship. . . . Could not its organization infuse into the proletariat relations of political dependence, and put its existence as a unified and distinct body directly in danger? Could it not also lead, by means of new inequalities, to a certain covert re-establishment of injustice and economic exploitation which would have to be suppressed? In fact, *all* democratic or proletarian dictatorships have never led to anything—directly or indirectly—but to the restoration of social inequities."[14]

The men who head the syndicalist movement in France are certainly not very great philosophers, but they are men of judgment and experience, who can be inept in the art of translating their impressions into scientific terms. But is it not truly curious to observe that their mistrust of political organizations reproduces—in a sentimental and obscure form—the distrust which G. Platon's profound study of philosophy and history inspires in him? Besides, this is not an isolated phenomenon, and several times again we will see that the "pure syndicalists" have more to teach us than they have to learn from us![15]

Our century has been rich in political experiments; almost always the expectations of the reformers have been disappointed; all the attempts to constitute an administration independent of the interests of political parties have been useless. In France, administrations become more corrupt as politics becomes more democratic. It is possible that this is simply a coincidence; but then again we must explain the reason for this progressive corruption.

The behavior of political professionals in all countries is such that many people hope to see all political organization vanish. This is a noble dream which has enchanted religious souls and utopians; but it is not enough to recognize an evil and to want to make it disappear to be rid of it.

It is here that we should interject the materialist conception of history: the study of politics does not allow us to recognize fundamental causes and does not enlighten us completely. This hierarchy, which the proletarian revolution boasts of abolishing,[16] corresponds in some respects to an economic differentiation; and it is this which must be fully exposed. This differentiation has not always been the same; the struggles have not always had the same goal. It would be very wrong to believe that classes existed in ancient times identical to modern classes. Outside the limits defined by a very conditioned mode of production, historical materialism does not lend itself to being included in the general empirical laws discovered by science. Thus this distinction must be sought in the present.

The contemporary hierarchy has as its principal basis the division of labor into intellectual and manual categories. It is too bad that in 1847 Marx did not examine this question in detail. This explains why the *Communist Manifesto* remains rather vague on the composition of the proletariat; but later, after he had delved deeply into economic problems in an original way, Marx stressed forcefully the importance of this separation.[17] It is thus that industrial economics came to the aid of history and philosophy.

With the energy of desperation, bourgeois democracy clings to the theory of ability[18] and strives to utilize the people's superstitious respect for learning; it uses the most unscrupulous means to heighten its prestige; it multiplies diplomas and strives to transform the slightly educated person into a mandarin. Parasites stand out by an immoderate and deceptive enthusiasm for knowledge, ride the coattails of great scientific pontiffs, serve them as heralds, and demand fat pensions for them.[19] These parasites hope to obtain the esteem of naïve people and to profit from it.

I do not want to enter into a detailed study of intellectual work here; we must apply to this question Marx's reflections on other distinctions in work. He says,[20] "The distinction between skilled and unskilled labor is often based on pure illusion, or at least on differences which have long since ceased to have any reality and only live through tradition." It is useless to fight prejudice, but at the present time a change is taking place which tends to spoil the prestige of the intellectuals. Observation teaches us that a profession rapidly loses its prestige when it undergoes feminization. Laboratory research, scholarly work, the patient and laborious pursuit of mathematical solutions are things particularly appropriate to the feminine genius: those who doubt this have only to refer to the experience of American schools. It is with good reason that so many intellectuals attempt to separate women from the liberal professions; but undoubtedly truth will conquer and then all the subterfuge of "talent" will come into full view.

This does not mean that all differences in places of work will disappear; for every right makes distinctions[21] and there will be, as today, people who are more skillful and faster than others, but *the differences will be judged in quantitative terms,* all tasks having become of the same kind and consequently measurable. Socialism will not abolish "general functions which originate from the difference existing between the movement in unison of the productive body and the individual movements of the independent members of which it is composed."[22] But experience shows that there is nothing exceptional in qualities of leadership and that they are found very commonly among manual workers, perhaps even more than among intellectuals:[23] the great trade unions of England easily found capable leaders in their own membership;[24] the leaders of French syndicates have strongly confirmed the conclusion that I have drawn here: they have seen that the domination of the public powers was founded on the supposed superiority of the intellectuals; in combatting the dogma of intellectual capacities, they have directed the workers onto the path pointed out by Marx.

III

In order to understand the full import of the problem at hand, we should examine the objections which are usually made to the syndicalists: they are reproached for being at times too absolutely exclusive: has not Kautsky shown that the Social Democracy cannot reject the intellectuals who come to it? He says, "This question is already settled in the *Communist Manifesto,* and also by the fact that the founders of the German Social Democracy, Marx, Engels and Lassalle, were members of this class. Those who accept the theories of Social Democracy and take part in its fight for freedom are welcome to its ranks."[25] What Kautsky says cannot be heedlessly applied to all countries. Conditions are not the same everywhere. In Germany there is a socialist organization which forms a sort of bureaucratic state within a state,[26] with paid functionaries. In order to have effective propaganda in the press, it is necessary to seek out professional writers just as one asks a good lawyer to plead a trial. A situation must be created for these writers "which corresponds not to a proletarian life, but to a modest bourgeois one."[27] In France, intellectuals claim that their true place is in the parliament and that dictatorial power would come to them automatically in the event of success. It is against this "representative dictatorship of the proletariat" that the syndicalists protest. They rightly think that it would not produce the happy results the theorists imagine would be engendered by the dictatorship of the proletariat.[28]

Marx and Engels[29] are not convincing examples of this parasitic intellectualism; they are the exceptions to the rule, because very superior men escape the limits of class. In the *Communist Manifesto* Marx notes that a part of the nobility used to identify with the bourgeoisie. He says that likewise "nowadays a part of the bourgeoisie passes into the proletariat; and that this is especially true for a certain number of bourgeois ideologues who have risen to the theoretical level of the whole historical movement."[30] It is necessary to discount the ideologues, who, by their temperament, can hardly play a political role, seize power and become the masters. Marx does not say that the proletariat will do what the bourgeoisie did in 1789; he knows well that the situation is very different: the Third Estate could offer ambitious nobles "political dignities," for it did not intend to destroy hierarchy; it intended only to improve it for its own benefit. Today the Social Democracy can offer only employment to the bourgeois who come to it.

Kautsky has examined very carefully the common interests between the intelligentsia and the proletariat; he recognizes that on an all-important point—the dissemination of education—"the interests of the proletariat are diametrically opposed to those of the intelligentsia. Already from this point of view, if we disregard all the others, an appeal to interests is not the best means of making this class as a whole come to socialism."[31]

The intellectuals have professional interests[32] and not general class interests. These professional interests would be injured by the proletarian revolution. Lawyers would undoubtedly find no place in the future society and it is not likely that the number of diseases will increase. Progress in science and the better organization of assistance have already had the effect of diminishing the number of doctors utilized. In big industry many high-level employees could be eliminated if large stockholders did not need to place clients. A better division of labor would allow, as in England, the concentration of the work (now done badly by too many engineers) in a small group of very learned and very experienced technicians. As the character and intelligence of the workers improve, the majority of the overseers can be eliminated.[33] The English experience abundantly proves it. Finally for office jobs, women compete actively with men; and these jobs will be reserved for them when socialism emancipates them. Thus, then, the socialization of the means of production would mean a huge "lock-out."[34] It is difficult to believe that the intellectuals are unaware of a truth as certain as this one!

These badly paid, discontented or idle intellectuals have had the truly inspired idea of introducing the ill-fitting term "intellectual proletariat." They can thus easily slip into the ranks of the industrial proletariat. Kautsky points out that they are like members of a medieval guild.[35] They also strongly resemble workers working at home, having all their equipment, but often idle due to insufficient clientele. They are attached to the petty bourgeoisie and strive to direct socialism onto paths favorable to their interests; their "socialism is at the same time reactionary and utopian," like that of the petit bourgeois.[36] Further, they could be compared to Romans of the period of the decline (so different from our proletarians) living off society, while modern society lives off the proletariat.[37]

While the socialization of the means of production will usefully employ all the forces of the work of the producers—that is, of the true proletarians—it will eliminate the work of the great majority of false proletarians. A more incisive opposition would be difficult to imagine and this opposition must appear especially glaring to those who are used to dealing with historical materialism.

The true vocation of the intellectuals is the exploitation of politics. The role of the politician is very like that of courtier and does not require any industrial aptitude. We need not try speaking to them of eliminating the traditional forms of the state: in this respect their "ideal" is reactionary, however it seems to "good people."[38] Intellectuals want to persuade the workers that their interest is in bringing them (the intellectuals) to power and accepting the hierarchy of ability, which subordinates the workers to politicians.

The syndicalists are rebelling, and rightly so. They sense very well that if the worker accepts the command of *"people outside of the productive corporation,"* he will always remain incapable of governing himself and be subject to external discipline.[39] The words may change,[40] but the thing will not: the exploitation of the worker will continue. Marx has described in excellent terms this state of insufficient development of the proletariat. "The tie between their individual functions and their unity as a productive body is found *outside of them.* . . . The coordination of their work seems to them ideally to be the province of the capitalist,[41] and the unity of their collective body seems to them practically to be *his* authority—the power of a foreign will, which subjects their acts to his goal."[42]

IV

In the last pages of the *Poverty of Philosophy,* Marx traces the development of the proletariat, such as it appeared to him in 1847, in the midst of the English disturbances. He himself says that he points out only "several phases" of this development. We should notice especially in this description that the proletariat is at first regarded as a class *for* the capitalists, against whom it puts up its organizations of resistance and that, only later, does it become a class *for itself.* "The interests which the proletariat defends *become* class interests. But the struggle between classes is a political struggle."[43]

These brief statements have not sufficiently attracted the attention of socialists. It is quite regrettable that language permits confusing the various meanings of the word "politics" with an ease often abused by polemicists. It is applied sometimes to the party agitators who seek to capture state power for the greatest profit of themselves and their co-members in order to exercise vengeance or in order to impose religious (or irreligious) ideas. It is also applied at times to measures of a general order with the object of modifying, in a notable way, the existing juridical system. Thus to change the mode of dividing inheritance, permitting trusts, augmenting the freedom of bequests, authorizing the creation of "homesteads," giving more liberty to women—these are all called political measures.

In order to transform the chaotic mass of the proletariat into a class for itself, an immense work of decomposition and recomposition must be accomplished. Marx believed that this work should be accomplished beginning with the organization of societies of resistance. But in 1847, his thinking was not yet perfectly precise; besides, he believed the world was going to enter into an extremely long period of revolutionary agitation, in which nothing could be foreseen with any degree of success. When he wrote *Capital* his thinking was more developed and he said in his preface: "Abstractions are made from loftier motives, while their own interest commands the present ruling classes to get rid of *all the legal obstacles which can hinder the development of the working class,*" so that the social revolution does not take a barbarous form. In his *Critique of the Gotha Program* in 1875 he asked that the state not be charged with the education of the people, but that it only endow the schools.

Marx's thought leaves no doubt: the transformation must come about by an internal mechanism: the new right must be created by an internal mechanism in the bosom of the proletariat, by its own resources. What must be asked of the public powers is to give the facilities to proceed to this transformation of the people by itself. It is with this goal that the workers enter into the electoral arena. The reason for the political struggle is thus well determined: there is no longer an arbitrary "ideal" end in view, such as that sought by political revolutionaries.

Now let us examine in a more precise way what experience teaches us about this formation of the proletariat into a class for itself; that is, let us ask what are the new juridical aspects under which economic relations presently appear to the workers. Like Marx, we take the resistance as a starting point: we must question whether the coalition does not give rise in the worker's soul to juridical principles in contradiction to those consecrated by tradition.

Law, as it is formulated by liberal codes, hardly recognizes anyone but the isolated worker; each individual can quit work; workers can have an agreement to abandon the factory together, but the multiplication of an individual fact does not change its character.[44] Each striker can take up his work anew when he judges it suitable; the boss can deal with other wage-earners, and this contract contains nothing reprehensible or blameworthy. Such is the theory applied by the courts in the name of the "freedom to work."

For syndicalists these propositions are false. The sum of workers forms a body; the interests of all are the same; no one can abandon the cause of his comrades without being considered a traitor. It is solidarity that characterizes the strike in the consciousness of the workers, and Marx defines this cohesiveness very well in saying that "the coalition has as a goal to end competition" among employees.[45]

The French law of December 27, 1892, on conciliations implicitly recognizes the existence of this solidarity. Indeed, taken strictly from the individualist point of view, there is no conciliation to be attempted; the strike has broken every lawful connection between the employer and each of his workers.[46] Before the strike there were only individual contracts; how can they be transformed into obligations which would bind the employer and a *body* with which he had never dealt? It is for this reason that very often industrialists do not wish to appear before the conciliation magistrate: they do not want to recognize the existence of a body which would have a monopoly on the manpower in their factories, just as, formerly, a guild used to have a monopoly on production in our cities.

Legislators have not dared to go very far in this direction; they are instituting a procedure in which delegates, nominated by the workers, take part, but they accord no authority to the agreements reached. The delegates cannot even impose on their constituents the agreement which they signed. A bill was introduced by Jules Guesde on February 8, 1894, to give a constitution to the workers' groups, which should be compared "in the management of the interests of their members to the capitalist

stock companies." The authors of the proposal drew from this principle
rules related to the exercise of the rights of the majority to impose a
strike on the minority; but they did not concern themselves with the
conditions of the normal life of this corporation. It is not very likely that
this idea will soon result in something practical.[47]

The workers believe that all strikers should be allowed back, and they
do not hesitate to make the greatest sacrifices to obtain the reintegration
of their excluded comrades. I find this principle expressed in a very
concise way in a transaction which occurred in Limoges. "The under-
signed recognize that in the matter of strikes, when the conflict is over,
the workers on strike without exception should resume their original
work."[48]

The inquiry on trade unionism which Paul de Rousiers has made
furnishes us very valuable information on the degree to which the *esprit
de corps* of English workers has been increased. Thus in 1897 it was
thought that "blacklegs" (strike-breakers) would rapidly disappear.[49]
Collective bargaining becomes more and more the rule: employers and
workers submit to rules which are as binding as if they were based on
law. Collective bargaining is, for Paul de Rousiers, necessitated by the
conditions of modern industry.[50] Finally, in the regions where the syndicates are well organized, discussions on the application of pay scales no
longer take place between workers and agents, but between officials of
the unions and employers.[51]

This constitutes a whole system of new rights which developed in the
midst of innumerable battles and difficulties; the workers needed to
have above them an authority divided into parts; consequently, however, it was uncertain in its plans; at times it was a violent authority and
at times it was more benevolent.[52] The influence of the political conditions in England is undeniable in the history of trade unionism, but
this influence has been indirect. Judicial obstacles have been raised,
concessions have been granted to the syndicates to act and popular education has been developed; but workers can boast of having won their
case themselves, of having produced a new organization in the bosom
of the unorganized proletariat and one independent from all bourgeois
organization.

Usually the syndicates have maneuvered skillfully to bring public
opinion to their side. It is indeed a political struggle—what takes place
between enemy groups in order to obtain public favor. It is a political
struggle often more effective than the one in parliamentary assemblies,
for laws are inoperative as long as public opinion does not support
them. The unions have gained universal respect: they have proved to
employers that they are "well-organized and responsible associations."[53]
Thus they have won effective recognition of their *ability*. They have

come of age by demonstrating their power. In England, the union movement is very far from having attained full maturity. More than once, unions which seemed very well launched have dissolved, or at least declined when the members no longer felt the urgent necessity for the union, when they believed that the goals had been attained, or when they found the obligation for constant payment too difficult.[54] One must have "intelligence, a certain breadth of ideas or public spirit, as the English say; that is to say, that these interests, though collective, are no less immediate so as to convince the worker to repeat the weekly deduction . . . [from] his wages."[55] Therefore, all observers agree in recognizing that the trade unions have been an excellent school for workers whose morality has been transformed; the syndicates are everywhere composed of the best elements of the whole trade. Experience has shown that there is no advantage in multiplying memberships to the detriment of quality. "In absorbing weak elements, one becomes weakened," said one important member of the mechanics' union to Paul de Rousiers.[56] Hence the result that many workshops by preference hire unionized workers who seem to offer guarantees which one ordinarily expects to find in men who have been selected by criteria of a moral nature; even for dock work, employers find it in their interest to deal with union men.[57]

In several fields in which industry has not become completely modern, for several exceptional professions, corporative aspects are still found in the unions. Paul de Rousiers believes that these vestiges of the past will disappear.[58] In general, the syndicalists do not pursue a selfish goal intended to give them privileges. They pursue a general goal, the realization of a settlement from which all workers will profit—even those who have made their struggle more arduous by their apathy or cowardice. An intelligent evaluation of their particular interests in the course of industrial conflicts leads the big unions to assume the protection of all the workers whose lives are affected by work stoppage. Thus the mechanics, during the Clyde strikes in 1893, not only sustained their own members but also gave help to non-unionists and to members of organizations too weak to stand heavy expenses.[59]

English unions have been very divided for several years on the question of "benefits": the oldest ones collect assessments and give help to members in case of sickness, unemployment or accident; they even give pensions to the aged. They are simultaneously societies of resistance and societies of mutual assistance. This system has shown excellent results as long as it has been confined to unifying elite workers receiving high wages; thus, the union of mechanics requires a levy of 2 fr. 50 a week, the carpenters, 1 fr. 25. When the old syndicates gradually opened their ranks to auxiliary workers, to the "unskilled," few of these workers could profit from the new order because their resources were too feeble. When the attempt was made to form syndicates with badly paid workers, such as agricultural workers or dockers, the difficulty was much greater, because levies of a penny per day were already high enough to discourage many workers. Thus the idea spread that it was necessary to limit the role of unions to resistance, and to eliminate benefits.

The tactics of the new unions are justified perfectly by the exigencies of the situation. But people have tried to give it a theoretical basis—wrongly so, in my humble opinion. Experience having shown how difficult it is to keep workers in syndicates, it seems strange to abandon the mutualist idea. Besides, even in the dockers' union, which was at first conceived in a spirit entirely opposed to that of the old trade-unionism, it was very quickly recognized that it would be useful to give family aid of 100 francs in case of death.[60]

In this question, as in all practical questions, we must keep our sense of proportion. The rules of the old unions were not flexible enough; dues for all benefits should not be made obligatory, so as not to alienate the less fortunate; only unemployment or health insurance need be mandatory, but types of assistance vary according to circumstances. If quality is an essential element of success in social struggles as well as in battles, numbers must not be neglected entirely. The question of principles does not appear to be in doubt: to reduce the syndicates to societies of resistance only is to pose a formidable barrier to the development of the proletariat; to open the workers to surrendering to the authoritative influence of bourgeois demagogues by reducing the importance of economic forces which can contribute to maintaining the autonomy of the working class;[61] to prevent it from elaborating new juridical principles in accordance with its own manner of living; in a word, to refuse it the possibility of becoming a class *for itself*. The mutual societies founded by the syndicates do not function on the same principles as bourgeois banks; instead of being inspired by capitalist models, they maintain an appearance of proletarian solidarity.[62]

The more there are distinct connections in the unorganized and confused milieu of workers, the more one is sure new elements of social reorganization are being carefully prepared. There is much talk of organizing the proletariat: but to organize does not consist in placing automatons on boxes! Organization is the passage from order which is mechanical, blind and determined from the outside, to organic, intelligent and fully accepted differentiation; in a word, it is a moral development. It is reached only by long practice and experience acquired in life. All institutions are formed in the same way; they do not result from decisions by great statesmen, any more than by scholars' calculations. They are made by embracing and condensing all the elements of life. On what grounds would the proletariat then escape the necessity of "developing itself" by this method?

One thing has always astonished me: the aversion of many Marxists to cooperatives. They maintain that the workers, once occupied with minute details of grocery and bakery, would be lost to socialism and would cease to understand the class struggle. From this desertion would come, at least in Italy, the increasing influence of the petit bourgeois mentality in the Socialist Party.[63] What is the evidence for this lamented desertion? Only one thing: the bad composition of the Italian Socialist Party, and this bad composition has led to numerous articles in *Critica Sociale*. The test of practice is the true test of ideas: if the workers perceive that their leaders are not capable of directing them, they abandon them as soon as they leave the realm of vague manifestoes and come into contact with economic life.

The leaders of the Socialist Movement are supposed to serve men, just as theory exists for practice. What would happen, then, if, after the social revolution, industry should be directed by groups who are today incapable of managing a cooperative?

I do not think that the social revolution could resemble a scene from the Apocalypse. At times the old idealists who believed in the supreme influence of education are scoffed at, and it is very seriously proclaimed that men will be transformed under the influence of the new economy! But has great progress thereby been made? How do we know that this change will take place within the boundaries in which we hope to see it take place? How do we know that a new economy will be able to function by itself? Is not the force behind all this education being hidden from us—the "benevolent despot" imagined by so many philosophers? In any event, the idea is very utopian. It is in the bosom of capitalist society that not only the new productive forces, but also the relations of a new social order—what can be called the moral forces of the future—should develop. Before these moral forces have attained a certain maturity, when they are still indistinct, we live apparently according to rules of the past; but in pushing these rules to their limit, in putting them to new and unexpected uses, they are worn out and gradually destroyed.[64]

Undoubtedly cooperatives are not specifically socialist institutions; they can even be directed with the aim of combatting socialist propaganda. But all institutions present the same *formal* character: they are only worth what is put into them; but they can more or less lend themselves to socialist influence. They can facilitate or indirectly hinder the proletarian movement.

If the cooperatives resulted only in making material life less harsh for workers, wouldn't this already be an enormous accomplishment? Experience had already shown Arthur Young, the celebrated agronomist

of the eighteenth century, that the best paid workers were the most inclined to agitation.[65] All writers now recognize that poverty is a great
obstacle to socialist progress. But cooperatives have a still more direct
effect in that they steer the worker away from the mentality of the shopkeeper, that great constituent of bourgeois democracy; that is no small
result.[66]

Syndicates can have a great influence on the cooperatives by under-
writing them, especially at the time of their formation: it rests with
syndicates to infuse the cooperatives with the proletarian spirit, to prevent them from being transformed into simple overseers, to make everything that recalls capitalist association disappear. The essential objective
is for the cooperative to develop new juridical notions in the working
class: the concepts of seller-buyer, lender-borrower are those that dominate the lives of workers in their relations with shopkeepers. These
concepts should disappear in order to make way for ideas deriving from
mutuality and solidarity.

In a book by Georges d'Avenel there is an item which will seem trivial
to more than one reader, but which I find very important. "In the statutes [of the *Moissonneuse*] voted in general assembly, 'free union' enjoys the same respect and confers the same rights as 'legal marriage.' At
the death of a member, says Article 15, his widow, his 'companion,' or
his children can effect the transfer of his stock to their name."[67] That is
indeed a new law promulgated and applied, in opposition to the old
law, and in opposition to the parts of this law which are ordinarily considered fundamental. It is useful to recall that one of the first manifestations of early canon law seems to have been the decree of Pope Calixtus
authorizing "Christian unions" in cases where imperial law forbade "lawful weddings."[68]

V

The English trade unions are far from comprising as large a proportion
of the working class as is commonly believed. A director of a docks company said to one of Paul de Rousiers's collaborators: "Trade unionism
includes at the most a sixth or seventh of all workers; there is no cause
to worry too much about what this minority can do." But, points out the
author, how does it then happen that employers are so troubled during
strikes?

"The moral influence of trade unionism extends well beyond the approximately 1,500,000 men who represent its numerical strength; these
1,500,000 men are like a peacetime army of laborers; in times of war
the voluntary enlistments rise. . . . It is fortunate that the non-unionists
are gradually acquiring the habit of lining up behind the union leaders,"

because the leaders generally succeed in preventing the mob from committing excesses.[69]

Many people believe that the remarkable results obtained in England justify the idea of restoring the obligatory guilds. I have already said that Paul de Rousiers considers the guild an outdated economic form, incompatible with the conditions of large, modern industry. Because excellent results have been achieved by the organization of a fair number of workers, we must not conclude that things would go even better by organizing them all: sophisms of this sort are frequent in the social science practiced by beginners. The success of trade unions arises from a certain selectivity in the trade bodies; this selectivity justifies, according to Paul de Rousiers, certain acts which we are in the habit of condemning and of ascribing to the "tyranny of the syndicates." In the building industry the unions seek to exclude the non-unionists from the great building sites and they generally fare so well that they succeed in taking in the great majority of workers. Thus our author evaluates these measures inspired by guild traditions: "Brought back to its true proportions, the tyranny of the syndicates . . . loses this terrifying quality which certain imaginations readily attribute to it; above all, it is not general and it is always exercised on an extremely limited group of little interest."[70]

At the present stage of development attained by many workers' societies, the new principle is not yet entirely detached from guild traditions; therefore, I am not citing the example of the building workers as an irreproachable example. I only want to show that rather questionable acts can seem justified by the superior ability of the syndicalists. The syndicalists give their time and their money without hope of purely personal rewards; thus they acquire the incontestable right to govern their group. It does not seem like a very good idea for the proportion of syndicalists to become extremely high in a trade, not only because selectivity is diminished but also because then the closed shop mentality develops. Obviously one cannot make a hard and fast rule; the most advantageous proportions vary from one occupation to another, according to a thousand individual circumstances.

We are faced with a truly new principle which upsets all the ideas theoreticians have tried to popularize for a century. "Government by all citizens" has always been a fiction, but this fiction was the last word of democratic science. No one has ever tried to justify the extraordinary paradox whereby the vote of a *chaotic majority* brings about Rousseau's infallible "general will." Often, socialist writers, in spite of their contempt for eighteenth-century utopians, reiterate Rousseau's idea: they say that the state will no longer exist because when classes have disappeared there will be no more oppression in society, and then public administration will truly represent the whole people. These are declarations without a hint of proof.[71] Besides, as a condition of his paradox, Rousseau posed the disappearance of all intrigues and factions: but that is an extremely improbable hypothesis. For, in fact, history is the story of the political factions that take over the state and exercise their predatory craftiness within it.[72]

What we find here is not a novelty in the strictly formal sense. The novelty resides in the mode and the aim of selection. The old groups were, above all, political—that is to say, constituted principally for the conquest of power; they welcomed all men of daring who were very poor at working for a living.[73] The new groups are professional. They have as a base the mode of production of material life and they have industrial interests in mind. According to the principles of historical materialism, they are capable of supporting the socialist structure.

These explanations were necessary to justify a resolution of the Congress of the French Workers' Party held at Romilly in 1895: "The congress pronounces itself in favor of a law binding all workers in the same occupation, syndicated or not, to the decisions of the syndicates in the matter of wages or prices and, in general, in all working conditions." This resolution passed almost unnoticed,[74] and its importance has barely been understood in France. It tends to legitimize what has become practice in English unions; it sanctions the principle of government by selected professional groups; that is, the new political principle of the proletariat. An organized equality[75] which is just and real would be substituted for a purely ideal and utopian one.

But principles of this kind do not pass into practice simply by decree. The unions must prove their juridical ability. The fact that the principle can by this time be recognized is already a step in the right direction; better yet: the unions have entered into battle in order to conquer new powers piece by piece. In this struggle, they find themselves in agreement with the established powers by virtue of the principles of bourgeois democracy.

Democracy hardly values *freedom to work* as economists define the term; coercion does not frighten democracy; in general radicals rather like to control authority; they have a taste for policing things and their hand is not light. It seems simple to them that economic difficulties be regulated by the decision of public powers. Thus they would willingly accept compulsory unions regulated by the commune; the municipal authority would make general rules in order to establish the conditions of collective bargaining.[76]

Many people believe that employment bureaus should be municipalized: at present they are not free enterprises; they are "offices," just like the offices of assessor, transport agent in Les Halles, etc. In order to promote the interest of the workers as well as to avoid immoral abuses, one wonders if it would not be preferable to change the operating method of these offices and have their work done by municipal employees. In many cities, free placement bureaus have been established. The expansion of this measure is not the kind that displeases the radicals. But the unions have understood very well that if they could take over the administration of employment bureaus, this conquest would be very important for them, not only because of the authority that they would have over the workers in the trade, but especially because they would have seized from the traditional political authority a bit of its power.

Several years ago, minor delegates were created to make up for the inadequacy of administrative surveillance; the old democratic tradition was followed for their designation; the unions were left aside. It was the same when it was necessary to organize pension funds and relief; direct election was called for instead of giving the syndicates a new field of activity. In fact, the syndicates are striving to conquer this power of surveillance indirectly, by influencing the voters; when they have acquired this power in a general and indirect way, the legislator will be forced to acknowledge them and to suppress the fiction of a useless vote.[77]

Everyone complains of surveillance of industrial shops; the inspectors are too few and their good will (when they have it) is destroyed by administrative inertia or even curbed by public powers. The radicals' solution is very simple: multiply the bureaucrats in order to give employment to intellectuals out of work.[78] The socialist solution is simpler and more economical: charge the unions with inspection; one would thereby be assured that it would be serious and practical.

Finally, is it not obvious that the unions should be much more qualified than municipal employees to be concerned with all questions of assistance? Here again their involvement would be more efficient and less expensive than that of established bodies.

Such are the first conquests which the unions can pursue in the political domain. They must gain these powers little by little, by demanding them constantly, by interesting the public in their efforts, by denouncing abuses unremittingly, and by showing the inability or impropriety of public administration. Thus they will succeed in taking all life out of the old forms, preserved by the democrats, and will leave them with only the negative function of supervision and repression. Then a new society will have been created with completely new elements and with purely proletarian principles. Societies of resistance will have ended by increasing their field of action so much that they will have absorbed almost all politics.

Here, according to the materialist conception of history as I under-

stand it, is the definitive struggle for political power. This is not a struggle to take over the positions occupied by the bourgeoisie and to assume
its mantle; it is a struggle to drain the bourgeois political organism of all
life and to transfer everything useful that it contained into a proletarian
political organism created along with the development of the proletariat.

VI

A very difficult subject remains to be treated and one that I would not
perhaps have attempted if I had not found some propositions in a recent
book of Durkheim's[79] which are of such a kind as to consolidate historical materialism. The weak part of socialism is the moral part: it is not
that many socialist writers have not written eloquently on this subject;
but oratorical amplifications are easy when it concerns morality. The
same things are repeated almost always, and up till now all the homilies
had little influence on men.

It would be criminal to encourage a social revolution which would
result in imperiling what little morality exists. In a speech which has
been quoted frequently by French newspapers, given at Montigny-sur-
Sambre, E. Vandervelde said: "If the workers triumphed without having
accomplished the indispensable moral development, their rule would be
abominable and the world would be plunged anew into suffering, brutality and injustices as great as those of the present."

Undoubtedly it is inexact to say that the social question is a moral
question, as understood by certain philosophers. But, we must also say
that economic transformations cannot be realized if the workers have
not acquired a superior level of moral culture.[80] The very notion of the
interdependence of phenomena, which creates the basis of historic materialism, makes this obvious: however, we often see Marx's disciples
showing astonishing carelessness whenever a question of morality arises.
This is due to the fact that they have recognized that the principal
remedies proposed by the philosophers are ineffective. Durkheim writes,
quite correctly: "When it is said of an individual or social malady that
it is completely moral, it is usually meant that there is no effective
remedy for it, but it can only be cured with the help of exhortations
and methodical objurgations and, in a word, through verbal action. . . .
No one sees that this is tantamount to applying to the mind the beliefs
and methods that the primitive man applies to the physical world. Just
as he believes in the existence of magical words having the power to
transmute one being into another, we believe . . . that with appropriate
words, character and intelligence can be transformed . . . We think that
if we fervently proclaim our desire to see a particular revolution accomplished, it will happen spontaneously."[81]

Molinari appeals to the religious influence;[82] Durkheim believes it to be ineffective: "When it is no more than a symbolic idealism, than a traditional but debatable philosophy *more or less estranged from our daily preoccupations,* it is difficult for it to have much influence on us."[83] He believes also that education has only a very limited influence: "The artificial environment of the school can only preserve the child for a time, and feebly at that. As real life influences him more, it will come to destroy the work of the educator."[84]

We understand that more than one socialist, after having noted, with Durkheim, the impotence of the methods advocated to moralize people, has reached a skeptical conclusion and has written that the future world would take care of itself. Undoubtedly we do not have to determine what will exist later on; history has no means of predicting. But the question is asked for the present and it is urgent. However, we must recognize that it is badly posed. It is not a matter of knowing what is the best morality, but only of determining if there exists a *mechanism capable of guaranteeing the development of morality.*

Durkheim, asking what mechanism could halt moral disintegration as revealed by the continuous increase in the number of suicides, sees hope only in professional groups. "In dispersing the only groups that can steadfastly rally the individual wills, we have destroyed with our own hands the designated instrument of our moral reorganization."[85] "Since [the corporation] is composed of individuals who perform the same work and whose interests are similar, or even identical, there is no more propitious ground for the formation of ideas and social feelings."[86]

From the renaissance of the corporative régime, modern society would obtain that moderate integration which, according to Durkheim's interpretation of the statistics on suicide, would be so beneficial for the citizen.[87] But the professional association in which the administrative spirit tends necessarily to dominate is definitely inferior, in this aspect, to the union in which are grouped workers who have given proof, to a particularly high degree, of productive capacities, of intellectual energies, and of devotion to comrades. In such a syndicate, liberty is encouraged and, by reason of the necessities of economic struggles, the will to solidarity is always firm.[88] We have then good reason to think that syndicates could be powerful vehicles of moralization.

Paul de Rousiers's collaborators, in the book already frequently quoted, have given us numerous examples of the moral progress realized under the influence of trade unionism. Concerning the dockers, changes have been very remarkable although their association is not the most prosperous. Many have abandoned their intemperate habits and several have even become "teetotalers."[89]—The union leaders spend a great deal of time combatting drunkenness. Knight, the secretary-general of shipbuilders, does so all the more commendably as his comrades have the reputation of being inclined to drink.[90]

Experience has shown that laws and police are powerless to halt alcoholism: in Belgium the Workers' Party understood that it was a question of life or death for the proletariat, and it has begun a very energetic campaign against alcoholism. With the help of constant surveillance by comrades it does not seem impossible to succeed: today one goes to the carbaret as a point of honor, in order to do as the others and show oneself a "good fellow." Instead, the bistro bar should be abandoned as a point of honor. This is not something beyond the strength of the unions: but in order for them to fill this role, they must be stronger and more disciplined than at present.

Two other serious problems are posed today: the protection of the wife against her husband, and the protection of the child against his father. I have no faith in legislation, inspection or the police; the workers should carry out their inspection and policing themselves. This is relatively easy since the woman is an industrial worker and can thus be a member of a union which will help her when her husband treats her in a way that he himself would not want to be treated by his boss.[91] Through the woman, the union watches over the child, the hope of the proletariat, who should be introduced very young into socialist groups.

Here again we see the importance of the benefits of the old trade unions. The woman who has retired from the shop remains a member of a workers' group, still takes part in its deliberations, has interests in the relief funds instituted by the syndicate, and consequently always has power to back her up. The child can be engaged at an early age if the union has various forms to aid its members, to watch over him at school and during his apprenticeship.[92]

Thus the syndicate is revealed as one of the strongest pedagogical institutions which can exist, however undeveloped it is.[93]

CONCLUSION

This study gives us a beautiful illustration of Marxian doctrines; the leaders of the syndicalist movement were unacquainted with his theories and usually even had but vague notions of historical materialism. Their strategy was at times open to criticism because they were obliged to learn by practical experience and no one could give them advice. Today things have developed enough to make it possible to understand the role that the unions have been called upon to play.

Today we see very clearly that the proletariat cannot be freed from all exploitation by modeling itself after the old social classes, by sitting at the feet of the bourgeoisie as they did at the feet of the nobility, by adapting the old political formulas to its new needs, or by seizing public power in order to profit by it, as the bourgeoisie in all countries has done.

If, as Marx said, the proletarians can only take possession of productive social forces by abolishing "the methods by which they gained a part of the revenue and consequently . . . the whole existing system of revenue sharing,"[94] how can it be asserted that they can preserve the quintessential bourgeois means of appropriation, that is, the forms of traditional government? Such a conclusion would be the negation of all historical materialism. Finally, how could the division between the governed and the governing disappear if society did not contain forces, developed over a long period, capable of preventing the return to the past?

Concerning the state, the action of the proletariat is twofold: it must struggle within the existing framework in order to obtain social legislation favorable to its development. It must use the influence it gains either in public opinion or in the structure of power to destroy the existing political organization: one by one, seize from the state and the community all their powers in order to enrich the budding proletarian institutions—especially their syndicates.

The proletariat must work henceforth to free itself from everything except inner direction. It is by movement and action that the workers must acquire juridical and political ability. Its first rule of conduct should be: *to remain exclusively worker,* that is, to exclude the intellectuals whose leadership would have the effect of restoring hierarchies and dividing the body of workers. The role of the intellectuals is an auxiliary role: they can serve as employees of the unions.[95] They have no role as leaders now that the proletariat has begun to be aware of its *reality* and to form its own organizations.

The development of the proletariat includes a powerful moral discipline exerted on its members: it can be exercised through its syndicates, which are supposed to remove all the forms of organization inherited from the bourgeoisie.

In order to sum up my thinking in capsule form, I say that *the whole future of socialism rests on the autonomous development of the workers' syndicates.*

CHAPTER 3

The Ethics of Socialism [1]

I

The ethics of socialism presents the greatest difficulties. Usually writers concerned with it seek to show how the social question should be resolved, instead of interpreting the Socialist Movement. However, this movement has now acquired such large dimensions and such definite characteristics that it can be studied as a natural phenomenon. We must not limit our discussion to the opinions of well-known socialist writers, for experience shows us that the people often ignore the direction of those who believe themselves to be their leaders. And finally, as Merlino says, the *socialism of things* is much more interesting than the *socialism of socialists.* [2]

Anyone who has studied history knows that it is impossible to unify any great social movement under a single principle, or to attempt to define a period through an abstract formula; this formula never exactly applies to the facts it claims to explain. There is always a mixture of two contrary principles; these principles correspond to two systems of tendencies and sentiments that come together, collide and combine, without the actors of the drama being aware of the complex role they play and of the heterogeneity of their motives for action.

It is very easy to recognize two opposing ethical conceptions in contemporary socialism: one is that of natural law, the other of historical law. The first, inspired by the traditions of the liberal bourgeoisie, is related to the French Revolution; the second, developed principally under the influence of Marx, derives its principles from the study of the social conditions produced by large-scale industry. One must not believe, however, that there is any perfectly pure school; no socialist has always remained faithful to a unique doctrine.

Natural law has furnished excellent ammunition to the men who have attacked the established powers. Natural law has been utilized by the most diverse groups, because it gives only negative results and its action is purely destructive; when the day of the revolution arrives, the best-placed social group for receiving the succession of power restores authority for its own profit.

The first socialists used the weapons against the bourgeoisie that the bourgeoisie had used against the old privileged groups. Socialists invoked the principles of the eighteenth century and maintained that the workers' "fourth estate" must be favored.

The laziness of our minds is such that abstract logic, tradition and analogy have a lot of influence over us; finally, political language was made by natural-law theoreticians. To these reasons of an intellectual nature we must add another of a sentimental sort to explain the permanence of natural-law tenets: in a society permeated with the hierarchical spirit, there are many men who want to imitate the upper classes; it is entirely natural that future democratic transformations be imagined along the lines of the transformation which gave power to the third estate.

The true Socialist Movement—the one that corresponds to the second or historical system of tendencies, and the one I want to examine now, can be defined as follows:

It is simultaneously a revolt and an organization; it is a creation peculiar to the proletariat, which class emerged from large-scale industry. This proletariat rises up against hierarchy and property; it organizes groups for mutual aid, unified resistance and cooperation. It wants to impose on future society those principles that it elaborates in its bosom for its own social life; it hopes to bring reason into the social order by abolishing the rule of society.

Marx's *Inaugural Address to the International Workingmen's Association* (1864) proclaims that the great aim to be attained is *economic emancipation* of workers; Marx explains that this emancipation consists in the suppression of class opposition and in the organization of cooperative labor; he says experience has shown that bosses can be dispensed with, and work for wages must disappear in the face of the *superior form* of associated labor.

Before going further, let us observe that Marx has often been accused of having reduced the social question to too much of a strictly economic problem, in the search for material improvements. In an article published this year on the books of Merlino, Professor S. Talamo wrote:[3] "For socialists in general, the worker question is an entirely economic question and even more exactly, a question of food." It is certain that the error (if there is an error) does not originate in Marx: he remembered what Hegel wrote on the opposition of the master and the servant and on the process by which reason appears, at which time this class opposition is overcome. The disciple did not purely and simply reproduce the thought of his predecessor, but he was inspired by it and perhaps even exaggerated the influence that reason should have in future society.[4]

In what follows I will take as a starting point the studies done by Marx, because no one except him has yet tried to give a philosophical interpretation of the Socialist movement.

II

Let us first say a few words about the general ideas of Marx and Engels on law and morality because the Marxists have greatly obfuscated these questions; they have forgotten too often that it is essential to go back to Hegel in order to understand Marx well. Hegel had considered the *system of needs* as the first stage of civil society; it is natural, then, for Marx to have said that society rests on an economic infrastructure. When we reflect on the intimate ties between the thinking of Marx and Hegel we are surprised that Marxists have put so much effort into defining the abstract connections of dependence between law and economics: the notion of system does not at all correspond to the relations of products, consequences and reflections that have been proposed for interpreting the Marxist doctrine.

Rudolph Stammler[5] said that economic *matter* cannot be studied without juridical *form;* that the economic phenomenon consists in a repetition of facts understood under one juridical definition; that *economics alone* would be reduced to technology. He has maintained, consequently, that economics cannot explain law.

If we refer to the theory of surplus value which is so important in *Capital,* we see that Marx's reasoning is not far from Stammler's. At each stage of the productive process he defines precisely the applicable juridical rules; he considers the juridical system as a framework on which the economic movement is built. Moreover, the problem is posed in an ethical rather than in an economic form; Marx depicts archetypal personages, such as those who, in the eyes of the law, stripped of individual qualities, offer no quantitative differences in their means of action; all capitalists are grouped in the capitalist class, which works like a single individual; all workers are reduced to a uniform type. What Marx is undertaking is a metaphysical inquiry; in a way, he obscures the differences between law and economics in order to determine the general tendency and essential principles of capitalist society.[6]

It has often been stated that there is no effort by Marx to establish a moral system. I believe that until now the question has not been posed as it should be.

Through Engels we know that in the last years of his life Marx was strongly convinced of the necessity for completing his studies with a theory of the family. After his friend's death, Engels published a work whose true value has not been recognized; it has been viewed as merely a vulgarization of the hypotheses of Lewis Henry Morgan. The truly interesting thing is the principle posed by Engels: he says that it is not enough to consider the mode of production of material life, but that it it also necessary to consider the mode of reproduction of the species. This assertion has been called a play on words.[7]

The essential aspect of Engels's thesis is very important: besides the *juridical relations* in which production comes about, it is necessary to take into account *affective relations,* manifested in the family. It does not seem that the Marxists have utilized this doctrine until now.

In the history of institutions the family can be viewed from three points of view:

(1) It is a group ruled by a leader; Jacques Flach[8] has often pointed out that legislation on the family is closely correlated with the principles of political legislation. Socialists generally want family authority to disappear completely, and that is why they want children to be raised by the state.

(2) It is a grouping of economic interests. Socialists want to make this aspect of the family disappear; and that is why they insist on the economic independence of women.

(3) It is an affective grouping. Engels envisions the family reduced to this in the future; this simplification may seem excessive because social phenomena tend rather to become more complicated than simplified; but what interests us here is the great importance that socialism attaches to affective relations; and this importance is made clear by the exclusion of the two other types of family connections.

In several places Engels stresses what the sexual union should be; he marks as essential traits devotion, reciprocity and respect. He rejects legal coercion so that the huband and wife are not soiled by the disputes of divorce. He believes that a new morality will arise when new forms of sexual union are introduced; he rejects with horror the idea that marriage be transformed into a mere accidental union; he sees very clearly that family life is closely tied to ethics.

It would not be difficult to present the various parts of moral life in the form of a system;[9] three stages could be recognized:

(1) the family considered in the essential affective aspects;

(2) *good will,* which is in opposition to the family because it applies to outsiders' feelings that were first observed in the bosom of the family;

(3) *humanitarian justice,* which forms the unity of the two first stages and which gives such a particular aura to the family when it has been recognized as sovereign.[10]

These parallels clearly illuminate the principles of morality; I will limit myself to two observations. Love teaches us with what energy man carries out acts devoid of any legal obligation. While the history of jurisprudence is the history of ruses thought up to elude juridical rules, the history of morality shows us that the notion of *virtue* is identified with the absolute submission to free engagements. On the other hand, love reveals to us the deep separation between law and morality; love does not take into account "juridical masks." The personality created by history, and who expresses certain social relations, disappears; there remains only the man, the "sensitive individual," talked of by writers of the eighteenth century.[11]

III

Everyone knows how difficult it is to understand the formation of historical law; the difficulty is such that it has often been thought necessary to imagine a fictitious framework intended to unite various phases of development. For example, proponents of this approach have attempted to relate all historical process to an evolution in logic; or rather, they have compared humanity to a living being. Images have been borrowed from physics and thermodynamics. These are artificial means which do not truly illuminate the question.

Two essential principles should be considered in the study of contemporary socialism: that of the *class struggle,* and that of the *historic mission of the proletariat.* Marx's disciples, having to struggle against adversaries who invoked natural law, have often thought it fair to ridicule all ethical considerations and to stress solely the material side of the struggle. They have even gone so far as to regard legal institutions as Machiavellian devices, used by the ruling classes to assure the maintenance of order for their own class interests. The moral bases of the socialist cause have been left in the shade and one talks of a victory of the proletariat without being concerned with the ethical qualities of the conflict. This doctrine, which merits the label of materialism in the worst sense of the word, has found its most complete expression in the work of Achille Loria,[12] who considers law and morality as "connective institutions" intended to assure the domination of the strongest. Far from protesting against these paradoxes, the Marxists have accused Loria of having stolen them from Marx!

In order to understand clearly what Marx meant by the class struggle, it is useful to refer to the dramatic scheme given in *Capital* of the great battle engaged in England for the limitation on work by women and children.[13] "The creation of the standard work day," he said, "is the result of a long and dogged civil war between the capitalist and the working classes." In the *Inaugural Address to the International Workingmen's Association* he said that the ten-hour bill was not only a practical success, but that it was *the triumph of a principle,* that a new conception of economics had been introduced into English society. In another way, this great conflict could be compared to the Thirty Years War, and the ten-hour bill to the Treaty of Westphalia: the law in both cases received new fundamental principles, and soon important results followed, not only in England but in all civilized countries.

There is still another distinctive passage in *Capital* which perhaps shows better the ethical nature of the class struggle. Marx, after having stated the reasons given by employers or workers to combat and defend the principle of standard workdays, adds,[14] "There is an antinomy here: right against right. Both carry the seal of the law that regulates the exchange of merchandise. Between two rights who decides? Force." Thus, during the class conflict, the two classes outline juridical systems to defend their claims; each class conceives in a special way the "policing" needed by the state for the benefit of particular interests in the role of common interests (as Hegel says). For the employers, the prosperity of the country is tied to the blind play of the law of supply and demand; anything attempted against this "natural law" would disturb order, would be contrary to science and would constitute an abuse of police power. For the workers, production should be controlled by state supervision; overwork destroys the substance of the working class and constitutes an abuse that should be suppressed by policing in order to safeguard the future of the country.

The class struggle acts, then, on juridical systems; one can say that it is a struggle between two principles, *a struggle about rights;* each of the systems is characterized by the *political idea that each class has of the role of law* and by the general consequences of this idea for the economy of the country. Marx can say that capitalist economics relies entirely on the free play of supply and demand, and that labor economics relies entirely on social regulation.

It is clear that all class struggles do not have such clearly defined traits as these. I have taken examples from England in a period when the classes had reached a high degree of organization. A long evolution is needed for classes to reach such advanced forms and to be thus imbued with ethical ideas; but it is clear that it is only in the most developed state that true social laws can be recognized; aggregates that are still badly defined show us only accidents without law.

In these last few years it has been thought necessary to complement the theory of the class struggle with that of mutual aid; this was thought to be a way of moralizing the social conflict. Examples of mutual aid among animals have been sought rather inappropriately. The history of socialism shows us that this doctrine is included in Marx's. The International proclaimed thirty years ago the necessity of opposing the solidarity of the workers in one country and the fraternity of workers of different countries against the capitalist forces. Contemporary socialism is occupied everywhere with grouping workers in various ways, and it strives to foster common ways of thinking in them. If Marx spoke often of the victory of the proletariat, it is because he saw everywhere the increasing solidarity of the workers, while capitalists remained divided. Finally, we know through numerous passages in his works that the union of reason and sentiment is, in his opinion, the mark of the full development of a class.

IV

Many people, deceived by associations of ideas deriving from language, have said that socialism, by referring constantly to the class struggle, appeals to the sentiment of hatred and to violent instincts; modern civilization would be threatened by an unleashing of savage passions.

a) Hatred is a feeling of considerable importance in the history of religions and in the development of patriotism; but it has become foreign to contemporary socialism.

Hatred can unleash upheavals, destroy a social organization and throw a country into an era of bloody revolutions; but it produces nothing. Our forefathers could afford to believe that after overthrowing power it is enough to allow things to take their natural course for the reign of reason to begin. We have gained too much experience to accept this naïve optimism; the position of authority does not long remain vacant; tyranny quickly succeeds tyranny. Socialists no longer want to leap into the unknown.

Hatred finds much less sustenance in historical law than in natural law. When we say to the poor that the holders of power (either political or economic) are thieves who for centuries have been usurping what does not belong to them; when the poor are called to rise up in order to retake what is owed them; when the existence of superior classes is depicted to them as the only obstacle preventing the happiness of the people, they soon come to believe that the most extreme violence is allowed against the enemies of humanity. The excesses of the Revolution have shown us to what extremes men of a gentle nature can go when they have acquired a violent hatred of this kind, based on a passionate conception of natural law. Present socialism is so far from this way of thinking that the Marxist school has often been reproached for teaching a sort of fatalistic indifference and for thus numbing the energies of the people.

b) Many difficulties arise from the imperfect idea socialists still have of the "evolution of the revolution," which is so often discussed lately.

Three stages can be distinguished.

(1) Revolution is a series of accidents happening in a short period—acts of violence following one another at random, which bring about important consequences, especially if circumstances are favorable to the blossoming of new ideas and if practical reforms are executed.[15] Thus 1848, with its unforeseen events, incoherencies of governments, upheavals and repressions, ended by ushering in a profound transformation in ways of understanding social questions.

(2) An important change appears in the notion of revolution when innovators no longer put their principal hopes in acts of violence, but come to believe that they can utilize the existing forces of the state and use them for a purpose entirely different from that for which the present society organized them. This is the revolution of the ballot box which Engels discussed at length in the preface to *Class Struggles in France*. The opposition between this stage and the previous one is so perceptible that many socialists believe that the ballot box revolution constitutes the abandonment of all of the old principles; the leaders of the workers' syndicates have some difficulty in believing that the proletarian movement will end in parliamentary procedures; they feel in a more or less confused way that this sort of a solution is unacceptable, while parliamentary socialist leaders seem to want to stop at this stage.

(3) The notion attains its full development when the ethical spirit completely penetrates the revolution. Violence always remains, but it is no more than the necessary effort to fell old branches, to give air to young creations full of life and to assure victory to institutions that have proved themselves. It is only an anticipation of the unanimity which will form forthwith and which will keep reforms intact.

In real life these divisions do not exist with the succinctness which can be given them in a philosophical analysis; if revolutionary development continues, it does not negate the previous stages, which subsist in subordinate forms and are often greatly altered. Immediate violence is found at the origin of the history of law, and it is found again and again throughout history; but its importance varies and its effects are more or less fearsome. As history unfolds, violence loses its quality of blind and irresistible contingency; at the same time it becomes less bloody. At first it is a matter only of *overthrowing* a regime; little by little, innovations are proposed—giving to rough creations a dimension that they could not have without triumphing over the repression of the traditional state. This evolution begins with a stage wherein the old *juridical form* is preserved because a new ethics capable of being affirmed independently has not yet been developed: it is the ballot box stage which is still full of violence and in which brutal revolution is thought to be vanquished because certain forms of government are respected. As the history of institutions teaches us, it is necessary to pass through this required stage of formalism in order to arrive at a new rule of law. The third period is the one in which contemporary socialism enters with its workers' organizations: we find in it law in action; it is the *stage of the living ethic*.

The scientific bias, so long dominant in socialist schools, is connected to the ballot box phase. It was believed that the functioning of power would be most simple because it would consist merely in applying scientific precepts. I will not dwell on this point because scientific bias is in low repute nowadays.

V

The motivating force of the whole Socialist Movement is the opposition between morality and law, which comes about whenever consciousness reaches a certain degree of maturity, when m n dares to see and reflect, and when he thinks about debatable applications of juridical rules. Then the *historical mandate*, the basis of all social organization, enters into conflict with the *human claim*, which morality teaches us to consider. This opposition can long rest without effect,[16] but there are always cases when the pleas of the oppressed individual seem more sacred to us than traditions, the necessities of order, the principles on which society rests. At that point historical law is shaken and considered unworthy of man. Morality does not give us any means of constructing a new juridical system; it brings only negations. In accordance with our habits of mind, education and general tendencies, we outline new forms of law.

Renan has often pointed out this opposition, which is of such great importance in history: he said that Rome and Greece founded the state, law, philosophy and science; but their civilizations were too harsh.[17] "Israel would bring an addition to them, an important correction, the care of the weak, the *obstinate demand for individual justice*." And elsewhere he wrote:[18] "Israel first gave form to the cry of the people, to the plaint of the poor, to the obstinate demand of those who thirst for justice." It has been debated whether the origin of this moral protest was truly Israelite; it hardly matters, for today we are imbued with this moral spirit. Besides it is not likely that the Jewish influence will henceforth disappear from the world.

In this moral preparation, which nourishes the class struggle, three very important elements can be distinguished:

(1) The desire to assure to the greatest number a greater respect for human dignity through more just laws, and a more effective control of the application of laws through a more refined moral consciousness.

(2) The protest of the oppressed, invoking their birthright against historical superiorities. It is here that the individual is truly pitted against the state.

(3) The hope of making the upcoming generation more happy, more enlightened and more morally sensitive. Then the sentiment of *ethical progress* is realized completely.

Too often we forget that these elements do not derive from human nature, but from certain historical conditions. It is thus very essential to know why contemporary society presents favorable conditions for this moral movement, without which socialism would not exist. We live on resources accumulated by our forefathers, and it is necessary to know whether we uphold morality sufficiently in the modern world. I think many socialists today regard the future with a certain distrust; for almost all Marxists regret intensely the exaggeration with which the beauties of materialism have so long been vaunted.[19]

It is quite likely that man does not have a very marked tendency toward progress, and that our ancestors were deluded on this point as on many others. Moreover one must not presume that man can act under the influence of an abstract idea, that he waxes enthusiastic for the happiness of future humanity. After the first trials of contemporary socialism, the notion of indefinite progress was abandoned for the pursuit of an immediate realization of a better state: Hegel perfectly interpreted the new idea when he said that the goal of our action should not be a goal which forever eludes us. Socialism has thus transformed the notion of progress; but it has often been wrong to show us a terrestrial paradise very near at hand; today we are beginning to believe that the "great day" is still far off. What will become of progress?

The idea of progress, as I have defined it, affects those very near to us, the children whose lives we want to better and for whom we do not hesitate to sacrifice our pleasures. I believe the Socialist theoreticians have excessively neglected the study of the family[20] from this point of view; but very fortunately, practice has been better than theory. In places having large-scale industry the workers are very concerned about their children, seek to have them educated and want to assure them a better fate than the one they themselves have known. We are thus led

to attach very great importance to the role of women in the development of socialism, for this sentiment of progress is much more powerful
in women than in men. Therefore it can be stated that if socialism
perished it would probably be because of woman's doing.[21]

A way has been sought to dilute the effects of the sentiments I have
just described by granting honorific satisfactions and material improvements to the workers. In order for socialists to hold out against the
efforts of the capitalists, the proletariat must acquire a clear idea of its
"historic mission." Theoreticians have not written much on this subject,
but the people have almost always understood clearly the role they had
to fill. Besides, Marx has given excellent general directions on this
subject, which reveal the development of the historic mission.

(1) In the first stage, the working classes of the most industrially
advanced countries are the "champions" of the whole proletariat; not
only do they undergo often powerful experiences for it, but their victories have repercussions on neighboring countries. English legislation
has served as a model; and the Continental workers have obtained reforms that their own strength would not have been able to impose.
Thus, the International says that theoretical and practical cooperation
of the highly industrialized regions is necessary for the emancipation
of work. The internationalism of the workers comes about at the time
when this necessity is understood.

(2) The proletariat gives its support to that faction of the bourgeoisie
which defends democratic institutions; the struggle takes on a paradoxical quality here, and seems contrary to the very principle of the
class struggle. Several socialist writers have said that it was deception
to uphold the exploiters of the people; and conservatives have more
than once sought to profit from conflicts of interest in order to fight the
liberals. From the moment when the masses have been touched by the
socialist spirit, they do not hesitate; they do not listen to the theoreticians; they march beside the bourgeoisie without haggling. The disinterested quality of struggle appears here.

(3) When the efforts of the proletariat have been futile, when government forces are too strong for the criminal designs of power to be
stopped, then the International recommends protesting and demanding
the rights of justice and morality. More than one socialist theorist would
not hesitate to label this demand "ideology" or "utopia" were it not a
rule given by Marx himself.

In the third stage, the mind is completely free from class concerns:
all the interests and juridical systems capable of protecting workers,
and the political reforms intended to increase their influence in the
future, have vanished. We are in the presence of pure feelings of revolt

brought on by the violation of normal rules of conduct. The mind is completely freed; the extreme limit of ethics has been reached.[22]

VI

The best theories are only valid insofar as they can be applied; the goal of ethics is to fix rules for normal conduct; Aristotle's ethical treatises are studies on the behavior of a respectable Athenian. Morality thus understood is very closely connected with the institutions of the country, and it is not without reason that the ancients considered morality as a part of politics. This way of looking at things seems inadequate today because we no longer consider the "city" as a unity and we always refer to its division into classes.

The rule of behavior is not a rule that can be deduced from philosophical theories; it is only in practice that we can see how man's behavior is evaluated in fact. It is easy to observe that behavior is mainly judged according to the correlation between it and certain institutions considered essential for a class. There is certainly room for distinction here; but it can be said that in countries where socialism has attained a certain maturity, normal socialist conduct is the one that is favorable to the progress of socialist institutions. This approximate rule seems to me to cover the developments described below.

An observation comes to mind first of all: one must not believe that the progress of institutions consists in any material advantage realized for the benefit of a workers' organization; a material advantage could in certain cases result from lies and duplicity. That would lead to the regression of the institution. When I speak of institutions, I am speaking of organizations imbued with the socialist spirit. The soul should never be separated from the body.

For a long time, socialist theorists frowned on institutions; notably, they maintained that cooperatives are not true socialist organs. This outlook has been all but abandoned by everyone, for indeed one must not stop at exterior forms. They can be very similar while functioning completely differently. In Belgium, there are Catholic societies and socialist organizations with very similar statutes, founded to satisfy almost identical material needs; however, the results are hardly alike! Institutions should be compared above all in their *psychological contents*, that is to say, by the feelings that they develop in their adherents.[23]

Institutions exercise a powerful educational force; and from this point of view their importance cannot be exaggerated, for it is necessary, as I have already said, to enlarge the heritage of moral ideas that we have received from our forefathers. When we study a cooperative, it is much less important to know what remittance is given to the members than to know what they have gained in morality; we should know if they have become more capable of understanding their interests, of managing their own affairs and of appreciating proletarian solidarity at its real value.

When socialist institutions were still barely developed, socialists attached a great importance to the description of cities of the future. It can be said, as a general rule confirmed by many facts, that the hope of a perfect life disappears to the degree that men are concerned with institutions. Thus millennialist prophecies ended by no longer being interesting to anyone except a few exalted Christians from the period when the Church was first organized. The same phenomenon takes place today in socialist circles and should be examined closely.

This transition from the hope of the perfect life to the practice of a tolerable life animated by the new spirit constitutes what should be called *"the passage from utopia to science"*; for science proposes only those ends which are attainable by our present strength, only those problems whose elements of solution exist. Marx says that a problem is posed only at the time when the solution has become possible. Today the proletariat is everywhere concerned with practice and is little interested in dogmatism; it strives to take advantage of all the elements it finds in capitalist society in order to create its own institutions, to obtain better conditions of life and to bring changes in legislation. Thus it is truly doing scientific work; it is this which has been called "the Movement."

People have wondered if the old hopes would disappear completely, or dissolve, as the Movement acquires importance; several writers have thought so and have written: "The Movement is everything and the end is nothing." This tenet of Bernstein caused a great commotion in Germany. There was a very confused discussion among socialists about this. It is an ethical question of the greatest importance.

Behavior should be considered from two distinct points of view: one should examine the exterior, to find its effects on society and to define it by its correlations with institutions; but it is also necessary to examine the interior, to treat it as the *behavior of free men* and to seek to understand the psychological state corresponding to a *just decision*. Is not the aim of education to fix in our minds an *intention* so firm and so dominant that we succeed in deciding without hesitation, and carry out (as Hegel says) our duties as something interior, of our own, without the aid of reflection? This interior aspect, this collection of feelings, this fixed and dominant intention, should be examined by the philosopher at the same time as the exterior: the two points of view can never be separated.

At first glance it seems impossible to define a psychological state of this type; the more the intention has acquired fixity and force, the more it escapes the examination of our consciousness; but experience has taught us to define causes of this nature by means of effects which are realized in very simple cases when causes reach their "full perfection." Christian education is based much more on the legends of the hagiographers than accounts of critical historians. These legends provide an illustration of Christian virtues pushed to the heroic state. The habits we wish to develop are thus clearly presented to our consciousness under the form of examples, wherein the right intention produced its most characteristic effects.

Likewise, it is possible for us to judge our socialist intentions by thinking of a regime where bourgeois traditions no longer would exist or in which hierarchy and property would disappear: this regime has been viewed as a final state. It is useless to discuss this "final state" at any length. It suffices for us to portray only its general appearance so that we can judge the similarity of psychological states corresponding to this regime on the one hand, to our present psychological states on the other.

We need not establish formal comparisons between the present and this "imaginary end" to find to what degree an existing institution resembles or differs from true socialism. Errors of this kind have often been committed which show that the opposition of the external and internal points of view has not always been understood. Quite uselessly, men have debated whether or not socialists, in realizing certain reforms, have abandoned their ideal. *All questions of quantity are in vain here.* Intention cannot be measured; it conserves its quality, however minimal the effects. This is a principle that Christian teaching popularized long ago.[24] Socialist intention can be realized in the creation of a small workers' society.

Renan has said:[25] "We have to explain life and give it a purpose. . . . We must give men a reason for living and for living well without offering them any false promises or inducements." We do not deceive men when we recommend that they involve their lives in a network of socialist institutions or by giving socialist significance to their actions. Consequently it is of small importance whether communism arrives sooner or later or whether it ought to be preceded by more or less numerous stages: what is essential is that we account for our own conduct. The "final end" exists only in regard to our internal life. Recently, Faguet wrote, "The socialist regime is not only utopian, as is ordinarily said; it is *achronian:* it is not placed in time." The eminent writer is deceived: the final regime imagined by socialists cannot be fixed at a determined date by a sociological prediction; it is in the present. It is not outside us; it is in our own hearts. Socialism is being realized every day,[26] under our very eyes, to the extent that we are able to conceive what socialist conduct is, to the extent that we know how to direct institutions and, consequently, to the extent that the socialist ethic is formed in our consciousness and in life.

When these principles are well understood, we will cease to be deluded by the expectation of a revolutionary cataclysm and by communism, both of which are ever more remote; then we will transform the old sociological doctrines into ethical ones.

VII

Has socialism sometimes tried to formulate rules of conduct? It is rather curious that in the *Communist Manifesto,* written by Marx and Engels in 1847, we find practically nothing on this subject. The two authors limited themselves to noting the decomposition of the bourgeois ethic. The practical advice contained in this celebrated document is related almost exclusively to the policy that the representatives of the working classes should follow in case of a victorious revolution. Seventeen years later, Marx wrote the *Inaugural Address to the International Working-men's Association,* which is no less important than the *Manifesto* of 1847, and from which it differed totally from an ethical point of view. In the interval, Marx had moved to England. He took part in the great development of the new-model trade unions and saw what the cooperative societies had produced. In 1847 he could have known only a few weak associations. Thus, his ethical ideas became more precise as the workers' institutions grew and showed their own characteristics.

The first rule of the International is of capital importance, for it permits the immediate separation of proletarian socialism from reforms attempted by the state, the Church or philanthropists. "The emancipation of the working class ought to be the work of the laborers themselves." Here, appeal is made to sentiments of energy and responsibility: the workers ought not to demand an improvement of their condition, to plead their cause before a tribunal of the ruling classes and hope that something will be given to them by virtue of a natural right. They ought to organize themselves and blame only themselves if their courage, solidarity and sacrifice make them incapable of attaining a better condition.

The principle of the abolition of all class distinction, already posed in the 1847 *Manifesto,* forms the object of the second rule; socialism does not seek a partial emancipation of the proletariat; it does not represent the interests of a new "Fourth Estate" behind which would lie a "Fifth Estate," as has often been said, and is beginning to be repeated today. Here we are in the presence of a purely ethical notion, denying all juridical distinctions, opposed to the maintenance of any traditional right. Today many writers hesitate before the difficulty of realizing such a precept and, in a recent book, Van Kol expressed the opinion[27] that the disappearance of classes was only *probable*, that perhaps we would see an inferior proletariat reborn, that following a victorious revolution, the Fourth Estate could perhaps bestow privileges upon itself. We are a long way from the International which said, "The struggle for the emancipation of the working class is not a struggle for privileges or class monopolies, but for the establishment of equal rights and duties and for the abolition of all class rule!"

Undoubtedly this *final end* will be difficult to realize; this total and simultaneous emancipation perhaps appears chimerical to our contemporaries habituated as they are to the idea of evolution. Here we are outside of science; we are posing an ethical principle of considerable value, which should remain unshakable, in order to direct all our thought and to orient our action in the direction of socialism.

I have already spoken of the third rule relative to economic emancipation and have said what meaning ought to be attributed to it. I will not stop here to discuss the solidarity of the workers because I have already discussed this. But we should weigh well the value of the two declarations which preceded the statutes. In the early 1864 text we read, "They regard as a duty, to demand for all men, the rights of man and of the citizen. No duties without rights." In the definitive edition, this precept was simplified: "No duties without rights, no rights without duties." Basically the thinking is the same and the International wished to protest the oft-expressed doctrines on the predominance of duties over rights, at the same time that it wanted to realize the exercise of political power for all men.

Finally, "all societies and individuals who adhere [to the International] will recognize as the basis of their conduct toward all men—without distinction of color, creed or nationality—Truth, Justice and Morality." Here it is not a question of a purely theoretical declaration, or of an appeal to abstract principles of natural right as has often been said. Marx poses a practical rule. He asks that men and nations respect the customs regarded as necessary to the honorable life between men of the same race, religion and country.

Have socialists remained faithful to the principles of the International? Here we should make a distinction between true socialists and socialists of a somewhat bourgeois nature. This separation ought not to be based on origins, for there are among the bourgeois some ideologists whose spirit has become purely proletarian, as Marx noted in the *Manifesto* of 1847. Generally, socialist writers oscillate between bourgeois and proletarian tendencies; but the workers and the men who participate effectively in the workers' movement have remained faithful to the principles of the International. We can easily perceive this truth by following the action of the group called the "Allemanists,"[28] which has been almost completely free from bourgeois influences. On the masthead of its journal, *Le Parti Ouvrier*, we find the first rule of the International. It is enough to read this organ to see that a truly working-class spirit animates it completely.

In a recent event almost all the Allemanists marched with an admirable ardor for the defense of Truth, Justice and Morality! This proves that in proletarian groups the ethical idea has *not* lost its importance— at a time when socialists who appeal to science are asking if law and morality are not words devoid of meaning! With the proletarian socialists we saw march the great orator who has shown that in the bourgeois classes there are always men capable of understanding the socialist movement and of representing it in times of decisive crises: the admirable conduct of Jaurès is the most beautiful proof that there is a socialist ethic.

CHAPTER 4

from
Critical Essays
in Marxism

Necessity and Fatalism in Marxism[1]

In reading the works of the democratic socialists one remains surprised at the certainty with which they "arrange" the future; they *know* that the world is moving toward an unavoidable revolution, the general results of which they discern. Indeed, some of them have such confidence in their theories that they end at quietism:[2] "among Marxists there is a widespread opinion that social evolution is like a natural process which fulfills itself independently of every human effort, and before which individuals can do nothing but fold their arms and wait until the fruit is ripe enough to harvest." Professor Sombart says that this quietism is contrary to the spirit of Marx; but the issue is to know whether or not the concept of a necessary revolution and an inevitable future results from what Marx wrote. Moreover, the works of Marx, according to the Professor from Breslavia,[3] who seeks to distinguish the essential from the non-essential things in them, are full of contradictions. I believe as he does that all that Marx and Engels wrote about the revolution, which they believed imminent, is not of great value and should in fact be classified among those accidental happenings that have disturbed the views of the two heads of modern socialism. But one must not conclude from this that such accidents are to be neglected, since they have had a considerable influence on the exposition of socialist doctrines, and one knows that it is *almost always the form and not the substance of a teaching which determines the direction followed by a school of thought.*

Believing in the imminence of a revolution, Marx did not at all concern himself with what the capitalistic society would become thirty years after his death. Some empirical evaluations based on the course of contemporary economic phenomena sufficed for him. The man of action always feels a great aversion to analyzing his own ideas; he does not succeed in establishing clearly the distinction between convincing hypotheses and what is fit for demonstration; the nature of the acceptance which he obtains matters little to him. The meticulous precautions suitable for scientific research leave him almost indifferent. In Marx's work we can see striking contrasts among its various parts. His prudence continuously increased as intellect got the upper hand over his revolutionary instinct.

Quite often Marx's language lacks precision, for he does his utmost to embrace the totality of the historical movement all at once, and *to consider it in all its complexity.* The intellect does not have the means to express such a synthesis. Can the artist himself, perhaps, represent nature in all its features when he has thoroughly comprehended it?

The rigid limits of scientific definitions are not well suited for the expression of a multiform thought which professes to correspond to the infinity of human actions. Therefore, Benedetto Croce was right in saying[4] that it is dangerous to take the Marxist formulas literally, and that they often seem false while they are in fact overloaded with truth.

I

First of all, we must ask ourselves how a school which proclaims itself highly materialistic can pretend to confine history within the boundaries of a system created by that very school: every forecast of a destined transformation, every calculation of a necessary order, every demonstration founded on the self-manifestation of ideological antagonisms—all this belongs to idealism. But without stopping at appearances and at traditions, let us try to probe the genuine thought of the master.

The *Communist Manifesto* seems totally impregnated with idealism, full as it is of symbols and images. Marx could not have treated otherwise a work addressed to men of action. For example, here we read that feudal relationships became obstacles to the development of productive forces, and therefore "they should have been demolished and were."[5] Here is an explicit enough statement! But it is necessary to compare this document with the *Poverty of Philosophy,* published a short time before, in which one finds the same idea expressed in quite a different way.[6] "As it is important above all not to be deprived of the fruits of civilization and of the acquired productive forces, it is necessary to smash the traditional forms in which they have been generated." Here we no longer see an abstract necessity, but real sentiments which instigate conquest; the preservation of the productive forces is of interest not to history but, on the contrary, to the class which has produced them and wants to enjoy them. If the feudal regime of property should have been destroyed, it was not because its maintenance was contrary to the laws of history, but rather because it bound and oppressed men capable of realizing their claims. One finds in the same work a passage[7] which seems at first a bit more difficult to explain: "because the oppressed class can emancipate itself, it is impossible for already developed productive powers and existing social relationships to exist side by side any longer. . . . The organization of the revolutionary elements as a class presumes the existence of all the productive forces which can develop in the bosom of the old society." Here one is not dealing with a scientific law; we could not arrive at an exact definition of the terms. How would we know that *the measure is full*? How would we measure the breadth of the field open to the unfolding of the productive forces? We should not forget that this was written in 1847, when Marx believed that the revolution was imminent, while capitalism was still in the first stages of its development on the European continent. We were dealing therefore with a very personal opinion, which experience would show to be in error.[8] Marx did not intend to formulate a law in the strict sense of the word, but only to give advice which might put the revolutionaries on guard against the illusions of the revolution conceived according to the *old style*. He announced the principle of the necessity of an economic preparation and taught that the emancipation of the proletariat depends upon circumstances outside our will, upon conditions which result from industrial development. To express this restrictive rule, to act upon beliefs in an effective manner, Marx gives his advice the form of an absolute law which governs history. There was nothing unsuitable in his expressing himself on the subject in too absolute a manner, since cautionary advice is rarely followed to the letter. More than once Marx still had to abandon himself to chimerical hopes. On the other hand, inexact language, which would not have been suitable for announcing a scientific law, suited advice perfectly.

At a lecture[9] in Paris, on the occasion of the fiftieth anniversary of the *Communist Manifesto*, Vandervelde said that experience no longer allows us to regard as true the three great laws enunciated by Marx in 1847: the iron law of wages, the law of capitalist concentration, the law of the correlation between political power and economic power. But was this last theory so rigorously exact even in 1847? We read in the *Communist Manifesto*:[10] "Today the power of the state lies in a committee which administers the social concerns of the bourgeois class." In 1850, Marx wrote:[11] "Under Louis Phillipe it was not the French bourgeoisie which was ruling, but a faction of it: the bankers, the financial barons . . . and a part of the landed property owners reconciled with them. . . . The really industrial bourgeoisie formed a part of the official opposition." In the *Manifesto* he makes an issue, above all, of that part of the bourgeoisie which is concerned with industry!

Therefore it is not necessary to push too hard the interpretation of the sentences which give the text a scientific rigor.

Vandervelde says that the socialist propagandists quite unwillingly abandon these three laws that they regard as veritable axioms superior to every rational argument. The *iron* law of wages has undergone some rather unique alterations. Accepted for a long time as the exact expression of the conditions of the working class, it has taken on an entirely new significance in the hands of Lassalle, who transformed it from a commonplace of political economy into a fundamental and rigorous law, suitable for serving as the basis for his state socialism. The power of the state was for him the only power which might be capable of creating a barrier to the formidable determinism of wages. Marx attacks the iron law and at the same time calls his rival's whole system into question. But if the Marxists officially reject this *Lassallian error*, in practice they, like Lassalle, know how to make use of it precisely in order to demonstrate to the workers that political action is the only kind of action which may bring about an improvement in their destiny. There is perhaps no other issue on which the socialists have exercised the system of the *double doctrine*[12] as widely.

After Marx's death, the law of the increasing concentration of wealth (which, like the iron law of wages, he borrowed from contemporary economic literature) was found to be increasingly deficient. It would never have occurred to him that anyone might regard what were only purely empirical relations as eternally true laws. But some zealous disciples could not bring themselves to abandon a formula which they read in the work of the master and which seemed to them sacred and immutable. They continue to imagine that current phenomena are purely accidental and they superficially cover the natural tendency of the economy.[13] And how do they ever know this tendency? By means of faith? As for Marx, instead, one did not deal with anything but his general observations of the phenomena which were taking place around him—observations valid only within the limits of the time to which they referred.

In 1850 Marx announced a fourth law, of no less importance than the three preceding ones. He announced that a new revolution would arise from a general and inevitable economic crisis. This theory is popular in Germany, where there are many who are awaiting such a crisis. Mr. Bernstein has vigorously combatted this way of thinking about the social revolution. Engels informs us[14] that this professed law of history was deduced from the study of a single crisis; it is not by means of such simple processes that one can arrive at proven scientific discoveries, and nothing prevents us from believing that Marx was not deceived about the value of this doctrine. Perhaps, with the doctrine, he simply wanted to give some practical advice to the revolutionaries, inducing them not to involve themselves in dangerous attempts and indicating to them which conditions might be favorable for appealing to popular action.[15]

II

In the preface to the second edition of *Capital*, Marx observes that historians (of any philosophical point of view) tend to give an idealistic appearance to their expositions. It is quite necessary for them to represent the unified whole of real movements by means of abstract formulas in such a way that this ideal reflection of material life may seem to be a deductive construction. Marx used the term "dialectics" to describe a systematic scheme through which what is *material* becomes transformed and *transposed* in the minds of men.[16] The expression chosen by Marx seems to me rather unfortunate; taken in a certain way it creates the belief that events constitute the arbitrary side of history, while the dialectical picture in which one summarizes their unity represents the general laws, or, as Proudhon said,[17] the eternal, invariable thought. In such a way we return to the concept of a necessary order, if not among things, at least among what is most essential in them.

Thus, thinking can find a foundation, and the future can be deduced from the past. It would be easy to show how (without realizing it) the Marxists have been victims of the dialectical illusion, and have reasoned in the same way idealists do.

In general we do not remember that the sociologist and the physicist, while they indeed appear to employ analogous methods, instead proceed along completely different lines. In order to facilitate his own research, the sociologist makes successive reductions, rather than abstractions. He separates from the unclear whole the important facts, the dominant characteristics, the general principles, trying to translate his reductions into clear and brief formulas, which are then quite often mistaken for necessary laws of the historical order. On the other hand, the abstractions of physics and the laws which express their intimate correlations are useful for practical application, whatever may be the direction in which we practice our activity. We view the abstractions of physics as absolute, because they are not subordinated to our will, to the ends toward which we direct our thought. The reductions of sociology and the dialectical schemes which summarize them are

made in order to be used in particular problems. We regard these reductions as subjective because they depend upon the direction which
we give to our thought. If we want to avoid all confusion and preserve
a true scientific character in the sociological reductions, we must always
define the purpose in view of which we announce them, and the philosophy of action which must illuminate the path of sociology. This is an
essentially Marxist point of view. Marx never was a slave to the dialectic, to formulas and to social science. With extraordinary facility he
changed his method of exposition according to his needs, and he knew
that (because of the necessity for action) some imaginary correlations
are substituted for *sociological reality* inaccessible to the understanding. The question is so important that it will still be well to insist a
bit on the psychological principle that dominates this way of understanding sociology. We can represent the opposition which exists between physics and sociology by means of the following scheme: at the
center we might place everything that belongs to opinion, to current use
and to empirical rules. This is the region of common sense. It is from
this that the mind starts to move toward science and it is indeed to this
area of common sense that the mind must return before directing itself
toward action. From one side we find the abstractions by means of which
the physicist is freed from cosmic accidents, from traditional processes
and from anthropomorphic analogies, in order to reach the precision
and the mechanical automatism of scientific methods. On the other
hand, we find the explanations of the social movement by means of the
reactions which human groups exercise upon each other, and finally the
laws of the imagination already sought by the great Vico.[18]

Common sense confuses all these things: it anthropomorphizes physics and mechanizes sociology, extending to everything that it touches
the mixed processes which we use in daily life—processes which have
a considerable psychological value, but which must not be taken for
scientific processes. In this region everything is interpenetrated; formulas are true and false, real and symbolic, excellent in one sense and
absurd in another; everything depends on the use we make of it. But,
whatever they are used for, the formulas of common sense are indispensable, because science is too abstract to be able to guide action.[19]
From what has been said up to now it is easy to understand that the
alleged Marxist laws belong to this region of common sense and that
they must be interpreted prudently. The reductions of sociology are
perfectly suited for the uses of common sense—even the most extreme
among them which, because they have made too great an abstraction
from reality, appear to be so empty.[20] The broad expositions of dialectical schemes are indispensable for pedagogy, and this pedagogy must
connect our knowledge to some associations of popular ideas. Without

current usage, without the psychological automatism which intrudes into this usage, the memory that is not supported by habit would be abandoned without a guide.[21] Without the use of formulas that might seem vague or erroneous to the scientist, men of action never would attain durable results. We have often observed that unintelligible dogmas provoke heroic acts. It is useless to argue with people who are accustomed to reducing everything to great principles which do not evoke a single real image and which produce their effects automatically without leading to a single act of reflection. These principles seize the imagination with an extraordinary tenacity and sometimes succeed in dominating the mind absolutely. It would be childish to condemn the processes that have their roots in the laws of our mind, but critical thought must never allow the processes of common sense and those of science to become confused.

III

These reflections will provoke people into understanding the true meaning of the concept of reciprocal dependence[22] in Marxist sociology.

When the groups of facts and of formulas have been reduced, it is easy to construct schematic tables that might, for every determinate class of phenomena, depict the dominant character of each epoch. The ancient authors defined each one of the arts for each century in such a way. Hegel conceived extremely succinct, analogous summaries for art, for religion and the law among each people.

These schematic tables rather clearly show the reciprocal dependence existing among the sociological elements in the same period. We can apply the same method to all branches of human activity, comparing, for example, productive forces, modes of production, social relationships and the entire ideological structure[23] that corresponds to economic life. In one table of this type the first column contains the information about the principal productive forces, and, to the right of each of them, one finds the indication of the corresponding elements in other columns, just as in a table of trigonometric lines one finds the logarithms of the sines, cosines, tangents, etc., corresponding to the arcs. Referring to this mode of forming tables, we can say:[24] "The mill operated by hand will correspond to feudal society, while the steam mill will give instead industrial capitalism." This is more or less true, provided that one is satisfied with correlations between social categories.

The dialectical illusion consists in wanting to see in these tables something more than relatively accurate summaries; they become concepts which express the action of an unknown law that governs the course of history. Thus we naturally end up in absolute determinism: the belief that the productive forces determine the elements of the other "columns" while in reality there is not a single fixed rule for passing from the supposed determining element to the determined element.

In the dialectic there are only general categories of understanding, and a hypothesis is introduced in order to create some mysterious connections among them.[25] In context, the example quoted earlier shows that Marx wanted simply to demonstrate how a great transformation in productive forces corresponds to a great transformation in the whole society. Men wanted to find the expression of profound principles in this very simple proposition. The sentence was detached from its context and considered separately as the abstract enunciation of a great historical law. It was said that according to Marx, productive forces determine social relationships by virtue of a still unknown law which science will discover later.[26] We must admit that if this was Marx's idea, he chose rather badly the example he cites: the mill operated by hand exists in countries with the most diverse systems, and it is far from being true that it is characteristic of feudal government or of any other determined form of civilization.

I believe, therefore, that Charles Andler is completely wrong when he cites this formula[27] as a conclusive proof of the deterministic doctrine in Marx, though I recognize that he has done nothing except follow the interpretation usually adopted by the Marxists.

Like all the notions of common sense, the notion of reciprocal dependence is contradictory: on the one hand, it gives rise to theories about the coordination of functions and about their harmony. On the other hand, it induces us instead to study the contradictions and antagonisms of these functions. Marx, who has so vividly brought to light the correlations among historical categories, has also made their discordances stand out. He says, for example:[28] "Because the oppressed class can liberate itself, it is impossible for already developed productive powers and existing social relationships to exist side by side any longer." This opposition, which manifests itself in a violent way during crises, exists all the time in a more or less pronounced way. I do not think it would be in conformity to the spirit of Marx's notion of reciprocal dependence to profess to divide history into organic (or constructive) and critical (or negative) epochs, as the Saint-Simonians do. This division is a purely arbitrary distinction which would violate the unity of human logic—a distinction which was able to deceive the men of 1830, because at that time historical knowledge had advanced little. All the well-known historical periods were classified among the critical periods, while supposed constructive characteristics were relegated to nebulous and imperfectly known times, such as classical antiquity before

Socrates, or the Western world from the establishment of the Church up to the fifteenth century. To us, instead, nothing appears less constructive than these periods, which we are really only beginning to know.

Reciprocal dependence is thus manifested as a simultaneous attraction and repulsion. The productive forces would determine the social relationships and would at the same time be in contradiction to them, would make them rise and at the same time would cooperate in destroying them. All this presents no difficulty to anyone who adopts the point of view already indicated above—that is, for anyone who does *not* want to see some prophetic indications about the mysteries of history in Marx's precepts but only some brief descriptions made with the processes of common sense, in view of determined, practical conclusions, without any pretense to scientific rigidity.

The Marxists have written much maintaining that the mode of production determines the mode of distribution and exchange. Stammler[29] and Andler say that this determination does not exist; everything depends upon the perspective (which can be true or false) that is adopted according to circumstances. Marx states, for example,[30] "The mode of exchange is regulated in accordance with the mode of production. Individual exchange corresponds to a determined mode of production, which, in its turn, corresponds to class antagonisms"; hence, there cannot be individual exchange without such antagonism. Here is a sentence which seems quite conclusive. Nonetheless, a few pages later in the same work,[31] we read: "The individual exchanges are in accord only with the small industry of past centuries and with its corollary of just proportion, or else with large industry and its whole retinue of misery and anarchy." Here are two modes of production that are as different as possible yet correspond to one identical form of exchange. The reason for this is that there is no exact determination of one thing by means of another, but only some concordances and discordances that alternately are revealed with respect to the questions examined. If we take these formulas as abstract expressions, or as laws according to which societies develop, they are full of errors and contradictions. If, instead, we examine them from the point of view of common sense, they are perfectly intelligible. In the same way, when the occasion seems favorable to them, the Marxists know very well how to insist on what is contradictory between the actual mode of production and the mode of distribution which was, in their opinion, characteristic of small industry. In this regard Marx sounds like Stammler.[32] The same reflections apply also to the professed determinism which would cause distribution to result from production.

IV

To give a clear idea of *relationships* as Marx understands them, we must penetrate to the very root of sociology and see in what way the concepts, *determined* and *indetermined*, apply to facts—to the objects of direct observation. To make this study we shall begin by investigating the nature of economic science.

In the modern industrial world there is no trait more characteristic than free competition. Certainly it has never been realized as one finds it described in books. But in a large number of cases the theoretical type is not so far removed from the actuality, so that science has not been able to take the type as the principle which dominates the general and deep-seated laws of society. Absolutely free competition assumes that individual wills do not agree, that they remain anarchic and that nothing resembling a *combination* can develop.[33] A world constituted in this way presents the greatest disorder and has the appearance of a group of corpuscles tossed at random in space, in the way ancient atomists imagined. We know that the phenomena in which chance is manifested in its fullest extent do not, however, cease to supply average results capable of being studied scientifically. The economists were not slow to discover that industrial anarchy seemed to conceal some regular forms that were obedient (so far as it seemed to them) to laws no less certain than those of physics. It is useful to note that economic science might not have been developed until men sought to study the social influence of predominating wills, that is, until economic science was psychological; instead it arose all at once, as soon as free competition reached a certain stage and anarchy was able to dominate individual wills, permitting the laws of chance to prevail. In Ricardo, economic science takes the appearance of a mathematical theory which regulates not the observed facts (which depend upon chance), but the tendencies concealed beneath the flux of everyday, accidental events. Scientific work has continued along the same line. Apparently Marx often was forced to give economics a mathematical appearance. The economists as well were pushed along this route, seeking to subject all the economic categories—not excluding that of needs—to mathematical treatment.[34]

In his pamphlet on Feuerbach,[35] Engels depicts history as is done today, and says: "In spite of the aims which individuals consciously propose for themselves, it seems nevertheless that chance reigns in the final analysis. For the most part, the numerous goals which individuals try to reach interfere with each other and oppose each other." We know today that chance does not always operate in the same way; it is in the economics of free competition that it produces the effects most similar to those which it causes in the physical sciences. It is there that one finds to the highest degree this indetermination of facts, united to the reciprocal determination of the tendencies (or average, regularized results). This science of economics seems to be the only social science truly purged of every psychological element, that is, from every free action; therefore it is the only one capable of being treated mathematically. The idea of chance is strongly repugnant to our habits;[36] and there are many who prefer to have recourse to more bizarre hypotheses, rather than to accept the facts just as observation presents them. At any rate we must make a choice between the idealistic course and the materialistic course: the idealist claims to explain everything, but adds nothing to our knowledge—that is, to our power over things—for he gives the name "explanations" to unverifiable, hence objectively ineffectual, theses. The materialist, on the other hand, keeps to observation and endeavors to draw from the totality of facts some indications that are useful in a practical way. Chance is operating whenever the result is not produced automatically, according to the predetermined plan which we had in mind, bringing about a movement. Engels formulated an idea of the future socialistic society that absolutely excludes chance.[37] He thought that men would act with deliberate purpose, keeping to maturely calculated "plans," without getting into a struggle over them, as they do anarchically today. Once they were the masters of their economic organization, no longer deceived by any fetishism and seeing clearly the true nature of the relationships among themselves, men would become conscious masters of nature, which would truly be subjugated to them. Actually, between man and nature there are only a few practical relationships abandoned to chance; that is, in which the results do not correspond to any act of will that may have seen the end effectively reached, or that may have done what was necessary for reaching it. In the present society, in the midst of antagonisms, the influence of the will is minimal. We find ourselves carried along in a general movement which, though born from chance, nonetheless seems no less imperious than if it had derived from a physical law. In this way anarchy presents itself to our understanding in the form of necessity. We are free, but we are hardly able to accomplish any one thing among those which our mind perceives as desirable. Engels said repeatedly that the transition to the future society would be the passage *from necessity to freedom.* We would be emancipated from the pressure exercised upon us in some mysterious way, owing to all the anarchic activities which oppress us and prevent us from living in conformity to a deliberate plan.

Durkheim, the learned professor at Bordeaux,[38] clearly recognizes the importance of the notion of necessity in Marxism. He says, in fact, that he succeeded in understanding sociology in much the same way as Marx. We know that for him a sociological phenomenon is characterized by external coercion of the consciousness.

Often the industrialist could ask for nothing better than to sit back and relax, but, driven by competition, he is obligated to combine new operations, to venture speculations, whether he seeks to take possession of the advantages resulting from a new invention, or wishes to profit from a momentary extension of the market or suddenly to enlarge his means of production. Then, unexpectedly, crises may occur which are brought about by sometimes trivial incidents at the moment of the greatest apparent prosperity. Industry ends by resembling meteorological phenomena quite a bit more than it resembles arrangements resulting from the general spirit of the industrialists.

It does not occur to anyone to look for the ideological reasons—the laws of history—which have led the heads of factories to employ steam engines, dynamos or the Bessemer process. These revolutions present themselves as irresistible currents, which everyone must follow under pain of ruination, but which cannot be explained by means of scientific or moral prejudices. The causes are infinitely varied and prosaic. Always on guard in the midst of a tumult of wills, in the midst of industrial struggle, we cannot pause to seek the psychological forces acting upon individuals; this is uninteresting. For the historian there remains only one undoubted fact—the necessary economic development. By this he does not mean that there exists a law by virtue of which, during a certain period, in certain determined conditions, Bessemer steel necessarily had to undergo the expansion which it has "taken." It means only that the owners of the foundries were obligated to transform their shops in order to use the new invention, precisely as if the property of the material suddenly had undergone a sharp change. Here necessity does not refer to the order in which the industrial processes succeed one another, but on the contrary, to the decisions of the industrialists who see themselves obliged to adopt the new processes as soon as they have been discovered. Marx says[39] that "the legislation on factories is a result of big industry, such as the railroads, the automatic machines, and the electric telegraph." Andler[40] sees in this sentence a determinist formula; I am not of this opinion.

Marx wished to express two things: first, that factory legislation developed parallel to big industry—a fact which brings to light the reciprocal dependence of social phenomena; second, that such legislation cannot be explained as resulting from forces directed toward a goal of social reform, and depends, like the great inventions, upon an infinity of causes. We know, in fact, that this legislation results from struggles among political groups, from personal disagreements, from compromises of every type, which have ended by determining an irresistible current in the direction of the regulation of work. Some revolts, some popular manifestations, and literary publications instigated a general movement of compassion and a universal disapproval of the excessively cruel owners. We find here a set of obscure, often opposing, causes which, however, are not worth analyzing. Here we find a *set* analogous to that which we have discussed in connection with the great inventions. We can say that the outcome is "necessary," because it does not reveal the free reaching out to an end chosen by the will for reasons consistent with the result.

If we can justify Marx's words in the manner previously indicated, we must recognize nevertheless that they may give rise to some misunderstandings and that it would be expedient to substitute a less ambiguous term for the word *necessary*. Here, in fact, it is synonymous with "blind" and "unconscious."

V

We should never lose sight of the fact that it is in the economic order and under the regime of free competition that chance furnishes "average" results, capable of being regularized in such a way as to draw attention to tendencies analogous to mechanical processes; these average results can be suitably expressed in the form of natural laws.

At the same time that we depart from this idea in which chance gives birth to a type of necessity, the mind regains its freedom and again becomes more or less capable of realizing its ends.[41] It is not, then, without reason that Marx has placed the system of economic phenomena at the base of the social structure. The general course of these phenomena (above all in the modern world) resembles the course of natural phenomena; they appear to our consciousness as representatives of conditions that are just as necessary as those imposed by the course of nature. Nevertheless, if we examine things thoroughly, there exists a very considerable difference between economy and nature.

In reality the economy is subject to chance; the regular laws which seem to govern it are nothing but appearances, have no value except for convenience sake and then only in certain instances. Economic facts can be represented schematically by means of a great number of points marked on a sheet of paper, in the midst of which a regular line, representing their general course, is traced. Nature, on the contrary, presents immovable principles, and if we could analyze these phenomena precisely, we would perceive in each particular case the realization of a principle.

Economic laws conceal the fact of fundamental chance from us, while physical laws often are concealed beneath an apparent chance; economic laws do not apply to an isolated case, physical laws, on the other hand, apply to any case whatever.[42] The former cannot be of use except within the limits in which the observations were made, the latter, instead, are valid for every time and place.

Too often the sociologists talk as if facts were governed by laws, while these laws do nothing but express roughly the grouping of certain facts. "There was," says Marx,[43] "the age which belonged to the principle and not the principle which belonged to the period. In other words, it was the principle that made the history and not the history that made the principle." When this illusion has taken root in the mind, we begin to believe that the social movement will, in one sense, reveal itself by observation of the past, with the necessity of a natural process.

This concept appears extremely erroneous to Sombart;[44] but we still must look for the origin of an illusion which seems so contrary to the spirit of historical materialism, and see to what extent Marx is responsible for the error of his followers. Marx started from a hypothesis which in his time could have appeared almost indisputable. That is, he said, as did the most celebrated economists, that the industrial world tended to develop more and more in the direction of the greatest competition among capitalists. He admitted, therefore, that from the point of view of the capitalists, one would never meet with a firm, collective will, while the proletariat would not cease to organize, to unify itself and to acquire a will always more conscious of its own ends. Such hypotheses lead us to regard the future revolution as a natural necessity resulting from an irresistable process. But was such a hypothesis correct?

This unlimited competition generating chance and necessity was a simple possibility. What reason is there, in fact, for supposing that the capitalists might not begin to acquire a class consciousness sufficient for creating a certain discipline? Because they would not be able to take measures to combat the proletarian organization? The conditions which make the revolution the necessary result of a natural process are not in themselves inevitable, as we now clearly see: no one is in a position to say what can result from the attempts at social reform. Marx did not formulate the problem as we do, because he believed in the proximity of a catastrophe; but it is necessary for us today to take account of what has happened since the time in which he wrote *Capital*.

The words which Marx used to express the analogy between the economy and nature certainly have contributed in large measure to developing the fatalist illusion, above all through the use of the term "necessary." It would be childish to deny that this illusion exists in the Marxist school. Sombart[45] says that the theoretical socialist always must add this reservation to his predictions: "Assuming that the energy of the resolution or of the realization does not diminish."

To me this reservation seems insufficient, because it is not enough to want something, but it is also imperative that circumstances permit the will to be carried out. Now, in our case, the circumstances presumed by Marx are the indefinite extension of competition and the absense of any unity of views in the capitalist class. These are rather aleatory conditions. Ordinarily we do not regard an economic law as proportionately less exact when the observations to which it refers occupy a longer interval of time.[46]

An empirical formula is made to represent in a convenient way the central part of a group of facts, but it gives less exact results in extreme cases and leads to the absurd when we try to apply it beyond certain limits.

When the practical man seeks great precision, he breaks down the whole into smaller groups and constructs more formulas. When we wish to embrace too much with one formula alone, we often achieve nothing but some expressions with no applied value. We should not put too much trust in the historians and sociologists who claim to contemplate the past with the eyes of an eagle and to give us general theories about it; they cannot rise above commonplaces and, proceeding without scientific intuition, they do nothing but bring to light some secondary characteristics.

Here we find an experimental argument against idealism and determinism. These doctrines claim, in fact, to gather together principles (reduced formulas) into a vast system, various parts of which would be bound to each other, and in which it would be possible to follow a historical development according to a logical plan. These claims are not sustained except in the case in which the principles would apply perfectly even to the extreme limits of the historical periods. But in reality, instead, these principles lose all value in the stages of transition. At the very moment when we are showing how the preceding stage gives way to the subsequent one, both of them are far removed from reality! It is difficult to understand that some Marxists as orthodox as Georgy Plekhanoff can admire Saint-Simon for having said that[47] "from the well-observed past we can deduce the future." Saint-Simon believed that the principles would follow each other according to fixed laws. He was, therefore, completely idealist and determinist, for he believed that the power of men might influence only the modalities and the rapidity of the transformations.

These are hypotheses having no justification[48] and they are contrary to the principles of historical materialism.

Idealism and determinism produce a fictitious and deceptive continuity. Marx teaches us to seek historical continuity in what is truly real— that is, in men furnished with the means to act upon nature. Men are "the authors and the actors of their own drama,"[49] and "social relationships also are produced by men just as are cloth, linen, etc."[50] The continuity of history manifests itself in two ways: by means of the development of productive forces[51] which come into being side by side, or by means of the development of men whose minds become transformed according to psychological laws. This psychological part has been quite neglected by the Marxists, who have, in general, remained aloof from the contemporary philosophical movement. In Marx's time psychology was little studied by the Germans[52] and few had comprehended the treasures contained in the work of Vico.

VI

If the reductionist formulas of history conceal the true nature of phenomena from the eyes of an inattentive observer and hide fundamental chance beneath an apparent social physics, reality nonetheless comes to light from time to time, manifested in an obvious way. Revolutions, accumulations of conclusive actions and great men escape all determinism. Literature reproduces the embarrassment in which writers find themselves in appealing to providence, the destinies of the people and to the mysteries of the inclination. These are some of the political expressions for what we prosaically call "chance."

Cournot gives some excellent examples of these chance occurrences that really are the masters of history.[53]

The explosion of great discoveries in navigation coincided in the beginning of the modern era with the culmination of Spanish power. To us today the discovery of deposits of precious metals in California coincided with a very powerful industrial preparation. If it had taken place sixty years earlier, the history of Europe might have been different. The regular course of the century was violently interrupted by that "great accident," the French Revolution. "In the same way, the natural and regular course of the French Revolution was formed; it was then disrupted by a still more fortuitous accident, which consisted in the appearance of an extraordinary man capable of pushing his audacity to the point of wanting to dominate the revolution and his century."

It suits our purpose to examine here a rather unusual idea: some sociologists, always concerned with the existence of fundamental laws (derived from the knowledge of grand historical events), ask themselves what would have happened if certain fortuitous coincidences had not occurred. To me such questions seem devoid of sense, when they are examined in such a general form. I cannot understand how Cournot was able to write on the Revolution:[54] "There are sufficient grounds for believing that Europe would have arrived a little sooner and by means of considerably less painful experience at what we can consider an advancement in its constitution and in its government."

For the needs of practical life, common sense proposes such questions, but it does so within the limits of its domain and with the clear persuasion of the problematic value of such a procedure. To transform a doubtful point of common sense into a scientific problem is to ignore the true character of science. In Germany there is wide discussion of the role of force. (Since only the state has the ability to impose unique events on economic development, *force* is viewed as the influence of chance events upon the economy and upon legal relationships.) Lassalle had based his whole system on the interference of the state. He believed that in the realm of free competition, necessity ruled absolutely; that the proletariat had become chained to necessity with steel bonds which could not be broken by any private collective effort. Therefore only the state would be capable of introducing chance events into the economic realm. In point of fact, experience shows that the intervention of the state is not that effective, and Engels[55] was able to write that the state can only retard or accelerate a movement without ever being able to alter its nature. We understand that Engels wanted to oppose Lassalle's principle with a new principle, but it would be impossible to demonstrate the truth of Engels's statement. We can only think that Engels's formula summarizes well enough what common sense can say about the principal forms of state intervention in contemporary Europe.[56]

A rather obscure image of Marx often is cited:[57] "Force is the midwife of every old society which is about to disappear, force is an economic *agent*," or, to translate the text with greater accuracy, the "*power*," the force, behind the progress of economic development is "squared" or raised to some other superior "power." The two images, then, express exactly the same idea: that of a sociological acceleration. But it would be a mistake to transform these formulas into abstract laws of history; they take up a paragraph again in which Marx explains how the rising bourgeoisie has exploited the state's concentration of organized violence.[58] Nothing indicates that Marx believed in a law of fated development upon which force might act only as an accelerating influence.

When Marx describes the formation of the capitalistic era, he shows that accidental circumstances or extremely diverse origins are brought together in a completely fortuitous way. He even points out[59] the curious fact that the various causes are not found in a group except in one country alone, England, and that this country was the last to enter the great movement which carried away the old civilization. Here is a history of primary importance, in which no *determinant* of any type is verified.[60]

Let us take a more simple transformation, that which came about in all of Europe, and which caused the change of the conditions of agricultural life. Here, also, Marx does not establish any law of development. On the contrary, he shows[61] different phases taking place in a diverse order and in different historical epochs. Only in England does he find a complete whole and what he called a *classical* form. Force, then, does not come solely to accelerate a movement whose parts are already determined and classified; it creates these very parts and dominates them completely.

The Marxists tend to imagine the social structure as being sustained by technological organization which would more or less determine the essential characteristics of history. Perhaps we will be able to find a greater regularity in this intimate organization; will we perhaps be able to find there a system in which the various parts generate themselves successively? It is of the greatest importance to know if the history of industry presents some series which resemble something fated. Andler has observed very well that the Marxists do not explain the development of technology; and history, moreover, shows that this development is full of contingencies. I do not deny that this judicious observation is a very strong objection to the fatalistic conceptions of many Marxists, but it seems to me that Marx has accurately noted what is contingent in technical progress. Also in our time of science and free competition there are often causes extraneous to the normal course of industry which intervene to bring about industrial transformation. He points out in particular the legislation concerning factories and strikes— that is, force and chance.[62]

I believe that the fatalist prejudice derives in large part from the false idea of science formed by the socialists. They imagine that science resembles a mill into which problems flow and from which solutions come out. The function of science is infinitely more modest. It endeavors to comprehend and to perfect the tests and the attempts of the empiricists. Its point of departure can be an invention owed to chance, since man does not yet possess the complete inventory of all the possible combinations which could serve as instruments of labor.[63] I do not suppose that such an improbable hypothesis can be discussed reasonably. Therefore chance will always be at the basis of technical invention.

CONCLUSION

In this study I have done my best to divest historical materialism of the mysterious and paradoxical character attributed to it by the excessively orthodox Marxists, more eager to draw attention to the importance of so-called discoveries than to find inspiration in the spirit of their master. If we want science to accept what is scientific in Marx's work, we should dispose of the contradictions and false interpretations: we must likewise complete it and improve it.

This work is not without difficulty, because the principles of historical materialism have not yet been subjected to a sufficiently solid criticism.[64] Today Marxists, not knowing how to reply to their adversaries, throw themselves into vague declamations and give their principles such precise meanings that they cause every interest to be lost to them.[65] We should proceed in a different way, and, when we find an error or a lacuna, acknowledge frankly that there is an error and a lacuna.

I have tried to direct my criticism according to these principles and I have taken the notions of *necessity* and *fatality* for consideration because these are the ones which orthodox Marxists have abused the most, and consequently the ones which require immediate revision. I believe I have demonstrated that these notions are incompatible with the principle of historical materialism and with the teaching of Marx, and I believe that I also have shown the origin of the contradictions of the school, in which, by neglecting to specify what "necessity" meant, simple opinions, referring to particular cases, have been mistaken for universal laws of history.

Is There a Utopia in Marxism?[1]

Several years ago such a question would have appeared ridiculous to practically all socialists. They were convinced that the doctrines of Social Democracy were unquestionably scientific. Frequently the disciples of Marx and Engels were accused of exaggerating the role of science—the better to separate themselves from utopians. When

Serverio Merlino published the booklet, *L'Utopia collettivista,*[2] many believed that this brilliant writer was amusing himself by creating a paradox.

A small work by Engels popularized the idea that there is a fundamental difference between "scientific socialism" and "utopian socialism." In almost all of the Social Democratic works, this same distinction is put forth and developed on every social question. It is worth pointing out that at the time of Engels's youth the word *Wissenschaft* corresponded only loosely to the meaning of the word *science*, as we understand it today. Engels had not read much contemporary philosophy. He had only general and rather vague ideas on modern science.[3] Thus not much importance should be attached to the terms he uses. The expression "scientific socialism" flattered current ideas on the omnipotence of science, and it flourished.

Professor Sombart, at the University of Breslau, has shown that two contradictory parts should be distinguished carefully in Marx's work.[4] His historico-social doctrine is evolutionist, while he never stopped preaching revolutionary agitation and announcing the imminence of bloody revolutions. Merlino has directed lively attacks against the "catastrophic theory." Bernstein has provoked a great flurry among his German colleagues, challenging them to renounce illusions which are now outdated and inviting them to profit from the English experience; to work for the improvement of the workers' lot.

In the following pages I examine especially what is called "orthodox Marxism," that is, the doctrine of Social Democracy. I will analyze, then, the part of Marx's legacy that Sombart considers outdated.

I

First of all it is well to say a few words about utopian literature and the various *types* of which it is composed. The utopias of old were almost always literary exercises, moral tales, satires of society put in a mild and suggestive form. This genre shocks all our scientific sensibilities, but in past times it was believed very useful to contrast to real life an ideal unattainable to the masses, intended to stimulate reflections on the relativity of laws and customs. This system of moral teaching was highly developed by the Church. In reading certain works of theologians and the Church Fathers, we could believe that Christianity is irreconcilable with civilized societies. However, the Church has been quite capable of accommodating itself to all of the social situations created by history. If Christian orators glorify poverty and abuse the rich, it is because they want to show God's infinite mercy, which allows the rich to combine the enjoyment of an easy life on earth with the hope of a benevolent future life—infinite mercy since the life of the rich is contrary to principles.

Today we have no need of paradoxes of this sort in order to understand that law and morality are relative things in the real world and that they are evolving.[5] Catholic scholars find that sermons of the old type are dangerous. They were not dangerous when property was not yet threatened. Thomas More's contemporaries do not seem to have judged his *Utopia* as revolutionary. Many such works had as their object to contrast the complexity of civilization and the greed of speculators to the simple existence and moderation of peoples living in agricultural and pastoral societies. More's work has been justly compared to idealistic pastoral novels. I believe that Le Play is the last author to have had the extraordinary idea of finding the practice of true virtue in the life of the nomads of the Great Steppes of Asia. The utopias of this first type are generally "reactionary," in the Marxist meaning of the term, since they seem to be attempting to inspire man to reverse the course of economic history.[6]

The second class of utopias seeks the abrupt and accelerated transformation of society. This second group of utopias gives rise to parties or schools that can be divided into two types. The systems whose influence is the most lasting, which exercise a powerful educational influence on the public, are the quiet ones which leave no glittering mark on politics; they are especially influential in their period of decline, when the dogmas of the first hour are worn out, and when the second generation leaders blend into common life. Thus Saint-Simonism disseminated many ideas that served as catalysts for reform plans.[7] In England, the Owenists held an important position in the history of cooperatives and trade unions. Other utopias give rise to poltical movements, make a lot of noise and disappear without leaving any significant trace. Babouvism belongs to this type.

Finally, there exist utopias which are incorporated into the programs of the principal parties. Democracy has a *credo* as abstract and as obscure as that of any religion; its trinity, "Liberty, Equality and Fraternity," offers as many mysteries as the enigmas of the Apocalypse; it promises inexpensive government, the elevation of talents to civic esteem, the integrity of administrators. These are a bundle of illusions, which still have a stranglehold on men's minds, even though the experience of all democracies has shown that the facts contradict the principles.

There are three important traits in all of these utopias. The present world is viewed from a deeply pessimistic point of view; it is bad; it cannot be anything but bad; no correction can be made without generating new evils. Emancipation will take place through a sudden (or almost sudden) renewal; by a catastrophe making the causes of the evil disappear; by the emancipation of the oppressed finally rid of their masters. Then an excellent world will begin and all of the most perfect institutions will be realized with an ease bordering on the miraculous; the good will be as natural as the bad used to be.[8] Democrats do not possess strong enough words to depict the horrors of the monarchy. They are convinced that everything will be perfect on the day a revolution puts power into the hands of their friends. In countries enjoying republican institutions, utopia is still more naïve, for the overthrow should result from a simple displacement of a majority in parliament, and this displacement depends on the chaotic votes of a mass of electors attracted by phantasmagorical programs. Tactical skills are useful in producing this miracle—this political alchemy. In France many socialists admit that they are deceiving the peasants by offering them "deceptively seductive programs."[9] The important thing is not to make them socialists, but to have them named deputies—aligning themselves in the socialist ranks!

Socialism has taken its utopias of "renewal" and political "catastrophe" from the democratic tradition, from which it has never been seriously emancipated. A terrible struggle has ensued on this subject between socialists and anarchists, with the latter denouncing the corruption and ignorance of all governments, showing the improbability of social renewal obtained through a parliament and advocating the organization of working classes into societies capable of improving the lot of workers.

Social science obviously cannot dispute the metaphysical principle of pessimism, any more than it can the poetical description of the future world; but it is able to discuss the question of whether the condition of the proletariet can be improved and is really improving in our present society. It can examine the probability of a liberating catastrophe. The studies made on these two points have not been very favorable to the tenets of Social Democracy. Marx had already abandoned the ideas of the old socialists on the iron law of wages, revived by Lassalle. His disciples often still use this law in their propaganda. But from the scientific point of view there is no longer any doubt. The most prominent Social Democrats have come out in favor of the development of cooperatives and syndicates. The more we advance, the more the idea of a social catastrophe appears inconceivable. This is a purely utopian view, to which, however, many German socialists adhere.

II

We know with what fervor Fourier attacked Owen's ideas. He called him a charlatan, a mediocre sophist, a false philanthropist and a reckless man. He denounced the crack-brained notions, the trickery, the quibblings, the "utopias" of the Owenist "sycophants." He was amazed that not one of those reformers had thought of putting the solution of the social problem up for competition; he became indignant against the prejudices of the public which scorned his "scientific discoveries." Fourier truly believed that he had contributed to science and had perfected Newton's work. Indeed many of his contemporaries believed that he had discovered the fundamental laws of society. The Social Democrats, as well, claim to be contributing scientists to science and they scorn utopia; perhaps their claim is no better founded than the Fourierists'!

Fourier said that Owen abandoned society to chance, with his heedlessly made reforms.[10] "Before admitting only a semi-liberty in love, it is necessary to introduce counterbalances that even the new society will be unable to create before the end of 15 or 20 years of practice." He believed that he had found a "social dynamic" which he often compared to celestial mechanics. The members of a "phalanx"[11] form a system very similar to the planetary system; by the free play of their gravitational pull, they form a stable group, activated by regular movements, varying only once every hundred years. The gravitational attractions are regulated by the passions, that is to say by forces which are practically independent of individual reason. The phalanx can be conceived of, then, as an automatic mechanism, an organism, or a planetary system. Each individual is motivated by necessity.

All of these beautiful inventions, which make us smile today, used to seem admirable because the utopian had never before imagined a system with so sure an operation and so resembling a combination of natural forces. On the contrary, the old utopians appealed to good will, to the marvels produced by education, and to the primordial virtues of human nature—they all relied on purely moral means, while Fourier alone relied on a "science of forces." He could maintain that nothing was left to the imagination; for he claimed to realize only the first stage of harmony, and in order to reach it, he needed only the forces of observable passions. He wanted to utilize all of the human passions and to take into account the proportions in which the various characteristics appear through observation. The "butterfly," the "cabalist" and the "composite" passions[12] exist at present as they would exist in the Fourierist society; but today they are restrained and do not produce their complete effects. Fourier called them the mechanizing or distributive passions because they are the ones that establish the natural stability of the system.

There is no scientific element in any of this psychology, and today we know it. The principle of the stability of the system was the weak point of Fourierism. We know what discussions were stimulated by the problem of the stability of the planetary system. It would have been truly extraordinary for a community of men, exercising various professions and possessing ordinary passions in the normal proportions, to be able to constitute an almost stable group. If this postulate is abandoned, all of Fourierism disappears. The unhappy experiments of Fourierism have shown that divergent forces were strong enough to dissolve the society. The phalansterians resembled comets much more than planets. Marx leads us to entirely different considerations. He did not conceive of society as a collection of atoms subjected to gravitational forces but as a kinematic chain formed of solid elements acting by mutual pressure. In the words of Professor Reuleaux, we go from the "cosmic" to the "mechanistic" conception. It is no longer men who are studied, but groups whose feelings, desires and juridical notions were formed historically and were solidified in a firm enough way for scientific observation to be possible. Individual psychology does not form, then, the foundation of sociology, which studies complex beings without trying to delve into first causes, just as the chemist takes the simple bodies given by nature without needing to make hypotheses on their formation.

Generally Marxists have not understood clearly the enormous difference between Marx and Fourier; like the old phalansterians, many of them are fooled by Fourier's fantastic mechanics; they believe that the phalansterian system has a physical aspect and is consequently materialistic. The automatic stability, in spite of the improbability of the hypothesis, pleases them, because it requires no moral ideas, and for a very great number of Social Democrats *morality is an abominable monster*. Therefore Fourier is treated with much more respect than the other early socialists by these writers. Some of them even have quite an admiration for him.

We should define as utopians all reformers who cannot ground their plans in the observation of the social mechanism. Marx thought that the revolution would result from a development of the social mechanism by the interaction of the proletarianization of the workers and the concentration of wealth, by the increasing unification of revolutionary forces, and by the incorrigible anarchy of the capitalist forces. This description corresponds rather well to what Marx observed in England. It is generally acknowledged that this schema was correct in past times. As he believed the revolution to be imminent, he did not put his disciples on guard against the possibility that the historical development of the social structure that he studied was a chance occurrence. The revolution did not take place, which shows that he was mistaken in his evaluation of social forces; but this error of fact is not enough to place him in the ranks of the utopians.

But if he was mistaken only about fact, his disciples have committed a serious error of principle, and have been utopian. They have not observed that the *social mechanism is variable*, especially in our era, because of the rapid transformations that take place in industry,[13] and that there are no means for constructing the social mechanisms of the future; that only those that can be observed can be discussed. Without being satisfied with these qualifications, orthodox Marxists have decided that the mechanism would continue to exist qualitatively just as Marx had described it and that its elements would be modified quantitatively in a uniform way according to the empirical law observed (in a partial way) at the beginning of large-scale industry. These two propositions are scientifically demonstrable; they recall the reasoning of the ancient philosophers on inertia. The movement of a body, left to itself, continues, they say, in a straight line, with a constant speed, because there is no reason for it to change its speed or direction! Experience shows us that the capitalist system is changing rather rapidly before our eyes. Orthodox Social Democrats make extraordinary efforts of imagination in order not to see what is clear to everyone; they have abandoned the terrain of social science to pass into utopia.

Visualizing the revolution and its aftermath is another matter. In discussions on the revolution we find symbols and dreams that are usually unintelligible; society is spoken of as an active being, capable of thinking and of conducting itself! We are told that the proletariat will exercise dictatorship, will make laws, and then will abdicate! All that is purely utopian, not only in substance but also in form. In order to remain on the realistic terrain of Marxism, it would be necessary to talk, not of society and the proletariat, but of the economic and political organizations whose functioning is known and which can be discussed. Society and the proletariat are passive bodies; the state, local government, cooperatives, syndicates and mutual aid societies are active bodies which follow reasoned plans of execution.

Socialists who give us abstract formulas, who talk to us of the socialization of the means of production or of the administration of things, are no less utopian and consequently are no less unfaithful to Marx's method. It should be explained how mechanisms are depicted which actualize notions that in themselves are rather vague. These formulas can be applied to the most diverse regimes. Is it a matter of bringing us back to the missions of Paraguay? The Social Democrats have laughed greatly at democratic symbolism: they have shown that behind the great principles of Liberty, Equality and Fraternity there could exist real states far removed from what the promoters of the Declaration of the Rights of Man thought they were producing. The same criticism can be leveled at all abstract social dogmatism, and notably at that of orthodox Social Democracy.

Besides, it seems that the insufficiency of the doctrine has been recog-

nized by Social Democrats. A long time ago Brousse accused Marx of
being utopian because Marx did not explain how communism could be
brought about; Brousse said that the transition from utopia to science
would truly be made by adopting his system of "public services." His
ideas first met violent resistance; but, little by little, French Marxists
rallied to them.[14] Their communism was transformed into an exploitation
of industries by the state or by the community. This mechanism is very
easy to visualize. I believe that it is even this facility of visualization
that has caused the success of this doctrine: but the simplest thing
intellectually is not always the most practical, and social questions never
have simple solutions. I am not discussing Brousse's system; I am limiting myself to mentioning its success.

III

Georgy Plekhanoff, one of the best known Social Democratic writers,
says: "Whoever seeks a perfect organization starting from an abstract
principle is utopian";[15] and he adds that in the eighteenth century "the
abstract principle which served as a basis for the inquiries of the utopians was that of 'human nature.'" This is not very clear; he finishes his
thought further on: "It is not 'human nature' that explains historical
movement; it is historical movement that diversely 'fashions' human
nature."[16]

Socialist society, as it was conceived by Engels, was supposed to be
as perfect as the societies dreamed up by the utopians. A few years ago,
the Social Democrats became more prudent and have since expressed
doubts on the possibility of realizing this New Jerusalem. One of the
renowned writers in the party, the Dutch deputy Van Kol, expresses
himself thus:[17] "It is probable that victory will put an end to all class
struggle, that goods will be held in common, and that liberty will be
the lot of all." Elsewhere he regards as very probable[18] that in socialist
society a Fifth Estate will be formed, which could be oppressed by the
Fourth. This caution is very laudable, but it reduces to nothing all of the
ideas that Marx and Engels had expressed on the process of transformation. For they assumed that the proletariat forms an indivisible class
and that the revolution will suppress all class division.

Against the abstract views of Marx and Engels on what should be,
Van Kol opposes an important observation of fact. He observes that the
Social Democrats today manifest their antipathy for the unfortunates
who live at the bottom of society; the division of the proletariat has
already taken place, in his opinion; and we can no longer say with
Marx that the revolutionary proletariat, having nothing beneath it, can
only be liberated by totally suppressing class division. In fact, the
proletariat of the Social Democrats is a Fourth Estate, which has in-

feriors it does not seem disposed to liberate, and according to Van Kol this Fourth Estate could grant itself privileges.

Our author even goes so far as to say that the wretched classes find their only defenders in the anarchists![19] We know with what ferocious hatred the Social Democrats harass the anarchists; from this it could be concluded that the Fifth Estate should not expect to be treated too gently by the upper proletariat if the latter ever succeeds in ruling. Thus the social mechanism is very different from what Marx and Engels had described: their perfect classless society becomes a utopia just as the unity of the proletariat is a theorist's illusion, which, because of abstraction, excessively simplified the social problem. If they did not start from the "abstract principle of human nature," they started from "the abstract principle of the unique proletariat," and reasoned in a purely logical way without considering the facts. That is indeed utopian.

Is it true that the Social Democrats have really abandoned utopian ideas on "the principle of human nature"? In a lecture on historical materialism several years ago, Paul Lafargue said that man has always sought to realize an ideal of peace and happiness "which has been in the human consciousness for millions of years. [This] is the remembrance of that golden age, of that terrestrial paradise spoken of by religions, a faraway memory of that communist period that man had to traverse in order to arrive at private property."[20] In various circumstances revolutionaries have tried to realize this ideal and have been defeated; but today economic progress allows us to emerge from instinctive strivings in order to create this communist world. This whole hypothesis should be considered utopian, according to Plekhanoff's definition of the word, for it assumes the pre-existence of an idea of the future society in the psychological structure of man. It is based on the least possible scientific theory of human nature: nothing is more contrary to the conception of modern psychology than this atavistic recollection, which finally coincides with the results of the evolution of the most advanced civilization!

We must not assume that Lafargue's paradox was original; almost all Social Democrats believe that private property has brought about the downfall of humanity and hope that the revolution will bring back the nobility of primitive sentiments.[21] And Sombart says that "the old dreams of paradise lost and regained—of the golden age of early humanity—disturb the harmony of the new system."[22]

We find again the notion of the primitive powers of human nature under another form in what Charles Bonnie says concerning Fourier:[23] "Utopia is but the source whence socialism draws its strength and *must always do so;* for men of genius have constructed sources which are far from being exhausted." A little further on he adds:[24] "The utopians are truly long-sighted persons, and the middle ground escapes them; they have seen it excessively enlarged in the details of the very present.

However, they have neglected the introduction of the forces which should bring on the advance of the phenomenon—not exactly as they had predicted, but in the same direction. From the study of a present state the utopian *can calculate* the future; but he cannot foresee the accident which will bring on the fall."

This passage, written by an orthodox French Social Democrat, brings us far from the realm of science. This sympathy for Fourier and for the utopians in general would be inconceivable in a man who is concerned with approaching social questions scientifically. There we see very clearly that this *Wissenschaft* of Engels's disciples has nothing in common with the science of scholars. No physicist has ever had the idea of studying the poets or the alchemists to find the theories or the solutions that his research would then make precise. The utopians have drawn their reforming conceptions from the ideas on human nature that they were formulating and that were being formulated around them. If the Social Democrats are often in agreement with them and find astonishing forecasts in their books, it is because they proceed in the same way. Human nature has a common basis, which has not varied much for a century,[25] and successive utopias are much more similar than we might at first believe. The difference between the new and the old socialists lies especially in the fact that the former add contributions borrowed from science to their "social poems"; but that is only a top dressing intended to please a public having an unlimited faith in science.

We must not be duped by sonorous words. There is no procedure for *seeing* the future in the present, even with presbyopic eyes, and no procedure for calculating the future. The utopians have only been able to express desires and regrets—desires and regrets that can still be found in the works of contemporary socialists. In vain do they accumulate blunt and abstract terms; they are not scientific so long as they do not limit their ambition to dealing with well-posed problems by means of scientific methods and by clearly defining materially operational solutions.

Plekhanoff condemns all these procedures which lead Marxism back to utopianism. He believes that the *substance of psychology* is continually changing. This thesis needs to be examined closely; for we are going to see that when it is not clearly understood it gives rise to new views just as utopian as those of the past.

IV

The psychology of the eighteenth century was not very advanced. It was generally believed that the science of man is a kind of physics which can be determined once and for all by observation; but Plekhanoff is against this idea. Since human nature is not immutable across the centuries, the natural order or the fundamental law of societies cannot be deduced from a psychological study. Today we know that psychological substance varies a lot according to exterior circumstances. Marxists have seized hold of this commonplace and have transformed it into a great principle. They have affirmed that the conditions of life *fashion* and *determine* our thoughts. It is very clear that such a thesis cannot be proved; it cannot be expressed even very imprecisely except in a *literary form*. It would be impossible to say by what rules we could pass from the knowledge of the historical world to the knowledge of our intellectual acts. To affirm that human nature changes historically is what experimental science does. To affirm that it is fashioned and determined without being able to give the rule of this fashioning or determination is not at all scientific.

Marx has often stressed the interdependence of social phenomena, but he took care not to go further by replacing this *rational idea* on the unity of things by a particular definition of a determined connection between parts. He sought to establish a certain order among the diverse regions of social science, and naturally he conceives of this order according to Hegelian models. But what is the value of these procedures? That question does not seem to have been completely resolved yet. Benedetto Croce does not voice his opinion,[26] but seems (like Lange) to admit that the principle of Hegel's tripartite divisions is psychological.

What seems most certain in psychology today is that exterior conditions act on the human mind only in a subordinate way to the formal laws of our mental development: on the one hand, psychological forms succeed one another regularly in passing from the instinctive to the intellectual, from sentiment to reason, from empirical action to science.[27] On the other hand, the logic of imagination, as well as that of reflective thought, can be found in all times and in all countries. These are two fundamental principles, already recognized by Vico, the understanding of which modern science is working to perfect. As we see, they give no indication about the contents of the mind; psychology allows us to classify, group and connect phenomena, but does not give us facts.

Marx treats sociology similarly: he classifies sociological elements, but he does not define them and does not claim to deduce one of them from another. He stresses notably the transition from economics to law and politics, which greatly illuminates history. In this (ideal) process, the mind increasingly emerges from necessity to liberty, from the individual to the universal. The Hegelian origin of this idea is undeniable; it is not difficult to see that it is based on psychological laws.

Unfaithful to the thinking of the master, almost all Marxists claimed to be *demonstrating* how institutions are derived from the economy. They proceeded in two different ways. They often regarded law as a mechanism created by crafty people in order to hide the reality of things. They presumed self-interested (not to say shameful) motives in important historical personages and they called this way of "tricking" history the "historical materialism of Marx"! Today these jokes are no longer even discussed. The second procedure leads us back to utopian abstractions.

It has been maintained that every description applicable to the systems of organized labor should at length become applicable to every other part of the social system. Here is how Lafargue applies this principle (without announcing it) in a pamphlet on *Communism and Economic Education:* Today production is carried out in common. The division of labor requires the gathering together of great collectivities of workers; in stores "the most varied products are *placed in common";* the corporation *"places in common* the petty capital possessed individually." In these diverse examples, the expression "placed in common" corresponds to very different realities, but the "common" label is found everywhere. Thus we should rediscover it in the other considerations relating to economics and law. "The placing in common of the means of production," says Lafargue, "must inevitably lead to the placing in common of the means of enjoyment"; and further on: "The inevitable development of economic phenomena generates the means of resolving the *antagonism* between the *communist method* of production and the *individualist method* of appropriation. That is to say that while it was *communizing* the means of production and exchange, economic evolution was preparing the *communization* of the means of enjoyment."

Here we are indeed in the realm of the most artificial abstractions, of those that seem especially worthwhile because of verbal analogies. They are the words that regulate things, the signs that move history. Experience certainly seems to have shown that the work of the collectivities assembled under one discipline can be allied with the most diverse legal systems; that, consequently, distribution can be described in terms of categories very different from those of production.

At the end of his pamphlet Lafargue passes into the realm of facts and says that the proletariat is organizing itself in order to resolve the social question in communist terms. He claims that this solution is inevitable and is required by economic evolution. That is to say by the abstract theory of the interdependence of phenomena, leading to the similarity of categories. His thinking is expressed perhaps more clearly still in the following passage:[28] "The death sentence [of the wage earning classes] is sworn. Proletarians *have the mission of carrying out the economic sentence.* Not only has capitalist production decreed the abolition of the wage-earning classes; but it gives the proletariat *the material means of fulfilling its mission.*" Thus history is primarily commanded by the innate logic of concepts (as is sometimes said); and the directives of logic are carried out because there exists at the same time a force capable of transforming society and people who are interested in changing it in the direction indicated by logic.

I believe that these ideas are not at all Marxist: but it must be recognized that they are based on the principles posed by Engels, principles which have been accepted by all of the German Social Democracy. Engels had no doubt about the importance of logic in social evolution. In the last pages of his pamphlet "Socialism from Utopia to Science," he describes to us the progress of history as Lafargue does. *Antagonism* is pushed to absurd lengths. *The mode of production rebels against the form of exchange.* The bourgeoisie is shown henceforth incapable of directing productive social forces. . . . The bourgeoisie is recognized as a useless class. . . . Proletarian revolution is a *resolution of antagonism.*

It is indeed true that Marx sometimes described social struggles in symbolic form, without expressly naming the actors of the drama. He said, for example, that productive forces enter into conflict with relations of property when the traditional legal institutions disturb the development of these same productive forces. But the meaning of this passage from the preface of the *Critique of Political Economy* is unmistakable when it is compared with the corresponding passages found in the *Communist Manifesto*[29] and especially in the *Poverty of Philosophy:*[30] it is a question of conflicts between classes, between the one that produces and wants to acquire the profits of the productive forces and the one that possesses by virtue of ancient title.

When we think like Engels and Lafargue, we admit that history is carried out in order to satisfy the exigencies of our logic; we are idealist, in the Hegelian sense. Marx had written against this Hegelian philosophy of history in 1859 that it is not our manner of understanding that determines the quality of our manner of being, but on the contrary our social life which is translated into concepts. The most ingenious companions, the most irreducible antagonisms among categories, the most imperious logical rules are no help for anyone who wants to apply Marx's true conceptions to real life.

V

Logic plays a considerable role in the work of the utopians, and therefore their methods merit close examination.

Utopians always make a long and acerbic criticism of the existing world. They lay bare the caprices, vices, and contradictions with which society is permeated; they then suggest corrections. In general a writer who devotes a long time to the criticism of customs and institutions should be distrusted. The criticism is usually highly developed the better to hide the weakness of plans; this procedure almost always indicates utopianism.

Fourier, to whom we must always revert when we treat these questions, owes a great part of his popularity to the truly amusing manner he adopted to describe the foibles of his contemporaries. Furthermore he did not intend to create a social science, in the present meaning of the term "science." "Questions of social politics," he said,[31] "will always be insoluble as long as we speculate on civilized regimes, which are intellectual labyrinths, vicious circles in every sense; but why not try to *invent a new society?* That would be a good task for so many writers who are beating the bushes for a new subject." It seems to me that this advice has been too abused and that there has been no dearth of inventors of new societies since 1829.

Merlino has clearly shown the method used by many socialists in their utopias:[32] "They reason by antitheses. Having demonstrated that evils and injustices are derived from an existing institution, they jump to the conclusion that it should be abolished and replaced by an institution based on the diametrically opposite principle." Fourier, who had pretentions to scholarship, reproached Owen for having proceeded in this way by denying religion, property and the family.

He found it absurd to try to reduce society so much[33] and to pretend to imitate primitive customs.

Utopians generally proceed like Owen by way of simplification: they make a complete list of the faults which society presents and which (in their eyes) inspire justifiable complaints; they abolish everything that seems to be the cause of these evils and everything that produces contradictions. Property generates relations that are too complex even to be reduced to a satisfactory logical system, entailing no drawbacks. This very complexity then leads to abolishing property and to a certain degree to imitating savage peoples. The mind of savages has not yet reached the stage of development of attaining clear juridical ideas on property: it is this insufficiency of law that has been transformed and interpreted[34] as a law of common property.

Almost all Social Democrats believe that a day will come when society will be able to do without the legal system, when anarchic communism will reign and when the most complete liberty will be established on earth. This idea is expressed several times in the already cited work of Van Kol, as a perfectly natural idea, having no need of justification. Vandervelde says that he aspires[35] "to the anarchist community, overflowing with brotherhood and wealth, in which everyone, doing as he likes, as in *The Abbey of Thélème*,[36] would give according to his ability and would take according to his needs"; and he adds: "There is no ideal so pure that it cannot be realized in the future." It would be well to know whether this "ideal"(?) is truly worthy of man, whether it is as pure as the great Belgian orator believes and finally where it comes from. These are questions that I will not examine here and I will limit myself to observing that never has there been proposed a more masked utopia than this one.

Let us return to the socialist world, which should succeed the capitalist one: there are great difficulties in trying to understand its functioning. Van Kol tells us that administration will be entrusted to the best of the best, that the leaders will represent the collective will, that all the citizens will be firmly committed to no other goal but the good. How can we be sure that all of these marvels will come about? Information about the institutions which would facilitate the realization of the socialist program is sketchy. It is not known whether the social mechanism will be capable of sustaining the future world; we are back to utopianism.

This utopianism is based on the presupposition that there will be a perfect harmony among men, so good that all wills will join together spontaneously in order to realize a reasonable plan of common life, just as if the city were a living and intelligent being. Aristotle long ago[37] objected that Plato's *Republic* would reach perfection if it were reduced to one individual, but that real societies are very complex.

This unity could be achieved in two ways: either by the transformation of men into atoms which are moved by forces whose laws are regulated to attain the proposed goal, or rather by a reduction of men to pure intelligence. The first system was Fourier's; although it appeared scientific to our forefathers, it no longer stands up under discussion. The second is that of the anarchists and Social Democrats.

In the last pages of his already quoted work on utopia and science, Engels says that humanity will truly emerge from the animal era; then sociological laws will no longer be exterior conditions as imperative as natural laws; man will employ his forces with full knowledge of what he is doing; free initiative will be fully exercised; men will act out their history as fully conscious beings; the reign of liberty will begin. The word "freedom" should be understood in the sense of purely intellectual action; if nature is fully subordinated to men, who possess at the same time full knowledge of relations and full power of execution, the *mind* will have overcome nature. Thus it is not surprising that authors who are enthusiastic about such a future have said that future man will be like a god.[38]

In *Capital* Marx speaks also of a period when intelligence will be sovereign.[39] "The religious reflection of the real world can only disappear when the conditions of work and everyday life present man with clear and *rational* relations with his peers and with nature. Social life . . . will not be drawn out of the mystical cloud that hides its appearance until the day when the work of freely associating men comes into evidence, working consciously and masters of their own social movement."[40]

Here Marx agrees with Engels; he too admits that later on men will possess the clear knowledge of all social relations; that they will become pure intellects capable of understanding the character of social movements by their causes. For him religion is only a poetic and provisional expression of physical and social relations. It forms a prescientific system with no more reason for its existence when science is fully established. Its affective element disappears when intelligence has triumphed in the human being.[41]

Utopians are all more or less intellectualists. They all more or less obviously deny feeling in social life. Fourier thought that he was bringing into play all the motive forces of human activity, but the passions that he described had no psychological reality. They were fictitious forces obeying laws that he had invented for the purpose of realizing a predetermined plan and, consequently, they were products of the intelligence.

There is a confusion in the utopia of the Social Democrats that does not exist in the others. We never know exactly of what period they are speaking. Does it concern the society which will immediately follow the capitalist world? Or rather does it concern the communist society that is shown to be far in the future? Marx seems to be alluding to this future in the passage on religion in *Capital*. In 1847 he had visualized the social movement in a very simple form: a period of disturbances and of popular dictatorship, then the communist period. In 1878 Engels, in his oft-cited pamphlet, thought along the same lines; however, Marx, in his 1875 *Critique of the Gotha Program*, admitted a greater complication; he had distinguished between the two stages—collectivist and communist—recognized today by almost all Social Democrats. Are the psychological states of these two regimes substantially different? Writers have hardly touched on this question.

The intellectualist hypothesis is as necessary for collectivism as for communism. We find it from the beginning, at the time when the social structure is about to change; this change comes about logically. The bourgeois class becomes useless; it is disappearing; class distinction becomes an anachronism and is abolished. The political authority of the state has no more reason for being and it dies out; the organization of production by society according to a predetermined general plan becomes possible and desirable and it is realized, etc. Thus speak Engels's disciples. The greatest miracle that could ever be recorded in history would be the voluntary abdication of dictatorial powers. Such a phenomenon cannot be understood without the intellectualist hypothesis. This dictatorship ceases when it is no longer necessary for the happiness of men!

Several writers—among them Van Kol—admit that things will not happen so simply. How will democracy be able to produce results so different from those that it has always provided when its power will be unlimited? How will the administration have all the virtues attributed to it? Van Kol says that the state will disappear only very late.[42] But since the state has always been an agent of oppression, why will it cease to be one? All this is impossible to understand without the intellectualist hypothesis.

The same author tells us that society necessarily must progress[43] in the future world: this is indeed a strange thesis, but one which can be understood by referring to the intellectualist conception. It can be stated with certainty that progress in intelligence has been made because knowledge is constantly being enlarged, at least since the origin of the capitalist era. The question of knowing whether progress (even reduced to the progress of knowledge) would continue to operate under a system deprived of capitalist competition offers no difficulties for anyone who accepts the intellectualist hypothesis.[44] "Scientific, artistic and aesthetic needs will be stimulated and satisfied to an unknown degree." Until now scholars have done much less for progress than inventors supported by the capitalists, but the reverse will occur very naturally in a society in which intelligence is sovereign.

VI

Merlino has made a very important contribution to the study of the above problems by showing that they should be approached differently. There is no scientific proof that collectivism must come after capitalism and be supplanted by communism. For Merlino, it is not a matter of two *successive economic regimes*, but of two juridical principles which must co-exist in order that true justice in society may be ensured. "To each according to his works" and "to each according to his needs," are two rules, each of which has its *raison d'être*.

Marx was led to suggesting solutions incompatible with science because he was governed by two main persuppositions: he believed that one system supersedes another by making earlier systems disappear almost completely; like Hegel he believed that the development of the

Spirit dominates history. In the passage from individual production to capitalism, then to socialism, he saw a progression from the individual to the universal—a transformation of the consciousness of the workers, attaining an understanding of increasingly general relations—a more perfect combination of interests, forces and ideas, passing from anarchic chance to intelligent organization.

It is impossible to demonstrate that such logical arrangements can govern history. Vico made a similar error in admitting that psychological processes can govern history. In our very complex societies all products of human nature exist in a state of combination. We have seen that Marx thought religion must disappear in the face of science: experience hardly confirms this view; religions always find elements of rejuvenation in the mystical. If it is true that on the one hand they develop from sentiment to intellectualism, on the other they re-create themselves just as continuously as they decompose—so much so that at every period the various stages of rejuvenation and decomposition are mixed. What is so true for religion is true also for every other manifestation of psychological activity.

Marx, like almost all his contemporaries, thought that the forms of large-scale mechanical industry would be imposed on production by making small manufacturing disappear. Nowhere do we see articles of clothing[45] manufactured in a general way according to principles analogous to those observed for spinning and weaving of cotton material. Agriculture resists experiments in large-scale cultivation wherever the nature of the ground allows a very intensive cultivation and requires a great economy of material. After having proclaimed the benefits of extended property, almost all economists recognize that it is small property that best corresponds to the necessities of intensive cultivation. Vandervelde[46] observes that in Belgium small farming is becoming more and more prevalent. In the Piedmont, Luigi Einaudi does not find that the division of land is being changed. The present division depends on conditions which are not very susceptible to change.[47] "The physical condition of the soil and the diversity of culture account for all of the vast organism of the agricultural economy of the Piedmont. It is futile to attempt to try to coordinate all of the sparse sections of agricultural zones and to bring them under a single law."

A special characteristic of Marx's communism does not seem to have been noticed: it is not complete. It leaves standing the most primitive of the forms of production of the means of subsistence, the one productive form representing the most complete anarchic waste in the minds of the old utopians: it preserves the family household, the creation of products out of nature for domestic usage and not for exchange. Van

Kol thinks[48] that "common households, houses like barracks, with open tables for common meals and uniform clothing would displease us," at least until the time when "a more elevated conception of communism and fraternity" will reign.

The Social Democrats have been forced to admit that the general plan of production, dreamed of by Marx and Engels, will not be actualized soon. They have proposed an intermediate stage in socialist development. They speak rather readily of a "partial collectivization," in which all small and medium-sized industries would be preserved in private form. Indeed they add that this stage would be provisional,[49] but they are no more masters of the future than anyone else. They recognize the principle of the coexistence of inferior and superior forms of production.

Finally, almost all Social Democrats have recognized that citizens should not be completely absorbed by collective workshops and that they would enjoy enough leisure to be able to devote themselves to freely chosen occupations. Without this vestige of individualism, progress would remain rather doubtful.

The seeming simplicity of the Marxist solution disappears when we examine the problem more closely. It becomes obvious to everyone that the economy is not everywhere the same, but that diverse systems coexist. It is still more certain that law could never be limited to cover only one principle corresponding to a single mode of production. Private property, collectivism and communism, instead of characterizing three successive epochs, can very well be notions that social science ascertains simultaneously in developed societies.

If one accepts this point of view, every trace of utopia in Marxian concepts disappears; there is no longer any need to abandon science in order to immerse oneself in dreams of the future. It is useless to seek problematical laws to regulate history; we remain on the solid ground of facts and utilize the mass of materials observed, classified and interpreted by Marx. But then, one asks: what is socialism, if not the research into society described in obscure terms by Engels? The answer is simple: Socialism is the workers' movement, the revolt of the proletariat against ruling institutions. It is the organization which is both economic and ethical at the same time, which we see forming before our eyes, and whose purpose is to struggle against bourgeois traditions.

Polemics on the Interpretation of Marxism: Bernstein and Kautsky[1]

I

For several years, socialists in all countries have felt the need of renewing their doctrines. Officially, Marxism constitutes the basis of all their claims; but Marxism has degenerated noticeably in the process of vulgarizing itself, and we often have difficulty in finding Marx's doctrines in it. The rare persons in France who are interested in these questions have been able to follow, in the *Devenir Social*,[2] a serious attempt to infuse Marxism with the latest developments in contemporary science.

In 1897, Serverio Merlino published in Italy a book entitled *Pro e contro il socialismo*[3] in which he showed the necessity of reforming the excessively narrow precepts of socialist orthodoxy. Early in 1898, Eduard Bernstein wrote some articles in the *Neue Zeit* entitled "Problems of Socialism" which provoked lively discussion. The French public knows of this controversy only through reviews. The *Devenir Social* ceased to participate in this renewal of socialism at the end of 1897 and the journal disappeared at the end of 1898.[4]

Early in 1899, Bernstein published a popular book intended to reveal his essential ideas to the public at large; its success was considerable. The director of the *Neue Zeit,* the official journal of the German Social Democratic Party, Karl Kautsky, replied to Bernstein in a work that has just been translated into French. The reading of the two volumes is difficult because the Bernstein is translated into pathetic French and in the Kautsky book, it is all but impossible to find anything more than the quibbles of a superficial polemic. Furthermore, both authors assume that their public is perfectly up-to-date on the ideas that have been popularized by the German Social Democracy so that the relevance of their discussions often escapes the French public. Here, I will not enter into an examination of anything that does not have a directly scientific interest. Everyone easily understands that if Bernstein is attacked so wrathfully in Germany, it is not solely out of a passion for scientific truth; I will confine myself to two indications which seem to me to be symptomatic of this lack of concern.

Wilhelm Liebknecht has not spared insults to Bernstein,[5] whom he has called an insignificant man from the political and scientific point of view; but he underestimated the real strength of the Bernsteinians, and he went overboard. In the preface to his book, Kautsky fervently summons Liebknecht, the dean of the Social Democracy, to his senses, and does not hesitate to write that Liebknecht's judgments on the value of Bernstein are those of a man who does not have even a superficial knowledge of the *Neue Zeit!*

At the 1899 Hanover Congress, August Bebel attacked Bernstein violently, but he did not dare to propose a resolution explicitly condemning his ideas. The matter remained in the realm of generalities which everyone could accept. Moreover, two months later in Berlin, Bebel gave a speech that could have been attributed to a Fabian.

In order to understand this controversy thoroughly, we must remember that the Germans want to defend the rightness of their position by saying that it is taken because of lofty motives, and they love to imagine that they have gone to the root of things. Engels understood the idiosyncrasies of his compatriots perfectly when he taught that Marxism is the quintessence of modern science. For a long time, he had been in business and had made a handsome fortune in cotton. He knew the great importance of words, etiquette and publicity. That is why in his work, *Anti-Dühring* (1878) he applied himself to giving a metaphysical aura to his ideas. From this work, a pamphlet was extracted, which has been translated into the pompous title of "Socialism from Utopia to Science." This pamphlet has become the catechism of Social Democracy in every country.

The books of the Social Democrats are always difficult to understand. Every minute one is struck by Hegelian formulas[6] which the authors understand badly; they distort them or even give entirely fantastic interpretations. The sterility of this socialist literature has been noted many times. The Social Democrats themselves recognize the fact, and several of them, including Paul Lafargue,[7] think that this sterility will endure as long as capitalist society does; during these years of trial, socialists ought to confine themselves to popularizing Marx and Engels.

Two grave consequences result from this: first, all free interpretation is regarded as a danger for the faith of the masses who might lose their absolute confidence in the masters; second, the Social Democrats, being powerless to derive anything from their precepts for the purpose of guiding them in difficult cases of practical life, are led to resort to a central authority which exempts them from the need of thinking for themselves. We have had a fine example of this "clerical spirit" in the responses sent to the *Petite République* by the heads of the International Social Democracy concerning the "problem of conscience" raised by the entry of Alexandre Millerand into the cabinet. Nearly all the correspondents were bogged down in abstract formulas on the class struggle, but almost everyone recognized that the most absolute principles can give way in exceptional cases—of which the central authority of the party is the judge. De Maistre would be satisfied; his theory of the supremacy of pontifical authority is justified.

Bernstein's book has produced an effect analogous to that of a Protestant sermon amidst a Catholic population.[8] He asks socialists to throw their doctrines overboard in order to observe, understand and, above all, play a truly efficacious role in the world.

At the beginning of his reply, Kautsky states that Bernstein's is the first truly sensational book in German socialist literature. It has been read and favorably reviewed by illustrious professors.[9] Kautsky has difficulty in consoling himself about such a scandal, for he is unable to understand that a philosophical or scientific work can be lauded for non-partisan reasons. Scholars and economists rarely have the opportunity to praise the works of Social Democrats, but the reasons for this are far removed from party spirit.

Before entering into an examination of the ideas under discussion, let us note that the theories that Engels had taken from Lewis Henry Morgan on the primitive family are ignored by the two adversaries. This has an important result: henceforth socialism will no longer depend on hypotheses about promiscuous Hawaiian tribes and other fine things of this kind. This is an advance that will not please certain French writers who are drawn perhaps as much to the promiscuity of primitive women as to the primitive communism of goods, and who indeed hope to see both of them reappear in future society.

II

In the pamphlet of which I have spoken, Engels says:[10] "These two great discoveries—the materialist conception of history and the revelation of the mystery of capitalist production by means of surplus-value— we owe to Marx. They made a science of socialism, and it is now a question of elaborating this science in all its details." There is general agreement today that we should attribute to Marx a third thesis relative to the dialectic of history; this agreement results from the chapter Kautsky devotes to method and from the lecture given by Jean Jaurès on February 16, 1900.

Like Jaurès, I will begin by speaking of the theory of value, because Bernstein thinks that it ought to be placed apart from the purely socialist doctrines of Marx.[11] "Whether the theory of value is exact or not," he said, "has no importance for the demonstration of surplus-labor (*Mehrarbeit*). It is not, in this connection, a proof, but a simple means of analysis and exposition. And further on, he writes that it is[12] "a key, an ideological image . . . a key which, utilized by Marx, led to the revelation and demonstration of the movement of capitalist economics in conditions of clarity, logic and lucidity never attained until then. Only, at a certain stage, the demonstration falls apart, and this failure has been the stumbling block to almost all the disciples of Marx."[12] Finally, he notes that, according to Engels, Marx's economic theory does not constitute a justification of socialism.

The great difficulty presented by this question results from the Marxists' refusal to present the theory in a clear and truly scientific form. Nevertheless there are only six pages of text to comment on! Kautsky discourses at great length on the Austrian (and associated) doctrines upon which Bernstein relies; but in fourteen pages devoted to value he sheds no new light.[13]

In Marx there is no theory of value[14] in the commonly accepted sense of the term, but a theory of economic equilibrium reduced to the instance of a vastly simplified society. It is assumed that all industries are equivalent and all workers are reduced to a uniform type. An hour of work with a team of ten men will produce the same thing everywhere. In any and all fields it will create the same intensive scale of a kind that has its equivalent in merchandise of comparable value. Value is the ultimate factor on which differences in exchange are based; its quantum is proportional to the time employed. As a result of the perfect symmetry presented by *homogeneous capitalism,* values are also the rate of exchange.

When we wish to go over the real facts and consider different branches of production, we must recognize that values determined by the expended time of unskilled laborers no longer correspond to the rate of exchange. Marx tries to proceed to a representation of economic phenomena by making use of methods he used in the most abstract case. In different fields, the quantities of liquid capital (salaries) are not proportional to the quantities of fixed capital (primary materials, coal, equipment). In the most highly perfected industries, fixed capital takes on a greater importance. However, Marx continues to make accounts in values measured by time,[15] without concerning himself with instrumental differences. He allows that a day's labor for a simple worker, after having produced the values equivalent to material consumed in the mechanical process, and the value corresponding to the existence of the worker, engenders a surplus value or net product which is the same in all industries.[16] Next, he divides the total mass of surplus values into the proportion of the capital employed and obtains the average rate of profit. The overvalued cost of production in this proportion becomes the price.[17] Thus, we obtain a representation which seems to have no other utility than that of showing the *possibility* of reconciling, by some ingenious artifices, the theory of value with the market price.

All of this is unproven. Marx operated as certain physicists had done formerly. He made it seem that explanation was possible, but he did not give the scientific formula for explanation. This doctrine was published after 1894, and although it forms a part of the "treasures"[18] which exist, according to Kautsky, in the posthumous work of Marx, no one has been able to use any part of it to promote progress in science. For my part, I think that Marx shelved this part of his work because he did not find it good.

Marx's methods present two very great disadvantages which prevent us from using them to resolve the problems of contemporary economics: First, the total value does not change when the productive force of labor changes, so that one must always calculate in *abstract time;* this gives rise to not a few misunderstandings.[19] Second, it assumes a uniform production that takes account of extra profits with difficulty—whereas they play the greatest role in contemporary society.

Marx seems to me to have been seduced by the Ricardian labor theory of value because of the ease with which it allows us to represent the general conditions of various societies in the same way. Several times he returns in his work to the comparison that can be established among a communist, a slave and a capitalist society. These comparisons are always greatly clarified through the use of the concept of labor time. Socialists have greatly stressed the resemblance between the *salariat* and serfdom. In both cases, they say, the laborer is occupied in working part of the week to produce the wealth of others. The difference is this: the employee does not see the phenomenon clearly, while to the serf it is entirely obvious.[20] Socialists have thus been led to say that the profit of the capitalists is "non-paid labor," and this expression has had a great vogue.

The comparisons between the *salariat* and serfdom and the expression "non-paid labor" precede Marx. For a long time, the phrase was popular[21] in England to designate the lengthening of the work day that certain employers imposed on their workers without augmenting their wages;[22] this was natural in a country where labor had always been considered from a juridical point of view as something for which the law fixed payment between master and servant. Everything that surpasses the traditional length of the working day is thus taken by the master into the portion which belongs to him, and we see that the laws of manufacture were regarded as an application of this means of conceiving social relations.[23] On the other hand, English socialists[24] who represented themselves as disciples of Ricardo greatly stressed the fact that capitalist profit would be a deduction of part of the product of the labor of the worker. There is a *very considerable equivocation here on the meaning of the world "labor":* sometimes the activity of the society with all of its resources is considered, and then it is obvious that all wealth is the product of labor; sometimes one speaks of the labor of the worker as an abstraction made of the resources of his employer, and then it is inexact to say that wealth is produced by *his* labor. In Marx's eyes, the capitalist purchases the work force—labor power—and becomes master of the product, because the product results from a mixture of things which have become his own.[25] The right to the integral product of labor could not find a place in this juridical conception. On labor considered as a general activity of society, there is one part which produces the costs and another which produces the profit. As society is transformed by Marx into a correlation of masters and servants, we can say that the first part is paid labor while the second is unpaid labor; but these obscure formulas are equivocal and should be banished from science.

If these precepts are bad from a scientific point of view, they are excellent for propaganda and can even be heard from the mouth of Jaurès, who, thinking he was defending Marx's ideas against Bernstein, said[26] that the capitalist retains a part of the worker's labor, and improperly extracts a certain quantity of work from him. Guesde takes no oratorical precautions: the works of charity of the master are[27] "a partial *restitution* of all the goods created (by the laboring classes) and of which goods they are increasingly dispossessed."[28] "Marx has demonstrated that capital was only *unpaid labor* and that the worker was consequently eternally robbed"; social emancipation must at first assure *"the end of this robbery."*

Generally it is not put so bluntly, but the Marxist theory of value is always presented to the people in such a way as to *seem* to produce pessimistic conclusions.[29] It is because of this that a doctrine which no longer has any scientific usefulness and which engenders much misunderstanding is maintained so assiduously.

III

Like the theory of value, historical materialism consists partly in philosophy and partly in equivocations designed to act on rather unenlightened minds. To separate these two parts should be the essential work of the disciples of Marx and this is what Bernstein wants to do, just as many others have done; but the procedure is very difficult, all the more so as neither Marx nor Engels has ever given a clear and detailed explanation of his ideas.

A most perspicacious critic, Benedetto Croce, believes that we should regard the materialist conception of history only as a framework for social analysis.[30] One can cite many passages in which Engels spoke of it as a working tool that Marx and he adopted after about 1845, following studies that had been undertaken separately. Engels often refers to Marx's pamphlet, *The Eighteenth Brumaire of Louis Bonaparte*, as a perfect model of the application of the method. Kautsky[31] also considered this work to be the true model of a historical account from the Marxist point of view. For anyone who studies this treatise, there cannot be the slightest doubt: Marx did his research in the spirit described by Benedetto Croce. He attempted to connect historical explanations to the economic differentiations disclosed by an analysis of civil society; but this was not a great innovation, and it is easy to see that Proudhon tried to do the same thing in studying the same revolutionary events as Marx did in a work entirely in his own time.[32]

In taking this simple example, it does not appear that there is anything very original in the work of Marx. Kautsky does not wish to content himself with it, because he sees clearly that historians had taken account of economic points of view for a long time. Certainly there is in Marx a special doctrine on the system of history, but it is not easy to discover, and interpreters so far have not succeeded in giving a truly scientific account of it. The literal meaning of the technical terms that Marx used in his preface to the *Critique of Political Economy* in 1859 almost always eludes them. However, it is to these several very obscure pages that one must refer in order to grasp the true thought of Marx.

Enrico Ferri gives the following definition of historical materialism:[33] "Economic conditions—which result from energies and ethnic aptitudes acting in a given territorial milieu—are the *determining base* of all the social, juridical and political manifestations of human life, *individual* and social."

This is a paraphrase of Marxist doctrine, but it is a very free paraphrase. Thus, Marx did not speak of individual life; he is only concerned with collective manifestations; he does not say that economic conditions are a *determining base,* but that the relations of production (which from the legal point of view are the relations of property) form the economic structure and the *real base (reale basis)* on which the juridical and political superstructures are mounted. In *Capital,* to express an analogous idea, he uses the Hegelian term *Grundlage,*[34] whose meaning is clear.

Professor Antonio Labriola has devoted three essays[35] to elucidating the idea of historical materialism. In one essay after another, Labriola departs from Marx's original views. Here is how Labriola expresses himself in his last work:[36] "The *means of social life*—which are, on the one hand, the conditions and the instruments, and, on the other, the results of variously specified kinds of cooperation—constitute (besides what the milieu offers) the matter and the stimulus of our interior formation. From this, secondary habits arise which create in us a feeling of our 'selves' as part of customs and of institutions, the state, the Church, historical tradition, etc. In these correlations of practical association from *individual* to *individual* are found the root and the objective basis of all the different expressions of the public consciousness." Elsewhere he recognizes[37] that economics does not permit us to take dispositions of the mind into account.

Labriola ends with a *psychological conception of history.* Kautsky does not accept this conception; he claims that one must first *posit determinism* as a necessity to which the historian must submit.[38] "What is science? The knowledge of the necessary and natural relations of phenomena. . . . The progress of science consists in restraining the domain of chance and in extending that of recognized necessity. The great merit of Marx and Engels has been to bring *historical facts* into the domain of necessary facts and thus raise history to the level of a science with more success than their predecessors."[39] I do not know if the author fully realized what he wrote: it is a little strange to affirm that there is a determinism when at the same time one cannot give the *rule of determinism.* No discussion is possible on declarations as vague as Kautsky's. He tells us that:[40] "The historians of the 'Marxist school' are unanimous in recognizing that all their research confirms Marx's description of the historical processes in the preface" of 1859. Unfortunately he does not go into detail about this school. Langlois and Seignobos, who in their *Introduction aux études* have so carefully examined the various ways of understanding history, make no mention of this school. Kautsky cites only one Marxist historian, Lafargue, who is a paradoxical journalist rather than a man of science. It is Lafargue who tells us[41] that Socrates and Plato were "profound politicians" who founded "the morality of the bourgeoisie, which can only result in putting words and acts into contradiction."

As opposed to Bernstein, Kautsky maintains[42] that Engels's posthumously published letters contain no corrections of the old interpretations. While maintaining the necessity of connecting every manifestation of the historical life of peoples to economic bases, of thus traversing the whole scale of social correlations in order to attain the farthest limit from one instance to another, Engels recognized that ideological factors have their own reality and a partly autonomous power once they are fixed by institutions. Bernstein says: "Historical materialism does not then in the least deny the independent movement of political and ideological factors."[43]

Jaurès claims to side against Bernstein, but he appears to go much further in his attenuations. He accepts historical materialism only on the condition of leaving so little of it that the doctrine has nothing truly Marxist remaining in it. At first he recognizes that Engels's letters have brought in a new element:[44] "I know that there are Marxists in France who are a little shocked by the apparent correction of the traditional interpretation of Marxism by Engels. They have said: 'But this is the ruin of Marxist theory.'" And here is how he interprets the correction to be made: "There are forces called 'science,' 'the Church' and 'democracy,' and each of these forces has its own internal logic, its 'own law of development' which would lead it to an end that could be designated in advance, if its development were not contradicted, driven back or pushed further by the dominant economic forces."

Kautsky avoids difficulties with subtleties of language. He says[45] that the ideological and political forces of which Engels had spoken are "products of earlier social forms and consequently also of earlier modes of production." We have not made much progress when we replace easily ascertainable facts with unintelligible words. How and according to what rule can one deduce these "products" from economic facts? This is the same insoluble question that I have already posed concerning the word "determine": we are promised *science* and are given only *words*. We are not given new ways of acting on the world with a clear will. New veils are interposed between reality and our eyes.

IV

Bernstein does not focus on these theories for purely speculative reasons. He discusses them because they have great practical interest; he wants the idea of "historical necessity" to be abandoned. He does not believe that the world advances toward a predetermined regime, and that is why he is hostile to the materialist idea.[46] *The materialist is a Calvinist without God.* . . . He believes—and he must believe—that from any given moment everything that happens henceforward is determined in advance by the whole of existing matter and by the reciprocal relations of the forces which it engenders." Marx and Engels believed that the world must soon emerge from what they called "prehistory" in order to enter into a period in which humanity would be freed from the old historical chains. But Bernstein rightly asks that we not confuse wishful thinking with sociological sections of the work of the masters.[47] Unfortunately, it is certain that this fanciful construction of the future interests the Social Democracy much more than all of the research into the past. Indeed the party draws a large part of its strength from the belief in the dogma of social palingenesis. Jaurès admits it:[48] "The workers must feel themselves helped by the logic of history. They must feel that they are carried, so to speak, by the internal reasoning that develops in reality, and they must view themselves as a complementary force which ends up by emancipating the human dialectic."[49]

If social predestination is rejected, there results, as Bernstein says,[50] an increase in the duties of social democracy. I myself believe that the result is total transformation. If social palingenesis is inevitably brought on by the immanent law of the capitalist regime, the working classes do not have to collaborate in the transformation. They must only seek to profit from the favorable events which will unfailingly occur. They must unite and discipline themselves in such a way as to be able to seize public power at the right time, in order to expel the bosses and to profit from the industry created by capitalism. The essential question is to have enough power to become masters of the political arena, and Kautsky never seems to doubt this principle. For Bernstein, on the contrary, the problem for socialism is to develop in the working classes a superior culture, which would allow them to administer the productive forces and which would prepare for a regime that is more just than the present one. Today, the proletariat is far from possessing this culture.

This education of the proletariat can only be accomplished through economic institutions (syndicates, mutual aid societies, cooperatives). Therefore, it is bad to judge these institutions, as does Kautsky, as being only (or especially) a factor in the electoral force of the party.[51] According to one's point of view, there are very different ways of administering these institutions.

For Kautsky and his partisans, every action is judged in relation to what they call the "final end." But how can we evaluate the value of a current action or a social reform as a means toward a regime placed in an *indeterminate future*? When men believed in an imminent palingenesis, they could reason on the degree of effectiveness of a determined tactic. But how can we predict what will result from our present-day conduct with regard to a socialist solution which is perhaps separated from our regime by "many forms of intermediate societies"?[52] The response will depend on our ideas about predestination. The Social Democrats have no doubt: all action that has a favorable influence for the electoral struggle is surely favorable for the final end, and this question is generally easy enough to resolve. However, when we accept Bernstein's way of looking at things, we should ask what the educational value of a given practice is. The education of the people is something much more difficult to direct than electoral politics. What is essential for Bernstein is to develop the idea of justice in the people. His adversary seems to have doubts about the value of such propaganda to lead the workers to socialism.[53]

We know that Social Democrats generally have a great disdain for ethical considerations.[54] They treat morality with as much contempt as the Voltairians treated religion (which is no worse for wear because of it). While Bernstein writes:[55] "The degree of development attained now gives to ideological factors and more particularly to ethical factors a freer field than ever before," Kautsky responds, "There is no place in historical materialism for a morality that is independent of economic forces and superior to them."[56] It is like dreaming to read such an audacious declaration! Is it, therefore, true that the social reforms made during this century have been accomplished without moral concerns having played a great role? And what then was Marx thinking when, in the preface to *Capital,* he spoke of lofty motives which are added to considerations of clearly understood economic interests in leading the ruling classes to dispel obstacles which hinder the development of the working classes?

At the present time all countries are concerned with perfecting their social legislation, and every unprejudiced person will subscribe to this precept of Bernstein:[57] "The necessities of techno-economic development determine the development of other social institutions less and less."[58]

In addition to legal action, there is a more direct action of the State in directing and controlling the economic movement of the country. In the construction of railroads, the subsidies to shipping and colonization corporations, commercial agreements, technical schools, the popularization of knowledge about international commerce, services of inspection of goods and health inspection, I do not find purely capitalist concerns. In the modern state, there is a great augmentation of collective force exercising an efficacious control over the economy. Bernstein expresses this idea, saying that[59] "some peoples protected a more considerable part of their existence from the influence of a necessity contrary to the will or independent of it." Indeed, not only has the modern state intervened at every point in economic life, but again it has succeeded in realizing rather completely the ends that it proposed, despite the resistance of the unconscious forces that it encountered. This is a completely new state of affairs, for in the past the attempts made by governments to direct development ended in failure, and social legislation remained a dead letter. This does not prevent Kautsky from affirming the contrary and maintaining[60] that at the time when custom and routine were completely dominant along "with primitive economic institutions," men were "much more masters of the conditions of production than with capitalist economic institutions."[61] Naturally he proves it, for everything can be proved!

There are social groups which play a large role in this modern development. They correspond to what the Germans call *Intelligenz.*[62] Kautsky is greatly concerned with them, and in his book he returns to their role three times.[63] Sometimes he recognizes that cultured men[64] have ideas that are favorable to social reform; sometimes he asserts that[65] "the mode of capitalist production has made [of the intellectuals] wage-earners in the service of the capitalists. Never have the ideologues depended so much on economic forces as today." Kautsky's problem stems from the fact that he clearly perceives that in Germany educated men do not appear to have any taste for social-democratic ideas.[66]

However, Kautsky hopes that the intelligentsia will come over to the Social Democracy, because there is an overproduction of graduates in the schools, and consequently there are many who are displaced (the party has already gained[67] sculptors, commercial employees and musicians). I doubt that these déclassé recruits augur well for the future. I would remind Kautsky of what Marx wrote in 1873 on the lawyers without a case, the doctors without patients, the students of the billiard halls and the commercial employees who found a *career* and an outlet in the groups in Italy formed by Bakunin; but he would answer that the adherence of these malcontents is a precious asset in the electoral struggle (perhaps the most precious of all) and that consequently they are *excellent* for Social Democracy. Are they "good for the working class"? I adhere to Marx's opinion on this point.[68]

V

We now come to the third Marxist theory. There is no agreement on the meaning of the term "dialectic," but it seems that the dialectic is a very important thing. First of all, I take from Jaurès the following definition:[69] "The dialectical conception of Marx consists in saying that society is . . . a development of social forms producing one another by continual necessity in which human society reconciles contradictory systems within itself. . . . While production has an increasingly *social* character,[70] property retains an individual character . . . and communism appears to be the means of resolving the internal contradiction of capitalism. . . .[71] Thus, Marx is right in saying that there is an internal dialectic of history."

I do not know where Marx has put forth this doctrine. In the preface to the *Critique of Political Economy* he considers the revolution as a "transfer of property," which passes from the hands of an incapable ruling class into the hands of the productive class formed under domination of the old class. The new class does not want economic progress to be arrested by outmoded juridical relics. I do not think that there is in Marx any other idea that is closer to Jaurès's, and this one is not very close!

Engels has indeed said that the socialist revolution will produce the resolution of all antagonisms between the mode of production and the mode of appropriation. It is only "at the end of present-day prehistory" that he counts on seeing such a solution of antagonisms realized. But on what grounds did he hope for such a result? We discover this in the part of *Anti-Dühring* where he claims to show that there is produced in the

world a series of conditions each one of which denies the preceding
one and which succeed themselves according to a rhythm of apparent
recurrence.[72] The plant is the negation of the seed and the fruit is the
negation of the plant. "All geology is a series of negated negations; that
is to say, a series of ruins which succeed one another and of new bases
of mineral formation." All peoples at first had communal property which
disappeared when this system impeded production, and private property
will disappear because it will hinder modern production. "Ancient
philosophy was an instinctive and immediate materialism" which was
replaced by idealism,[73] and modern materialism has replaced idealism.

To what extent does this represent the opinions of Marx? That is what
we must look for. Only one passage is ever cited wherein he seems to
reason like Engels. In the penultimate chapter of *Capital,* in that apocalyptic text that we will discuss at length, he said that private *capitalist*
property (*kapitalistische Privateigentum*) was the first negation of private *individual* property (*individuelle Privateigentum*) founded on personal labor (*auf eigen Arbeit*); that capitalist production begets its
own negation with the necessity of a natural process; that there will be
individual property (*individuelle Eigentum*) on the basis of cooperation
and common possession (*Gemeinbesitz*) of the land and of the means
of production.[74] The question arises: did Marx deduce the hypothesis
of the future regime from this dialectic? Kautsky[75] says not, and I have
myself voiced the same opinion.[76] But it is certain more than one reader
was mistaken about this, and Jaurès most of all, since he affirms with
conviction that the concept of the dialectic permits prediction of a distant future.

The example of Jaurès shows us that Bernstein is correct in pointing
out the danger of this method, which consists more in making brilliant
analogies than in instituting scientific analyses.[77] "We fall back into the
pitfalls of the auto-development of the Idea. . . . When it is a matter of
simple things, experience and logical judgment generally protect us. . . .
On the other hand, the more an object is complicated . . . the less these
formulas can protect us; for all criteria of evaluation become all the
more difficult." And does not Kautsky also allow himself to be duped by
"Hegelian words" when he writes[78] that Marx and Engels, far from
having mixed irreconcilable ideas as Bernstein believes, have "brought
about the *reconciliation* of utopian socialism and the workers' movement
on a *higher level*"? It seems to me that one could apply this notion of
"reconciliation" in many other cases, and I do not see what reason
Kautsky can use to oppose those people who speak of reconciling private property with the collective interest.

The danger is especially great for men with a revolutionary temperament: they choose their hypotheses about the future, not because of the

likelihood of their imminent realization, but because of their intense opposition to the present. Thus Marx was led,[79] according to Bernstein, to deceive himself so gravely in 1847 (and Engels in 1885)[80] on the imminence of a revolution:[81] "The natural heir of the bourgeoisie could only be its antagonist, the proletariat—that essential social product of the bourgeois economy." Kautsky protests[82] against this interpretation. According to him, the two masters of socialism were simply deceived by the forces at work. The two explanations are not incompatible, and it seems quite natural to me that in the writings of Marx and Engels, revolutionary illusions were fostered by the abuse of dialectical *negations*. Besides, how else can we explain that Marx in 1844 had been able to write that *through philosophy* Germany had attained a degree of maturity which placed it on a level with the more advanced countries on the course of modern development (either in political or economic relations)? Such an illusion would have been impossible for anyone who had not replaced the study of material things by oppositions among abstractions.

In any case, Kautsky, in defending the dialectic so energetically, very carefully avoids explaining what it is and how it can be used.

The dialectic has a fundamental fault: it introduces a paradoxical discontinuity into history, which prevents us from grasping the real evolutionary mechanism.[83] It considers only *perfect states* almost as would a physiologist who focuses on the egg and then the adult without trying to follow development from one to the other little by little. We are in the presence of a series of *catastrophic metamorphoses*—each one characterized by the qualities that society presents when it is far removed from periods of transition.

Such a conception completely neglects "the estimation of the ground to be covered," and this estimation is of capital importance in judging the value of a social hypothesis.[84] "From this estimation too comes the following contradiction: that bothersome minutiae go hand in hand with an almost incredible neglect of the most palpable realities." Under the influence of dialectical concerns, the study of real relations and practical solutions is naturally set aside.

The greatest mistake of the theorists of the dialectic is in placing social transformation in a mysterious realm and consequently culminating "in a veritable supernatural belief in the creative power of force."[85] Thus, for reasons very different from those that guided Blanqui in France, Marx and Engels were veritable Blanquists for a great part of their lives; this conclusion has greatly offended the Germans. As Sombart has recognized,[86] there is a dualism in Marxism; but Sombart has not analyzed the question as thoroughly as Bernstein, who tells us the real reason why "Marxism appears in many different perspectives over very short intervals."[87] It is the confidence in the value *of similarities and of oppositions of abstract words* which maintained the revolutionary and Blanquist illusion from which we must be definitively emancipated.

VI

The three great theories discussed above still give only a very incomplete notion of the social theories of Democratic Socialism, and the greatest part of the two books under examination revolves around the discussion of the *Catastrophic hypothesis.* In the penultimate chapter of the first volume of *Capital* Marx explains how he understands the future and the end of capitalist society. Capital is concentrated into fewer and fewer hands, progress accumulates and the interests of the people become increasingly unified. At the same time, the totality of misery (*Elend*), hardship (*Druck*), servitude (*Knechtschaft*),[88] degeneracy (*Entartung*) and exploitation (*Ausbeutung*) of the working class increases. But at the same time there is an increase also in the resistance (*Empörung*) of the working class, which grows unceasingly and which is trained, unified and organized (*geschult, vereinst und organisiert*) by the mechanism of the process of production (*durch den Mechanismus des Produktionsprozesses*). Monopoly becomes a chain (*Fessel*) on the modes of production; the capitalist armor will be broken and the expropriators will be expropriated.[89] Formerly the popular masses had been deprived of proprietary rights by a few usurpers. Now it is a question of expropriating the usurpers. This second transformation will be incomparably less difficult and drawn out than the first. We should add to this that Marx had noted that the revolution of 1848 followed a commercial crisis and was halted the minute that business revived. He attached an extraordinary importance to the proximity of these events. At the end of the year 1850 he wrote that all revolutionary attempts had become impossible for the moment, and that new revolutionary agitation had chances of success only after a renewed crisis, the revival of which was, moreover, assured. In 1873, at the end of the preface to the second edition of *Capital,* he recalled that periodic crises culminate in a general crisis of which he believed he saw the symptoms. He hoped that by the "universality and intensity of its action, it would infect the speculators of the new Prusso-German Holy Roman Empire with the dialectic." He was unable, I think, to express his prediction of the expected catastrophe more explicitly in a book printed in Germany.

The text of the penultimate chapter of *Capital* obviously gives us a description of an observed state and not the result of a theory. For it does not establish any connection among the five stages of the workers' oppression any more than between these stages and the resistance movement: the phenomena are described just as Marx saw them. It is a question of knowing where and when he made these observations.

In another part of *Capital* we find a similar description.[90] There it says that wealth concentrates at one pole, while at the other pole we find increasing misery (*Elend*), painful labor (*Arbeitsqual*), slavery (*Sklaverei*), ignorance (*Unwissenheit*), brutality (*Brutalisirung*) and moral degradation (*moralische Degradation*). These two passages ought to be compared; in both, it is a matter of isolated facts which are sometimes ascertained separately and sometimes together in the diverse strata of the clases being studied. They are concerned with simple empirical statements of phenomena which have no theoretical connection.

But there is a great difference[91] between the two texts. In the latter, Marx did not have the true proletariat in mind, but the classes who did not have an asured occupation, or even did not work at all—living on the fringes of organized labor and descending to the lowest rank in the scale of property or even coming very close to crime. On the other hand, in the first text, Marx speaks of the whole laboring class; the workers are more or less affected by one or another of the five forms of oppression, but they are all thus affected and all organize to resist the capitalists.

In the *Communist Manifesto* he presented a picture that is quite analogous to the one that we are examining here, and he said[92] that the workers fall into an ever-worsening situation—that wage earners are unable to live without assistance. This corresponds well to the situation of the workers in England depicted in 1845 by Engels in the *Condition of the Working Classes in England* and that he and Marx in 1847 regarded as the prototype of the worker in a capitalist regime. But in 1867, the year that *Capital* was published, when trade-unionism had already become strong, it was no longer true to assert that repression and subordination were increasing, and in his book Marx himself noted the renaissance of the English working classes (*physisch und moralische Wiedergeburt der Fabrikerarbeiter*). Therefore, our text makes complete sense only if we apply it to the events of around 1847.[93]

In this text, just as in the *Manifesto,* Marx shows himself very vague about details on workers' associations. He says that the functioning of capitalist workshops is sufficient to provoke their reunion in a *mechanical* way. The rapidity with which the great (and temporary) Trade Union was established misled him concerning the enormous difficulties presented by durable proletarian organizations; in 1847 no one had had any experience with these difficulties.

Moreover, there are verbal analogies between our apocalyptic text and the *Manifesto;* thus the relations of property are designated as being a fetter (*Fessel*) which will be broken because these relations are irreconcilable with the progress of the means of production. The old regime *must* be annihilated and it *is*. In the *Manifesto* Marx wrote: "*Sie mussten gesprengt werden; sie werden gesprengt*" and in *Capital:* "*Sie muss vernichtet werden; sie wird vernichtet.*"[94] In the former, society forges the arms which must kill it; in the latter, society produces the means of its own extermination. Again we can see that in our text, the French word "exploitation" is used to denote capitalist direction and the profit resulting from it in a pejorative sense as in the *Manifesto*.[95]

I have already indicated the exceptional use of negation. It would be strange for Marx in 1867, when Pecqueur was no longer being read, to appeal to his authority in order to say that maintaining the old piecework production would amount to "a decree of universal mediocrity" and yet not to give a reference to the book which contained this phrase.[96]

Thus, I think that this text is a fragment which, like many other old sections, was introduced into *Capital* and that Marx thought worth preserving because it presented the schema of the class struggle in a very lively way.[97]

Bernstein observes[98] that in order to interpret this famous text, it is necessary to take into account the footnote found at the end which refers to the *Manifesto:* "the return to the *Manifesto*," he says, "reveals to us the very real survival of a vestige of utopianism." I think that this reference is all the more natural as the text is very similar to that of 1847 and written in the same spirit as the *Manifesto*.[99] Marx wanted to complete his account calling for the means with which the extermination (*Vernichtung*) of the old regime and the expropriation of the capitalists will come about. Referring to the early writings of Marx and Engels, Bernstein said: "These writings always exude a Blanquist (i.e., Babouvist) odor. Proletarian *terrorism*, which could only have been a destructive force, given the conditions in Germany, is presented as a prodigious force which would precipitate economic development."[100] In 1847-50, Marx and Engels were concerned with reviving the French Revolution with all of its popular disturbances. The proletariat would not have been able to take power, but it would have continually burdened weak governments until the time when it would be strong enough to execute the communist plan. Kautsky cites[101] an extract of a declaration made by them on September 15, 1850, at the Communist League: "You have 15, 20, 50 years of social struggle to maintain, not only to change social conditions, but to transform yourselves and make yourselves worthy of power."

Thus it is playing with words to pretend, as Kautsky has,[102] that the theory of collapse does not exist in the Social Democracy. This total

Critical Essays in Marxism   165

collapse undoubtedly will not consist in an "evening session of Parliament"[103] as he jokingly calls it, but in a long *terrorist regime* imitating 1793. This was certainly the thought of Marx and Engels early on. It is the thought which is seen in the apocalyptic text, and Bernstein had the great courage to say so.

VII

The discussion on which Kautsky focuses does not throw any great light on the questions raised above. Since socialist ideas on transformation of property relations have never been clearly formulated and result from popular interpretations of various fragments, it is always easy for a subtle polemicist to contest everything that stands in his way. We could have hoped that Kautsky would profit from the opportunity open to him to give a truly scientific form to theories of social transformation. Not at all; he seems to have had only a single concern: to reserve an escape for himself and to allow the propagandists to take from Marxism as many formulas as can be used for various propaganda needs.

A) Kautsky[104] repeatedly recognizes that the material situation of the workers has improved. He thus rejects the literal interpretation of the thesis of "increasing misery,"[105] but he does not want to abandon Marx's words because these words can be of service. He asserts that Marx intended to speak of "relative social misery,"[106] that he meant to express the disproportion which exists between *desires* and *means*. Such an interpretation is insupportable. Kautsky nowhere produces any text of Marx which allows us to think that he used the word *Elend* in the sense of a *malaise* resulting from a psychological phenomenon.[107] The text that I have cited above and compared to the apocalyptic text has physical misery well in mind. Kautsky is obliged to resort to Lassalle and Rodbertus to find the notion that he arbitrarily attributes to Marx!

Furthermore, in this question we should be very careful not to confuse the various strata of the popular classes. Marx and Engels never intended to concern themselves with the *Lumpen-proletariat*, when they speak of the working class. Thus, it is quite useless to recall that, according to Sidney Webb, the misery of the English poor has probably not diminished. Also, everyone who is concerned with the working classes knows that at the bottom of the social scale there is a nearly irreducible stratum which benefits neither from material improvement nor the moral progress made by the working masses.

To prove that *malaise* increases, Kautsky says that marriage is decreasing,[108] but this phenomenon ought to be explained by the ardent

desire that men have for the comfortable life and by their very strong
belief that they have the power to improve their position by conserving
their independence despite the old customs.

It is not necessary to be a great scholar in economic science to discover[109] that the bosses want to have labor at the best possible bargain
and to adorn this truism with the pompous name of a "tendency" of the
capitalist era! But it is necessary to know how the workers can struggle
succesfully against this; in Germany they have struggled very badly,
because the Social Democracy has lulled them with grandiose words,
has long turned their heads with the class struggle, and has made them
dream of extravagant political rewards. It was debated at length[110] not
long ago whether or not the sacrosanct principle of the class struggle
allows the typographers to bargain collectively for a five-year contract!
The purists have maintained that such contracts weaken "class consciousness."

Kautsky called attention to the competition that child and female
labor gives to workers. He is happy that the laws have curtailed the
former,[111] but he does not want the latter to be curtailed. In the
Congress on the Protection of Workers held in Zurich[112] in 1897, the
Social Democracts passionately upheld the necessity of allowing women
into the factory. In France, when the Corporative Congress of Rennes[113]
voiced unfavorable pronouncements on female labor, Guesde[114] protested against this "Proudhonian" idea that women ought to be supported by men; he called this making women into the "proletariat of
men"! Kautsky recognizes the grave disadvantages of female labor[115]
but the Social Democracy, in wishing to keep women in the factory, is
pursuing a political and ethical end, the ruination of the family under
the specious pretext of preparing for a superior organization of sexual
relations of the future.[116]

B) At every turn, socialist literature before 1848 speaks of the
pauperism and the financial feudalism of England. Marx has not added
much to what this literature included, and it is by a strange mistake
that he is credited with the invention of theories which were commonplace in his time. In 1838 Pecqueur offered the opinion[117] that industrial
Europe had two possible futures: either it would reproduce the sad
spectacle of England; or industry might take a democractic form
through the formation of small share groups and by the introduction of
a representative government in the factories. In 1842, in the preface to
his *Théorie nouvelle,* he appears more pessimistic. He believes that
Europe is in full moral decline; that before it disappears, our civilization is destined to pass through the deceitful, Parliamentary and mercantile regime of England and that we will have "our industrial and
territorial aristocracy, our bands of proletarians hungry and degraded

by the ignominious stigma of legally fixed wages." The idea of an alternative could not be admitted easily by Marx who, in his more Hegelian moments, believed that "capitalism had its own law" and that a given name corresponds only to a perfectly developed form. The English model was, for him, the model to which all countries should conform in proportion to their industrial progress.[118]

The concentration of fortunes appeared to him, then, under a very simple form of "landlordism." Capitalist magnates, as he says, are the leaders of all the branches of industrial activity; concentration of revenue and the enlargement of enterprises were then regarded as synonymous. Today, it is entirely different, and it has become impossible to compare Marx's forecasts with reality, because there is no basis of comparison between two absolutely different regimes. It is clear that if the Lyon railroad belonged to a family of capitalist magnates it would be something entirely different from what it would be if it belonged to a company having widely dispersed shares.

The enlargement of industrial operations in Germany is under a form which seems somewhat abnormal because that country has recently entered into the period of large-scale industry and because from 1882 to 1895 (dates of the two censuses compared by our authors) there was a prodigious productive and commercial take-off.

Marx and his disciples were hardly concerned with the technical reasons that produced the formation of great enterprises. This is curious in Marx, who attached such great importance to conditions of technology. In his long dissertation, Kautsky does not speak of this crucial question at all. Pecqueur, in 1838, saw clearly that the steam engine is, as he said, an "agglomerator," and Professor Reuleaux,[119] in our day, regards the use of steam as one of the most compelling causes of enlargement. Industries which utilize heat are obliged to work at a rapid rate and with huge apparatuses in order to use fuel effectively. Almost everywhere advantage is found in using great mechanical speed and consequently in accelerating the daily productivity of various jobs. Here we have technical explanations that have great weight.

For a long time it has been asserted plainly that production on a large scale is always more economic, and that there results from it a marked advantage for the great industrialists or the great proprietors. This reasoning does not work in the case of land: Vandervelde, in his studies on landed property in Belgium, published in the *Annales de l'Institut des Sciences Sociales* of Brussels, has shown that concentration of property ownership is produced in that country for two reasons: (1) because the land yields little today, a rich bourgeois can acquire great domains in order to transform them into parks; (2) because speculators buy land on the edge of towns for their increased speculative value, not their revenue. Concentration in this case occurs mainly because the great lands cease to be a means of production!

Bernstein gives good reasons for the maintenance of small industry. Certain crafts lend themselves as well to middle-sized or small industry as to large industry, and often small factories finish pieces that are half-completed by large industries. Often (as in a bakery) it is in the interest of the public to be served by small shops. Finally, for a rather long time, objects of luxury have been fabricated in small numbers. It is when these objects are "democratized" that they are absorbed by large industry. Everywhere experience shows that the little *boutique* is holding its own.

Kautsky commits several gross errors of reasoning. (1) He does not see that our modern society is much too complex to be self-sufficient with a single system of production; that there is a relatively fixed segment of our needs which corresponds to small industry and that consequently, the latter could not grow as speedily as large industry; this is true above all in a country like Germany which has been thrown brusquely into the whirlwind of modern life. (2) Kautsky argues as if large-scale commerce had not had a long-standing influence on production. Marx clearly recognized that it is large-scale *commerce* which has stimulated new forms of the organization of labor. In particular, small production should not be confused with the old collective manufacture that LePlay rightly associated with large industry,[120] and which usually tends to be transformed into a mechanical factory. (3) Finally, if there are cases in which the small entrepreneur is a simple wage-earner doing piece-work, it is not possible to make this comparison in as general a way as Kautsky did.[121]

In the end, the problem is extremely complex. There are divergent causes at work here, and it is anti-scientific to claim to express (by a unique law) facts which depend on such varied forces of nature. This does not prevent Kautsky from affirming triumphantly:[122] "Never has a theory received such a striking confirmation as that which Marx's theory has found in the census figures." But where then did Marx demonstrate his laws of concentration? And would he have been able to predict contemporary technology, the new steel metallurgy, the new methods of soda manufacture, the new compound steam engines, the application of electricity, etc., etc.? There is no procedure for deducing a technique from a past technique, therefore no precision is possible. Let us recognize, to his credit, that Marx, who was more perspicacious than his disciples, understood the complexity of the technological structure of modern industry on more than one occasion. A project that should tempt Marxists is to formulate a theory of this structure in showing how the systems of production are superimposed.

However, Kautsky recognizes that Marx's predictions with regard to agriculture have not been realized. He consoles himself by thinking[123] that the peasantry is losing social importance every day.

Like many socialist writers, Kautsky is extraordinarily confused on the subject of agriculture; he sometimes confuses profit and rent; and if we follow his terminology, the Sicilian *latifundist* could be called a capitalist!

Here are several more very imprecise assertions. It is not correct to assert[124] that the capitalist mode of production tends to separate property from exploitation (that separation would be rather the results of feudal survivals) any more than it would be to regard[125] the progress of rural cooperation as a manifestation of capitalist concentration (this would be like confusing communal goods with capitalist property)[126] or to see in the cartels[127] a simple maneuver to exploit the public. Bernstein is much more correct when he admits that *under certain forms* cartels are able to act to limit crises.[128]

C) Modern society contains two new classes which benefit from what Marx called "surplus value": they are the stockholders and the officers of industrial corporations. Kautsky does not wish to call them *Besitzende* (propertied classes), but words mean nothing here. The expression in question seems to me to be sufficiently just because the men of these classes enjoy the fruits of capitalism without being owner-entrepreneurs. What shocks him above everything else is that Bernstein allows himself to write that the middle echelons are maintained in society—which "evidently contradicts the *Communist Manifesto*."[129]

Truly one must be strangely blinded by the partisan spirit not to admit with Bernstein that corporations have conspicuously dispersed the ownership of their securities. Neymarck's statistics on the parceling out of stocks leave no doubt in this regard.[130]

Kautsky, indeed, wants to acknowledge that the management class never ceases to grow, and that it is able[131] to compensate for the losses of the middle classes. These are men participating in surplus value, and in fact many among them[132] are strongly hostile to the proletariat. Thus there would be no hindrance to merging them with the *Besitzende*.

D) I will not dwell on the theory of crises, because Marx really wrote nothing important on the subject, and because the ideas he had on their frequency are very vague. Whatever Kautsky thinks[133] about the subject, he took his ideas on cycles from his predecessors. In *Capital*[134] Marx put forth the opinion that the decennial cycle tends to shorten. Experience does not seem to have confirmed this view, and the idea of periodicity is, today, very much under attack, while Marx considered it a "mechanical necessity." It would have been interesting to discuss in detail what Engels wrote[135] in the notes of the second volume of *Capital* on the subject of the new forms that crises can assume. Kautsky glosses over it very lightly because he is anxious to conserve the idea of *a universal crash resulting from universal overproduction*[136] all the while declaring that Bernstein is wrong in crediting the Social Democrats with the belief in this terrible and final crisis.[137] According to Kautsky, if the class struggle has not yet destroyed capitalism[138] at the present time, it will succumb to this irremediable overproduction through "decomposition"(?): this "decomposition" can only be the great crisis, the "universal crash." All the rest is vague, because the author is careful not to disturb the progagandists who do not need to use very scientific arguments. Such are the handicaps of the situation of the seer of a political party.

E) Like all Social Democrats, Kautsky is very much persuaded that the *conquest of power* would allow the realization of all desired social changes. We know that this is one of the so-called discoveries of Marx; such a banal idea is as old as the world. But what many people do not know is that the celebrated formula of the International which regards economic reform as an *end* and the political struggle as the *means* is already an old formula.[139] Several times, Kautsky asserts that the conquest of power is the great question; but he recognizes that the present moment is not favorable, that we live in a period of[140] "political reaction and industrial prosperity" during which "the laboring classes think that they can obtain more by the syndicalist and cooperative movement than by political activity." According to him, the success of Bernstein's book depends on this temporary situation, and this book is incapable of disturbing the foundation of a doctrine[141] "based on the study of *all the facts* of the history of our society."

This is an interesting contention and it merits further elucidation. We should ask what causes (in relation to Marxist principles) this political stagnation to occur. The reason seems to me very simple; while the workers are found in conditions such that they can improve their lot by their reasoned activity, they cease having the superstitious respect for the mysterious power of political force which is easy to inculcate in them during periods in which they are crushed by economic calamity. The *religion of political magic* always dissipates somewhat when man feels free to rise to a superior position. All this is very clear.

VIII

Bernstein has the great merit of fully illuminating the fact that Marx conducted his scientific research with a view to justifying preconceived socialist precepts, and that his preconceptions prevented him from writing a completely satisfactory work.[142] "When Marx touches on points where the final end is put seriously in question, he becomes vague and uncertain. . . . In such a case, we see that this great scientific mind was the *prisoner of a doctrine*."

I think that we could go further and wonder to what degree Marx was seriously "communist" and to what degree he was in accord with Engels. I find in these two doubts the explanation of many of the obscurities which baffle the reader. He entered the League of Communists in 1847 and wrote their *Manifesto,* and left it in 1850; then Wittich's friends accused him of being a bourgeois. His personal ideas were very close to those of Fernand Pecqueur: the social appropriation of the means of production,[143] the call to all to cooperate in production by means of the instruments placed at their disposal,[144] the individual possession of the products of labor; all this is found in the "Projet d'association nationale et universelle"[145] drafted by Pecqueur in 1842. In 1875 in his *Critique of the Gotha Programme,* Marx did not dare to deny communism completely, but he postponed it to such a distant and indeterminate date that he suppressed it in fact. This did not prevent Engels, in 1878 in the *Anti-Dühring,* from speaking of communism as the regime to which capitalism would inevitably lead: for Engels, communism was rather simple and very crude, a gigantic "factory" administered by businessmen having full powers, like the heads of English services.[146]

These observations help us to understand why the *Manifesto* of 1847 is so often bizarre and obscure. It has been asked if it reflected Marx's ideas well. Above all, this document seemed to have had the purpose of summing up the notions which had currency in socialist circles. Sometimes the author gets out of trouble with a play on words.[147] Everyone is struck by Marx's embarrassment in speaking of the family and country and it is obvious that he could not express his whole thought. This document remained unknown for a long time, and when it was unearthed, an originality was attributed to it that it did not have at the time of its publication. In 1872 Marx and Engels, writing a preface for the new edition, declared that certain parts had become outdated but that they did not believe that they had the right to touch an historic document. They announced that, perhaps later, they would do an introduction which would restore things in perspective; Marx lived another eleven years but he did not write this introduction.

IX

In Marxism there is a great foundation of subjectivism; the manner of understanding social relations and of directing practical activity depends, in large part, on the character of the writer. The dispute between

Bernstein and Kautsky (and above all the way in which their polemic is conducted) should largely be ascribed to subjective causes. It has rightly been pointed out that they do not seem to understand each other. Kautsky's counter-critique is very often aimed blindly. Indeed, I think that they do not understand each other, and it is important to deduce the reasons for this.

Bernstein lives in England amidst men involved in the great capitalist movement. He is a Jew who has a very acute understanding of business and who thinks—just like Marx—that socialism would have no meaning if it did not continue and did not perfect the work of capitalism in directing more scientifically the ever-accelerating productive forces. Thus it should not be astonishing to see him thinking like a veritable Englishman: he approves[148] of the German intervention in China because it will permit the defense of German commerce against Russia. He finds it puerile[149] to condemn the exploitation of tropical countries by German colonists, while not condemning the consumption of tropical products by the Germans. Like Demolins, he says to the sentimentalists: "Superior civilization has superior rights. This is not conquest but exploitation of the soil which creates the historico-juridical title to its utilization." He asks his friends to reflect[150] on the need for a solid army, capable of taking the offensive in the modern way. It seems to him[151] absurd to forbid labor to children over fourteen when the work does not harm their health.

On the other hand, Kautsky is a South German, a "small-town boy" full of good intentions and very often dominated by the remembrance of pastoral romances. He forcefully inveighs[152] against the waste of modern societies, which constantly change stripes. Undoubtedly he misses the good old days when one kept one's wedding costume for life. He deplores[153] the extension of the great cities and the costly works of municipal government that they demand as well as the "loss of pastureland" which results from this separation of town and country. He denounces[154] the revolutionary mania of our epoch "which knows nothing stable." A conservative would not speak otherwise. Kautsky wants a highly productive industry without the psychological conditions which assure its outlets and without the demographic and technological conditions which permit it to exist and progress. He believes perhaps, like certain socialists, that capitalism will have soon finished its work and that the world will be able to repose in a stable regime of maximum happiness! In any case he fears this fever of expansion. He thinks that he recognizes[155] that capitalists use a very large part of the net profit to increase their machinery and he does not perceive that if this is truly the case on a very great scale, it proves that capitalists are still able to direct production. According to Marx's doctrine, they will be the masters as long as they justify their *ability*. At this point, we would not know how to replace them because they have so shown themselves to be the hardy pioneers of industrial progress. The question of administration greatly concerns Bernstein, who is in England and who views the world of business at close hand.[156] He fears the difficulties that overall direction of modern production presents. Kautsky does not seem to find this very difficult; we need only let routine carry on. Undoubtedly the machine will be greased, the boilers stoked as in the past, but all this is not to direct industry.[157]

As for the procedure that will be used to create the new order of things, it will supposedly be of such simplicity that anyone who comes along will be able to decipher it.[158] The state will take possession of the great monopolies; it will "socialize the trusts";[159] it will suppress unemployment;[160] it will make life impossible for the capitalists "who will have to bear the risks of their industry without being the masters of it," and then the capitalists will try to have their factories bought out quickly. Political despotism is acknowledged cynically: "in other words, capitalist production and power in the hands of the proletariat are two incompatible things." Thus, Bernstein is right when he expresses the fear[161] that socialization would "result in a vast destruction of the forces of production, *senseless experiments*, and unreasonable violence." It is well to remember Proudhon's phrase cited by Bernstein:[162] "Then you will know that it is a revolution that is instigated by lawyers, accomplished by artists and led by novelists and poets."

If events occur as Kautsky predicts, the difficulties will be enormous. Indeed, he writes that capitalism will end in a general and immediate overproduction, and that the countryside will continue to be depopulated to the benefit of the cities. Then we should not continue what capitalism does. There should be a complete change of production and a return of the urban workers to the land. I suppose that Kautsky has never reflected on the frightful difficulty that is presented by the exodus to the countryside. In any case, it seems obvious to me that he does not conceive of socialism in the same way as Marx—as a continuation of the work of capitalism, as a means of developing the productive forces created by capitalism and which had become too powerful to be directed by individuals. In his works there is something (and even something rather important) which comes close to Kropotkin, the Russian anarchist, whose ideal is the peasant life.

The idea of the "good old days" seduces Kautsky's Germanic imagination. In his eyes, capitalism is a monster which uproots the peasant-proprietor-artisan in the patriarchal life led in the bosom of an economically self-sufficient family, free from the necessity of resorting to commerce. In Kautsky there is a great deal of what has been called "collectivist troubadourism."[163]

Kautsky and Bernstein do not understand each other when they use the same words: when the latter speaks of democracy, economic responsibility, public liberty and personal guarantees, his adversary proclaims himself in agreement with him.[164] But the practical meaning of the concepts escapes him, because he does not understand the mechanism of the institutions of a free people. Thus he ends up by contesting a very correct observation of Bernstein.[165] The latter says: "the more ancient democratic institutions are, the more also the rights of minorities are recognized and respected." Kautsky asks[166] where this is verified! Time and adaptation to institutions are nothing for him who truly has the *magic cult of force*—and the rights of minorities could not be recognized by a fanatical partisan of revolutionary dictatorship.[167]

The specifically German characteristics are not revealed solely by the cult of force, but again by the exaggerated idea that Kautsky has of the effect of events which occur in his country. Bebel believes that it is Germany which will be the initiator of the social revolution,[168] but doesn't Kautsky really go beyond the pale when he writes[169] that the events of 1870 constituted "a most fortuitous European revolution"?

Writing that statement in a book intended to be read by Frenchmen is to conceive internationalism in a peculiar way. It is true that a doctor of the German Social Democracy may permit himself many liberties!

CONCLUSION

One's impression after reading each of these two books is very different. With Bernstein, one likes to think that Marxism constitutes a philosophic doctrine still full of the future, that it suffices to free it from badly made commentaries and to develop it, while taking recent occurrences into account. With admirable good faith and great ability, the author pursues the task of rejuvenating Marxism: from superannuated formulas or false impressions, he calls it back to the very spirit of Marx; we are talking about *a return to the spirit of Marxism*. With Kautsky, it is the complete opposite. Marxism appears as a very old thing, a compilation of disparate theses that the disciples keep from exposing too much. For them it is above all a matter of defending words, appearances and petrified formulas. Nowhere do we find a scientific philosophy concerned with refining the sense of its affirmations and with giving a sure means of putting it into practice. Kautsky, far from wishing to dissipate equivocations, attempts to profit from the confusion the social questions contain in order to embarass his adversary; he makes an *anti-critique*.

What is value? What is the materialist conception of history? What is the dialectic? What is the theory of classes?[170] What is the role of the proletariat, and what is that of the bourgeoisie? What is the theory of crises? What is the role of the state? On all of these fundamental questions, Kautsky has been able only to argue against Bernstein's observations, but he has been incapable of teaching us anything.

Undoubtedly Bernstein has not given us a new philosophy, but his goal was not that ambitious. He only wanted to urge us into thinking for ourselves, all the while keeping the core of Marxism.

Bernstein is preoccupied above all with practical results. To him it seems wrong—and contrary to the spirit of Marxism—to have a dogma which is no longer related to the rules of practical activity recognized by all reasonable men.[171] This is why he has written his book, and this is why he had no need of stating a series of theorems. It is sufficient for him to emancipate the mind and to smash formulas that are contrary to practice.

If the Social Democracy were comprised of men sufficiently *emancipated from superstition,* undoubtedly Bernstein would have the great majority grouped around him. His book would be received as a deliverance; but it does not seem certain to me that the spirit of the German masses has become very free yet. The conserver of old symbols, the defender of the old abstractions, the *master of the old aphorisms* is able to capture them easily and there is no hiding the fact that *the triumph of Kautsky would signify the definitive ruination of Marxism, henceforth stripped of all scientific interest.*

CHAPTER 5

from
The Illusions
of Progress

FIRST IDEOLOGIES OF PROGRESS[1]

I   The dispute between the ancients and the moderns. Morals at the end of the seventeenth century. The philosophy of Fontenelle. The political origin of the ideas on nature. Pascal versus superficial rationalism. Cartesianism and society people.

II   The idea of a pedagogy of humanity. The popularizers. Condorcet conceives of popular education on an aristocratic model; his illusions with regard to the results of education.

I

Historians have traced back the question of the doctrine of progress to the dispute between the ancient and modern writers, which caused so much furor at the end of the seventeenth century. It might seem very odd to us today that such a purely literary conflict could produce such consequences, for nowadays we would hardly be willing to admit that artistic progress can exist at all.

Nothing appears stranger to us today than the manifestations of bad taste on the part of men like Perrault, who systematically ranked his contemporaries above the great men of antiquity or the Renaissance—who preferred Lebrun to Raphael, for example. . . .

The argument between the ancient and modern writers at the end of the seventeenth century had consequences that infinitely surpassed the realm of art. French society, proud of its new conditions of existence and persuaded that it had reached or even surpassed the most famous periods celebrated by historians, thought it no longer had to seek models in other countries. It was French society that would henceforth serve as the model to all civilized men; it was French taste alone that would decide the value of intellectual works. In all things, French society meant to revel in the fruits of its own civilization without being criticized by anyone.

At the end of the seventeenth century, the religious questions that had previously impassioned the country left everyone indifferent, to the point where Bossuet and Fénelon preserved from publication important controversial works. Massillon's sermons were concerned only with morality.[2] It has often been thought that the persecutions against the Jansenists and the useless quarrels of quietism had an influence on this decline of religious ideas.[3] I do not believe this is a satisfactory explanation.

In the last fifteen years of the seventeenth century, life was very merry. Formerly Jansenism had furnished a means of raising problems of Christian destiny, of combatting the solutions brought forth by the casuists, who preached easy religion, and of justifying an austere discipline.[4] Now, people wanted largely to profit from the well-being permitted by the new era, and, henceforth, Jansenism was found to be quite tiresome. The number of its apologists in good society diminished, and Port-Royal was abandoned to the furor of its enemies. Thus I do not believe that we should attribute the lowering of the moral level to the persecutions of the Jansenists; I believe rather that we may attribute these persecutions to the lowering of the moral level. There remained, however, several families who preserved the old ways and affected an outdated morality. They were all the more haughty as they were more isolated. In these families, Jansenism remained as an often fanatic protest.

At that time everyone was shocked by the disintegration of feminine morality and also by the indulgence with which good society treated the emancipated women. "Mademoiselle de la Force [who attracted attention as the mistress of the actor, Baron] was on familiar terms with the Princesses of Conti as well as with the Vendômes."[5] In a letter dated November 19, 1696, Dubos said to Bayle that women no longer wanted to have children as their lackeys but rather "the tallest and best-looking young men," and that they no longer had maids but valets.[6]

Boileau had the courage to attack these women, but his satire caused an enormous scandal. Arnauld, who was in Belgium living with his old ideas, applauded the poet's severity, but his friends warned him that his commendation produced a very bad impression.[7] I suppose that Bossuet passed judgment against Boileau because he sensed the danger of overtly defying the opinion of good society. We know that Bossuet was more than once accused of leniency toward the morals of the great. According to Brunetière, this lenient attitude was due to the fact that Bossuet had only "remained on the fringe of society" and had not lived in it, as Pascal had. "Both in society and in the life of the court, Bossuet always saw only what others let him see or made him see."[8]

It is very remarkable that Bayle inherited from Christianity a pessimistic view of man, so that Brunetière was able to say he had maintained religious morality in the process of de-Christianizing it. According to Bayle, man ought to resist the instincts, an idea that later seemed scandalous. With Fénelon, the idea of the goodness of human nature entered into serious literature.[9] It corresponded so well to the most profound tendencies of the time that an optimistic conception of man soon dominated. We might say that fear of sin, respect for chastity, and pessimism all disappeared at about the same time at the end of the seventeenth century. Thus Christianity vanished from the scene.[10]

This society was not able to do without a philosophy, because it had inherited from preceding generations the habit of reasoning and, in particular, the habit of applying juridical reasoning to all questions. Thus it was that discussions on grace, predestination and the sacraments could occupy such a dominant place in French history for half a century. Such a society could not abandon itself to happiness without justifying its conduct; it had to prove that it had the right not to follow the old maxims. For if the society was not able to give this proof, was it not liable to be compared to the son who is in such a hurry to enjoy the paternal inheritance that he devours all resources for the future? Hence, they were very happy to find able apologists who could solemnly establish that it was all right to amuse oneself without fear of the consequences:[11] this was the origin of the doctrine of progress. Fontenelle had the honor of revealing the possibility of such a philosophy to his contemporaries.

Nobody would have dreamed of disputing the fact that the conditions of life under Louis XIV had become softer for the upper classes than they had been under the preceding monarch. Henceforth people had the right to ask themselves the following questions: Could it not be assumed that forces that had produced this improvement of life resulted from the new constitution of societies by a sequence of events as natural as those found in the physical world? If these forces continued to operate, would they not have an accelerated momentum in the social world, just as a weight is accelerated by gravity in the material world? If this is so, why worry about the fate of new generations, which are destined to have a fate that is automatically superior to ours? Brunetière has correctly observed that the idea of the stability of the laws of nature is an element in the theory of progress.[12] We should determine, however, whether this idea came from physics or ought to be explained solely in historical terms. The second hypothesis seems closer to the truth.

The contemporaries of Fontenelle (who popularized the idea of the stability of the laws of nature) were above all impressed by seeing to what extent the royal majesty was able to rise above mere chance in a seemingly definitive way. They were inclined to relate all social movements to the impetus society received from royal authority. They, then, must have regarded royal institutions as a constant force adding some new amelioration each day to improvements already acquired. The conception of an acceleration of improvements thus must have seemed to follow in a clear-cut and necessary way. The law of the acceleration of weights might conceivably have occurred to Galileo as a consequence of political analogies; in his time, the monarchical power had already become absolutist enough for people to see a type of constant force.[13]

According to Brunetière, the idea of progress heavily depended on two important Cartesian theses related to knowledge: knowledge can never be separated from its application, and it is always increasing.[14] It seems, indeed, that we ought immediately to infer limitless progress from such premises as these, but I think it is wrong to attribute to them the scientific scope that a modern writer could give them. In the seventeenth century, they originated from political ideology rather than true science, so that, in measuring their historical importance, we should start by observing the political phenomena.

From the time of Descartes, it was easily seen that the new model of governments, with their concentrated power and their regular administration, were in a position to execute their plans in a most precise way and that they could thus realize a union of theory and practice. Furthermore, the royal power seemed infinite. So many extraordinary changes since the Renaissance had taken place because of the will of the sovereign power, especially in religious matters, that nothing seemed beyond the power of the king. Science could never be unavailable to rulers who had affirmed the completeness of their divine right. Science had to grow with the power of those who needed it in order to reign. After the revocation of the Edict of Nantes in 1685, these considerations were much stronger than in Descartes's time. The quarrel between ancients and moderns exploded two years after this great event, which event so clearly demonstrated the omnipotence of the crown.

Neither do I agree entirely with Brunetière about the influence of popularization in this matter. According to him, men at the end of the seventeenth century marveled at knowing so many things. Brunetière thought that, instead of occupying themselves with the care of their consciences as their fathers had done, they preferred science to religion[15] and abandoned Bossuet's point of view for Fontenelle's. In contrast, I consider scientific vulgarization to have had a great, although not direct, influence in the formation of the new philosophy; the taste for popularization helped above all to establish a tight link between the thinking in the salons and Cartesianism. The result was that the literary argument over the ancients and the moderns took on a scope one would not have expected at the beginning—it became a landmark in the history of philosophy. Fontenelle, who was at the same time a literary partisan on the side of the moderns, a very skillful popularizer, and a Cartesian fanatic, could thus strongly influence the development of ideas, a circumstance in peculiar contradiction to his own mediocrity.

In order to understand this question thoroughly we should cast a rapid glance at Cartesianism, looking for the reasons that made it a philosophy of the salons. Here we have a very remarkable example of the adoption of an ideology by a class that has found in it certain formulas to express its class propensities. There are few phenomena more important than such adoptions for the true philosopher who studies such doctrines from the point of view of historical materialism. The creator of a system operates like an artist who interprets everything around him with extreme freedom. If this system has a sufficient number of links with current ideas, it can endure and become the favorite doctrine of a later generation, which will find in it something entirely different from that which pleased its contemporaries. It is on this adoption that the definitive judgment of history rests. Often this judgment upsets the order of values the first followers had attributed to the various parts of the doctrine; it can bring to the fore what they had regarded as secondary.

Descartes's reign began rather late, and Brunetière even says that "the Cartesian influence on the seventeenth century is one of the inventions, one of the errors with which Victor Cousin infested the history of French literature."[16] For a long time, the great theologians did not even seem to have understood what role the Cartesian philosophy would play. They saw that the unbelieving men of the world (who were called *freethinkers*) were not receptive to the arguments used by the scholastics to prove the existence of God and the immortality of the soul. They thought that the Cartesian explanations would have more success. Bossuet expressed this point of view in his letter of May 21, 1687, to a disciple of Malebranche and in one of May 18, 1689, to Huet.[17] Once the fundamental principles were accepted, the theologians thought that the general body of religion did not present any great difficulties.

It is likely that Pascal wrote the *Pensées* against the Cartesians.[18]

He was not a professional theologian and, therefore, had no confidence in scholastic proofs, but he did not appreciate Descartes's theories any more than he did those of the Sorbonne. Rather, Pascal took the vantage point of religious experience, which requires a God who is always present, and he understood that Cartesianism only believed in an absent God. The reasons Bossuet considered sufficient to defeat atheism appeared very weak to Pascal. Bossuet judged everyone like himself, and he failed to see the immense difference between the priest living in the midst of the sacraments, on the one hand, and the laity, on the other.

The pious priest who realizes a religious experience every day is inclined to be convinced by explanations that seem feeble to more worldly men living outside of this experience. Pascal wrote for men who had retained a goodly portion of sixteenth century ways. These new pagans —violent, imperious, and capricious—were not, however, completely shut off from any possibility of returning to Christianity, because they regarded the miracle as a distinct possibility; now, a miracle is a material experience of the divine presence in the world. The miracle strongly attracted Pascal's imagination, but there was no place for it in the Cartesian philosophy, which purported to submit everything to universal mathematics.

Descartes seemed to encourage those who considered experience of miracles impossible. Hence the oft-quoted sentence of Pascal, "I cannot forgive Descartes; he would have liked to have been able to leave God out of his entire philosophy,[19] but he could not resist having Him snap His fingers in order to set the world in motion. After that, he had nothing more to do with God" (fragment 77 in the Brunschwig edition).

Sainte-Beuve understood very well that it was by drawing man away from God that eighteenth-century philosophy fought against Pascal. According to Sainte-Beuve, it was Buffon who, in creating a science of nature, refuted Pascal most thoroughly.[20] We know that Diderot studied natural history passionately in the hope of rendering God completely useless.[21] Descartes, therefore, is to be thanked for having prepared the way for the Encyclopedists by reducing God to a mere trifle, while Pascal is discredited. Condorcet excelled in the art of making a great genius look ridiculous, all the while showering him with praise. Sainte-Beuve said, "Pascal was portrayed as a victim of a sordid superstition; Pascal's vital and tender piety was overshadowed by the emphasis on bizarreness. The repeated discussions of the *amulette* date from Condorcet's comments."[22]

It does not seem to me that present-day admirers of Pascal are always correct in their way of interpreting him. For instance, Brunetière asserts that Pascal tried to reduce the influence of reason.[23] But we must

not confuse the scientific use of reason with what is usually called
rationalism. Pascal attacked that fradulent practice mercilessly, not only
because he was a Christian, but also because his mind could not admit
pseudo-mathematical reasoning to be used for answering moral questions: "I have spent a long time studying the abstract sciences, and the
lack of true communication to be gained from them made me averse to
them. When I began to study man, I saw that the abstract sciences are
not suited to him and that I was more estranged from my human condition than others who remained ignorant of these sciences" (fragment 144). We must understand that, in Pascal's eyes, the mathematical
sciences form a very limited area in the whole field of knowledge and
that one exposes oneself to an infinity of errors in trying to imitate
mathematical reasoning in moral studies.

Pascal's highly rigorous mind was offended by the fantastic and often
fradulent procedures used by the Cartesians to enable them to give the
impression of explaining the whole world. He speaks of the *Principes
de la philosophie* with extreme contempt, likening them to the theses
of Pico de la Mirandola, *de omni re scibili* [concerning every known
thing] (fragment 72); he writes the scornful words, "Descartes is useless
and dubious" (fragment 78). Furthermore: "We must say generally, 'it
comes about by form and motion,' for that is true. But to say which
form and which motion and to assemble the parts of the machine, that
is ridiculous. For it is useless, uncertain, and painful. And if it were
true, we do not think that all of philosophy is worth one hour of
trouble" (fragment 79).

Pascal protests in the name of true science against the pseudo-physics
suited only to satisfy the curiosity of those who frequented the fashionable salons. Later, Newton makes the same point; he asks the geometricians not to make hypotheses to explain gravity. We know that this
reform raised many objections; even today, some "enlightened" soul
never fails to deplore our ignorance of the "causative laws" of celestial
mechanics. Pascal did not yet have enough knowledge to say to his contemporaries: The proof that all your pseudo-philosophy is in vain and
not worth an hour of trouble is that I have solved all astronomical problems without it.[24] He could not oppose the illusions he believed to be
all around him except by protesting as a man of genius. As he wrote
only for himself, he did not restrain himself from expressing all the bad
humor he felt on seeing the enthusiasm inspired by the elaborate and
deceptive Cartesian mechanisms.

It is difficult to know what conclusions Pascal would have arrived
at if he had been able to complete his work. His meaning was often
unclear, and this has allowed commentators to attribute certain opinions
to him which were very likely not his. I find no great mystery in the

famous passage from fragment 233, which is so often regarded as a repudiation of reason: Pascal said to the freethinkers who claimed that
they did not know how to arrive at faith, "Follow the way of believers,
who begin by doing everything as if they believed—taking holy water,
having masses said, etc. Naturally this will make you believe and will
also stupefy you [*vous abêtira*]." Pascal contrasts the practices of piety
to those of literature. It is very probable that, in order to strengthen
this contrast here, he intentionally uses one of the pejorative expressions
[*abêtir*] that has always been used by freethinkers to discredit piety.
The freethinker answers him: "But that is exactly what I fear." "And
why?" says Pascal. "What have you to lose? But to show you that this
method leads to faith, it does so by weakening the passions, which are
your greatest obstacle." Thus it is obviously a question, not of making
the freethinker stupid, but of leading him to think dispassionately. Indeed, earlier in his book, Pascal assumed that the freethinker would
decide in favor of religion if he could freely appreciate the advantages
of the choice proposed to him, but that passions kept him a prisoner of
his own bad habits. At the end of the fragment, he talks of the humble-
ness of Christian life, and here I see a synonym for stupefied thinking
[*abêtissement*]: "You will not partake of foul pleasures, delights, or
glory." The question would be to know in what measure this devout
practice can produce the results Pascal expected. Perhaps it would be
truly salutary for men used to living in a society in which one boasted
of unbelief. Above all, Pascal was concerned with changing men's associations. In any case, his advice to the freethinker did not imply any
contempt for reason.

In the 218th fragment, I cannot see the slightest indication of the
indifference with which Pascal supposedly considered the work of his
contemporaries to revive the theory of planetary movement. "It is well,"
he said, "that we do not go thoroughly into the judgments of Copernicus, but this . . . ! It is important for all of life to know whether the
soul is mortal or immortal." Pascal thought that society people should
better spend their time in reflecting on our destiny beyond death than
in expatiating on astronomical problems that exceed their competence.

If we take an overall view, we can see clearly that Pascal was offended by the superficial character of Cartesian ideas. They were infinitely better suited to conversation than to true scientific study.

Why, however, was there such a need for "scientic" conversation?
Because as I have said above, men of the seventeenth century were
used to analyzing causes. Cartesian science was not so confused with
mathematical technique that men of society, having received a good
liberal education, could not converse with professionals. Descartes was
adept at improvising explanations, whether of known natural facts or

of new experiments people submitted to him. A good intellect familiar with Cartesian reasoning could find an answer to anything: this characterized a good philosophy for the habitués of the salons.

There is, it seems to me, a close resemblance between Cartesian physics and the sophistry of the casuists. In both cases, elaborate mechanisms placed between man and reality prevent the mind from exercising its proper functions; ingenious, plausible chimeras are invented. The frivolity of the rationalists of high society was nourished at the ruinous expense of true reason.

All Descartes did in formulating his famous role of methodical doubt was introduce aristocratic modes of thought to philosophy. Brunetière very correctly notes that writers of noble origins have very little respect for traditions.[25] It seems that this similarity of Cartesianism and the skepticism so dear to the hearts of men of quality was one of the major reasons for the success of the new philosophy.

People unacquainted with the methods of experimental science are fully satisfied only if someone succeeds in connecting the explanations (in an inoffensive manner) to other principles their common sense accepts with ease. They do not see that such a process involves a great deal of deceit. Taine cites this phrase of Malebranche as characteristic of the Cartesian spirit: "In order to attain truth, it is sufficient to pay attention to the clear ideas that each man finds in himself."[26]

Thus intelligent men did not fail to embrace Cartesianism when it was presented to them. Indeed this philosophy justifies the pretension men of society have always had to speak of things they have not studied with an imperturbable assurance, all because of their "natural enlightenment."

About thirty years after the publication of the *Pensées*, Bossuet discovered the danger for religion of this wordy rationalism (Cartesianism): "Under the pretext that we must admit only what we understand clearly (which is very true with certain limitations) everyone takes the liberty to say: 'I understand this, I don't understand that.' . . . Without regard to tradition, any thought is boldly put forth . . . so long as Father Malebranche will only listen to flatterers or men who, for lack of having perceived the essence of theology, worship only its beautiful expressions. I see no cure for this sickness."[27]

This letter is extremely important, for it shows us a bishop upset by the audacity of men who treated theology as a frivolous subject. These men were more concerned with beauty of language than reason, and they failed to penetrate questions, which they preferred to judge by common sense. In this letter we have a protest against popularization. Everything connected with Cartesianism presents the same quality, which was recognized by Pascal: it is literature that leads to nothing useful and nothing certain. The whole value of this philosophy lies in its elegance of exposition.

By the terms that Bossuet uses, furthermore, we see that this concerns a totally new situation. The author sees that a great battle against the Church is being prepared under the name of Cartesian philosophy. At this time, in fact, Fontenelle had just published his famous work on the plurality of worlds; this is the beginning of the true reign of Descartes.

In examining them closely, we easily recognize that the fundamental ideas of Cartesian philosophy correspond perfectly with the state of mind of that time. Cartesianism was resolutely optimistic,[28] a fact which greatly pleased a society desirous of amusing itself freely and irritated by the harshness of Jansenism. Furthermore, there is no Cartesian morality, for Descartes reduced ethics to a rule of propriety prescribing respect for the established usages; since morals had become quite lenient, this was very convenient. Descartes never seemed to have been preoccupied with the meaning of life.[29] As a former student of the Jesuits, he must not have reflected very much on sin, and his disciples were able, like Renan, to suppress it.[30] Sainte-Beuve said that Descartes relegated faith, "like the gods of Epicurus, into some sort of intermediate realm of thought."[31] This suited those who hoped to be freed from the yoke of Christianity.

II

Henceforth, French philosophy was to remain marked by highly typical rationalist characteristics, which would make it very amenable to Parisian intellectual society. The Cartesian physics could be abandoned and even pronounced ridiculous in the following century, but Cartesianism would always remain the prototype of French philosophy, because it was perfectly adapted to the inclinations of an alert aristocracy proud of its ability to reason and anxious to find ways to justify its frivolity.[32]

The doctrine of progress would always be an essential element in the great movement that would continue up to our modern democracy, because this doctrine permits the enjoyment of the good things today in good conscience without worrying about tomorrow's difficulties. It pleased the old, idle aristocratic society; it will always be pleasing to the politicians elevated to power by democracy, who, menaced by possible downfall, wish to make their friends profit from all the advantages to be reaped from the state.

Today, as in the days of Fontenelle, the dominant society demands a "complete science of the world" that will allow it to expound opinions on all things without having to go through any special instruction in them. What is called science in this society is really a way of inventing nature in the tradition of Descartes; it has no relation to the probing in depth of the problems posed by genuine science, which is founded on prosaic reality.[33] The cosmological hypotheses of Spencer or Haeckel amuse the *literati* today just as mythological stories entertained former aristocracies, and the consequences of the enthusiasm inspired by modern stories are considerable. Their readers, after having resolved all cosmological problems, like to consider themselves capable of resolving all daily difficulties. From this state of mind comes the stupid confidence in the resolution of "enlightened men," which remains one of the ideological bases of that excessive attachment to the modern state.

Today the idea that everything can be submitted to a perfectly clear analysis is about as strong as it was in Descartes's time. If someone considers making a protest against the illusion of rationalism, he is immediately accused of being an enemy of democracy. I have often heard people who pride themselves on working for progress deplore the teachings of Bergson and point to them as the greatest danger confronting modern thought.[34]

For our democrats, as well as for the sophisticated Cartesian intellects, progress consists neither in the accumulation of technical methods nor even of scientific knowledge. Progress is the adornment of the mind that, free of prejudice, sure of itself, and trusting in the future, has created a philosophy assuring the happiness of all who possess the means of living well. Human history is a sort of *teaching* that shows how to pass from the savage state to aristocratic life. In 1750 Turgot said: "Considered since its origin, mankind appears to the eyes of the philosopher as an immense entity that, like each individual, has *its childhood and its progressive growth*."[35] In resuming the unfinished work of Turgot, Condorcet entered still more into this train of thought; he tries to describe to us the history of the education of humanity.

From this point of view, the great question that comes into focus is how to teach men to reason well. From this arises the extraordinary importance attached to logic; Condorcet presents Locke as one of the great benefactors of the human mind: "Finally, Locke seized on the course that would guide" philosophy. His "method soon became that of all philosophers, and in applying it to morals, politics, and economics, they succeeded in making almost as sure a development in these sciences as we find in the natural sciences."[36] Among Condorcet's projects for a mankind regenerated by revolution was his dream of perfecting our "vague and obscure" language. He thought that if men had received an incomplete education, they needed a precise language all the more;[37] hence he intended to reform popular language on the model of the impoverished language then used by high society. He also hoped that a universal scientific language could be created which would succeed in rendering "knowledge of the truth easy and error almost impossible."[38]

These preoccupations were very natural in men whose aim was to provide society people with a digest of knowledge and to transform everything into agreeable conversational subjects. To Condorcet, this vulgarization appeared to be one of the most honored products of the eighteenth century. The length of the passage and the solemn tones he affected well reveal the importance the author attached to the propagation of philosophy: "In Europe, there formed a class of people who were less concerned with a thorough uncovering of the truth than with propagating it. They . . . gloried in destroying popular errors rather than extending the limits of human knowledge—an indirect way of serving the progress of mankind which is neither less perilous nor less useful. Collins and Bolingbroke in England and Bayle, Fontenelle, Voltaire and Montesquieu in France and the schools they founded all fought in favor of truth . . . using all styles of writing from wit to pathos . . . attacking in religion, administration, custom, and law everything that bore the character of oppression, harshness and barbarism . . . finally adopting as a war cry, 'Reason, Tolerance and Humanity!' "[39]

It would be impossible to herald in more enthusiastic terms the passage from literature to journalism, from science to the rationalism of the salons and debating societies, from original research to declamation.

When Condorcet became an important political figure, he judged that the time had come to have the *people* participate in the progress of enlightenment. His ideas on public education have considerable importance for us because, in studying them, we can obtain an accurate picture of the nature of the eighteenth-century notion of progress. We should understand this notion as it applies to society; that is, in all its complex and living reality. A short analysis of Condorcet's proposals is, therefore, necessary here.

Condorcet thought it obvious that if one could show the people how to reason in the same way as those who frequented the salons of the *ancien régime,* world happiness was assured. His plan for secondary education with this end in mind is not regarded by present-day specialists as a very successful one. Compayré, though he greatly admires Condorcet's ideas, thinks that the Convention was misled in following him too closely on this point. The *écoles centrales* failed because they were "badly defined establishments where the instruction was too extensive, the curriculum too turgid and, it seemed, the student had to teach himself to discuss *de omni re scibili*."[40] It seems to me that Compayré did not understand Condorcet's thinking very well.

Condorcet did not want to produce farmers, manufacturers, engineers, geometricians and scholars; he wanted to produce "enlightened men."[41]

In his report, he revealed that he was inspired by eighteenth-century philosophy when choosing academic subjects. He wished to be "free from all the old chains of authority and custom." This philosophy, "in enlightening the contemporary generation, presages, prepares, and advances the superior reason to which the necessary progress of the human race calls future generations."[42]

We now know what it means to be inspired by eighteenth-century philosophy and to form enlightened men: it is to popularize knowledge in such a way as to put the young republicans in a position to hold an honourable place in a society based on the ideas of the *ancien régime;* it is to want democracy to model itself on the defunct aristocratic society; it is to place the new masters on the same social level as their predecessors. To obtain these results, it was necessary to give a smattering of all kinds of knowledge; and it was for this reason that the *écoles centrales* were conceived. Condorcet spoke of the classical languages with scorn: Greek and Latin ought no more to serve the men who aspire to shine in a democratic society than they served those who shone forth in the salons of the *ancien régime.*[43] Here we have the last echoes of the quarrel between the ancients and moderns. It was the latter who had triumphed in Condorcet's world, and our reformer takes his ideas from the past.

Condorcet believed that, contrary to the results from the old colleges, it would be very easy to obtain much more satisfactory results in the new schools through the use of synoptical tables,[44] of which he speaks in the following terms: "With the aid of a small number of these tables, which can be easily mastered, we will show how men who never rose above the most elementary education will be able to find at will the knowledge of details useful in ordinary life whenever they need them; how, also, by using these same devices, elementary instruction can be made easier in all matters in which this instruction is based either on a systematic order of truth or on a series of observations or facts."[45] Indeed, by such a method, it is possible to have students skim through an encyclopedia. And if they have been drilled to speak at random *de omni re scibili,* they can be made capable of writing articles for the newspapers or of giving parliamentary speeches on subjects about which they have scant knowledge.

Thus we arrive at the ultimate in vulgarization. Condorcet's methods are also the methods dunces use for preparing their examinations: what a lovely democratic ideal!

Our author tells us what goal he hoped to attain by means of public schooling. It is worth a short account: "We can teach the entire mass of the people everything each man needs to know for household economy, the administration of his affairs, the free development of his skills and faculties, knowledge and exercise of his legal rights, knowledge of his duties so as to enable him to fulfill them, and the capability of judging his actions and those of others according to his own understanding. No man would be unacquainted with the elevated or delicate sentiments that bring honor to human nature."

Let us interrupt our thoughts here awhile and note that Taine was shocked to see what uniformity the eighteenth century assumed in humanity. "People were considered to be only well-trained puppets and usually trumpets through which an author blares his declarations to the public. Greeks, Romans, medieval knights, Turks, Arabs, Zoroastrians, Peruvians and Byzantines are all only outlets for tirades. The public makes a success of all peasants, workers, Negroes, Brazilians, Parsees, people of the Malabar Coast who come to harangue the public."[46] As an audience for literature, "it seemed that there were only salons and the *literati*."[47] It was a matter of vulgarizing the manner of expressing "the elevated or delicate sentiments that bring honor to human nature," to such an extent that there would be a version of Madame Geoffrin's salon in the smallest hamlet. Then the world would be transformed according to the model novels and tragedies have created to the applause of a frivolous literary public.

We will now continue our description of the benefits of elementary instruction. "We should not be blindly dependent on those to whom we must entrust the care of our business or the exercise of our rights; we should be in a position of choosing and overseeing them." But contemporary experience shows that the vulgarization of knowledge does not make the people capable of choosing and supervising their so-called representatives, and it is hardly paradoxical to assert that, the more we march with the wave of democracy, the less efficient this supervision will be.

The newspapers manufacture political opinion just as they manufacture a style, a literary reputation, or the commercial value of a drug. Democracy has systematized certain methods that existed before it came into prominence, but it has invented nothing. In this, as in all aspects of democracy, we find the ideological heritage of the eighteenth century. The similarity between the current press and the world of the old salons does not occur to us because we are shocked by the grossness of our contemporary newspapers and because we view the past a little too much through legend. Basically, there is not much difference in ability between our great modern journalists and the Encyclopedists. As for their customs, unfortunately, they resemble each other in an astonishing way. In both the current press and the salons, one finds satisfaction with superficial reasoning, a great show of noble sentiments, and an admiration for science.[48] There is no reason to expect that the opinions of the modern press should be any better in quality than those manufactured by the philosophical salons.

We are not saying much when we assert that education is not useful to the proletariat, since it has as its object the popular participation in the reasoning methods taken over by the bourgeoisie from the aristocracy. I suppose that our great pedagogues agree with me and that it is precisely for this reason that they corrupt the primary schools with so many of their old ideas. Condorcet hoped that education would abolish all illusions having a magical quality. He said that people "should no longer be duped by the popular errors that torment a life with superstitious fears or illusory hopes. They should defend themselves against prejudice with the sole force of reason, and they should withstand the allures of charlatans who set traps for their fortune, health, liberty of opinion or conscience under the pretext of enriching, curing or saving them."

In these last words, Condorcet is obviously alluding to Cagliostro, Mesmer and the *Illuminées* who had such great success at the end of the eighteenth century. Up to the present time, such charlatans have not had a notable influence on the people, but this may be because the people hardly know them. Indeed, it is very doubtful that the type of education they are given could preserve them from these follies. The most genuine scholars of our times have been dupes of the spiritualists, and yet we cannot deny that Crookes and Richet know the scientific method! No one could foresee what could be produced by an adept vulgarization of occultism by the popular press.[49] We should not forget that Benoit Malon was adept at these extravagances, and he was not far from joining them to "integral socialism," which would not have lost much in this mixture.[50] The ease with which all of the inventors of new remedies find a large clientele in the bourgeoisie shows that the most absurd beliefs can obtain some credit if only they assume a scientific appearance.

It would seem that Condorcet was a better prophet with regard to Catholicism. Indeed, he alluded to Catholicism in the first lines of his last fragment. It is generally agreed that the development of the primary school is very dangerous for the Church. Twenty-five years ago, Renan wrote: "Popular rationalism, as the inevitable result of the progress of public instruction and democratic institutions, causes the churches to become deserted and multiplies purely civil marriages and funerals."[51]

The educational policies of the Third Republic have placed the Church in daily conflict with the official representatives of democracy. The Church took up the cause of its teaching orders, whose interests were endangered by lay teaching. The Church conducted violent campaigns in the hope of abrogating laws republicans regard as unassailable. Not a single defeat discouraged the Church, and she still hopes to triumph. Clericalism thus remains an enemy of democracy, which tries to usurp the faithful from the Church. The republicans have been denounced as "enemies of God"; as a result, academic competition has produced a battle against beliefs. Skepticism has become an essential element of the republican program, since the public schools have been successfully defended only through the use of anti-Catholic propaganda.

The Church made this propaganda easy because it entrusted its defense to sacristy-haunting petit bourgeois, who thought it a good idea to teach the people things educated Christians would find offensive if addressed to their children: the doctrine of providence has sunk to the level of the intelligence of savages, their conception of nature is that of fetishists, and the Miracle has been dishonored by a charlatanism worthy of drug peddlers. Primary schooling has permitted placing in the hands of the people, books and newspapers that show them that the men of *La Croix* and *Le Pélerin* laugh at them. The clerical press, in its blindness, has given its adversaries an easy way of demonstrating the stupidity, bad faith, and crass ignorance of the writers who call themselves the *friends of God.*

The popularization of scientific knowledge certainly creates serious difficulties for Christianity, which has sometimes excessively connected its theology to the medieval concept of nature. These difficulties have been made particularly acute in France in the wake of the struggle undertaken by the Church to preserve its teaching orders. That part of the bourgeoisie which possesses a slightly more elevated culture is much less hostile to the Church than are the people, because these bourgeois have not been called upon to equate the Gospel with *Le Pélerin.*[52] The priests who address themselves to this group almost always take the precaution of declaring themselves adversaries of the sacristy-haunting petit bourgeois, who conduct political campaigns among the poor classes.

CHAPTER 6

from
Reflections on Violence

INTRODUCTION: LETTER TO DANIEL HALÉVY[1]

My dear Halévy....

My *Reflections on Violence* has greatly annoyed many people because of the pessimistic idea on which the entire study is based; but I also know that you most certainly do not share this impression. You have proved brilliantly in your *Histoire de quatre ans* that you scorn the deceptive hopes on which the weak-spirited humor themselves. We can therefore freely discuss pessimism, and I am happy to find in you a correspondent who is not vulnerable to that notion without which nothing very great is produced in the world. I have long believed that if Greek philosophy did not produce great moral results, it is because generally it was strongly optimistic. Socrates was sometimes unbearably optimistic.

Our contemporaries' aversion for any pessimistic notion undoubtedly arises largely from our education. The Jesuits, who have created nearly everything that the University still teaches today, were optimists because they had to fight against the pessimism that dominated Protestant theories and because they popularized the ideas of the Renaissance. The men of the Renaissance interpreted antiquity philosophically and thus were led to understand the great achievements of tragic art so badly that our contemporaries have had great difficulty in rediscovering the pessimistic significance of this art.[2]

At the beginning of the nineteenth century there was a symphony of moaning and groaning that greatly contributed to making pessimism odious. Poets, who really were not always greatly to be pitied, claimed to be victims of human malevolence, of fatality or, better still, the stupidity of a world which did not succeed in amusing them. They willingly made themselves into Prometheuses called upon to dethrone jealous gods. As proud as the fierce Nimrod of Victor Hugo whose arrows, hurled against the sky, returned covered with blood, they imagined that their verses were mortally wounding the established powers who were so bold as not to humble themselves before them. The Jewish prophets never dreamed of so much destruction in order to avenge their Jehovah as did the men of letters in order to satisfy their *amour-propre*. When this style of cursing had ended, judicious men came to wonder if all this display of so-called pessimism had not been the result of a certain mental imbalance.

The immense successes gained by material civilization produced the belief that happiness would be created by itself, for everyone, in the near future. "For about forty years," wrote Hartmann, "the present century has only just been entering the third period of illusion. In the enthusiasm and enchantment of its hopes, it is rushing headlong into the realization of promises of a new golden age. Providence does not allow the predictions of an isolated thinker to disturb the progress of history by prematurely affecting too many minds." Also he thought that his readers would find it difficult to accept his criticism of the illusion of the happy future. The rulers of the contemporary world are pushed by economic forces into the path of optimism.[3]

Thus we are so badly prepared to understand pessimism that most often we use the word in an entirely wrong way; quite mistakenly we label disillusioned optimists as "pessimists." When we come across a man who, having been unfortunate in his undertakings, disappointed in his most justified ambitions and humiliated in love, expresses his unhappiness in the form of a violent revolt against the bad faith of his associates, the stupidity of society or the blindness of destiny, we are disposed to regard him as a pessimist—while nearly always we should see in him a disheartened optimist who has not had the courage to change the direction of his thought and who cannot explain why so many misfortunes happen to him contrary to the general order that decrees the creation of happiness.

In politics, the optimist is a fickle and even dangerous man, because he does not take account of the great difficulties presented by his projects. These projects seem to him to possess an intrinsic force leading to their realization all the more easily as they are destined, in his mind, to produce more happiness.

Rather often it seems to him that small reforms of the political constitution and most importantly of governing personnel are enough to direct the social movement in such a way as to reduce the horrors of the contemporary world to the satisfaction of sensitive men. From the moment his friends are in power, he declares that it is necessary to leave things alone, not to be too hasty and to rest content with what their good will suggests to them. It is not always self-interest alone which dictates his words of satisfaction, as has often been believed. Self-interest is strongly aided by pride and by the illusions of an insipid philosophy. Optimism moves with remarkable ease from revolutionary wrath to the most ridiculous social pacifism.

If he has an impulsive temperament and if, by some misfortune, he is found armed with great power allowing him to realize an ideal he has fashioned himself, the optimist can lead his country to the worst catastrophies, for he soon recognizes that social changes are not realized with the ease that he had counted on; he takes out his disappointments on his contemporaries instead of explaining the course of things by historical necessities. He attempts to do away with the men whose ill will appears to him dangerous for the public happiness. During the Terror, the men who spilled the most blood were those who had the most burning desire to make their contemporaries enjoy the golden age of which they dreamed and who had the most sympathy for human misery: sensitive, optimistic and idealistic, the greater their thirst for universal happiness, the more inexorable they were.

Pessimism is entirely different from the caricatures that are most often made of it: it is a metaphysics of morals much more than a theory of the world. It is a notion of an *advance toward deliverance* that, on the one hand, is closely connected to the knowledge gained from experience of the obstacles which resist the satisfaction of our imagination (or, if you wish, connected to the feeling of a social determinism); on the other hand, it is connected to the deep conviction of our natural weakness. These three aspects of pessimism must never be separated, although in practice one hardly ever takes account of their close connection.

1. The word "pessimism" is derived from the impression made on literary historians by the laments uttered by the great ancient poets on the subject of the ills which constantly plagued mankind. Few people have not been lucky at least once. But we are surrounded by hostile forces which are always ready to ambush us and to rush in and overwhelm us. Real sufferings arise from this, which stir the sympathy of practically all mankind—even those whom fortune has treated favor-

ably; therefore, sad literature has been successful throughout almost all of history.[4] But we would have only a very imperfect notion of pessimism by looking at it in this kind of literature. Generally, in order to evaluate a doctrine, it is not enough to study it in an abstract way, or even in isolated individuals, but we must see how it reveals itself in historic groups. This leads to adding the two elements discussed above.

2. The pessimist regards social conditions as forming a system chained together by an iron law to whose necessity we must submit *in toto* and which will disappear only if a catastrophe sweeps everything away. Thus, when this theory is admitted, it becomes absurd to blame the responsibility for the evils endured by society on a few evil men. The pessimist does not have the bloodthirsty madness of the optimist infuriated by the unforeseen obstacles encountered by his projects. He wouldn't think of making the happiness of future generations depend on slitting the throats of our present egoists.

3. What is most profound in pessimists is the manner of conceiving the advance toward deliverance. Man would not go far in the examination either of the laws of his misery or of the fatality which so shocks the innocence of our pride if he did not possess the hope of seeing an end to these tyrannies by means of an effort that he will make, together with a whole group of companions, to get rid of them. The Christians would not have thought so much about original sin if they had not felt the necessity of justifying deliverance (which should result from the death of Jesus) by assuming that Jesus' sacrifice had been made necessary by a hideous crime attributable to humanity. If Western man was much more concerned with original sin than were the people of the East, this is not solely due to the influence of Roman law,[5] as Taine believed, but also because the Latins, having a higher idea of imperial majesty than the Greeks, regarded the sacrifice of the Son of God as having realized an extraordinarily marvelous deliverance. The necessity of probing the mysteries of human misery and destiny springs from this.

It seems to me that the optimism of Greek philosophers is largely dependent on economic factors. It must have arisen in wealthy and commercial urban populations that could view the world as a huge shop full of excellent things on which their covetousness could satisfy itself.[6] I imagine that Greek pessimism originated from poor, warlike mountain tribes who had an enormous aristocratic pride, but whose circumstances on the other hand were quite impoverished. Their poets enchanted them by praising their ancestors and making them hope for triumphant expeditions led by superhuman heroes. They explained their present poverty to them by relating the catastrophies in which semi-divine old leaders had succumbed as a consequence of fate or of jealous gods. The warriors' courage could remain temporarily useless, but it would not always be so. It was necessary to remain faithful to the old morals in order to be ready for the great victorious expeditions, which could be very near at hand.

Very often Eastern asceticism has been held to be the most remarkable manifestation of pessimism. Certainly Hartmann is right when he regards it as having only the value of a foreboding whose utility was in reminding men of the illusory nature of vulgar possessions. He is wrong, however, when he says that asceticism taught men "the end to which their efforts would lead" which is the annulment of the will.[7] For deliverance has been something entirely different in the course of history.

With the advent of early Christianity we find a fully developed and completely armed pessimism: man has been condemned to slavery from the time of his birth; Satan is the prince of the world; the Christian, already regenerated by baptism, can enable himself to obtain the resurrection of the body through the Eucharist.[8] He awaits the glorious return of Christ Who will vanquish Satanic fatality and will summon His companions in struggle to the celestial Jerusalem. All of this Christian life was dominated by the necessity of taking part in the Holy Army which is constantly exposed to the traps set by the instruments of Satan. This notion gave rise to many heroic acts, engendered a courageous propaganda and produced a serious moral advance. Deliverance did not take place, but we know by innumerable testimonies of this time what greatness the advance toward deliverance can produce.

Sixteenth-century Calvinism offers an example which is perhaps even more instructive, but we should be careful not to confuse it with contemporary Protestantism, as many writers have. These two doctrines are at the opposite ends of the pole from one another. I cannot understand how Hartmann can say that Protestantism "is the resting place in the course of authentic Christianity," and that it made "an alliance with the re-birth of ancient Paganism." This judgment applies only to recent Protestantism, which has abandoned its own principles in order to adopt those of the Renaissance. Pessimism, which did not enter at all into the stream of Renaissance ideas,[9] was never affirmed so forcefully as it was by the men of the Reformation. The dogmas of sin and of predestination were pushed to their logical extremes; these dogmas correspond to the first two aspects of pessimism: the wretchedness of the human species and social determinism. As for deliverance, it was conceived under a very different form from that of the early Christians: the Protestants organized militarily wherever this was possible. They made expeditions into Catholic countries, expeling the priests, introducing the Reformation worship and promulgating laws of proscription against papists.

They no longer took from the Apocalypse the idea of a great final catastrophy in which Christ's companions would only be spectators after having long defended themselves against Satanic attacks. The Protestants, steeped in the reading of the Old Testament, wanted to imitate the exploits of the ancient conquerors of the Holy Land. Thus, they took the offensive, and wanted to establish the kingdom of God by force. In each conquered area, the Calvinists realized a veritable catastrophic revolution, changing everything from top to bottom.

Calvinism was finally defeated by the Renaissance. It was replete with theological concerns borrowed from medieval tradition, and there came a day when it was afraid of appearing too backward. It wanted to be on the level of modern culture, and it ended by becoming simply a relaxed Christianity.[10] Today very few people suspect what the men of the Reformation in the sixteenth century understood by free examination. Protestants apply to the Bible the procedures that philologists apply to any secular text. Calvin's exegeses gave way to humanist criticism.

The analyst who is content to list facts is tempted to regard salvation as a dream or an error, but the true historian views things from another perspective. When he wants to know the influence of the Calvinist spirit on morality, law or literature, he is always led back to examining how the thought of the old Protestants came under the influence of the advance toward deliverance. The experience of this great epoch shows very well that the man of spirit finds a satisfaction sufficient to maintain his ardor in the sentiment of struggle which accompanies this *will to salvation*. Thus I think that a conclusion could be drawn from this series of beautiful illustrations of pessimism—that the Wandering Jew is the symbol of the highest aspirations of humanity, condemned always to wander without rest.

II

My ideas still shock people who are, in some way, under the influence of ideas that our education has conveyed to us on the subject of natural right [*droit*], and there are few educated men who have freed themselves from these notions. If the philosophy of natural right is in perfect agreement with that of force (understanding this word in the special meaning I have given to it in Chap. 5, sect. 4),[11] it cannot be reconciled with my ideas on the historic role of violence. Scholarly doctrines on natural right would end up in a simple tautology, "what is just is good and what is unjust is bad," if it had not always been admitted implicitly that what is just adapts itself to actions which occur automatically in the world. Thus economists have long maintained that the relations created under the regime of competition in the capitalist order are perfectly just—as resulting from the "natural course" of things. The utopians have always claimed that the present world was "not natural enough"; consequently, they wanted to give a portrait of a society automatically better ruled and therefore more just.

I cannot resist the pleasure of citing several of Pascal's *Pensées,* which greatly disturbed his contemporaries and which have been genuinely understood only in our day. Pascal had great difficulty in freeing himself from the ideas of the philosophers of natural right; he abandoned them because he did not consider them sufficiently imbued with Christianity. "I have spent much of my life," he said, "believing that there was justice; and in this I was not wrong; for *there is justice insofar as God has wished to reveal it to us.* But I did not interpret it in this way, and in that I was wrong; for I believed that our justice was essentially just, and that I was capable of knowing it and judging it" (fragment 375 of the Brunschwig edition); "Doubtless there are natural laws; but this beautiful but corrupted reason[12] has corrupted all" (fragment 294); "*Veri juris.* We no longer have any" (fragment 297).

Moreover, observation showed Pascal the absurdity of the theory of natural right; if this theory were exact, several universally admitted laws would be found; but actions that we regard as crimes have been regarded as virtues in the past. "Three degrees nearer the Pole reverses all jurisprudence, a meridian decides the truth. In a very few years, fundamental laws change; right has its stages, the entry of Saturn into the constellation of the Lion marks the origin of a certain crime. Absurd justice delineated by a river! Truth on one side of the Pyrenees, error on the other. . . . It is said that we must return to the fundamental and early laws of the state, abolished by unjust custom. That is a game that is sure to lose all; nothing will be just on that criterion" (fragment 294; cf. fragment 375).

Since it is impossible for us to be able to reason about the just [*le juste*], we must turn to custom, and Pascal often comes back to this rule (fragments 294, 297, 299, 309, 312). He goes still further and shows how the just is in practice dependent on force: "Justice is subject to dispute, force is very recognizable and undisputed. Thus justice has not been able to be given force because force contradicts justice and has said that it was itself just. Thus, not being able to make what is just strong, what is strong is made just" (fragment 298; cf. fragments 302, 303, 306, 307, 311).

This criticism of natural right does not have the perfect clarity that we could give to it today, because we know that we must seek in the economy the kind of force that operates fully automatically and is thus able to identify itself naturally with right—while Pascal mixes all manifestations of force under a single type.

The changes that law undergoes in the course of time strongly impressed Pascal and they continue to disturb our philosophers greatly: a well-coordinated social system is destroyed by a revolution and gives place to another system that one finds just as reasonable; and what was formerly just has become unjust. Sophisms have been applied unsparingly to prove that force was placed at the service of justice during the revolutions. These arguments have been shown to be absurd many times, but the public cannot bring itself to abandon them, so habituated is it to believing in natural right.

Nothing up to and including war has been excluded from the domain of natural right: war has been compared to a trial in which a people lays claim to a right unrecognized by a malicious neighbor. Our fathers willingly admitted that God would decide the dispute, in the course of battles, in favor of the party who is in the right. The defeated party was treated as if it were a losing litigant in a trial. It had to pay the costs of the war and give guarantees to the conqueror so that he could enjoy his restored rights in peace. Today we are not without men who propose submitting international conflicts to arbitration courts; this would be a secularization of the old mythology.[13]

The partisans of natural right are not irreversible adversaries of civil strife or especially of tumultuous demonstrations. During the Dreyfus affair we have seen this clearly. When the public force is in the hands of their adversaries, the natural-right men rather willingly declare that it is used to violate justice, and then they prove that it is permissible to depart from legality in order to return to right (according to the Bonapartist formula); at the very least they try to intimidate the government when they cannot manage to overthrow it. But while they thus combat those who control the public force, they do not at all desire to do away with it, for they wish to use it to their own advantage someday. All of the revolutionary disturbances in the nineteenth century ended by reinforcing state power.

Proletarian violence changes the aspect of all conflicts in which it appears, for it denies the force organized by the bourgeoisie and claims to suppress the state which forms the nucleus of it. In such circumstances there is no longer any way to argue about the primordial rights of men. That is why our Parliamentary Socialists, who are children of the bourgeoisie and who know nothing outside the ideology of the state, are completely disoriented when faced with proletarian violence. They are unable to apply to it the commonplaces which usually serve them in speaking of force, and they view with alarm movements which could end in ruining the institutions under which they live: with revolutionary syndicalism, no more second-rate discourses on immanent Justice, no more Parliamentary regime possessed by the intellectuals; this regime is the abomination of desolation! So it is not necessarily surprising if they speak of violence so wrathfully. . . .

III

In the course of these studies, I have established something so simple that I did not believe it had to be emphasized: men who participate in great social movements represent their immediate action in the form of images of battles assuring the triumph of their cause. I proposed calling these constructions *myths*, the knowledge of which is so important for the historian:[14] the syndicalist general strike and Marx's catastrophic revolution are myths. I have given as remarkable examples of myths those which were constructed by early Christianity, the Reformation, the French Revolution and by Mazzini's followers. I wanted to show that it is not necessary to try to analyze such systems of images in the same way that one breaks down something into its elements; that they should be taken as a whole and as historical forces; that it is necessary above all to keep from comparing the accomplished facts with the images which men had adopted prior to action.

I could give another perhaps still more impressive example: the Catholics are never discouraged amidst the most severe trials because they imagine the history of the Church as being a series of battles joined between Satan and the Christ-sustained hierarchy; any new difficulty that comes into view is an episode in this war and must finally conclude in the victory of Catholicism.

In the beginning of the nineteenth century, the revolutionary persecutions revived this myth of the Satanic struggle which provided Joseph de Maistre with eloquent words; this revival largely explains the religious renaissance that occurred at that time. If Catholicism is so menaced today, this is due in large part to the fact that the myth of the Church militant is beginning to disappear. Ecclesiastical literature has greatly contributed to making it ridiculous. Thus, in 1872 a Belgian writer recommended restoring exorcisms to honor; he thought they would be an effective means of combatting the revolutionaries.[15] Many educated Catholics are aghast to see that the ideas of Joseph de Maistre contributed to the ignorance of the clergy, because the clergy avoided keeping abreast with an "evil" science. The Satanic myth thus seems dangerous to these educated Catholics and they point out its ridiculous aspects; but they did not always understand its historical significance.

Besides, the gentle, skeptical and above all peaceful habits of the present generation are not favorable to the maintenance of this myth, and the adversaries of the Church loudly proclaim that they do not want to return to a regime of persecutions which could restore their former power to images of war.

In using the term "myth," I thought that I was making a fortunate discovery, because I thus rejected all discussion with those who wish to submit the general strike to a detailed criticism and who collect objections against its practical possibility. On the contrary, it seems that I had a very wicked idea, since some people say to me that myths are suitable only to primitive societies, while others think that I want to attribute as driving forces of the modern world dreams analogous to those that Renan believed were useful for replacing religion;[16] but my detractors have gone further and have claimed that my theory of myths is a lawyer's argument, a false translation of the true opinions of the Revolutionaries—an "intellectualist sophism."

If this were so, I would be rather unfortunate since I wanted to remove all influence of the intellectualist philosophy, which appears to me to be a great embarrassment for the historian who follows it. The contradiction between this philosophy and the true understanding of events has often impressed Renan's readers. At every moment Renan was swinging back and forth between his own intuition (which was almost always admirable) and a philosophy which could not touch upon history without falling into platitudes; but, alas, too often he believed that he was obliged to think according to the "scientific opinion" of his contemporaries. The Napoleonic soldier sacrificed his life in return for the honor of working in an "eternal" epic, and of living in the glory of France all the while saying "that he would always be a poor man";[17] extraordinary virtues were shown by the Romans who resigned themselves to a frightful inequality and they endured great sacrifices to conquer the world;[18] "faith in glory [was] an unequaled value," created by the Greeks and due to which "a choice was made amidst the teeming throng of humanity, life had a purpose, and there was a reward for those who pursued the good and the beautiful"[19]—these are things that the intellectualist philosophy cannot explain. On the contrary, intellectualism leads to the admiration of the 51st chapter of Jeremiah, "the deeply sad, superior sentiment with which peaceful man contemplates the collapse [of empires] and the commiseration aroused in the hearts of wise men by the spectacle of people working for nothing, victims of the pride of the few." According to Renan, Greece did not see this,[20] and it seems to me that we need not complain about it! Besides, he himself praises the Romans for not having acted according to the ideas of the Jewish thinker: " 'They labored, they exhausted themselves—for nothing, for the fire,' said the Jewish thinker—yes, undoubtedly; but that is the virtue that history rewards."[21]

Religions constitute a particularly grave scandal for the intellectualist, for he can neither regard them as being without historical importance nor explain them; thus Renan has at times written about them in some very strange phrases: "Religion is a necessary swindle. The crudest means of throwing sand in the eyes cannot be neglected with a race as stupid as the human race, created to make mistakes, and which, when it admits the truth, never admits it for the right reasons. It is thus necessary to give it the wrong reasons."[22]

Comparing Giordano Bruno who "allowed himself to burn in Venice," and Galileo who gave in to the Vatican, Renan approved Galileo's actions because, according to him, the scholar has no need of bringing forth anything besides reasons to support his discoveries. Renan thought that the Italian philosopher wanted to complete his inadequate proofs by this sacrifice, and he uttered this scornful maxim: "One is martyred only for things of which one is not quite sure."[23] Here Renan confuses *conviction,* which must have been strong in Bruno, with that very particular *certitude* that teaching produces in the long run on the subject of the precepts that science has accepted. It is difficult to give a less precise idea of the real forces which make men act!

This entire philosophy could be summarized in this proposition by Renan: "Human things are a rough estimate without seriousness or precision," and, indeed, for the intellectualist, what lacks precision also ought to lack seriousness. But the historian's conscience could never completely rest and he quickly added this corrective: "To have seen [this] is a great achievement for philosophy, but that is an abdication of any active role for philosophy. The future belongs to those who are not disillusioned."[24] We conclude from this that the intellectualist philosophy is extremely incompetent in explaining great historical movements.

To the ardent Catholics who struggled successfully for so long against revolutionary traditions, the intellectualist philosophy would have tried in vain to show that the myth of the Church militant does not conform to the scientific constructions established by the most scholarly writers following the best rules of criticism; it could not persuade them. No argument could have shaken the faith that these men had in the promises made to the Church, and as long as this certitude remained, the myth was incontestable in their view. Similarly, the objections of the philosopher against the revolutionary myths would make an impression only on the men who are happy to find a pretext for abandoning "any active role" and to be revolutionary in name only.

I understand that the myth of the general strike greatly offends many judicious men because of its boundless character. The present world is quite inclined to return to the opinions of the ancients and to subordinate morality to the smooth running of public affairs, which leads to placing virtue in a happy medium. Insofar as socialism remains a *doctrine expressed entirely in words,* it is very easy to have it veer toward a happy medium. But this transformation is manifestly impossible when the myth of the general strike, which calls for an absolute revolution, is introduced. You know as well as I that what is best in the modern conscience is the torment of the infinite. You are not one of those who regard as fortunate discoveries the procedures which are used to deceive readers by verbal trickery. That is why you will not condemn me for having attached such great value to a myth which gives to socialism such high moral worth and such great honesty. Many men would not try to dispute the theory of myths if it did not have such wonderful consequences.

IV

The mind of man is made in such a way that it cannot rest content with observed facts; it wants to understand the reason for things. Thus I wonder if it would not be fitting to try to examine this theory of myths by using the insights that we owe to Bergsonian philosophy. The effort that I am going to submit is undoubtedly quite imperfect, but I think it is conceived according to the method that we should follow to clarify this problem.

First of all, note that the moralists almost never discuss what is truly fundamental in our individuality. Ordinarily they try to project our accomplished acts onto the balance sheet that society has drawn up in advance for the various types of action most commonly found in contemporary life. They say they determine motives in this way, but these motives are similar to those considered by jurists in criminal law; they are social evaluations which relate to well-known facts. Many philosophers, especially in antiquity, believed that they could relate everything to utility, and if there is a social calculation, it is surely there. Theologians place transgressions on the path which leads normally, according to average experience, to mortal sin; thus they know what degree of malice is present in concupiscence, and the penance that should be inflicted; the moderns teach readily that we judge our will before acting by comparing our maxims to general principles which are not without some similarity to the *Declaration of the Rights of Man;* this theory was very probably inspired by the admiration for the *Bill of Rights* placed at the head of the American Constitutions.[25]

We are all so greatly interested in knowing what the world will think of us that sooner or later considerations arise in our minds similar to those discussed by the moralists. From this it results that the moralists could imagine that they were truly appealing to experience in order to discover what lies at the basis of the creative consciousness when they were really only considering accomplished acts from a social point of view.

Bergson asks us, on the contrary, to be concerned with our inner selves and with what happens in us during the creative moment. "There are two different selves," he said, "of which one would be, as it were, the exterior projection of the other, its spatial representation and, so to speak, its social representation. We reach the first by deep introspection, which causes us to grasp our inner states as living beings, in a constant process of formation, as states which resist measurement. . . . But *the moments in which we are fully in possession of ourselves are rare* and that is why we are rarely free. Most of the time, we live outside ourselves; we perceive only a colorless phantom of ourselves. . . . We live for the external world rather than for ourselves; we speak more than we think; we are acted upon more than we act ourselves. To act freely is to recover possession of ourselves, it is to get into pure duration again."[26]

In order truly to understand this psychology, it is necessary "to carry ourselves back by thought to those moments of our existence when we made some serious decision, moments unique of their kind and which will never be repeated any more than the vanished phases of the history of a nation will ever return again."[27] It is quite obvious that we enjoy this liberty above all when we try to create a new man in ourselves for the purpose of shattering the historical framework which encloses us. At first, it might be thought that it would be enough to say that we are then dominated by all-powerful feelings; but today everyone agrees that movement is the essential aspect of emotional life, and it is thus in terms of movement that we should speak of the creative consciousness.

In my opinion, this is how deep psychology should be depicted: we should abandon the idea that the soul is comparable to a moving body which propels itself, according to a more or less mechanical law, toward various incentives given by nature. When we act, it is because we have created an entirely artificial world, in advance of the present, consisting of movements which depend on us. Thus our liberty becomes perfectly intelligible. Since these constructions include everything which interests us, some philosophers, inspired by Bergsonian doctrines, have been led to a somewhat surprising theory. For example, Le Roy says, "Our true body is the entire universe insofar as it is lived by us. And what common sense more exactly calls our body is only the least unconscious and most freely acting part of it, the part over which we have direct control and through which we can act on the rest."[28] We should not confuse, as this subtle philosopher does constantly, a fleeting state of our voluntary activity with the stable affirmations of science.[29]

These artificial worlds generally disappear from our minds, leaving no memories; but when the masses become impassioned, then a tableau can be described which constitutes a social myth.

Faith in glory, praised so much by Renan, rapidly dissolves into rhapsodies when it is not upheld by myths which have varied greatly according to the period. The citizen of the Greek republics, the Roman legionnaire, the soldier of the wars of liberty, and the artist of the Renaissance have not conceived of glory by appealing to the same system of images. Renan complains that "faith in glory is compromised by short-sighted views of history which tend to predominate nowadays. Few people, he says, "act with eternity in mind. . . . They want to enjoy their glory; they devour it during their lifetimes; they will not harvest it after death."[30] It seems to me that short-sighted views of history are not a cause but a result; they result from the weakening of the historic myths which were so popular at the beginning of the nineteenth century; faith in glory perished and short-sighted views of history began to predominate when these myths were disappearing.[31]

Revolts can be spoken of indefinitely without ever provoking revolutionary action as long as there are no myths accepted by the masses; that is what gives such great importance to the general strike, and that is why it is so odious to socialists who fear a revolution; they do their utmost to shake the workers' confidence in their preparations for revolution; and to achieve their end they ridicule the idea of the general strike, which alone can be a moving force. One of their great methods consists in portraying it as utopian; this is easy to do, because there are rarely myths perfectly free of any hint of utopianism.

Current revolutionary myths are almost pure; they permit the understanding of the activity, sentiments and ideas of popular masses who are preparing to enter into a decisive struggle; they are not descriptions of things but expressions of the will. Utopia is, on the contrary, the product of an intellectual labor; it is the work of theorists who, after having observed and discussed the facts, try to establish a model against which existing societies can be compared in order to measure the good or evil that they contain;[32] it is a composition of imaginary institutions, but offering close enough analogies to real institutions so that the jurist can discuss it; it is a construction which can be broken down into parts and of which certain parts have been set up in such a way as to enable them (provided we make a few corrections for adjustment) to be included in pending legislation. While today's myths lead men to prepare themselves for a battle to destroy what exists, utopia has always had the effect of directing minds toward reforms that can be put into effect piecemeal within the present system; thus we should not be surprised that so many utopians were able to become clever men of state when they acquired a greater experience of political life. A myth cannot be refuted since fundamentally it is identical to the convictions of a group, an expression of these convictions in the language of movement. Consequently, it cannot be broken down into parts which can be applied on the level of historical descriptions. Utopia, on the contrary, can be discussed like all social constitutions; one can compare the automatic movements that it assumes with those which have been ascertained in the course of history. We can thus estimate their probability. It can be refuted in showing that the economy on which it is based is incompatible with the necessities of present-day production.

Liberal political economy was one of the best examples of utopia that could be cited. A society was imagined in which everything would be reduced to commercial types under the law of the most complete competition. Today we recognize that this ideal society would be as difficult to realize as that of Plato. But great modern politicians owe their glory to the efforts that they have made to introduce something of this commercial freedom into industrial legislation.

We have described a utopia free of all myth, but the history of French democracy provides a very remarkable combination of utopias and myths. The theories which inspired the authors of our first constitutions are regarded as highly chimerical today. Often the value that had long been recognized in them is no longer conceded: that of an ideal upon which legislators, magistrates and administrators should have their eyes permanently fixed in order to assure a modicum of justice to men. With these utopias were mixed myths which represented the struggle against the Old Regime. As long as they were maintained, refutations of the liberal utopias could abound without producing any result; the myth safeguarded the utopia with which it was mixed.

For a long time socialism was hardly anything but a utopia. The Marxists have rightly claimed for their master the honor of having changed this situation: socialism has become a process of preparing the masses employed in large-scale industry who want to suppress property and the state. Henceforth there will be no more concern with how men will contrive to enjoy the beautiful future. Everything is reduced to the *revolutionary apprenticeship* of the proletariat. Unfortunately, Marx did not have the facts available to him that have become familiar to us. We know better than he what strikes are because we have been able to observe economic conflicts of considerable extent and duration. The myth of the general strike has become popular and has been solidly established in men's minds. We have ideas on violence that Marx would not have been able to formulate easily. Thus we are able to complete his doctrine, instead of commenting on his texts as did his unfortunate disciples for so long.

Utopia is thus tending to disappear completely from socialism; socialism has no need to try to organize labor since capitalism has already done so. Besides, I think I have demonstrated that the general strike corresponds to sentiments so strongly related to those necessary to assure production in a regime of very progressive industry, that the revolutionary apprenticeship can also be an apprenticeship of the producer.

When we are put in this realm of myths, we are secure from all refutation, which has lead many people to say that socialism is a kind of religion. For men have long been impressed with the fact that religious convictions are independent of criticism; from this it has been concluded that everything which claims to be above science is a religion. Also we note that today Christianity tends to be less a dogma than a way of life; that is, a moral reform which tries to go to the foundation of human life. Consequently, a new analogy has been found between religion and the revolutionary socialism which gives itself as a goal the apprenticeship, the preparation and even the reconstruction of the individual with a view toward a gigantic work. But Bergson's teaching has shown that religion is not the only thing to occupy the regions of the deepest consciousness; the revolutionary myths are as much entitled to a place there. Yves Guyot's arguments against socialism (treating it as religion) seem based, therefore, on an imperfect knowledge of the new psychology.

Renan was quite surprised to find out that socialists are beyond discouragement: "After each failure they begin again: the solution is not found, but it will be found. It never occurs to them that the solution does not exist; and therein lies their strength."[33]

Renan's explanation is superficial; he regards socialism as a utopia; that is, as something comparable to observed realities, and it is hard to understand how confidence could thus survive many failures. But alongside utopias there have always been myths capable of leading the workers to revolt. For a long time, these myths were based on the legends of the Revolution, and they preserved their complete value as long as these legends were not shaken. Today the confidence of the socialists is very much greater than before, since the myth of the general strike dominates every genuine workers' movement. A failure can never be taken as evidence against socialism since socialism has become a work of preparation; if there is failure it is proof that the apprenticeship was insufficient. It is necessary to return to work with more courage, persistence and confidence than before. The practice of work has taught the workers that it is through the process of patient apprenticeship that one becomes a true comrade; and it is also the only means of becoming a true revolutionary. . . .[34]

THE PROLETARIAN STRIKE*

. . . Syndicalism strives to use means of expression which fully clarify things, which put them in their natural place, and which accentuate all of the value of the forces put into play. In order to understand the syndicalist movement, oppositions should be accentuated instead of softened; the groups that struggle against each other should be clearly delineated; in sum, the movements of the rebelling masses should be portrayed in such a way that the rebels receive an overpowering impression.

Language is not sufficient to produce such results with any certainty; it is necessary to invoke groups of images capable of evoking, *as a whole and solely by intuition* prior to any deliberate analysis, the mass of sentiments which corresponds to the various manifestations of war entered into by socialism against modern society. The syndicalists resolve this problem perfectly by concentrating the whole of socialism in the drama of the general strike; thus there is no longer any room for compromise between the opposing parties through the eyewash of "official scholars"; everything is drawn up in such a way that there can be only a single possible interpretation of socialism. This method has all the advantages that, according to Bergson's doctrine, "total knowledge" has over analysis, and perhaps we could not cite many other examples capable of illustrating the value of Bergson's analysis in as perfect a way.[1]

There has been wide discussion on the possibility of realizing the general strike: it has been claimed that the socialist war could not be resolved in a single battle. To "wise men," both experienced and learned, it seems prodigiously difficult to set great masses of the proletariat in motion all together; the difficulties of detail presented by such an enormous struggle have been analyzed. According to the socialist-sociologists and the politicians, the general strike is a popular reverie characteristic of the early stages of a workers' movement. Sidney Webb has been cited as an authority who has decreed that the general strike was a youthful illusion[2] quickly abandoned by those English workers whom the proprietors of the "serious science" have so often presented as repositories of the true conception of the workers' movement.

That the general strike is not popular in England today is a poor argument to make against the historic significance of the idea, for the

* Chapter IV, section 1.

English distinguish themselves by an extraordinary incomprehension of
the class struggle. Their thought is still strongly dominated by medieval
influences: the guild which is privileged, or at least protected by the
laws, always seems to them to be the ideal workers' organization; it is
for England that the term "working class aristocracy" was invented in
order to speak of the unionists and, indeed, trade unionism seeks the
acquisition of legal favors.[3] We could say, therefore, that the aversion
England feels for the general strike ought to be regarded as a strong
presumption in its favor by all those who regard the class struggle as
essential to socialism.

Furthermore, Sidney Webb enjoys a greatly exaggerated reputation
for competence; he has the merit of having gone through rather uninteresting documents and having had the patience to compose one of the
most turgid compilations on the history of trade unionism in existence;
but he has an extremely limited intelligence which has been able to
dazzle only those who are little used to thinking.[4] The people who introduced his glory into France did not understand anything about socialism, and if he is really in the first rank of contemporary writers on
economic history, as his translator[5] assures us he is, it is because the
intellectual level of these historians is rather low. Moreover, many examples show that one can be an illustrious professional historian and at
the same time have a less than mediocre mind.

Neither do I attach any importance to the objections that can be addressed to the general strike which rely on practical considerations.
This only returns us to that old utopian mentality which tried to manufacture on the basis of historical models certain hypotheses on future
struggles and on the means of suppressing capitalism. There is no way
to predict the future in a scientific manner, or even to discuss the superiority that certain hypotheses have over others. Too many memorable
examples show us that the greatest of men have committed mammoth
errors in their desire thus to become masters of even the most immediate future.[6]

And yet we are not able to act without leaving the present, without
thinking about that future which always seems condemned to escape
our reason. Experience proves that some *constructions of a future undetermined in time* can possess great effectiveness and have very few
disadvantages when they are of a certain nature; this occurs when it
is a question of myths in which the strongest inclinations of a people,
a party or a class are found, tendencies which present themselves to the
mind with the insistence of instincts in all of life's circumstances, and
which give an appearance of complete reality to hopes of imminent
action on which the reform of the will is based. Moreover, we know that
these social myths do not prevent any man from learning to profit from

all the observations he makes in the course of his life and that they are no obstacle to the fulfillment of his normal business.[7]

This can be shown through many examples. The first Christians expected the return of Christ and the total ruination of the pagan world, with the setting up of the kingdom of saints at the end of the first generation. The catastrophe did not occur, but Christian thought would later make such great use of the apocalyptic myth that certain contemporary scholars insist that all of Jesus's preaching bore upon this single subject.[8] The hopes of Luther and Calvin on the religious exaltation of Europe were not at all realized. These Fathers of the Reformation very rapidly appeared to be men of another world. For contemporary Protestants, they belonged to the Middle Ages rather than to modern times, and the problems which most disturbed them occupy a very small place in contemporary Protestantism. Should we, because of this, dispute the immense result that arose from their dreams of Christian renovation? It is easily seen that the true developments of the French Revolution did not at all resemble the enchanting portraits which had so inspired its first partisans, but without these pictures how could the Revolution have triumphed? The myth was greatly mixed with utopias,[9] because it was formed by a society that was impassioned for fiction, full of confidence in "popularized science," and not very well informed about the economic history of the past. These utopias were useless, but one wonders if the Revolution was not perhaps a much greater transformation than those dreamed of by people who fabricated social utopias in the eighteenth century. Very recently Mazzini pursued what "wise" men of his time called a crazy dream; but there is no doubt now that without Mazzini, Italy would never have become a great power and that he has done much more for Italian unity than Cavour and all of the politicians of his school.

Thus it matters little whether or not we know to what extent myths contain those details that are actually destined to appear on the plane of history in the future; myths are not astrological almanacs; it is even possible that nothing contained in them will take place, as was the case with the catastrophe expected by the first Christians.[10] In everyday life, are we not accustomed to recognizing that reality differs greatly from the ideas that we had of it before acting? And that does not prevent us from continuing to make resolutions. Psychologists say that there is a heterogeneity between the ends realized and the ends given: the least experience of life reveals this law to us, applied by Spencer to nature in order to devise his theory of the multiplication of effects from it.[11]

Myths should be judged as means of acting on the present; any discussion on the manner of applying them materially to the course of history is devoid of sense. *It is only the myth as a whole that counts;*

its parts are interesting only for the emphasis that they give to the idea contained in the whole structure. It is not useful then to argue about the incidents which can take place in the course of the social war and on the decisive conflicts which can give victory to the proletariat. Even if the revolutionaries were entirely wrong in constructing a whimsical tableau of the general strike, this picture could be a very strong element in the course of preparation for the revolution if in a perfect way it welcomed all of the aspirations of socialism and if it gave to the whole of revolutionary thoughts a precision and a severity which they could not receive from other modes of thought.

In order to appreciate the significance of the idea of the general strike, we must abandon all of the methods of discussion which have currency among politicians, sociologists or those having pretensions to practical science. Everything that the adversaries are trying to prove can be conceded without reducing in any way the value of the hypothesis that they think they can refute. It matters little if the general strike is a partial reality or only the product of the popular imagination. The whole question consists in knowing if the general strike contains everything that the socialist doctrine expects from the revolutionary proletariat.

In order to resolve such a question, we are no longer reduced to arguing knowledgeably about the future. We do not need to devote ourselves to lofty considerations of philosophy, history and economics. We are not in the realm of ideologies but can remain on the plane of observable facts. We should question those men who take quite an active part in the truly revolutionary movement in the bosom of the proletariat, who do not aspire to rise to the bourgeoisie, and who are not dominated by medieval prejudices. These men can be mistaken about any number of questions of politics, economics or morality; but their testimony is decisive, sovereign and unchangeable when it is a question of knowing which images act upon them and their comrades most effectively, which images come closest to their idea of socialism and thanks to which reason, hopes and the perception of particular facts seem to present an indivisible unity.[12]

Thanks to them we know that the general strike is indeed what I have said: the *myth* which encompasses all of socialism; that is to say, an arrangement of images capable of evoking instinctively all of the sentiments which correspond to the various manifestations of the war waged by socialism against modern society. Strikes have inspired in the proletariat the noblest, deepest and most forceful sentiments that it possesses; the general strike groups them all into a general unified image and, by bringing them together, gives to each one of these sentiments its maximum intensity. Evoking very vivid memories of particular conflicts, it colors intensely all of the details of the composition presented to the mind. Thus we obtain that intuition of socialism that language could not give in a perfectly clear way—and we obtain it as an instantly perceivable whole. . . .[13]

THE MORALITY OF THE PRODUCERS*

III

Before examining the qualities which modern economy requires of *free producers,* we must analyze the components of morality. Philosophers always have some difficulty in seeing clearly into these ethical problems because they maintain the impossibility of unifying ideas which occur simultaneously in a class, but they nevertheless imagine that their duty is to unify everything. In order to succeed in hiding from themselves the fundamental heterogeneity inherent in any civilized morality, they resort to an infinity of subterfuges, sometimes relegating everything that bothers them to the rank of exception, importation or relic; sometimes drowning reality in a sea of vague terms; and, most often, using these two procedures to confuse the question more. I, on the contrary, believe that *a whole, whatever its nature, in the history of ideas cannot be well known unless all its contradictions are brought to light.* I am going to adopt this position, and I will take as my point of departure the famous opposition that Nietzsche established between two groups of moral values, an opposition about which much has been written, but which has not been properly studied.

A) We know how forcefully Nietzsche has praised the values created by *masters,* by a high class of warriors who, in their expeditions, fully enjoy freedom from all social restraint, return to the simplicity of spirit of the wild beast, become triumphant monsters who always bring to mind "the superb blond brute roaming in search of prey and carnage," in whom a hidden bestiality needs an occasional outlet. To understand fully this thesis we should not cling too much to theories which have sometimes been purposely exaggerated, but rather to the historical facts; the author informs us that he has in mind "the Roman, Arab, German or Japanese aristocracy, the *Homeric heroes* and the Scandinavian Vikings."

We should turn especially to the Homeric heroes in order to understand what Nietzsche wanted to explain to his contemporaries. It must be remembered that he had been a professor of Greek at the University of Basel and that he gained his reputation with a book devoted to glorifying Hellenic genius (*The Birth of Tragedy*). He observes that,

* Chapter VII, sections 3–5.

even at the period of their highest culture, the Greeks kept an awareness of their former temperament, that of *masters:* "Our bravery," said
Pericles, "has cleared a path for us on land and sea, everywhere erecting
imperishable monuments for good or evil." The heroes of Hellenic
legend and history fit the description of what he admires in "this
audacity of the noble races, a mad, absurd, spontaneous audacity . . .
their indifference to and their scorn of all physical comforts, of life, of
well-being." Is it not particularly of Achilles in the *Iliad* that one may
speak of "the terrible gaiety and the profound joy that [the heroes]
taste in all destruction, in all the sensual delights of victory and
cruelty"?[1]

It is certainly to the model of classical Greece that Nietzsche is referring when he writes: "The value judgments of the warrior aristocracy
are based on a strong physical constitution, flourishing health, without
forgetting what is necessary for the maintenance of this unbounded
vigor: war, adventure, hunting, dancing, games and physical exercises and
in general everything which implies robust, free and joyous activity."[2]

The archaic type, the Achaean type celebrated by Homer, is not a
simple memory; it has reappeared several times in the world. "During
the Renaissance there was a superb revival of the classical ideal, of the
noble evaluation of all things," and after the Revolution "occurred
all of a sudden the most stupendous and unexpected thing: the ancient
ideal appeared *in person* and with an unusual splendor before the eyes
and the mind of humanity. [At that time] Napolean appeared, a unique
and untimely man if ever there was one."[3]

I believe that if Nietzsche had not been so dominated by his experiences as a professor of classical philology he would have seen that the
master still exists before our very eyes, and that it is he who brings into
being at the present time the amazing greatness of the United States;
he would have been struck by the extraordinary parallels between the
Yankee, capable of any task, and the ancient Greek mariner, sometimes
pirate, sometimes colonist or merchant; above all, he would have established a parallel between the hero of antiquity and the man who dashes
off to the conquest of the Far West.[4] Paul de Rousiers has sketched an
excellent portrait of the prototype of the master: "To become, and remain, American, life must be regarded *as a struggle* and not as a pleasure; one must seek victorious effort, energetic and effective action, more
than amusement, more than leisure embellished by the cultivation of
the arts and the refinements peculiar to other societies. Everywhere . . .
we have discovered what makes the American succeed, what constitutes
his nature; it is moral value, personal, active and creative energy."[5] The
same profound scorn that the Greek had for the barbarian, the Yankee
has for the foreign worker who makes absolutely no effort to become

truly American. "Many of those people would be better if we took heed
of them," said an old Civil War colonel to the French traveler, "but
we are an imperious race"; a Pottsville shopkeeper called the Pennsyl-
vania miners a "population devoid of reason."[6] J. Bourdeau has pointed
out the strange similarity which exists between the ideas of Andrew
Carnegie and Roosevelt, and those of Nietzsche: Carnegie deploring the
wasting of money on the support of incompetents, Roosevelt appealing
to Americans to become conquerors, a race of predators.[7]

I am not one of those who regards the Achaean type sung by Homer
—the untamed hero, trusting to his strength and placing himself above
the rules—as bound to disappear in the future. If we have often believed that he will vanish in the future, it is because we have imagined
that the Homeric values were irreconcilable with other values born of
an entirely different principle; Nietzsche committed this error, an unavoidable one for all those who believe in the necessity of unity of
thought. It is quite obvious that freedom would be gravely compromised
if men came to look upon Homeric values (which are quite close to
those held by Corneille) as being suitable only to barbarian peoples.
A great number of moral problems would cease to force humanity to
progress if some rebellious person did not force the people to examine
their consciences. And art, which counts for something also, would lose
the finest laurel in its wreath.

Philosophers are ill disposed to admit the right of art to maintain the
cult of the "will to power"; they think that they should give lessons to
the artists without receiving any in return; they hold that only sentiments licensed by the universities have the right to reveal themselves
in poetry. Art, like the economy, has never bowed to the requirements
of ideologues; it disturbs their plans for social harmony. Humanity has
found too much freedom in art to dream of subordinating it to the
fabricators of sociological platitudes. Marxists are used to seeing the
ideologues take things in reverse and, in contrast to their opponents,
they should look upon art as a reality which gives birth to ideas and not
as an application of ideas.

B) Against values constructed by masters, Nietzsche contrasts the
system constructed by priestly castes, the ascetic ideal upon which he
has heaped so much invective. The history of these values is much more
unclear and complicated than that of the preceding values. The German
author tries to link the origin of asceticism to physiological causes which
I will not examine here. He is certainly mistaken when he attributes a
dominant role to the Jews; it does not at all appear that ancient Judaism
had an ascetic character; undoubtedly, like the other Semitic religions,
it attached some importance to pilgrimages, to fasts and to prayers
uttered in sackcloth. The Hebrew poets sang of a hope of revenge which

existed in the heart of the persecuted; but up until the second century of the Christian era, the Jews demanded that this revenge be with weapons.[8] Besides, with them, family life was too strong for the monastic ideal to become important.

No matter how steeped in Christianity our modern civilization may be, it is nonetheless obvious that even in the Middle Ages it was subjected to influences foreign to the Church, so that the old ascetic values were transformed little by little. The values most esteemed by the contemporary world and which it regards as the true "virtuous values" are not realized in convents but in the family. Respect for the human person, sexual fidelity and devotion to the weak constitute elements of morality of which all men of elevated sentiment are proud. Very often morality is reduced to that definition.

When one examines critically the many current writings on the subject of marriage, one sees that the serious reformers propose to perfect family relations in such a way as to assure a better realization of these virtuous values; thus it is requested that scandals of conjugal life not be exposed before tribunals, that unions not be maintained when fidelity no longer exists, that the protection of the heads of families not be diverted from its moral purpose to become exploitative, etc.

On the other hand, it is curious to note how much the modern Church ignores these values which Christian-classical civilization produced; the Church sees in marriage above all a chance for financial and worldly interests; it has an extreme indulgence for amorous intrigue; it does not want to allow a union to be broken when the household is a living hell, and does not take any account of the obligation for complete devotion. Priests come to terms nicely in order to procure rich dowries for impoverished nobles, to the point that the Church has been vulnerable to the accusation of considering marriage as a joining of gentlefolk living as bullies and bourgeois women reduced to the role of servants. If one remunerates it generously enough, the Church has unexpected reasons for divorce and finds means of annulling inconvenient unions for ridiculous reasons: Proudhon ironically asks, "Can a serious man, a serious mind, a true Christian, have concern for the love of his wife? . . . All well and good if the husband who asks for a divorce or the wife who desires a separation alleges the refusal of conjugal rights: then the rupture would take place, since the service for which marriage was granted was not fulfilled."[9]

Two very grave consequences have arisen because our civilization has come to the point of having nearly all morality consist of values derived from those observed in the normally constituted family: first, one wonders if, instead of viewing the family as being the result of moral theories, it would not be more exact to say that the family is the basis of these theories. Second, it seems that the Church, having become incompetent in matters which concern sexual union, must also be incompetent in morality. Indeed, Proudhon came to these conclusions: "Nature has made sexual duality as a vehicle for Justice. . . . To produce justice is the superior aim of bisexual division: procreation and what results does not come into play here except as an accessory."[10] "Marriage, by its principle and its purpose, being the very voice of human *right,* the living negation of divine right, is in formal contradiction with theology and the Church."[11]

Love, through the enthusiasm which it engenders, can produce the sublime without which there would be absolutely no effective morality. Proudhon has written at the end of his book on justice some pages which will never be excelled concerning the role which belongs to woman.

C) Finally, we have to examine some values which escape Nietzsche's classification and which concern civil relations. In the beginning, magic was involved in the evaluation of these values; amongst the Jews, until recent times, we see a mixture of hygienic precepts, sexual rules, advice on integrity, goodwill or national solidarity—the whole enveloped in magical superstitions; this mixture, which appears strange to the philosopher, had the most felicitous influence on morality as long as the Jews practiced their traditional manner of living; and one notices among them even today a particular conscientiousness in the execution of contracts.

The ideas current among modern moralists derive largely from decadent Greece. Aristotle, living in an age of transition, combined ancient values with the values which were increasingly dominant. War and production had ceased to concern the most distinguished people in the towns, who sought to assure themselves an agreeable life; the important thing was to establish friendly relations among refined men, and the fundamental rule was therefore that of the golden mean. The new morality was acquired mainly through habits which the young Greek had to take up by frequenting a cultivated society. Here we are in the realm of consumer morality; one should not be surprised if some Catholic theologians still find Aristotle's ethics excellent, since they too have the consumer perspective.

In the civilization of antiquity, the morality of the producer could hardly be more than that of the slave master, and it did not appear to merit long examination during the period when philosophy was cataloging Greek customs. Aristotle says that it does not require a very elevated and extensive knowledge to employ slaves: "It consists solely in knowing how to *command what the slaves must know how to do.* Thus, as soon as the master can spare himself this trouble, he delegates responsibility to a steward in order to devote himself to political life or to philosophy."[12] A little further on he writes: "It is therefore necessary to acknowledge that the master must be the source of the slave's particular virtue, although he does not, in his role of master, have to teach him his work."[13] There we are firmly in the realm of the concerns of an urban consumer, who regards as a serious nuisance any obligation to lend the least attention to the conditions of production.[14]

As for the slave, he will only need a very weak sort of virtue: "He will have the virtue necessary not to neglect his work through intemperance or laziness." It is advisable to treat him with "even more indulgence than children," although certain persons believe that slaves are deprived of reason and are not fit for anything except to receive orders.[15]

It is easy to observe that for a very long time the moderns have not thought that there was anything else to say about workers besides what Aristotle said of them: they shall be given orders, they shall be scolded gently like children, they shall be treated as passive instruments that have no need to think. Revolutionary syndicalism would be impossible if the workers' world were under such a "morality of the weak"; on the other hand, state socialism would get along perfectly with such an ethic since state socialism is founded on the division of society into a class of producers and a class of thinkers applying to production the doctrines of science. The only difference which would exist between this so-called socialism and capitalism would consist in the use of more ingenious procedures for obtaining discipline in the workshop.

The official moralists of socialism are working at the present time to create the means of moral government which would replace the vague religion that Gustave de Molinari believes necessary to capitalism. It is quite obvious indeed that religion is losing its effectiveness among the people every day; something else must be found to give intellectuals the means of continuing to live on the fringes of production.

IV

The problem which we are now going to seek to resolve is the most difficult of all those that the socialist writer can touch upon; we are going to ask ourselves how it is possible to conceive of the transition of the men of today to the state of free producers working in a factory without masters. We must state the question precisely; we do not pose it for an already socialist world, but only for our time and for the preparation of the transition from one world to another; if we did not make this limitation we would fall into utopianism.

Kautsky is highly concerned with what would happen the day after a social revolution; he proposes a solution which seems to me as feeble as Molinari's: if syndicates are strong enough to make present-day workers decide to abandon their workshops and to endure great sacrifices during sustained strikes against capitalists, they will doubtless be strong enough to bring back the workers to the workshop and to obtain excellent regular work from them, when it is recognized that this work is demanded by the general interest.[16] Kautsky does not appear, moreover, to have great confidence in the excellence of his solution.

Obviously no comparison can be established between a discipline which imposes on workers a general stoppage of work and that which can lead them to put machines into operation with singular efficiency. The error comes from the fact that Kautsky is much more of an ideologist than a disciple of Marx; he likes to discuss abstractions and believes he has advanced a solution when he has succeeded in grouping together words with a scientific appearance; the underlying reality interests him less than the scholastic decor. Many others, moreover, have committed the same error and have let themselves be duped by the variety of meanings of the word "discipline"—it is understood just as well to mean steady conduct based on the ardors of a profound soul as it is to mean external restraint.

The history of the old guilds does not supply any really useful information; it does not seem that they ever had the effect of inciting any progressive movement whatsoever; it seems rather that they served to protect routine. When one examines English trade-unionism closely there is no doubt that it is equally imbued with industrial routine, which derives from the spirit of the guilds.

Nor is the example of democracy capable of throwing any light on the question. Work conducted democratically would be regulated by orders, watched over by a police force and submitted to the sanction of tribunals distributing fines or imprisonment. Discipline would be an external restraint quite similar to what exists today in capitalist factories, but it would probably be still more arbitrary because of the electoral calculations of committees. When we reflect on the singularities which are presented by judgments in penal matters, we are easily convinced that repression would be exercised in a very unsatisfactory way. It is generally agreed that small misdemeanors cannot easily be judged by tribunals according to the rules of a rigorous judicial system; it has often been proposed that administrative councils be established to decree on the fate of children; in Belgium begging is submitted to an administrative arbitrariness that can be compared to the policing of morals; it is known that this policing, in spite of innumerable complaints, continues to be almost supreme in France. It is even noticeable that for misdemeanors, administrative intervention is becoming stronger every day because heads of penitentiary services are being granted, more and more, the power of reducing or even of doing away with sentences; doctors and sociologists preach widely on behalf of this system which tends to give the police as large a role as it had in the Old Regime. Experience shows that the system of the capitalist workshop is much superior to that of the police, so much so that it is hard to see how it would be possible to perfect capitalist discipline by means of democratic procedures.[17]

I think there is some truth in Kautsky's hypothesis; he felt that the motive behind the revolutionary movement should also be the motive behind the morality of the producers; here is a view fully in harmony with Marxist principles, but we can apply this idea in an entirely different way than Kautsky did. One should not believe that the action of the syndicate on labor is direct, as he supposes; its influence must result from mediation.

We arrive at a satisfactory result by starting from some very curious analogies which exist among the most remarkable qualities of the soldiers who fought in the wars of liberty, the qualities inspired by propaganda in favor of the general strike and the qualities which must be expected of a free worker in a highly progressive society. I believe that these analogies constitute a new (and perhaps decisive) argument in favor of revolutionary syndicalism.

During the wars of liberty, each soldier considered himself an important person with something very important to do in battle, rather than regarding himself as only a cog in a military machine entrusted to the supreme direction of a master. In the literature of that time, the free men of the republican armies are continually contrasted to the *automatons* of the royalist armies; these were not rhetorical figures manipulated by French writers. I am convinced, through an intensive and personal study of one of the wars of this period, that these terms corresponded perfectly to the actual sentiments of the soldier.

Battles, therefore, could no longer be put in the framework of a chess game in which the man is comparable to a pawn; they became compilations of heroic exploits accomplished by individuals who drew the motives of their conduct from their own enthusiasm. Revolutionary literature is not totally deceptive when it reports such a great number of grandiloquent words supposedly uttered by the combatant. Undoubtedly none of these phrases were pronounced by the people to whom they are attributed. The form is the product of men of letters accustomed to manipulating classical declamation; however, the content is real, in the sense that we have (thanks to the falsehoods of revolutionary rhetoric) a perfectly exact representation of the perspective under which the combatants viewed war, the true expression of the feelings it stirred and the very mood of the Homeric battles which then took place. I do not think that any one of the actors in these dramas ever protested the words which were ascribed to him; that is because each rediscovered his own intimate soul amidst fanciful embellishments.[18]

Until the time Napoleon appeared, war did not have the scientific character which later strategical theorists sometimes believed should be attributed to it; deceived by the similarity that they found between the triumphs of the Revolutionary armies and those of the Napoleonic armies, historians imagined that the generals before Napoleon made great campaign plans; such plans did not exist or had but a minute influence on the progress of operations. The best officers of that time realized that their talent consisted in furnishing their troops with the material means of expressing their enthusiastic outburst; victory was assured each time the soldiers could give free rein to all their spirit without being hindered by the bad administration of supplies and by the stupidity of people's representatives masquerading as strategists. On the battlefield, those in charge gave the example of the boldest courage and were merely the first combatants, like true Homeric kings: this is what explains the great prestige that was immediately acquired by so many sub-officers of the Old Regime, who were elevated to the highest ranks by the unanimous acclamation of the soldiers at the beginning of the war.

If one tried to discover the form of discipline in these first armies, one could say that the soldier was convinced that the slightest lapse of the lowest of the troops could endanger the success of the group and the lives of all his comrades—and the soldier acted accordingly. This assumes that no account is taken of the relative values of the factors which constitute victory, so that everything is considered from a qualitative and individualistic point of view. Indeed, one is overwhelmed by the individualistic qualities encountered in these armies, and one finds nothing which resembles the obedience discussed by present-day authors. Thus, it is not entirely inexact to say that the incredible French victories were due to "intelligent bayonets."[19]

The same spirit is found in workers' groups which embrace the general strike; indeed these groups envisage revolution as an immense uprising that can again be called individualistic: each one marching with as much ardor as possible, operating on his own account, scarcely concerning himself with subordinating his behavior to a carefully constructed overall plan. This characteristic of the proletarian general strike has been pointed out many times and it is not a characteristic without power to terrify greedy politicians who understand perfectly that a revolution led in this manner would do away with any chance for them to take possession of the government.

Jaurès, whom no one would dream of calling uninformed, has very well recognized the danger threatening him; he accuses the partisans of the general strike of fragmenting life and of thus going against revolution.[20] This gibberish should be interpreted as follows: revolutionary syndicalists want to exalt the individuality of the life of the producer; hence they go against the interests of the politicians, who would like to direct the revolution in a way that would give the power to a new minority; they undermine the foundations of the State. We are perfectly in agreement with Jaurès's interpretation and it is just this characteristic (frightening for parliamentary socialists, financiers and ideologists) that gives such extraordinary moral significance to the action of the general strike.

The partisans of the general strike are accused of having anarchist tendencies; indeed, it has been observed that anarchists have been entering the syndicates in great numbers for some years, and they have worked hard to develop tendencies favorable to the general strike.

This movement is understood perfectly when we go back to the preceding explanations; for the general strike, like the wars of liberty, is the most dazzling manifestation of the *individualist strength* in the aroused masses. It seems, moreover, that official socialists would do well not to insist so much on this point, for they thus risk inspiring reflections which would not be to their advantage. Indeed, one is led to think that our official socialists, with their passion for discipline and their infinite confidence in the genius of leaders, are the authentic inheritors of the royalist armies, while the anarchists and the partisans of the general strike would today represent the spirit of the revolutionary warriors who whipped the beautiful coalition armies so soundly and against all the rules of the art. I understand that endorsed socialists, controlled and duly patented by the administrators of *Humanité,* have little taste for the heroes of the battle of Fleurus;[21] these warriors were very poorly dressed and would have cut a bad figure in the salons of the great financiers; but everyone does not subordinate his thought to the conveniences of Jaurès's cohorts.

V

We are now going to try to point out some analogies which will show how revolutionary syndicalism is the great educational force possessed by contemporary society for preparing the work of the future.

A) The free producer in a highly progressive workshop must never measure his efforts in relationship to an external norm; he finds all the models presented to him mediocre, and wishes to surpass everything that has been done before him. Production thus is assured of improving in quality and in quantity; the idea of indefinite progress is made real in such a workshop.

The old socialists had an inkling of this law when they asked that everyone produce according to his abilities, but they did not know how to explain their rule which, in their utopias, seemed more suitable to a convent or a family than a modern society. Sometimes, nevertheless, they fancied that the people of their utopias would have an ardor similar to that which history tells us about certain great artists: this last point of view is not unimportant, even though the old socialists barely understood the value of this comparison.

Every time that a question relating to industrial progress is raised, art is looked upon as an *anticipation* of the highest production—although the artist, with his whims, often seems to be the opposite of the modern worker.[22] This analogy is justified by the fact that the artist does not like to reproduce stereotypes; *the infinite nature of his will* distinguishes him from the common artisan who mainly succeeds in the unlimited reproduction of types which he did not create. The inventor is an artist who wears himself out in pursuing the accomplishment of ends which practical people most often declare absurd, and who is easily regarded as mad if he has made an important discovery; practical people are like artisans. In all industries, one could cite considerable improvements which have originated in small changes effected by workers endowed with the artist's taste for innovation.

This state of mind is again exactly the same as that seen in the first armies which fought the wars of liberty and the same as that seen in the propagandists of the general strike. This passionate individualism would be completely missing in working classes receiving their education from politicians; they would no longer be fit for anything except changing masters. Bad leaders truly hope that it will be so, and stockbrokers would not give them any money if they were not persuaded that parliamentary socialism is very compatible with the pillages wrought by finance.

B) Modern industry is characterized by an ever-growing concern for exactitude; in proportion as the tools of production become more scientific, it is required that the product present fewer hidden faults and that it be of lasting quality living up to its appearance.

If Germany has not yet won its rightful place in the economic world by dint of its mineral-rich soil, the energy of its businessmen and the knowledge of its technicians, this is due to the fact that for a long time its manufacturers believed that it was clever to flood the market with inferior goods; although German production has been greatly improved for some time, it does not yet enjoy very high regard.

Here we can, once again, compare highly perfected industry and art. There have been periods during which the public especially appreciated the means by which illusions were created, but these methods have never been accepted in the *grandes écoles* and they are universally condemned by authorities on aesthetics.[23]

This integrity, which seems today as necessary in industry as in art, was hardly suspected by the utopians.[24] Fourier, an early utopian, believed that deception about the quality of merchandise was a characteristic trait of relations between civilized men; he turned his back on progress and showed himself incapable of understanding the world which was forming around him; like almost all the professional prophets, this alleged seer confused the future with the past. Marx was to say, on the contrary, that "cheating on merchandise is unjust in the capitalist system of production" because it no longer corresponds to the modern system of business affairs.[25]

The soldier of the wars of liberty attached an almost superstitious importance to the accomplishment of the smallest command. Hence, he felt no pity for the generals or the officials whom he saw guillotined after some defeat, charged with failure in performance of their duty; he did not understand these events in the same way as the historian of today; he had no means of knowing if the condemned had really committed treason; the lack of success could only be explained in his eyes by some very serious mistake attributable to his leaders. The lofty sentiment which the soldier had of his own duty and the excessive honesty that he brought to bear on the execution of the smallest command led him to approve rigorous measures taken against men who seemed to him to have caused the misfortune of the army and occasioned the loss of the fruit of so much heroism.

It is not difficult to see that the same spirit is found during strikes, when the defeated workers are persuaded that their lack of success is due to the villainy of certain comrades who have not done all that was rightfully expected of them; numerous accusations of treason are produced, because only treason can explain, for the defeated master, the overthrow of heroic troops; many violent acts must thus be attributed to the sentiment which everyone has acquired, that of the integrity which must be brought to bear in the accomplishment of tasks. I do not believe that the authors who have written of the events which follow strikes have reflected enough on the analogy between strikes and the wars of liberty, and consequently between these violent acts and the executions of generals accused of treason.[26]

C) There would never be great prowess in war if each soldier, while conducting himself as a heroic individual, aspired to receive a reward proportionate to his merit. When an assault column is launched, the men who march at its head know that they are sent to death and that glory will be for those who climb over their dead bodies, and enter enemy territory; nevertheless, they do not reflect on this great injustice at all and they go forward.

When in an army the need for rewards makes itself keenly felt, it can be affirmed that its value is at a low ebb. Officers who had engaged in the campaigns of the Revolution and the Empire, but who only served under the direct orders of Napoleon during the last years of their career, were very surprised to see so much attention paid to feats of arms which, in their youth, would have passed unnoticed: "I was covered with praises," said General Duhesne, "for things which would not have been noticed in the army of Sambre-et-Meuse."[27] This charlatanism was pushed to grotesque extremes by Murat, and historians have not sufficiently noted Napoleon's responsibility in this degeneration of the true warrior spirit. He was a stranger to that great enthusiasm of the men of 1794 which accomplished so many marvels; he believed that it was for him to measure all ability and to attribute to each a reward exactly proportionate to what he had accomplished; here already the Saint-Simon principle was entering into practice[28] and every officer was urged to make himself count. Charlatanism exhausted the moral forces of the nation, whereas the material forces were still quite considerable; Napoleon trained very few distinguished general officers and mostly fought with those whom the Revolution had bequeathed him. This inability constitutes the most absolute condemnation of the system.[29]

The paucity of information that we possess on the great gothic artists has often been noted. Among the stonecutters who sculpted images for cathedrals there were men of superior talent who seem to have remained indistinguishable from the mass of their fellow-workers. They produced masterpieces nonetheless. Viollet-le-Duc found it strange that the archives of Notre Dame have not preserved any details of the construction of this enormous monument and that in general the documents of the Middle Ages are very sparing in information about architects; he adds that "genius can develop outside the limelight and its very essence is to seek silence and obscurity."[30] One could even go further and wonder if their contemporaries suspected that these artists of genius were erecting edifices of imperishable glory; it seems very likely that cathedrals were admired by the artists alone.

This drive toward excellence, which is manifested in spite of the absence of all personal immediate and proportional reward, constitutes the *secret virtue* which assures continued progress in the world. What would become of modern industry if there were inventors only for things that procure them a more or less certain remuneration? The job of inventor is the most miserable of all, and yet it is never abandoned.

In workrooms, how often have slight modifications in work by ingenious workers resulted in bringing about increasingly profound improvements without the innovators ever extracting any lasting or appreciable benefit form their ingeniousness? And has not even simple piece-work managed to engender a slow but uninterrupted progress in productivity, a progress that after having temporarily improved the situation of a few workers and especially that of their patrons, ends by profiting buyers above all?

Renan wondered what causes the heroes of great wars to act: "The soldier under Napoleon told himself that he would always be a poor man, but he felt that the epic in which he was taking part would be eternal, that he would live in the glory of France." The Greeks fought for glory; the Russians and the Turks are being killed because they expect an illusory paradise. "A soldier is not made with the promise of temporal rewards. He needs immortality. Instead of paradise, there is glory, which is also a sort of immortality."[31]

Economic progress goes far beyond the immediate time in which productive advances are made and benefits future generations much more than those who create it; but does it yield glory? Is there an economic epic which can awaken enthusiasm in the workers? The impetus to immortality, which Renan saw as so powerful, is obviously without effect here, for artists have never been seen to produce masterpieces under the influence of the idea that this work would procure them a place in paradise (in the same way as the Turks have themselves killed in order to enjoy the happiness promised by Mohammed). Workers are not even completely wrong when they regard religion as a bourgeois luxury, for religion has no resources to improve machines and to yield means of working more rapidly.

It is necessary to pose the question differently from the way Renan proposed it. We should know whether there is, in the world of producers, any force of enthusiasm capable of combining with the morality of good work, in such a way that in our days of crisis this ethic can acquire all the authority necessary to lead society onto the path of economic progress.

The very keen sense that we have of the need of such a morality and the ardent desire that we have of seeing it realized should not induce us to accept phantoms as powers capable of stirring the world. The abundant idyllic literature of professors of rhetoric is obviously pure vanity. Equally vain are the efforts made by so many scholars to find past institutions to imitate, which would be capable of disciplining their contemporaries: imitation has never done much good and has often engendered many disappointments. Is it not absurd to think of taking from defunct social structures means to control a productive economy which is necessarily and increasingly in contradiction with preceding economies? Is there no hope then?

Morality is not destined to perish because its driving force will be changed; it is not condemned to become a simple collection of precepts if it can still ally itself to an enthusiasm capable of overcoming all the obstacles put in its path by routine, prejudices and the need for immediate enjoyment. But it is certain that this supreme force will never be found by following the paths that contemporary philosophers, experts in social science and inventors of *sweeping reform,* would have us take. There is only one force which can produce this enthusiasm today without which there is no possible morality; it is the power which results from propaganda in favor of the general strike.

The preceding explanations have shown that the idea of the general strike, constantly rejuvenated by the sentiments induced by proletarian violence, produces an heroic state of mind and, at the same time, pushes all the powers of the soul toward conditions which allow the realization of a freely functioning and immensely progressive workshop; we have thus recognized that there are great connections between the sentiments of the general strike and those which are necessary to induce continued progress in production. We have, therefore, the right to maintain that the modern world possesses the primary motivating power to assure the morality of producers.

I stop here because it seems to me that I have accomplished the task which I set myself; I have established, in effect, that proletarian violence has an historical significance completely different from that attributed it by superficial scholars and politicians. In the total ruin of institutions and customs there still remains something powerful, something new and intact; it is what constitutes, to properly speak, the soul of the revolutionary proletariat; and that will not be carried away in the general decadence of moral values if the workers have enough energy to bar the way to bourgeois corrupters by responding to their advances with a most intelligible brutality.

I believe I have brought to bear a considerable contribution to discussions on socialism; this discussion must henceforth deal with the conditions which permit the development of specifically proletarian forces, that is to say, *violence enlightened by the idea of the general strike.* All the old, abstract dissertations become useless for the future socialist regime; we pass on to the domain of real history, to the interpretation of facts, to ethical evaluations of the revolutionary movement.

The bond which I noted at the beginning of this research between socialism and proletarian violence now appears to us in all its force. It is to violence that socialism owes the high moral values by which it brings salvation to the modern world.

CHAPTER 7

from

Materials for a Theory of the Proletariat

INTRODUCTION

I

. . . Benedetto Croce, a highly respected authority as a critic of Marx, declared a few years ago that socialism is dead.[1] In his view, Marx had dreamed of a magnificent epic that inspired legitimate enthusiasm. On the faith of the best socialist writers, many young people believed that somewhere an heroic proletariat existed, the creator of a new system of values, called upon to found very shortly a civilization of producers on the ashes of capitalist society. In fact the German worker is in the process of becoming wiser; he is enlisting in the ranks of democracy, and instead of sacrificing everything to the idea of the class struggle, he is concerned, along with the bourgeoisie, with the general interests of his country.[2] The readers who agree with the eminent Croce that Marx's revolution is a chimera[3] will not be surprised to see that I felt much uncertainty when I was pondering how the essential aspects of Marxist doctrines could be realized. Those familiar with psychological research will certainly not regret that circumstances suggested to me that I examine the field of contemporary experience by approaching it from different directions, because I have thus had the opportunity of grasping many details which might have escaped an excessively one-sided observer. The multiplicity of the opinions which I have successively adopted will not fail to draw the attention of metaphysicians, who will find in them a particularly striking example of the freedom of the mind when it speculates on the results of history.

II

Today if I re-examined the questions which are treated in this work, I would follow the principles put forth in the 1910 appendix to the *Réflexions sur la violence*. Obviously I would sometimes reach different conclusions from those reached in a time when I was guided by the inspiration of chance discoveries; but the new formulations could no more be categorized into a general structure than can the disjointed pieces collected in this volume. Indeed, I wrote in the work just cited:

> In order to study the most important phenomena of history, social philosophy is obliged to proceed to a "diremption," to examine certain parts without taking into account all their connections with the whole; to determine, in some way, the nature of their activity by isolating them. When it has attained the most perfect knowledge in this way, social philosophy can no longer try to reconstruct the broken unity.[4]

By taking my inspiration from this theory, I have been able to dwell at length on proletarian violence while leaving aside the juridical aspects of the conflicts which lead to violent strikes, the political regime of the country and the institutions that enable the working family to improve its everyday conditions of existence.

Do not think that I pretend to have invented a *novum organum*. The method just discussed has long been used by philosophers for various purposes with some degree of success. However, it seems to me that its true significance has frequently been misunderstood. Rather than representing things, this method produces symbols in which phenomena participate, sometimes in a rather obvious way, sometimes in a distant and complex way, impossible to define.[5] According to my idea of metaphysics, reason has a double mission when we turn to civic matters: (1) Reason should be prepared to use fully our constructive faculties which, after we have practiced "diremption," can give us a symbolic knowledge of what history creates by means beyond our intelligence. (2) With the aid of this speculation, reason should clarify practice so as to help us guide ourselves as wisely as possible in our day-to-day difficulties. The merits of the method indicated here are placed in full light when we try to make historical phenomena enter the realm of

the free spirit. This symbolism fills them with life, exalts the psychological qualities that constitute the true cause of the importance given to
memorable actions by thoughtful people, whereas common rationalism
annuls these qualities in constricting reality within the bounds of skeletal
abstractions. Now art, religion and philosophy flourish only when they
are in contact with an overflowing vitality. This will be well understood
by examining some of the more notable creations suggested by history
to the free spirit.

(a) Greece raised the art of celebrating the great feats of her children
so high that Renan was inclined to attribute to her the invention of the
idea of glory. Greece was thus well deserving of civilization in endowing
it with a purpose in life that possessed "unequaled value." On the faith
of the masters of literature, the West believed that "the important thing
for man is what will be said of him after his death; that present life is
subordinate to the after-life; that to sacrifice oneself for one's reputation
is a wise motive."[6] Consequently its historians wrote to preserve the
memory of the valiant warriors who had accomplished acts of marvelous
self-sacrifice with a view to acquiring the right to the admiration of
future generations.[7] The example of Alexander shows that in the bosom
of a refined society, when the immense majority of enlightened people
are thinking only of securing themselves a peaceful existence,[8] at a time
when philosophy seems to have suppressed for all time ancestral worship, a prince can, thanks to the Hellenic aesthetic, revive the mythology
of conquering gods.[9] The Renaissance was intoxicated with accounts of
the wonderful adventures undertaken by individuals with indomitable
energy, to the extent that it too often forgot any thought of moral
criticism. The dreadful wars that marked the end of the eighteenth
century and the beginning of the nineteenth gave a supremacy to the
ideas of classical antiquity that had been lost since the fall of the Roman
Empire. Napoleon would perhaps have become a new Alexander if,
during the years when his legend could have been formed, romanticism
had not repressed what it called the paganism of the Renaissance in the
name of a Christian, Germanic and medieval aesthetic.[10]

(b) In the time of the barbarians the army leaders sought to increase
their strength by hurling magical curses against their enemies; by
humbly soliciting the support of mysterious powers whose intervention
primitive men feared; by promising a large share of booty to divinities
with crude appetites. As the religious spirit developed at the expense
of old superstitions, only beings who possessed the most perfect qualities
that the mind could imagine were placed above the world. Finally, in
grave circumstances, the actors of the dramas, either private or social,
were dominated by the idea that they were being watched by an infinitely just God, from whom no secret of the soul could escape, and

who takes pity on every misfortune. Renan has exposed this way of conceiving of the role of the supernatural in a passage that has perhaps not sufficiently attracted the attention of philosophers: "To act for God, to act in the presence of God, are conceptions necessary for a virtuous life. We do not ask for a reward, but we do desire a witness.[11] . . . Unknown sacrifices, misunderstood virtue, the inevitable errors of human justice, the irrefutable calumnies of history legitimize or rather inevitably bring an appeal to the conscience of the universe by the conscience oppressed by fatality.[12] This is a right which the virtuous man will never renounce."[13] In the course of these reflections, it appears that Renan was thinking of little else but the events of his own life; but the interest of his book increases greatly when it is seen in the light of history and applied to the religious aspects of mass upheavals. Notably, I believe that the sentiment of the divine presence gave life to Mazzinian politics in the time when it appeared to governments as only a pipedream of fanatics.

(c) The idea that there exists some finality in the whole of the contingencies whose details seem to depend on independent causes; the faith of human groups in a mission which has been entrusted to them; the certainty of a success pursued over a multitude of obstacles—there one has strength of the first order which, when projected in the midst of the chances of history, can group numerous wills in such a durable way that they fashion movements[14] adapted to their nature. When the Solomon monarchy collapsed, the Jews drew such elements of life from the marvelous promises popularized by the books of its prophets and psalmists, which were read avidly by the exiles, that they were never so sure of their Mosaic faith until after the loss of their territory. The Christian conquest would probably astonish our scholars much less if they contrasted with the discouragement aroused in the defenders of the old Roman institutions by the tribulations of empire, the feeling of power inspired in the Church by the conviction that it formed the advance guard of the army of saints. Catholicism, full of confidence in the help promised by Christ to the successors of the apostles, took beautiful revenge on the Reformation when Protestantism deserted the Biblical spirit of its foundation and sought to transform itself into the literary expression of an ideal nourished on scholarly vanities and capable of provoking, at the most, the vague hope of vague utopias which have no hold on truly strong souls.

Two very different meanings are given to the term "philosophy of history." According to ordinary rationalism, such a philosophy speculates on the morphological development of institutions, ideas or customs; if one takes the viewpoint opposite to the one we have taken in this study of the free spirit, it must be said that it is a matter of the control which a philosophy is capable of exercising on the living realities of history. Renan saw "in the Book of Daniel the first attempt at the philosophy of history";[15] for a long time the Greeks had been tracing schematic tableaux to define the successions of political forms of which the psychological development of a city can be composed. But Renan, rightly disdaining these abstractions and placing himself on the terrain of Christian origins, wanted to show that the Book of Daniel[16] is a document of primary importance for the philosophy of history, because it has suggested to the Christian conscience some of its more useful myths.[17]

III

The sound interpretation of the symbols examined here collides with the illusions accepted by a very large number of our contemporaries, who have been persuaded that it is possible to ascertain *scientifically* the general drift of the things which most interest civilization. They concede that it would be highly rash to announce the imminent arrival of a political event, considering that one could name numerous errors, sometimes enormous or even funny, committed by illustrious statesmen led astray by the untoward ambition to make such prophecies. But they firmly believe that a good understanding of the totality of the past would allow sociologists to gain perceptions of future totalities that were very likely. Our symbols have a greater clarity than any of the other expressions that could be included in a schematic description of the mass of centuries. That is why the professionals of historical scientism seize them avidly, without asking themselves the cause of this beneficial clarity.[18] Every pragmatic critic will observe that it is absurd to try to profit from *diremption* in order to obtain clarity and to forget what *diremption* is when one makes use of what it has produced. One is thus liable to fall into grave sophisms by using our symbols in conditions which are irreconcilable with the nature of their formation. Their meaning becomes vague, their usage arbitrary, and consequently, their clarity deceptive. As long as historical scientism exercises the influence on minds which it now does, it will be difficult to use our symbols without sharing some of the misunderstanding favored by this scientism. We are thus led to ask ourselves the reasons for the dangerous authority given to a theory which cannot at all be justified scientifically.[19]

In many authors it rather astonishingly resembles the most hazardous parts of Peripatetic physics. At times Aristotle wonders what would happen in the case of certain bodies going beyond the limits of the experiment to the point where some of their important characteristics could be called null or infinite. To guide him in these radical concepts he has only observations made without precise measuring instruments under the crudest and most imprecise scientific conditions and within the very restricted limits which the latter entailed for the ancients. The Greek philosopher wished to establish, by means of demonstration by the absurd, the impossibility of certain hypotheses contrary to the habitual observations of common sense. Today sociologists, who have the ambition of marching in the forefront of progress, take as points of departure several axioms of capitalist economics, viewed moreover with polemical intentions in mind. From this they jump into the abyss of prehistory, then take off into the heavens where they construct happy cities; they intend to lead their readers to believe that their dreams are perfectly scientific. Such aberrations make us think that the successes of historical scientism are connected to man's powerful psychological impulses to want to be deceived.

(a) In all countries, democracy seeks the destruction of the forces which still keep national traditions slightly alive. The constructions of the past are generally solid enough to resist the pamphleteers who relate to poor devils the absurdities, vices or wrongdoings of certain errant social authorities. The theories of the rational state, by which demagogues propose what the state logically ought to be (as against its development in history), are too abstract to be efficacious in themselves. But these methods of propaganda become quite formidable when the masses are persuaded that the laws of history will make inevitable the plans of the destroyers of history. What conservative writers call the venerable achievements of our ancestors would, to believe the demagogues, be reduced to worldly customs, conventional lies imposed by an absurd education, and to accidents due to the Machiavellian skill of the ruling classes. The seers of progress invoke the laws of history in order to make the proletariat believe that the old restraints could not be maintained for long after the proletariat, finally enlightened on the natural order of societies, and having acquired the clear conscience of its fighting power, has resolved to institute an era in which the will of the majority is sovereign. In the course of the nineteenth century the bourgeoisie was so disturbed by the fear of revolution that it accepted with resignation the demands of democracy, whose inevitable triumph was announced to it by numerous philosophers.[20] The leaders of the radical parties would indeed be naïve if they did not defend with great energy the sophisms of historical scientism which have been so advantageous to them. Their followers, whom they know so well how to fanaticize[21] by arousing their feelings of jealously,[22] by gorging them with utopias and by making them obtain a few minute advantages, regard as execrable reactionaries those who dare to deny that an irresistible force is drawing the modern world toward equality;[23] few bother to confront these outcries.

(b) Historical scientism has contributed a lot to the transformation of the spirit of the French peasant who, to the great surprise of Catholic writers, has become in a few years an irreducible anti-cleric.[24] The plebeian wisdom, which can be found in perfect form in the fields, is affected with a kind of thoughtlessness which is often encountered in timid minds. The common man does not launch into a new enterprise unless he is seduced by the mirage of enormous advantages, which appear almost certain and near fruition; this fact is known by unscrupulous financiers who attract the savings of little people whom they entice with the aid of wondrous prospectuses. Demagogues know this psychology at least as well as the speculators. They repeat frequently in their newspapers that science never ceases to create miracles that are destined to assure the ease of the greatest number when popular reforms are more advanced; that pious practices cannot procure any material advantages to the poor; that consequently little people would be wise to abandon a sterile faith in order to participate in political movements which offer many chances for profit. These arguments take on an extraordinary power when they are combined with the philosophy of history that teachers are charged with bringing to the smallest village. While the priest teaches that the Church is in the process of finally triumphing over all of Satan's powers, the schoolmaster declares that the Church is condemned to undergo more and more serious humiliations, as enlightenment becomes more widespread. The secular doctrine appears more probable to the peasants because its heralds are the harbingers of a scientific vulgarization which amazes them. Anti-clerical historical scientism is today a part of the repertory of the most enduring plebeian passions. Writers who wish to reach the multitudes are obliged to treat it with respect; more than one university scholar looks like an elementary school teacher fighting his parish priest.

(c) In this inquiry into the causes of the prestige of historical scientism, we must not neglect the rivalry which has been established for twenty years between socialists and demagogues, equally desirous of obtaining the allegiance of industrial workers. Marx and Engels had introduced the forecasts of their own imaginations into Hegelian concepts in such a way as to obtain a *monster*,[25] capable of fascinating those adventurous souls who risk navigating in the regions of the social Thule.[26] In 1876 Hegelianism had descended into the graveyard of defunct superstitions, whose gravestones no longer interested anyone except scholars endowed with a special sort of patience.[27] In claiming to be the disciple of a master who was often compared to the enigmatic

Heraclitus, the author of *Capital* assured himself the immense advantages which an obscure exposition procures for a philosopher who has succeeded in seeming profound.[28] Thanks to the persevering efforts of a school which was devoted, enthusiastic and free from any critical spirit,[29] myriad workers were persuaded that the founders of the socialism called "scientific" had described with the certainty of a Laplace describing planetary movements, the principal phases through which the evolution of capitalism would pass, the order of the crises which would shake it and the conditions of its final collapse. But as electoral preoccupations took on more importance in the socialist world, the details of orthodox Marxism were more neglected and only its conclusion was retained: the necessity for a political revolution. Demagogues profited very skillfully from this abatement of socialist thought which became less philosophical, in order to raise themselves in public esteem by appearing as devotees of philosophy. They have proclaimed that the politician should refer to the works undertaken by professors of sociology on the modalities of the revolution destined to suppress capitalism. Thus the university has found itself called on by democracy to give a scientific formulation to the abridged conceptions of socialism. Thanks to this purification in scholarly waters, historical scientism has won a new youth.

IV

There is much truth in William James's schematic tableau of the most widespread philosophical concepts, arranged around the two poles of rationalism and empiricism.[30] Nothing is farther removed from empiricism than the historical scientism studied above; the empiricist treats events as a naturalist treats fauna or land, making sure of the exact configuration of each detail, seeking to define a whole, not fearing to make hypotheses to fill in gaps that his data present. But he would never consent to foretell the future any more than a zoologist would ask whether man is apt to acquire complementary organs. In *Les Illusions du Progrès* I have indicated that after the wars of national independence, historical law, carrying in its wake, ideas of evolution, tradition and local jurisprudence, rose up against natural laws, which the intellectualists of the eighteenth century had so celebrated at the same time as ideas of progress, regeneration or creation, and universal reason.[31] The empiricist who studies human activities turns toward the past where he finds the completed thing, the material of science, history and determinism. Of course anyone has a perfect right to adopt a contrary attitude, to meditate on the future, to consider consequently life, imagination, myths and liberty. But it is absurd to act like the rationalists who, under the hallucination of their unitary prejudices, mix the two genres, and pretend to impose on the second the conditions of the first and thus lose themselves in historical scientism. William James seems to have been particularly shocked by the suppression of the real world effected by the rationalists in favor of an ideal, well-ordered one in which everything is clear. Placing himself on the side of the barbarians, he calls the rationalists overrefined, tender and delicate spirits.[32] It would be quite difficult to define these two groups; yet one cannot help but observe that rationalism shines brilliantly in free-thinking societies, in democratic committees and in literary circles which search for well-turned phrases from a lack of ideas.[33] In most cases rationalism is far from being a sign of intellectualism today. We will now examine how rationalism countermines our symbols.

(a) These symbols sufficiently resemble phenomena seen by common sense to be compared usefully to figures carved out of rock by sculptors with the intention of respecting the general appearance of these natural objects to imaginary spectators. The cosmogony of Plato's *Timaeus* was established according to a principle manifestly derived from this system, since the demiurge imposes geometrical forms (and the properties which correspond to them according to Plato) on primitive masses which were already disposed to acquire the qualities of a superior order they now possess.[34] Greek philosophers believed that the aesthetic genius of their race commanded them to show the possibility of subordinating to the intelligence the (until then) incoherent government of their cities, inspired by procedures used by artists (and by the Platonic demiurge) to overcome the crudeness of matter.[35] Protected by the prestige of the classical tradition, after the Renaissance utopias became a great literary genre which, by simplifying economic, political and psychological questions to the extreme, had a harmful influence on the formation of the revolutionary mind.[36] If it is true to say, with Renan, that our time is devoted to historical studies,[37] their influence has been sovereign only over a very limited elite—so much so that for the majority of our contemporaries the only institutions worthy of an enlightened society are those that give rise to abstractions capable of entering into the fabric of a good novel. The result is that men of letters enjoy very great prestige in the eyes of the apostles of revolution.

(b) When symbols have been pushed far enough along the path of antinomies, it is easy to forget from what historical roots they derive; hence they seem very like those fundamental notions of the sciences about whose origins very few people are aware. Both pass for ideals produced by our minds when they are excited by a prolonged contact with experiment. As philosophers are generally much more interested in the method used in the teaching of a doctrine than by the very essence of the doctrine, they have often believed that a system would merit an absolute confidence if it were capable of being presented as an imitation of ancient geometry, whose rigorous objectivity had never seriously been doubted until the nineteenth century. Descartes gained great glory when he set forth a metaphysical system deduced from postulates that to him seemed quite comparable to those of Euclid and Archimedes.[38] Societies do not offer us data that can be incorporated into such a system. That is why men of the seventeenth and eighteenth centuries regarded history as a rather humble field. As for symbols, when they could at least be arranged more or less easily into a dialectical progression like that of the *Elements,* they were treated as profoundly venerable realities. It then followed that if one day humanity became wise, it would hasten to submit itself to the leadership of masters of philosophy and entrust in their advice; it could then replace the miserable world of history by a world which, adapting itself perfectly to the scholarly disciplines, could be regarded as elevated to the level of the mind.[39]

(c) The prestige enjoyed by social rationalism is due in large part to our habit of dealing with some of the most serious political problems by procedures borrowed from judicial practice. Jurists, in academic arguments, in their conclusions for clients and in the grounds for judgments, ignore the psychological motives that cause individuals to act.[40] They hide real men under what they call legal persons, types of social groups that are supposed to live almost like automatons according to usages fixed in jurisprudence. In the application of laws, however, judges possess a certain arbitrariness which allows them to adapt the rigid forms of legal theory to circumstances, so as not to wound the feelings of equity of the public at large. But these rationalist artifices have been transferred to the discussion of social questions as a consequence of causes that I will outline. It is likely that at all times princes have denounced misdeeds, true or imagined, of peoples against whom they made war, in order to arouse the zeal of their subjects, to obtain the cooperation of hesitant friends and to discourage neutrals from supporting the adverse party.[41] Men particularly skillful in the art of politics must have rather quickly seen that there is a greater chance to obtain the desired results when one thinks only of abstract justice. However, this affectation of lofty serenity never prevented them from using, on occasion, sophisms, lies or flattery in the manner of lawyers seeking to win the sympathy of magistrates.

As it is a rather general law of history that societies imitate in their interior order what has been tried with success in the exterior life of the state,[42] the litigious methods of diplomacy have been applied to social questions in the hope that the opinion of honest men could exercise a determining influence over interested parties, the public authorities and the masters of the national economy. In the course of the imaginary trials which we thus support with the conviction that from them will come some favorable change in institutions, symbols very naturally occupy the place of juridical persons in real trials.[43]

Thus abstract theories, dependent on considerations belonging to the beautiful, the true and the just, become the object of a superstitious respect at certain times.

V

At the end of the Old Regime innumerable lofty minds composed descriptions of the natural state of societies whose elements were borrowed from many sources. These utopias seemed quite superior to what was seen in the real world; but readers of these wondrous novels did not quite know what conclusions should be drawn from this literature.[44] It was necessary to reach the time of the greatest intellectual weakness of Jacobinism for enraged politicians to believe that they could convert these philosophical dreams into proposals for legislation.[45] In general, it seems that the *literati* of the eighteenth century believed that they should, out of loyalty to the progress of enlightenment, admire all those books because they undermined what remained of the authority of medieval traditions; because they spoke with enthusiasm of an indefinable superior morality; because they justified in principle the practical reformers concerned with improving an administration clearly too often defective.

After the Revolution, the appearance of things changed completely. People had seen with disbelief that unheard of upheavals could take place without memorable battles, such as those which bloodied the Roman Empire, Germany and France after the Reformation, or even the England of the Stuarts; that the tempest had been limited to the ordinary exploits of bands of rioters more noisy than fearsome, organized by small associations of "patriots" led by men unworthy of leaving a name in the annals of their country; that, finally, the destiny of the most powerful modern state can depend on miserable machinations as well as on true civil wars. The people, called to give its opinion on numerous constitutions, based on quite differing principles, blindly approved everything that the dominant party presented to it. Thus the will of the infallible sovereign was found to be in fact at the mercy of a few adventurers brought to power by bizarre events. Upheavals, proscription and the emigration of many rich families caused only temporary inconvenience. Governed by excited *parvenus* who were intoxicated with their ephemeral power and always ready to launch armies to plunder

Europe, France was more respected by its neighbors than in the most glorious years of the reign of the Capets. A period of luxurious and lascivious hedonism had succeeded the anguish of the Terror with such speed that the hedonists who had known the Old Regime well could wonder whether the revolutionary cataclysm had not been simply an accident, a brief interruption of the progress toward happiness, caused by the imprudence of blind rulers.[46] Contrary to the very legitimate apprehensions of the magistrates, who feared that the foundations of law were ruined by measures taken to upset the position of traditional property, new juridical doctrines arose which were more favorable to property than those of the most famous writers before the upheaval. Suffering had swept away the world which believed that property is, to a greater or lesser extent, a creation of the legislator; the acquirers of the national wealth required that their property be protected unreservedly by ideology.[47]

Small civil quarrels, crises less serious in reality than appearance, material and juridical progress[48]—such was the outcome of the Revolution. Interpreting these extraordinary experiences from the perspective of the manipulators of abstractions, the rationalists, leaving aside all the complexity of history, said that the French *plebe* had fought in order to introduce into legislation the principles of natural law which the most significant thinkers of the Old Regime had, in vain, shown the masters of royal France: the "man" referred to in the Declaration of Rights is obviously a symbolic being, obtained by a *diremption*[49] and transformed by not-very-perspicacious theorists into the generating factor of the modern order. A generalization of these utopian views led very gradually to the assumption that each time that progress would be facilitated, the forces controlled by the interests, passions and imaginations of the poorest and most numerous class would introduce violently several fragments of theoretical systems into the body of fundamental social rules; this would be done with a view to making the beautiful, the true and the just, as conceived by enlightened minds, triumph over the blind forces of history.[50] Consequently, those who profess to give advice to the ruling classes on the wisest policies have taught that the truly great statesmen, foreseeing shortcomings in their successors,[51] bring about far-reaching reforms. These reforms would spare their country the pain of upheavals, provisional governments and their consequent economic disturbances. The utopians who appeared during the first half of the nineteenth century were inspired by these historical conceptions. They thought that if the informed bourgeoisie had to choose between the anticipation of very probable revolutionary troubles and well thought-out solutions to social problems, it would not hesitate to make great sacrifices in order to conciliate order with progress. Many distinguished

young people, in whom the study of science had inculcated an excessively great confidence in rationalism, let themselves be seduced by
these creators of so-called sciences.

It is in the nature of rationalism to eliminate (as much as possible)
the psychological forces it meets in its path. It thus followed that the
rationalists often shut their eyes to the plebeian forces, however weak,
which had upset the Old Regime, in order to reduce the Revolution to
a triumph of an idea over historical facts. A gigantic experiment thus
showed that the things recognized by philosophers as conforming to the
precepts of reason are destined to become real despite the fact that this
realization occurs amidst accidents which do not deserve the attention
of the rationalists. I will give two other remarkable examples of this
illusion:

(1) When large-scale production had begun to develop in England
it was easily recognized that the prosperity of manufacturing does
not depend on the intervention of the state as much as many skillful ministers had believed, and they had sometimes gone so far as to
treat industry as a sort of public service. Subtle writers even worked
to create a science which considered the relationships of seller-buyer,
capitalist-employee, lender-debtor in a market that no government
penetrated. If moralists, jurists and good administrators have many times
reproached them for placing their theories outside of historical reality,
by reducing human activity to the petty concerns of *Homo œconomicus,*
they did not seriously examine the legitimacy of the *diremption* which
was assumed by the construction of classical political economy. Petty
philosophers, devoured by the ambition to pass for great men, transformed this symbolism into a utopia which would, to hear them talk,
spread happiness throughout the world.[52] A vast literature has been
devoted, in the name of natural law, to demands for free trade, which
best symbolized to the masses the separation of production from the
state. Customs reforms have been effected only in the countries in which
powerful groups of interests have imposed them on governments. But
the rationalists continue to cry that some day they will slay the hydra
of protectionism by *raison démonstrative,* as Molière's characters would
have done.

(2) During all of the nineteenth century, men who boasted of being
the sons of '89 reproached Catholicism for seeking to create a privileged
position for itself, incompatible with the tenets of the modern consciousness. The publicists, who were called "ultramontanists," claimed that
they were only defending the necessary liberties of the Church; in fact,
they mixed with systems of public law a symbolism that assumes a
diremption. The liberals answered them by a theory of a free Church
in a free state, which they said would satisfy all the requirements of

natural law.[53] In the United States, the independence of religious sects
was established in order to make Christian teachings richer by the
multiplicity of their forms. But in France democracy has suppressed the
former concordat legislation in the hope of hurting religion; that does
not prevent many informed Catholics from arguing with their adversaries over the rules of worship using rationalist arguments, as if the
radicals cared about the good, the true and the beautiful!

The ideas that Marx formed on socialism were suggested to him by
the example of English industry. In England he had observed a working mass which could be practically regarded as released from all the
ties of solidarity that citizens of all other countries recognize as necessary. Consequently he could develop fully his theory of the class
struggle;[54] nothing was more legitimate than finally to proceed to a
diremption in order to study the qualities intrinsic to a militant proletariat. This proletariat could not carry out the mission assigned it by
Marx unless there existed in its heart a distribution of feelings strong
enough to lead each member, because of his special talents, to carry out
the particular task that harmonizes effectively with the common work.
Socialists have examined in only a very insufficient way the conditions
which further or hinder such a state of mind.[55] They have almost always
contented themselves with naïve sophisms which can almost be reduced
to this: the present regime cannot endure because it does not hold up
under serious criticism based on considerations relative to the good, the
true and the beautiful. Now there are no forces to be found in society
capable of overturning capitalism, outside of those contained in the
world of those workers who are placed by large-scale industry in un-
ceasing conflict with the employers. Thus, reason requires the working
masses to form an entity capable of carrying out the condemnation
pronounced by criticism. Social change could not have the absolute
character required by inexorable logic if the revolutionary class did not
possess qualities giving it a composition much more advanced than that
of any other class. Judging that it would be beyond their strength to
realize such a deep, mysterious and new reform,[56] the leaders of socialism content themselves with organizing proletarian political parties—
an easy enough thing. The rest is supposed to follow in due time, by
the natural play of minds, when the politicians have sufficiently explained to the electorate the laws of historical development. In the hands
of these socialists the Marxist theory of the proletariat has become one
of those abstractions regarded by rationalism as being more certain,
desirable and able to govern the mind in proportion as they have given
more services for the construction of systems. According to the rationalists, truly enlightened men must regulate their conduct by debating such
"super realities" and not by considering facts with common sense. That

is why social democrats shout that empiricism can do nothing against their doctrine, which they believe indispensable for giving a sanction to the judgments which rationalism pronounces on history. Thus we are brought to utopia![57]

VI

What Marx knew of Hegelian philosophy predisposed him to cherish Monist prejudices, according to which human genius could have no higher ambition than to introduce the noble discipline of unity into systems of knowledge, will or action. However, according to what he wrote at the beginning of the *Communist Manifesto,* no profound explanation of history is possible unless the point of departure is the development of the antagonisms which are produced between groups amenable to *diremption* (free men and slaves, patricians and plebians, lords and serfs, masters and journeymen, capitalists and proletarians). But Marx was intoxicated with the hope that a day would come when *diremption* would be without an object. The *Idea* that, according to Hegel, carries man toward reason,[58] will indeed, according to Marx, achieve its beneficent work in imposing the unity required by rationalism, where only plurality—the detestable fruit of chance, immoderate desires and general ignorance—reigned before. Marx understood that this passage from heterogeneity to homogeneity is not the same type of movement as that produced by a mechanism of antagonistic forces similar to those which he had recommended considering for a full understanding of the past. Transformations will result henceforth from ideological causes. The materialist theory of history is applicable only for the times which Marx called "prehistoric."[59]

The *Manifesto* of 1847 assumes that the power of the bourgeosie will be overturned by a coalition of Jacobins and proletarians.[60] The victors, in order to take full advantage of their successful campaign, will organize a democracy which begins by adopting measures of social liquidation, the nomenclature for which was borrowed by Marx and Engels from the literature of their time.[61] Finally, with the working class each day exercising more dominance over the state, the ideal of the *League of Communists* will enter into the history of institutions. This schematic tableau seems to have been intentionally presented in an enigmatic form. Marx, still only a young philosopher without reputation, could not express his ideas with complete freedom. Many of the members of the association for which he spoke thought that the transitory regime of democracy could be avoided, thanks to a revolution which would be conducted energetically enough to throw the workers into full communism.[62]

Marx's letter written in 1875 on the *Gotha Program* is much more informative than the *Manifesto* of 1847, because by then Marx had become the celebrated author of *Capital;* because a large party in Germany looked to him as its authority; and because the document was confidential and its editor did not have to deal tactfully with public opinion as much as if it had been public. There again Marx admits that the passage to communism would take place in two stages. At first society would be strongly imprinted with the traits of the old one, which would regulate the distribution of products according to the Marxist theory of value.

> In the advanced phase of the development of communist society, when the enslaving subordination of the individual to the law of the division of labor has disappeared and with it the opposition of intellectual and manual labor; when work is no longer solely the means of living, but the first need of life; when the forces of production have increased along with the integral development of the individual and when all the sources of public wealth are plentiful, then, for the first time, the narrow horizon of bourgeois law will be surpassed and society will inscribe on its flags: "From each according to his ability, to each according to his needs!"[63]

This is a formidable accumulation of very unusual hypotheses which cannot be realized unless our fundamental psychology undergoes the transformations which we will now outline.

The contrast of manual labor, reputed to be servile, and intellectual labor, supposedly noble, would seem shocking to sensible persons if some art were to be found in the practice of the common trades which today produce products devoid of all aesthetics. Work will be the primary need of life when we have learned to resort to tasks which are at the same time useful and aesthetic in order to overcome suffering, instead of demanding a fleeting escape in distractions.[64] The rapid development of productive forces will undoubtedly rest principally on the value of the aesthetic motifs which the promoters of innovations will make valuable, after material progress is no longer imposed by the necessities of competition. Thus our present civilization, which is so little concerned with distinguishing the beautiful and the ugly, would give way to a sort of idealized Greece, where aesthetic preoccupations would be very frequently decisive. At the same time there would be an essential difference in the manner of living celebrated by the ancients and that of the socialist era. While ancient philosophers believed the sage should be content with a modest life, proportionate to the conditions of the rudimentary economy of their time, we are promised a land of milk and honey,[65] which could include free consumption, according to many socialists.[66] If men of the future choose the communist method of regulating their civil relations, it is undoubtedly because it is, in Marx's judgment, the most beautiful, the truest and the most just method which the human mind has ever conceived.[67] The founder of scientific socialism hoped that the newspapers of social democracy would give the proletarians an education capable of thus assuring the triumph of rationalism in a hyper-Hellenic world.

I think that Marx must have established more than once a connection between the warriors of Plato's *Republic* and the workers of large industry whom socialism is organizing for a mortal struggle directed against the capitalist regime. He evidently believed that modern workers, dispossessed of property, deprived of a family establishment[68] and reduced to a salary which forbids any accumulation of money permitting joining the ranks of employers, are as well prepared for communism as the Platonic guardians, to whom the philosopher had refused the right of having lands, a family[69] and any monetary resources. But if we abandon these abstract analogies and face reality, we perceive that the nature of Plato's book discourages those who, on the faith of Marx and Engels, believe that history is in the process of preparing communism.

(a) First of all I would point out that the group on whom Plato imposes his law of communism is extremely narrow. Now Marx pointed out in *Capital* that to a certain extent simple changes in quantity lead to changes in quality.[70] From this it follows that if communism is good for Platonic warriors, it would have very few chances of suiting the organization of our proletarian masses.

In order that his guardians always keep in their consciences the contemplation of their military mission,[71] Plato forbids any reform in the discipline of the fairly narrow education[72] that he had ordered for them (Book IV, 424b).

In our industrial societies, in which, for the productive man, the tasks of production take much more time than does social activity,[73] material progress requires that very marked individualities bring their arbitrary initiatives into regions that seem best suited to order. Thus the countries on the path to great development lack the psychological block of submission, uniformity and immobility which was so favorable to communism in the Platonic world. Far from believing that the natural movement of societies would give rise to his ideal city, Plato teaches that this movement would inevitably end in the known political forms of oligarchy, democracy and tyranny, if it were abandoned to the play of temperaments as seen in the material world.

(b) It seems that Plato took pleasure in pointing out the improbability of his utopia.[74] For example, he declares that it could not func-

tion without philosophers at its head—and what philosophers! Men
who, after learning the elements of knowledge taught in the schools of
the time, raise themselves to the knowledge of *essences* (Book V, 480;
and Book VI, 484c-d). The explanation which he gives is so obscure that
he could have been accused of talking gibberish.[75] It is obviously one
of those Pythagorean enigmas, and we can console ourselves for not
knowing how to resolve it because solution would be absolutely useless.[76] Magistrates, imitating hunting-dog breeders who match sire and
dam with great care (459a), would pair men and women in the most
beneficial way for the beauty of the race (459d–460b); that assumes that
these heads of state would know the modern laws of eugenics, but all
the work of modern naturalists shows that there are very indefinite rules
regulating procreation. Then here is something even more extraordinary:
the decline of the perfect order created by Plato will begin, in his
account, when several errors have been committed in the choice of the
times propitious to good reproduction (Book VIII, 543b). In subordinating the prosperity of his republic to so many mysterious conditions, Plato wanted to make us understand that we would be committing
a gross error if we mistook for a legislative plan a fantasy that he had
imagined in order to illustrate, through a particularly convenient form,
his ideas on good conduct, education and the psychologies corresponding to various political regimes.

(c) If, instead of being one of the best writers of Greek prose, Plato
had been a pure rationalist, he would, in order to preserve only an
abstract monism, have omitted from his expositions all the pluralist
appearances which, in preserving a certain life in his invention, give it
an aura of reality like that of a novel. Then it would have been clear
that this Platonic city is not a real society, full of variety, but an
agglomeration of identical characters.[77]

In such a construction, with human actions magnified in an indeterminate way, the philosopher has the right to say that the just and the
unjust are easier to discern in his city than in the individual (Book II,
368e–369a).[78]

This reduction of society to a replica of a type has great importance
for the history of communist ideas. People who have failed in their
undertakings like to believe that their misfortunes àre due solely to the
malice of their contemporaries. They consequently believe that they
would unfailingly attain the ends which they pursue if they found sympathy around them instead of competition; thus they often aspire to the
communism which, as it is supposed to transform all men into reproduc-
tions of the thinking subject, promises them the power to create the
future according to the views of their intelligence.[79] Communism is well
suited to tender souls, remorseful hearts and all those who fear solitude

because their interior feelings would be repeated around them. This communism would bring much relief to their pain. Finally, an immense satisfaction envelops the individual who dreams of becoming the center of the world; experience shows that it is necessary to have the mind solidly anchored in practice in order to be completely free from this temptation of pride. Modern workers whose initiative is reduced by the capitalist regime are very sensitive to this imperial mirage presented to them by communism. This explains why politicians can find so many precious expedients in communist literature. More than once sophists led workers of revolutionary temperament onto opportunistic paths by shouting the passionate love which they supposedly feel for communism.[80] It would have been impossible for Marx to express the least doubt about future communism, although he probably did not have great faith in what his party taught.[81]

VII

It seems useful to me to present to the reader, at the end of this introduction, several reflections which Benedetto Croce expressed, at the beginning of 1911, on the results produced by Marxism. "I do not believe," said the illustrious Italian philosopher, "that one can overlook the following effects: the definitive abandonment of egalitarian and optimistic socialism, which had become ridiculous; the assistance that modern and 'historicist' socialism has given and gives to the parties who have struggled against every reactionary attempt, notably in contributing, for several decades, to the prevention of European wars; work legislation, improvements realized in material conditions of the working class and a certain intellectual restoration in the proletariat which is translated by a more concrete sense of social reality, expanded everywhere today. In the intellectual domain, modern socialism has participated in the philosophical awakening and in the elimination of positivist inanities; it has rendered stronger economic studies and economic culture. It has indicated new ways of considering history. These are some of the gifts which socialism has given to modern civilization."[82] All the men who have taken part in such a notable work can rest in the knowledge that they have led a usefully employed life.

July 1914

POST SCRIPTUM

This book was not printed until 1918; the war has posed new problems which I dare not broach at this time. Only one point seems certain: that the victory of the Entente was a triumph for demagogic plutocracy.[83] This plutocracy wants to suppress the Bolsheviks who frighten it; its military forces are sufficient to carry out this operation. But what will the plutocrats gain by the extermination of the Russian revolutionaries? Will not the blood of martyrs be effective once again? One must not forget that without the massacres of June 1848 and May 1871, socialism would have had great trouble in making this principle of the class struggle acceptable in France. The bloody object lesson which will take place in Russia will make all workers feel that there is a contradiction between democracy and the mission of the proletariat. The idea of constituting a government of producers will not perish; the cry: "Death to the intellectuals!" for which the Bolsheviks are so often reproached will perhaps end by imposing itself on the workers of the entire world. One must be blind not to see that the Russian Revolution is the dawn of a new era.

THE ORGANIZATION OF DEMOCRACY

I

For many years a multitude of writers, who are not generally distinguished by talent but who are versed in the art of making noise, have been asserting that if universal suffrage were organized according to the methods sanctioned by them, democracy would function in such a way as to satisfy the most demanding critics. This literature is almost always crammed with abstract considerations and is consequently rather vague and uninformative. Adolphe Prins's book, *De l'esprit du gouvernement démocratique*,[1] cannot be entirely overlooked because in it, the author intends to present to his compatriots constitutional reforms which seem to him to suit the social conditions of contemporary Belgium.

In order to read this book fruitfully, one must never lose sight of the following observations. Belgian politicians, except perhaps the leaders of the Socialist Party, are firmly attached to the institutions of liberty.[2] Educated Belgians would believe that they were lacking in the elementary duties of patriotism if they did not seem proud of the traditions of the old Flemish communes. The Belgian bourgeoisie does not feel the need of having a leader capable of making the national army play a great role in the world, capable of assuring the continuity of a foreign policy which comprises one of the most important elements of European equilibrium or of giving material interests guarantees in order to maintain necessary confidence in economic progress. Therefore the Bonapartist spirit does not exist in our neighbors to the north, who can criticize current parliamentary achievements without wanting to establish an absolute monarchy.[3] Moreover, Prins is not one of those rhetoricians who pretends to create an artificial order according to scholastic precepts. A high official of the Ministry of Justice, he is a practical man; he has been able to observe especially well how a bureaucracy functions in a regime of parties. His plans are thus realistic and liberal at the same time so that they can serve as the basis for useful discussions on modern democracy.

The elect of democracy occupy positions which, in an Old Regime government, would be entrusted to the King's men whose prior services would have deemed them worthy of controlling the administration, of advising ministers and of correcting the errors of the sovereign as necessary. The present-day bureaucracy, which has preserved many traditions of the old royal corps, would like the parliaments to conform to its customs to a certain extent. It is thus natural enough that the plans presented by Adolphe Prins aim above all to introduce into democracy ideas dear to bureaucrats.

A regular promotion in a hierarchy, arranged so as to assure just rewards for merit—that is the foundation of public law for the perfect employee of the state. The first years serve to make him aware of routine, the fundamental law of any administrative body. Young people who are destined to attain high ranks distinguish themselves then by showing, on a modest scale, the moral qualities which will be so necessary to them later on in order to lead. Would it not also be well for politicians to be obliged to pass through an apprenticeship? Our author thinks so; that is why he writes: "The exercise of local duties is for modern parliamentarianism what the training in the high courts was for recruitment to the Roman Senate, or the activity of the bourgeoisie in medieval corporations[4] for the recruitment of the leaders of our great towns; that is to say, a means of training for the most eminent administrators." In his opinion, then, the essential condition of parliamentary life is a strong local life. Those who are designated to apply the laws deplore that for "the sober and clear work of the past" is substituted an "inextricable mess." The solution of problems having a tremendous national interest is constantly subordinated to the maneuvers of politicians.[5] The work of parliaments is spoiled by an electoral system which permits candidates to have themselves elected on programs that are too abstract. The system would probably work better if elections were episodes in the functioning of local organisms as happened in England when the county and municipal corporations were electoral colleges. Prins writes that at the present time in England local powers still have the effect of diminishing the spirit of party,[6] so that they discuss matters in a truly objective manner. In the judgment of this high official (Prins), they are more valuable than the parliaments resulting from an unorganized electorate. Very often cabinet ministers have found it advantageous in drawing up difficult laws to organize commissions comprising representatives of all interests; in the *Supreme Labor Council,* established in 1892, including sixteen sociologists, sixteen industrialists and sixteen workers, the spirit of conciliation was manifested so forcefully that the country owed to this institution excellent practical measures "in a time of social trouble." A parliament appointed by curias of talent, capital and labor could probably satisfy the bureaucracy.

Here is how Prins conceives of the complete application of his theories to Belgium. The number of members in the communal councils would be increased so as to interest more citizens in the prosperity of town affairs. These assemblies would be composed "one-quarter by representatives of all electors over twenty-five years old who had resided three years in the commune; one-quarter by representatives of middle and higher education; a quarter by representatives of certain qualified voters occupying houses; and the last quarter by representatives of the large social interests whose management figures in the prerogatives of communal power.[7] Sheriffs would be chosen from the last quarter of the assembly by the majority of the three other parts." For parliamentary elections, account would be taken of both the population grouping and the social situation of the citizens. In the rural cantons there would be a curia of qualified voters and one of laborers, each one naming a deputy; in medium-sized cities, three curias would each name a deputy. Elites, qualified homeowners, all other citizens over twenty-five who had lived three years in the locality; in the large cities, four curias of elites (sciences, letters, arts, teaching with two deputies; law, justice, administration with three deputies; religious denominations recognized by the state with one deputy each; national defense with one deputy); four curias of capital each naming a deputy (property, industry, commerce, finance); five labor curias each naming a deputy (building, manufacturing, clothing and furnishings, typography and book binding, other trades); one curia of hygiene and public works, naming two deputies who are supposed to be instructors in health to the poorer classes.

II

The extreme complexity of this system should not frighten a reader of Proudhon.[8] Persuaded that good public administration is only possible if it is greatly inspired by juridical practices, which makes the plurality of interests conspicuous, he wrote at the end of his life: "A sincere and truthful representation in a country like ours presupposes an ensemble of institutions arranged in such a way that any interest, idea or social and political element can be introduced into it, express itself, have itself represented, *obtain justice and security,* and exercise its part of influence and sovereignty. For national representation, where it exists as a political condition, must not only be a part of a machine, as it was in the Constitution of 1804, a mechanism and a counter-weight as in the charter of 1814-30, the foundation of the governmental edifice as in the constitutions of 1793,[9] 1848 and 1852; it must be at the same time, so as not to be a deception, a foundation, a mechanism, a counter-weight and in addition a function—a function that comprises this whole of the nation in all of its categories of persons, territory, fortunes, faculties, talents and even poverty."[10]

In order to wholly grasp the nature of this concept, I think we must examine closely what Proudhon meant in speaking of a representation of poverty. Earlier he wondered if it was equitable to refuse all parliamentary rights to men affected by legal disqualification. He wrote, "The Church has its penitential office according to which the sinner should accuse himself if he wants to attain the remedies of the soul through the pardon of his sins. Now, the majority of citizens excluded from electoral lists are social and political cripples: how will they raise themselves, how will they obtain the justice that is their due . . . if they are forbidden to "plead" (if I dare to phrase it thus) in the exercise of the sovereignty of the people?"[11] What should induce the reflection of the philosopher here is the analogy between judicial forms and public law. Proudhon saw in legislative assemblies, law courts in which each group comes to plead his cause before people who have gained the habit of raising their minds above individual considerations[12] in order to reach solutions which are very likely rational.

The collective reason on which modern governments are supposedly based has as its organ every gathering "for the discussion of ideas and the seeking of right.[13] One precaution should be taken: that is to assure that the collectivity in question does not vote as one, by virtue of a particular feeling becoming common, which would only lead to an immense swindle, as can be seen in the majority of popular judgments. To fight as one[14] is the law of battle; to vote as one is the opposite of reason."[15] Legal truth can be compared to the provisional technical truth which is formulated in professional congresses.

Guided by his judicial preoccupations, Proudhon sees, much better than Adolphe Prins, the enormous difficulties presented by the purification of democracy. In the "Little Political Catechism" inserted in *De la justice,* one reads: "So long as democracy does not rise to the true conception of power, it can only be, as it has only been until now, a lie. . . . The Revolution consecrated this word[16] 'democracy' as a lode star; for sixty-six years we have been making a scandal out of it."[17] "As opposed to divine right, the Revolution poses the sovereignty of the people, the unity and indivisibility of the Republic; words devoid of meaning, suitable and useful only to mask the most horrible tyranny ... if they do not relate to the higher organism, formed by the relations of industrial groups, and to the commutative power that results from them."[18] "As all the constitutions since 1789 have made it, universal suffrage is the strangulation of the public consciousness, the suicide of the sovereignty of the people, the apostasy of the Revolution. . . . In order to make universal suffrage intelligent, moral, and democratic, it is necessary, after having organized the scale of services and assured the independence of the suffrages by free discussion, to have citizens vote by categories of function, conforming to the principle of the collective force which comprises the foundation of society and the state."[19] In almost the whole of this book, Proudhon regards democracy as a preparation for the republican regime whose principles he defined in one of the complementary notes.

"In order to establish the republican government in its truth, five conditions are required: (1) definition of economic rights; (2) balance of economic forces, formation of agrico-industrial groups, organization of public utility services (credit, discount, circulation, transport, docks, etc.) according to the principle of mutuality and gratuity, [at] cost;[20] (3) political guarantees: freedom of press and speech, parlimentary initiative, public accountability, extension of the jury, freedom of assembly and association, inviolability of the person, of the domicile and of the mails; complete separation of the judiciary and the government; (4) administrative decentralization, resurrection of communal and provincial life; (5) abolition of the state of war, demolition of fortresses and abolition of permanent armies. Under these conditions, the principle of authority tends to disappear; the *res publica* rests on the eternally unshakable base of law and local corporative and individual freedoms, whose interaction brings about national liberty. To tell the truth, the government no longer exists . . . it is this impersonality, the result of liberty and law, which above all characterizes republican government."[21]

III

The republican regime of which Proudhon dreamed will perhaps never be realized.[22] But it is quite probable that universal suffrage would cease to be a curse if the citizens were animated by a truly republican spirit; that is to say, if they regulated their economic relations according to equitable methods, at least in general; if they had a long practice of political liberties, and if they no longer had any idea of conquest. There is no reason to suppose that such a nation could have been educated by democrats. In *Justice*, Proudhon recognized that the constitutional monarchy can preside over the evolution of a society toward a state of law and liberty;[23] although he often forcefully denounced the faults of democracy, always under the delusion of the *raison d'Etat*,[24] it would have been very painful for him to admit that he was wrong to hope for so long for a republican transmutation of democratic life. I believe that is why he did not dare to complete his *Contradictions politiques*, in which this dreaded admission is implicitly understood many times.[25] In the fragment of his work published after his death, Proudhon points out the extreme facility with which one passes from democracy to despotism and vice versa; "and a sad fact," he adds, "is that the most ardent democrats are usually the most prompt to accommodate themselves to despotism and on the other hand that the courtiers of absolute power (when the opportunity arises) become the most enraged demagogues."[26] Consequently how can one hope that democracy will lead us to a republic? Rest assured that politicians endowed with such psychological dispositions will never make the proper reforms to restrain the influence of their arbitrary wills. When Proudhon called his disciples democrats, this word implied "the idea," he said on March 4, 1862, "that if we do not serve the omnipotence of the multiude, we work at its emancipation through law and freedom and that consequently we defend its interests."[27] Who then is the demagogue (or the parliamentary socialist) concerned with working for the emancipation of the proletariat through law and freedom?

Proudhon's republic contains too many libertarian, anti-militarist and federalist elements for it to be developed by our modern democrats, who have an unlimited confidence in the economic capacities of the state, are deluded by chauvinism and are as fanatical about unity as the most ultramontane Catholics. Proudhon believed that the state can usefully intervene in the economy in order to create new institutions (insurance, banks, railroads), but that it should immediately turn over management to citizens.[28] In 1860 he had seen the maneuvers of agents sent by the Emperor into Belgium in order to prepare its annexation; he advised the Belgians (like the Swiss) to avoid any act that French chauvinists could interpret as a provocation to justify a war of conquest. He was convinced that the treaties which guaranteed the neutrality of Belgium and Switzerland did not protect the two countries against the voracity of our democracy. Proudhon undoubtedly recognized the impossibility of attaining federalism through democratic development, for he seems to have believed that this regime should be imposed on France by victorious outsiders, just as the parliamentary monarchy had been imposed on our fathers. "I have only one fear," he wrote to Chaudey on April 4, 1862, "it is to see the dismemberment of France, and Paris deserted like another Versailles. But who knows whether at that price our nation could not be saved and become something once again? . . . In order to save the freedom and the nation, emancipate the populace, create peace and develop the principles of the Revolution in Europe, I see only one means: divide France into a dozen independent states and suppress Paris."[29] In the following section we will encounter other reasons preventing the linking of Proudhon's republic to modern democracy.

Democrats do not want administrations to function with the regularity dear to good employees; this is irreconcilable with their freedom as party leaders. They gladly denounce as reactionary those who, like Adolphe Prins, miss the order which formerly ruled in legislation. It would thus be quite useless to try to persuade them that they would be doing a worthwhile thing by organizing suffrage according to Prins's plans. But like all idealists, democrats often let themselves be taken in by dialectics; academic manipulations of abstractions inspire an extreme confidence in them because such exercises help them to dupe the people, who do not see what it is they are made to applaud. It would not be entirely impossible, therefore, to lead the people to accept voting systems whose real significance is not clearly shown. Thus it has been proposed to perfect our democracy by means of proportional representation as used in Belgium, the presidential veto of the American constitution, or the Swiss referendum, under the pretext of rendering more effective the control which citizens have the right to exercise electorally on the state. Joseph Reinach, who is the profound thinker of the proportionalist clan, shouts with all his might that if his pet project is not quickly adopted, the Republic will find itself exposed to imminent perils. The prestige of bold verbiage is so great in the political world that this crafty man has succeeded in having his views accepted by those whom he hopes would lose their parliamentary seats by the application of proportional representation.

Joseph Reinach obviously does not move about frantically through love of the democratic ideal, as he pretends. Having recognized that current parliamentary groups do not at all correspond to serious currents of public opinion, he believes that electoral majorities are at the mercy of chance.[30] He hopes that the introduction of the proportional system would cause such chaos in the radical organizations that his friends would have the possibility of returning to the parliament in great numbers—in spite of the ill-will of unscrupulous ministers, who would no longer be in a position to "construct" elections as easily as today. Democracy, which had the unhoped-for luck of securing a sort of dictatorship, does not want to compromise its situation by engaging in adventures. It will accept proportional representation only when it believes that it has taken enough precautions to no longer have anything to fear

from the stratagems of Joseph Reinach; besides, Reinach expects that
his reform will become useless if it is postponed for any length of time.

But what is the use of organizing democracy? Its apologists declare
that it is in order to enable it to accomplish its historic mission, to
create its own genius, to prove that it is capable of expressing human
reason. Once organized, it could resolve the enigma of development by
constructing the foundations of a future society intended to be regulated
according to the principles of the most perfect justice. On the contrary,
I believe that democracy requires no organization, in the scientific sense
of this term, considering that it is directed only by instincts of destruction. German Social Democracy, which claims to have received from
Marx a very deep knowledge of economics, politics and history, has
never been able to produce a doctrine worthy of occupying an honorable
place in modern philosophy. But it rightly credits itself with the glory
of possessing the most advanced form of contemporary democracy, because it has succeeded better than any other popular party in grouping
multitudes of devoted electors around its uncompromising negation of
national traditions. Thanks to the tireless agitation of the Social Democracy, the German proletariat longs for the day when the Prussian army,
the pedantic bureaucracy and magistrature derived from the old universities and the authority of the churches will all disappear. The
frivolity, incoherence and cynicism of Social Democratic propogandists[31]
have helped it extend its spiritual ravages into the most diverse *milieux*
more than well-directed reason could have done. All our current European democracies reveal phenomena equivalent to those seen in such
a particularly striking form in the bosom of German Social Democracy.[32]

When the negative character of democracy is understood we see that
in order to evaluate soundly the worth of the plans that are supposed to
perfect it, we should ask above all if such reforms are seriously capable
of restraining the legislative mania of our parliaments.[33]

From this point of view, the system of proportional representation
seems much less interesting than the referendum or the American veto.
In fact its result is to develop strong party spirit.[34] A fanatical majority
can be extremely dangerous. Even with a small difference between its
numbers and those of the opposition it would be better if the difference
were greater and the majority less disciplined.

IV

Political philosophy becomes muddled whenever it is concerned with
democracy, because in its scholastic cauldrons it mixes together abstractions deriving from very dissimilar concrete systems, placed between
two extreme types which I will try to define clearly by some of their
noteworthy characteristics. Primitive democracies, of which certain

vestiges could be observed in nineteenth-century Switzerland and in Algeria, were formed of families bound in the most solid way to the culture of a canton sanctified by ancestral tombs; they accepted with profound respect the decisions of "social authorities" who maintained the spirit of the race; religion imposed on them the obligation of following strict rules of morality.[35] In our modern democracies, almost everyone feels free from the past, is without a deep love of the home, and thinks but little of future generations; deluded by the mirage of speculative riches which would come from the cleverness of their minds rather than from a serious participation in material production, they think only of royally enjoying windfalls. Their true bailiwick is the big city where men pass like shadows; political committees have taken the place of the old "social authorities" destroyed by revolutions, whose descendants have abandoned a country forgetful of its past, and who have been replaced by people living in the new fashion. The enlightened classes find it definitely not philosophical to deny, out of religious scruple, the satisfaction of their passions whenever possible.

In order to understand Greco-Roman institutions well, it is often very useful to refer to what we know of primitive democracies.[36] In the course of their decline, the Hellenic cities became a lot like our modern democracies. The oligarchs who seized power from Athens at the end of the Peloponnesian Wars had no trait in common with the "social authorities" who had existed in the glorious days of the Republic.[37] Patrons of the arts, curious about all the exotic novelties, students of the Sophists, they were at least as revolutionary as the most impassioned demagogues. It is even probable that the cult of tradition was maintained more strongly in the world of artisans than in the wealthy classes.[38]

When Aristotle tried to apply the teachings of empirical political science to popular governments, he was thinking of reforms intended to make them more like primitive democracies.[39] Unfortunately few elements which allowed constructing a state according to such a program were any longer found in Greece. As a consequence, Aristotle's ideas are often rather vague. It seems that he especially admired the rural economy because it did not permit citizens to assemble too frequently; legislation would not then be in danger of being overturned at any time, as happened in the cities, where the artisans dominated; laws would appear as stable manifestations of human intelligence, superior to the accidents of particular wills. The Greeks had become too skeptical for one to hope they would make a tragedy of religious punishments. The Peripatetic ethic corresponds to the customs of bourgeois of good standing who have followed the schools of Socratic philosophers. Aristotle was the master of these secular moralizers whose work has been so obviously useless. In order for the law to conform to reason as Aristotle demands, it is obviously necessary for the mass to follow the advice of the most distinguished citizens (*beltistoi*) and not the suggestions of demagogues. There were no longer enough vestiges of the old structures for a concrete theory of "social authorities" to be constructed at that time. Aristotle is thus obliged to be content with several abstract and uninformative outlines.[40]

Proudhon's republic is far more interesting than the *politeia* of Aristotle, because the French philosopher understood much better than the Greek philosopher the importance of each of the conditions under which primitive democracies function.[41]

The evolution of Proudhon's ideas on property would be unclear if we did not understand that his meditations were leading him every day to see more clearly how law arose from rural economy. He felt the glory of the land more than anyone.[42] His love of the rural life was related to his deepest psychology. What will humanity do when it has become republican? asks the "Little Political Catechism"; and here is the answer: "It will do as Genesis said,[43] as the philosopher Martin recommended in *Candide,* it will cultivate its garden. When the cultivation of the soil, previously the realm of the slave, becomes the 'first of the arts,' as it is the first of the industries, man's life will take place in the calm of the senses and the serenity of the spirit."[44]

In writing his great treatise on *Justice,* Proudhon hoped to work at the construction of a more complete popular philosophy, as effective and no less austere than the Christian ethic ever was, from which ethic he saw the masses becoming detached. He applied himself to this work with an admirable passion, aroused by his notion of its necessity; its failure has shown more clearly than any metaphysical dissertation could have done that our democracies do not at all favor the blossoming of a true *republican* morality. He felt vividly that the world would not easily arrive at accepting the doctrines of the free justice that he preached and he was very anxious to give a provisory guarantee to morals.[45] That is why he proposed to the Church an unusual Concordat according to which the clergy would teach the ethic of Revolution under the veil of Christian symbolism.[46] "In three centuries Protestant Germany has effectuated its passage from orthodox Catholicism to philosophic morality, without any serious disturbance to the masses." Proudhon hoped that by means of his system one could "revolutionize minds and consciences without passing into the way of Protestantism and without getting lost in the profligacy of the religious visionaries and miracle-workers. . . . Outside of that I see no safety except in dictatorship and terror."[47]

It does not yet seem to have been remarked that Proudhon was preoccupied with institutions which could take the place of the old "social authorities."[48] That is why I am going to reproduce here several eloquent passages from the complementary notes in *Justice:* "Does one think he

has fulfilled his duty by abstaining from any reprehensible or illegal
action? . . . Our justice must radiate afar. . . . Like patriotism, justice
is nothing if it is not armed. For it is not only the enemy from within
that we must vanquish, it is also the one from the outside. This unpunished crime that you denounce with such bitterness is the crime of
those whom you call just; it is yours. It is your cowardice, oh good
people, it is your tacit connivance which encourages scoundrels. What
then do you blame on fate? What does providence owe you in recompense for an inept life, lived in idiotic fears? . . . We speak of tribunals instituted to act in our place: but tribunals touch only on the
minimum and the least dangerous part of offenses. The true causes of
depravity are carefully avoided by them. . . . How can the zealots of
law, of which there are always a few, not think of forming a coalition
against the invasion of unpunished crime, against the ineptitude of the
legislator and the tolerance of the judge, against the prevarication of
power itself? . . . What society lacks are "lovers of justice": Those whom
governments designate to carry out justice . . . are only semblances. But
then, once again, what are we complaining about when we point a
finger at social disharmony and when we ask the heavens for additional
justification? We are punished where we sin. The persecution of the just
is the punishment for their softness, not to say for their complicity."[49]
Proudhon was unable to give a concrete solution to the problem of the
organization of justice. Democracy with its political committees cannot
create "the lovers of justice" that he asked for; these "lovers of justice"
"organized everywhere in juries of honor with the right to pursue, judge
and execute their judgments," would have resembled conspicuously the
"social authorities" of past times. Would not workers' syndicates be apt
to play a similar role?

It is very regrettable that Proudhon was unable to study the old rural
democracies. If he had known them well, he would have shown much
better than can be done here how these societies resemble the republican utopia and differ from our modern democracies. Such comparisons
affect the philosopher infinitely more than the most scholarly abstract
dissertations. For too long a time socialism has followed a bad path,
inspired by the bad leaders educated by democracy. There is nothing
more essential for the future of the proletariat than to be initiated into
Proudhon's teaching. The disciples (or so-called disciples) of Marx, in
leading an impassioned campaign against Proudhon, have a large responsibility for the decadence of socialism. It is amusing that these
second-rate intellectuals have denounced as "bourgeois" this admirable
representative of the world of work whom Daniel Halévy was right in
calling: "an archetype of the peasant and of the French artisan—a hero
of our people."[50]

CHAPTER 8

from
The Utility
of Pragmatism

ON THE ORIGIN OF TRUTH

I   Interpretation of the Kantian theory of knowledge by Bergson who discovers a divine implicitness in it. Replacement of the formal God by an ecclesia docens. Formation of the Cité savante.

II   The experience of the Medieval Cité esthetique. Its separation from the general society of its time.—The traditions it maintained. Symbolism. Decadence of art after the dissolution of the medieval corporations.

III   The creation of order without legislative authority. False ideas that are introduced when science becomes acceptable. D'Alembert's faith. Opposition to the so-called psychic sciences which have no pragmatic controls.

IV   The Cité morale. Its strength in America. Its tradition. The inadequacy of William James's explanations on the subject.

V   The pragmatic interpretation of truth. The apprenticeship of moral life in Christian communities. The illusions of the theologians who are adversaries of pragmatism. Mathematics and theology. False traditionalism.

I

Before explaining my understanding of the origin of truth, it seems useful to call attention to Bergson's interpretation of the Kantian critique. "Spinoza and Leibniz had, following Aristotle, hypostatized in God the unity of knowledge. . . . For the ancients, science was concerned with *concepts,* that is to say, with kinds of things. In compressing all concepts into one, they therefore necessarily arrived at a being, which we may call Thought, but which was rather thought-object than thought-subject. . . . God was the synthesis of all concepts, the idea of ideas. But modern science is concerned with laws, that is, with relations. Now, a relation is a bond established by a mind between two or more terms. . . . The universe, therefore, can only be a system of laws if phenomena have passed beforehand through the filter of an intellect. Of course, this intellect might be that of a being infinitely superior to man, who would found the materiality of things at the same time that he bound them together: such was the hypothesis of Leibniz and of Spinoza. But it is not necessary to go as far as that, and for our purposes here, the human intellect is enough. . . . True, when he speaks of the human intellect, [Kant] means neither yours nor mine. The unity of nature comes indeed from the human understanding that unifies, but the unifying function that operates here is impersonal. It imparts itself to our individual consciousness, but it transcends it. It is much less than a substantial God. It is, however, a little more than the isolated work of one man or even than the collective work of humanity. It does not exactly lie within man; rather man lies within it, as in an atmosphere of intellectuality which his consciousness breathes. It is, if you will, a *formal* God, something that in Kant is not yet divine, but which tends to become so. It becomes so, indeed, with Fichte."[1]

I do not view the revolutionary role of Kant entirely as Bergson defined it because I find between ancient science and the science of Kant's contemporaries a very serious explicit difference which Bergson neglected to discuss. The Greeks have left us rather paltry compilations of usually loosely connected propositions whose proofs too often seemed to depend on a few lucky accidents and which were the sporadic fruit of the ingenious curiosity of men very little concerned with material progress.[2] Kant's contemporaries were developing methods allowing them to order their mathematical knowledge. Enthusiastic about what Newtonian astronomy had already produced, they were convinced that the normal development of the new geometry of nature provided serious future workers with all the instruments they would need to solve the most thorny problems.[3] Thus, with great confidence, they approached areas which, until then, had been left to empiricism, with the idea of wondrously transforming the old practices—thanks to the resources of "mechanical rationalism."

In the illustrious monuments of ancient science there was so much incoherence, chance and uselessness that the philosophers had a perfect right to treat this ancient science like an accumulation of meteoric dust coming out of vessels that can be called divine because they are beyond our reason. In the eighteenth century, science was characterized chiefly by the continuity that had recently been procured by some of the most extraordinary intellectual achievements in history; by the richness of the procedures of an infinitesimal analysis that is constantly being improved; by daily examination of questions which concern the prosperity of peoples.[4] Science had to be regarded as due uniquely to human reason. Kant, who wanted to put his philosophical teaching in perfect harmony with the noblest tendencies of his time, wanted to orient it, consequently, in the opposite direction from that adopted by the ancients.[5] He could not seek, as Bergson presumes, to halt modern dogmatism "on the slant which made it incline too far toward Greek metaphysics."[6] We should rest assured that he meant to cut all communication between knowledge and the divine.

If Bergson believed that Kant's theory implicitly contains the divine, it is because he perceived a serious deficiency in the *Critique of Pure Reason*. He remembered that philosophers, like the authors of bad tragedies, have the habit of making a *deus ex machina* intervene when they are embarrassed,[7] but the question is whether or not this artifice clashes too much with the conditions under which Kant formed his thought. Descartes judged it necessary to call on divine veracity to guarantee the existence of phenomena because, since in his time the Peripatetic heavens were no longer supposed to move the earth and since universal gravitation did not yet exist, philosophy did not know how to defend itself against the fantasies of romantically inclined inventors. Kant felt no need to seek help outside of science to verify the worth of modern scientific knowledge; according to the unanimous opinion of competent people, this knowledge found in the celestial mechanics of Newton a support as unshakable as that with which Aristotle, in creating his theory of the first immobile motor, had hoped to endow ancient scientific knowledge.

Today at the end of the profound revolutions which have upset physics, physicists wonder if they will ever discover a solid enough foundation on which a structure adapted to their experiments can be erected. Disorder has become as great as it was after the Renaissance; philosophers who want to save the idea of certitude at any price are inclined to inject the superhuman into the theory of knowledge as was done before Kant. Bergson brought to early Kantianism a view which seemed to him to allow twentieth-century Kantians to reconcile the order conceived of by the master with the anarchy of present-day thought.

The difficulty presented by Kantianism consists in Kant's failure to

explain the nature of that superior impersonal understanding at the level
recognized by experimental psychology in the operation of our minds.
The mystery is cleared up easily if we examine several eighteenth-
century ideas on the teaching of the sciences. The men of the eighteenth-
century wanted to preserve as much as possible the glorious tradition
of Euclid, Archimedes and Apollonius, by profiting from the resources
furnished by the new habits of reasoning to simplify the ancient didactic methods.[8] They were convinced that all of the fundamental parts of
physics could be submitted to the discipline of perfected Greek mathematics. They had no more doubts about the principles of modern physics
than about those of ancient geometry. Obviously the intellectual activity
of the schools is entirely impersonal; there they espouse, according to
methods similar to Euclid's, a science as consolidated as his, with the
full conviction that it deals with the absolute. One can say that the
student is steeped "in an atmosphere of [impersonal] intellectuality that
his consciousness would absorb." As for the professor, he "communicates
[to] individual minds [a oneness of perceptions] which is beyond him,"
with an authority recalling to a great extent that enjoyed by the great
inspired religious figures, imperial legislators or theologians of the Middle Ages.[9] Instead of comparing, as Bergson proposes, the cognitive
faculty described by Kant to a sort of "formal God," it is suitable to say
that it is seen in the activity of an *Ecclesia docens* possessing a Euclidian
science.

The Kantian theory of knowledge has become outdated since it has
entirely lost the historical basis that once gave it such great value. Science indeed no longer appears to us as a definitively constituted system
whose formulas would be decreed by the absolute experts of an *Ecclesia
docens;* it springs forth in the midst of the agitations of a *Cité savante*
["scholarly community"] which works unceasingly to recast its constructions with the aim of rendering them more useful. The philosopher
who wants to reduce science to a human level no longer turns to Kantianism, but to pragmatism. In order to understand pragmatism well, it is
consequently necessary to understand precisely the nature of the contemporary *Cité savante,* of which it is one of the ideological reflections.

I am convinced that a century ago no dreamer of the unlimited
progress of the mind would have yet dared to foresee what a huge number of people would in our time devote their lives to: (1) pursuing
research requiring as much ingenuity as patience with the aim of passing
from the minute observation of natural phenomena to theories worthy
of supporting them; (2) composing works for authoritative didactics,
for university teaching or for popularization which spread with an extreme speed the most recent acquisitions of knowledge; (3) realizing
on the colossal scale imposed on our workshops by capitalist competi-

tion the application of the laws just revealed by minuscule laboratory mechanisms.

The majority of these intellectual workers are grouped in clans, around proud barons whose names are commonly linked to one of the resounding discoveries that have contributed to making the achievements of science admired by a considerable public. As most often these leaders have only succeeded in obtaining their brilliant positions after undergoing harsh trails, they regard themselves as belonging to an elite derived from a selective process whose fairness should be universally admired. In their old age, they almost always appear all the more eager to uphold the positions that made their fame as they feel less capable henceforth of producing anything that equals the work of their youth. Very preoccupied with the dangers that threaten their glory, they strive to organize solid interest groups that can impose their precepts on coming generations. Faithful disciples are assured of obtaining, without much effort, those positions sought so avidly by mediocre people concerned less with the advancement of science than with money, honors and domination. Bold spirits, who scorn commending themselves to such powers in the hope that they would do better to follow personal paths, undergo the greatest difficulties in bringing their inventions before the circles which could best benefit from them.

There are jealousies among these science magnates that are as ferocious as those that the humanists, artists and philosophers of the Renaissance were accustomed to. The clans that they lead indulge in wars as rich in treachery as those of the barbarians. All of this perfidy prevents the *Cité savante* from falling into the Chinese somnolence dreamed of by Auguste Comte for a Europe converted to positivism.[10] Scientific systems often disappear with their inventors; everyone feels an immense relief when an academic tyrant, a Charcot, Pasteur or Berthelot is sealed in a magnificent tomb in the course of a grand ceremony replete with hypocritical rhetoric. His disciples who, in order to flatter him, had vilified independent researchers, now hasten to add to their teaching, as much as they decently can, a quantity of innovations formerly treated by them as suspect.[11] Often an important opinion dies before its inventor, when the clan whose property it was believes it necessary to contract alliances which oblige it to compromise on doctrines in order to defend its situation more effectively. The result of this organization of intellectual work is that scientific progress is realized through a succession of crises offering a rather striking analogy with those that accompany industrial progress, brought on by capitalist competition.

In the course of the immoderate struggles they wage against their detractors, the masters of science never forget for long that their interests command them to do nothing that could seriously compromise the prestige of science. They must let their most detested adversaries enjoy the advantage obtained by the title of "scholar," so that they themselves may thoroughly exploit the confidence of the public. That is why they join in a bloc, containing many of the faults the old guilds were justly accused of, whenever a "layman" is so bold as to criticize one of the heavyweights of the *Cité savante*. Thus the passions of a clique do not prevent the existence of a strong sentiment of class solidarity. Moreover, the idea of class for scholars does not rest solely on a utilitarian basis. Seeing that the extraordinary prosperity of modern production is linked in the closest way to the great discoveries of physics and chemistry, they take pleasure in imagining that all of the benefits of capitalist industry are due to the genius of their class. A pride, magnified by the flatteries of the clan, then compels them to imagine that they are called on to lead the world along paths of the highest social progress, as well as technological progress. In this way there is constituted a notion of the mission of science, which reinforces the class spirit in conjunction with public encouragement of this perversion of the souls of scholars.

The courtier poets, who, at the beginning of the modern era, were celebrating with such fluency the merits of the princes from whom they received stipends, are today surpassed in obsequiousness by the numerous hack writers who intoxicate the masters of science with absurd praises, in order to live at ease in the shadow of their protection in their capacity as authorized popularizers. Progressive politicians, who are disturbed by daily accusations of crass ignorance, try to ennoble their parties from time to time by having resounding honors decreed to some representative scientific personalities whose talent has not preserved them from vanity. The social quacks repeat at every turn that in the universities marvelous solutions in physics, history and philosophy are at hand, solutions which will very soon allow revolutionaries to transform into a paradise our unhappy planet, which has hitherto been condemned to work, poverty and grief; the working masses, infatuated by dreams of the free-wheeling life, venerate with a sometimes comical ardor men whom their newspapers have pointed out as the standard-bearers of science.

In the midst of the frightful triumph of moral materialism, artistic vulgarity and stupidity in all its forms, which we observe helplessly, the *Cité savante* attracts to it the instincts of discipline which, cultivated by classical education, are unused today. Thus it profits indirectly from the progress of democracy, which is working feverishly to destroy the prestige of the old "social authorities", restrict the influence of the Church by spreading impiety, and, by its low electoral practices, vilify the state. True scholars, without having many illusions about the real import of science, like to spread respect for the *Cité savante* which, like them, devotes itself to "intellectual work."

These observations seem to be sufficient to show that the "scholarly community" constitutes an oligarchy which is no less solid than it would have been had a law grouped scholars in a privileged corporation which would be given a monopoly over scientific research.

II

We have no right to think that we have an adequate understanding of an institution that is in the process of *becoming,* unless we can project the present movement into a clear picture of similar institutions whose results have been clearly shown. The promoters of social reforms claim to be inspired by this principle when they parallel what seems desirable in their own countries with what is found in peoples famous for their enduring prosperity. Unfortunately they usually consider only small fragments of life, which they frequently reduce further into abstractions designed to play a role in pretentiously scientific theories or which at times dress their false appearances with causal forces in utopian novels. We must strive, on the contrary, to obtain an overall perspective, after being familiarized with the minute details of the system viewed as a pattern. If historical questions had to be dealt with according to the same methods used to discover the laws of physics, the rule outlined here would almost always be impracticable. It is rare indeed for us to have complete information on the points that should be made more precise for reconstructing the past. But experience shows that interpretations established according to reasonable hypotheses are at times very helpful whenever we want to appraise the present soundly.

It is not easy to discover another organization that is similar enough to clarify the functioning of our exceptional *Cité savante;* however I think that it would not be imprudent to compare the nineteenth-century *Cité savante* to the *Cité esthétique* ["artistic community"] which produced so many admirable monuments from the twelfth to the fifteenth century. Besides, the study of this artistic community is strongly recommended to pragmatic philosophers to whom it could suggest many ingenious perspectives on the art of discussing the development of human activity.[12]

In the Middle Ages the workers guilds, which included a few men with talent of the highest order, imposed their building methods, their decorative tastes and their conception of what distinguishes a great work, on the sovereigns, the bourgeoisie and the clergy.[13] Between the cathedral builders and the ecclesiastical world there existed such a deep separation that the literature of the times teaches us nothing about the history of Gothic art. For want of written documents putting us on the trace of its early tendencies, the innumerable disputes concerning its origins have remained unproductive. Archaeologists now seem to have renounced the hope of ever explaining the practices which best define the originality of Gothic masonry.

They have thus given up trying to discover why, during the second half of the twelfth century, the great naves (Noyon, Laon and Paris) were covered with groined arches on a square plan of six compartments, although they were less suitable than the groined vaults on the oblong bay plan already used at Cluny.[14] The oldest system, which appears the most natural to us, returns to favor at Chartres, Amiens and Reims. The temporary success of the sexpartite vault was evidently due to reasons that cannot be known today—reasons which were cogent in the middle of the twelfth century.[15]

By never making the ribs penetrate into the vaults, the Gothic builders adopted a course that our contemporaries hardly understand, accustomed as they are to making the various elements of their construction as solid as possible. Consequently we can raise the question of whether the ribs had not first of all been broad camouflages for groins.[16] Whatever the case, it seems certain that it is only toward the end of the Middle Ages that architects regarded the ribs as a stone framework supporting the webbing.[17]

In all the churches of five aisles except for Notre Dame in Paris, the flying buttresses are double-arched, separated by strong piers resting in a somewhat disturbing way at times on columns which separate the two side aisles. One wonders if the first Gothic builders thought of holding up their vaults by means of various supports, or better, by means of widely grooved abutments.[18] If they had understood the science of equilibrium of vaults, as has often been assumed, the medieval builders would have developed the Paris system.

The isolation of the *Cité esthétique*, which has the result of depriving our archaeologists of information on the history of medieval art, was very useful to the artists of that period in allowing them an important independence. "When artists in society," writes Viollet-le-Duc, "form a sort of caste in which all members are equal, they find themselves in the best circumstances for the free development of art. As a caste, they acquired in the bosom of the civil order, a marked predominance— especially in the divided society of the feudal order. . . . The experience or genius of each member enlightened the corporation, but imposed neither doctrines nor methods."[19]

Such an aristocracy of professionals,[20] who had a long time to think about the resources offered to them by a vocation of which they were perfect masters, was able to create an art which merits, better than any other, to be called an "art of producers." They executed a plan of an unequalled daring, that of breaking resolutely with Romanesque practices (which could, however, still be applied to beautiful works),[21] in order to devise a new system, instead of returning to antiquity[22] whose remains they studied with a critical spirit.[23]

In searching through the woods, they discovered flora which allowed them to put motifs of a lively originality in place of the imitations of famous antique fragments, the interpretations of luxurious objects or the fantasies invented by calligraphers,[24] all things that art lovers of every period have admired because they seem to be placed above conditions imposed by the matter to be shaped.[25] They established a harmony[26] between building and sculpture which did not interest their contemporaries any more than it interests "enlightened" men of our time. By studying the details of their own statues, they rediscovered a number of aesthetic rules whose value has been appreciated by the moderns only when great collections of ancient Greek works have appeared.[27]

We would have but an imperfect idea of the autonomy of this *Cité esthétique* if we did not know that it possessed an extraordinarily strong tradition which protected it against external influences. In speaking of the transformations that architecture underwent from the twelfth century until the dawning of the Renaissance, Viollet-le-Duc defined, in the following terms, the intellectual work that was produced: "It is an uninterrupted chain of inductions, a single link of which cannot be broken, for they have all been forged in virtue of the principle which had formed the first. And we will say that it perhaps would be easier to study Gothic architecture starting from its period of decline and going back successively from effects to causes and from consequences to principles, than in following its natural progression.

"Most of us have in this way been led to the study of the origins of this art, that is by starting at the point of its decline, and going back to the source."[28] Thanks to their traditional genius, the Gothic artisans were able to take on gigantic compositions with complete success, while men who profess independence almost always fail in such enterprises. Certain very significant facts show that they carefully conserved some ancient doctrines that their traveling companions had probably received from isolated practitioners of Greek science encountered in the Orient.

I recognize that there is a certain amount of exaggeration in Viollet-le-Duc's hypotheses on the testing of proportions brought about by means of various triangles,[29] but the principle appears incontestable. The use of this method, going back to very remote times,[30] makes edifices based on the same geometry appear to be related, which makes aesthetic judgments easier to make.[31] We know from Villard de Honnecourt that the Gothic artisans drew their sketches of statues around rectilinear schemas. Viollet-le-Duc thought that the Greeks proceeded in the same way in composing the metopes of the Parthenon and the friezes of the temple of Thesius. These practices achieved expressions remarkably well-suited to monument sculpture.[32] It seems natural enough for architects raised in the cult of antiquity to have respected, from the Renaissance up until the nineteenth century, the Greek custom of never constructing façades with more than twelve columns;[33] but it is quite remarkable that this rule was applied in the Gothic naves of France;[34] this would be inexplicable without admitting an inheritance of ancient aesthetics.

I do not know if anyone has yet noted the similarities between the longitudinal sections of Gothic aisles and the façades of palaces built at a time when the taste for good composition reigned in French architecture. In the first cathedrals, we find two superimposed porticos, crowned by an attic (triforium), above which open rather modest windows that can be compared to high dormer windows (Noyen, Laon, Paris). Later, it was recognized that in order to utilize the resources that glassmakers provided to the decorative arts, following the principles of good composition, it was necessary to treat the window work (until then having a very small aesthetic role) as an important level. The galleries which never seem to have had much usefulness, were omitted.[35] The triforium became a mezzanine.[36] Finally it was connected to the window level by making it translucent in such a way as to achieve a composition which brings to mind the colossal order.[37] In reading what our best archaeologists—all more or less unacquainted with the concerns engendered by the study of architectural principles—write on these transformations, we understand that the values of these various systems of composition were absolutely unintelligible to the advisers of princes, the great merchants and medieval bishops.

The symbolism practiced by Gothic artists still belongs to that hidden life of aesthetic tradition which made their community independent of ecclesiastical scholars. The latter have left us puerile, laborious studies on the symbolism of religious edifices that are as far from the motives which could have affected the medieval masters as are the hypotheses proposed by modern dreamers with the purpose of deciphering the alleged puzzles of Gothic sculpture.[38] True symbolism ought to serve only to explain, for motives drawn from popular beliefs, decorative preconceptions which could not be justified on grounds of technique, aesthetics or liturgy. It would not be absurd to assume that the vertical lines were heavily accentuated with the intention of expressing symbolically the mystical impulse of souls;[39] but there are no facts to show that a connection between these two things was established in the

Middle Ages.[40] We should therefore probably view this theory as a literary invention with no more value than the theory that likens cathedrals to forests.[41]

There are some examples which seem to belong incontestably to symbolism. It has often been noted that the first bell towers had a disproportionate importance to that of the bells that they sheltered. It has been surmised that they were perhaps built partly for military purposes.[42] I think that they were certainly constructed very high in order to place under holy protection the great open country which surrounded them. Later, the effectiveness of their protective quality was augmented by topping them with spires, which very probably, in the beginning, represented the flame of a sacrifice.[43] The tower lanterns that were at times placed at the crossing of aisles were intended to diffuse the emanations of worship over the neighboring area,[44] according to the barbarians, who brought them into use in the fifth century.[45] The desire to protect the faithful, assembled at prayer, against demons led to multiplying religious images at the doors of the churches.[46] I think that the pinnacles were probably conceived more to serve as observation posts for celestial guardians than to increase the stability of the vaults. The great rose windows whose purpose has remained an enigma,[47] could well have been remembrances of the gladiators' nets.[48]

The façade of Notre Dame in Paris owes its beauty to its military symbolism, which connects it closely to the gates of Roman fortresses.[49] The Gallery of the Kings shows us defenders ready to crush any enemies who would advance on the square in front of the church. The high gallery, devoid of statues, was supposed to be inhabited by spirits entrusted with pushing back airborne enemies.[50]

The decline of art progressed rapidly after the artists abandoned the community of artisans to mix with courtiers, humanists and rich bourgeois. The pragmatic philosopher will not fail to note that the plutocratic oligarchies regard as particularly interesting those forms of art which are quite similar to activities in which they fancy themselves proficient. The men of the world feel themselves highly capable of directing theaters; they like to play salon comedies; their most seductive festivals are palliative operas. It is therefore natural that the scenic arts controlled aesthetics after the Renaissance. Painters composed great ensembles in which they grouped imposing choruses, inspired by episodes taken from famous tragedies, or they imagined erotic mythologies. Play actors who seem occupied with declaiming loud tirades or throwing themselves about like maniacs were sculpted in stone by geniuses.[51] Architects, instead of trying to construct well-planned buildings, painted vast decors that they applied for better or worse onto buildings whose interior arrangement generally did not correspond to their external appearance.

The official teaching still maintains a little prestige for what is called classical art, while the progress of our mercantile civilization favors other parodies of the productive arts. Music, for example, has occupied a very important place in the world since the time when every well-bred young lady could fill her house with piano noise. If the deplorable Catholic imagery continues to be in evidence, it is because it faithfully reproduces the edifying postures that the devout perform in the course of their worship services.[52] Men of the stock market support painters whose interests greatly resemble their own. That is why they pay very dearly for landscapes which remind them of sexual revels,[53] vulgar scenes of racing, backstage and café life—pictures whose bizarre execution denotes in their authors a very lively feeling of puffery. The so-called *avant-garde* painters are almost all perfect bourgeois whose spirit has never been touched by any poetry.

Architecture is probably the art that has suffered most in the conditions of contemporary society. Architects are asked to regard emporiums, palace hotels and rooms where tickets are bought as patterns of the most noble composition. They are confined to designing pretentious decorations, which are capable of emphasizing the glorification of money. If a *Cité esthétique* still existed, the ideas formed within it could not have any connection with the architectural practices governed by our capitalists. This art form, which has kept almost nothing of what made it great art, interests practically no one.

In the Romantic period, it was believed easy to revive medieval art, which everyone then claimed to admire passionately. Highly talented men constructed churches which gave rise to many deceptions. These costly monuments are now regarded as simple archaeological playthings. When we examine an old Gothic composition, we have the preconceived notion that it possesses a very marked poetic character because we assume that it is filled with a symbolism which was understood instinctively by all the members of the *Cité esthétique*. But when we are in the presence of a modern Gothic composition, we wonder why the artist has imitated some part of a celebrated monument instead of another equally admired piece. All poetry is suppressed by this comparative criticism, which is needed for the evaluation of Gothic art as revived by theoreticians. This example clearly shows the folly of talented men when they attempt to subject to their analytical intelligence that which belongs to historical development. Such an observation conforms completely to the principles of pragmatism.

The powerlessness of the mind that is free of traditions again appears very clearly in the results obtained by the schools that have been founded in our time for the purpose of arresting the decline of the arts practiced by the working world. Eighteenth-century philosophy had taught that rational education should be limited to facilitating the exercise of the faculties of the naturally good man who, above all, needs protection against the baneful influence of tradition. Regarding man as having been created sovereign, democracy views the reading of penny newspapers as amply allowing the ignorant to be the equal of the scholar in the political realm. It goes without saying that man is naturally artistic,[54] so that he would produce great works if he had enough manual skill to materialize his thought. Contemporary pedagogy has not succeeded in producing an elite capable of directing the workers in decorative arts as many eloquent writers had hoped. The schools created for the aesthetic formation of the people seem often to have contributed to uprooting from their class young men who would have made excellent workers, to precipitating the ruin of superior crafts and consequently further subordinating production to the fantasies of amateurs. Only the unconscious forces of history are in a position to provide an aristocracy of artist-producers. The errors I note here would not have been committed if our ruling classes had known pragmatism.

The history of medieval art could suggest to the pragmatic philosopher many other instructive ideas, but I will limit myself to discussing the following: The ideology of the Gothic community on the eve of its downfall was presented with conditions which, according to the doctrine of Charles Peirce, could have assured to it the highest degree of formal perfection; indeed this ideology was mixed with daily experiences which in the eyes of the producers brought out either magical values,[55] technical knowledge or the beauty of the system. The artisans never had any doubt of the significance of concepts accompanied by a considerable practical realization. The mind had not yet subjected the whole of reality created by inventors to its logical rules. Around what could be called a *center*, what could be demonstrated by principles and clearly explained, there existed a marginal area in which the laborer, guided by knowledge acquired during a solemn apprenticeship, performed his work unerringly. This supra-intellectualist zone became practically negligible at the end of the Middle Ages when the poetic spirit receded before the scientific spirit. In the beginning, there were many innovations which strongly resembled capricious accidents. The value that is attributed to them today began to be recognized only after a long application had revealed their advantages. They were interpreted through perspectives often quite alien to those of the first Gothics.[56]

III

At the heart of our modern *Cité savante*, order is established under conditions resembling those that suit the *Cité esthétique* rather than those observed in the political world. Very deep changes are often realized in it in a rather short time without there being a need for a legislator to promulgate reforms. Full of admiration for the marvelous adventures of certain contemporary scientific theories, many enthusiasts have ended by maintaining that absurdity will rule society so long as all activities are not given over to the anarchic initiatives of ingenious individualities.

Many times, doctrines destined to become fundamental have been introduced with such weak proofs that if a tribunal of scholars had been called upon to rule on their value, it would have proclaimed them rash.[57] They succeed in being accepted if they make their way in the company of extremely productive methods of investigation, if this association leads to results whose utility is manifested daily and if consequently they favorably impress ardent researchers.[58] Thanks to the competition of a large number of anonymous people, innovations are tested in the most varied ways. Under the control of a methodical teaching, syntheses appear which appropriately combine the elaborations of current knowledge with the good acquisitions preserved from the past. A language is created to translate the essential tendencies of the system into clear, sure and concentrated formulas. Thus, the period that can be called the "pragmatic stage" is replaced by the "classical stage" in which most often we no longer encounter the slightest trace of the ideas that had directed the first thinkers.

When competent men have become familiarized with the new methods of understanding natural questions, which were treated as revolutionary at first, ingenious professors, desirous of having the latest scientific progress accepted in the schools, create didactic systems. At the head of these systems appear certain propositions whose evidence forces itself, according to the professors, on those who make the path-breaking steps in this kind of research. The postulates appear incontestible to the majority of educated men in the "classical stage" for reasons which are historical and not, as is commonly taught, due to the affinities which exist between them and the unalterable foundations of our intellectual power. The prodigious applications which unceasingly enrich theories reinforce these principles in an implicit way, almost in the same way that the conduct of men of renowned prudence reinforces the principles of the conventional wisdom. The development of the scholarly community has erased from memory the objections that were thought so forceful at the time the new doctrines were introduced. The habits of mind that were created lead us to find simple, basic and obvious that which in fact has resulted from long reflections brought about through prolonged application.[59] But pragmatism does not lose all its effectiveness during the classical period.

(a) The form in which Greek geometry has reached us has greatly contributed to the spreading of false ideas on these questions. Our fathers were victims of an illusion similar to the one that persuaded the Renaissance that art could never free itself from ancient tutelage. They believed that it was necessary to seek evidence of true mathematical genius in the books that the schools preserved for them. The problems treated by the moderns—far more important than those of the past—are resolved by entirely new methods. But the intellectualists relate these differences to historical accident and think that the nobility of geometry would be misconstrued if it were not recognized that its foundation has a spirituality as great as the tradition bequeathed by the Greeks. In order truly to understand what science is, we need to think about the achievement of a dialectic whose most perfect model is found in the teachings of Euclid.

Under the influence of these prejudices, many mathematicians imagined that geometry depends entirely on several "mysterious sources of truth" of which a few men of genius had the intuition.[60] They thought that the time had come to submit the postulates to searching criticism, to determine their statements clearly and to discuss their value. Several of the most illustrious scholars investigated how geometry would be transformed if it were based on new principles that to them appeared just as satisfactory for logicians as the traditional principles.[61] Henri Poincaré has written essays on these subjects that are as ingenious as they are useless. If such interpretations of science were legitimate, pragmatism would have nothing more to do in a science which had become dialectic.

This manner of subordinating science to a didactic which claims to be inspired by monuments of Hellenic pedagogy could only be accepted today if it could be recognized at what point the obligations imposed on the Greek geometers by the prejudices of dialectical masters were cumbersome. In 1806 Delambre expressed the opinion that the Greeks must have had mathematical procedures, which have since been lost, to establish certain theorems which are explained in their books in a very confused way.[62] His hypothesis leads one to the assumption that proof of the Euclidian type is not as admirable as was long believed.

Michel Chasles noted, in the strongest terms, the serious drawbacks of the Greek mode of exposition: "The ancients," he said, "more zealous of convincing than of clarifying,[63] have hidden all the traces which could have revealed their methods of discovery and invention and which would have been able to guide the continuators of their labors. This was the cause of that timid and confused advance of geometry and of the incoherence of its methods in questions of the same kind; or, to speak more precisely, this was the cause of the absence of those sure and proper methods, found in modern geometry, in entire classes of questions calling for a certain generality."[64] Euclidian-style proofs cannot be justified completely by the conditions of the subject. Did it not depend then on accidental circumstances of Hellenic civilization?

The Greek geometricians addressed themselves to men of a singularly alert state of mind, very good judges of ingenious discourses who were unused to blending the theory of mathematical figures with extensive research in physics.[65] Such readers examined each proposition separately to see if it was artistically expressed. Nothing was more appropriate than to offer them proofs which recall the prolix discussions of the Platonic dialogues. Today didactics no longer is of any interest to us except as a very minor auxiliary of science. Science is composed of very general problems that have been raised in order to satisfy our desire to calculate phenomena. The means used to put young people in a position to enjoy the fruits of the achievements of their ancestors should be distinguished from the modes of activity of the scholarly community. Didactics is good only to open to apprentices paths which can lead them to mastery. Now that books on mathematics are opened only to find in them the instruments needed to resolve natural questions, not much attention is paid to the eloquence of the rhetoric of the ancient dialecticians;[66] consequently, proofs are reduced to only what is necessary in order not to arouse doubts in the critical spirit of beginners; it is above all important to lead them as rapidly as possible to a degree of familiarity with the methods so that they feel vividly the utility of what they are taught. One could say then that current pedagogy was inspired by pragmatism in abolishing prejudices that the superstition of classicism had imposed on our fathers on the subject of Euclidian-style proofs.

(b) It has often been said that d'Alembert, consulted by a young man on the very real difficulties presented by the elements of infinitesimal calculus, answered him: "Carry on; faith will come to you."[67] A few scholars have reproached the author of a *Treatise on Dynamics*, long regarded as a classic,[68] of having, on this occasion, reduced the dignity of teaching in order to take pleasure in imitating those impertinent gentlemen who get rid of importune solicitors with a joke. In my opinion he meant that by seriously taking part in the work of geometricians of the time in the most varied discussions of physics, the new mathematician would quickly forget that in the long-ago time of his introduction to complex analysis he was very confused. D'Alembert's maxim is unclear today because the conditions of study of this kind have radically changed since the eighteenth century. Today they are dominated by the functioning of engineering schools whose students need to possess a certain knowledge of methods in calculus to exercise their skill well. As they are not generally destined to become true armchair scholars, their teachers must know how to render the elementary expositions rapid, clear and convincing, so that these young people are not discouraged into abandoning their careers; but we should recognize that this result is obtained only by means of numerous sleight-of-hand tricks.[69]

It was an instinctive pragmatism which, in d'Alembert's time, was found at the basis of the certitude possessed by geometry after it completed its scientific apprenticeship. Pragmatism, which we "breathe," so to speak, in our industrial society, inspires in the best present-day professors sufficient boldness to dare to indulge in the games of their simplified pedagogy. We can say further that a spirit of anticipation of pragmatism exists in the most studious pupils; they accept with unequalled confidence, poorly established propositions in the hope of rapidly covering the ground that the ancients had painfully cultivated, in order to participate in the scientific production of the century.

(c) Pragmatism explains well the repugnance, so difficult to overcome, which men of ordinary intelligence feel for the occult fables which so often have led astray professors of universally recognized wisdom. Many academic harangues maintain that observation, manipulated by personages equipped with fine diplomas, was truly the oracle of modern culture, the sure condition of scientific progress and the primary motor of our creative evolution. If this is true, then science ought quickly to add to its realm those vast reaches of the supernatural on which numerous masters of research have already moved toward experiments that promise rich harvests. Men who are excited by the idea of greatly enlarging the perspectives open before the human mind answer the prudent men who object to the numerous failures of mediums, that according to Claude Bernard, "negative facts, however numerous, never destroy a single positive fact."[70] If, therefore, say the partisans of parapsychology, hardened skeptics refuse to admit the positive facts cited by the occultists (undoubtedly still rather few facts, but supported by some academic luminaries), it is because they are led astray by one of those harmful scientific dogmas noted by Claude Bernard.[71]

The pragmatist replies that if "psychic sciences" really exist, they ought to be able to undergo proofs that are similar to those that inventions in physics have undergone with consistent success. Now we have not yet heard talk about applications of these "psychic sciences" to the needs of everyday life. No one would contest the virtues of the divining rod if this tool worked as regularly as a compass. The clairvoyance of sleepwalkers would be recognized by every physician if these extraordinary women were employed daily in clinics to diagnose hidden injuries.[72] If mental telepathy is not a farce, why doesn't it compete with wireless telegraphy?

The experiments that the scientist organizes (necessarily rather limited in number) with the purpose of increasing the glory of his laboratory, are not always as conclusive as is ordinarily believed. The master and his assistants strive to obtain a desired result.[73] They do this using a method that is conceived in order to perfect an initial observation of uncertain significance. Through pride, they are strongly inclined to ever larger claims without having to fear anything more than quickly forgotten academic squabbles in case of imprudence. Suggestion acts on them strongly and at times exclusively in order to lead them to see what their impassioned minds want them to see. Criticism of such works, like that of all those produced by individuals having only slight responsibilities of a purely intellectual order, results from psychology as much as physics.

The laughable adventures of the rise and fall of N-rays reveal how easily a scientific insanity can triumph in contemporary science. Many *French* observers successfully repeated Blondlot's supposed discoveries. The academic reviews were, for two years, filled with increasingly absurd communications; a 50,000 franc prize was awarded to the illustrious professor at Nancy whose glory seemed no less than Déroulède's. Today it is confessed that the "French" rays constituted a pure product of mental suggestion and contagion and that they never existed.[74] Scholastic control was thus shown to be powerless, the highest scientific authorities having consented to share the illusions of a colleague.

The only proof that a pragmatist can regard as decisive is provided by the enormous mass of endeavors directed by a multitude of men who want to exploit a discovery commercially and who are outside of academic hierarchies. The phenomena ruled by the law that is being tested are not the same in factories as they are in laboratories—a supreme end whose passionate pursuit can intoxicate the intelligence—but only *means* mixed with many others in schemes which will enrich or ruin the entrepreneurs. The slightest success attracts to the new production many of those adventurous individuals who are always looking for opportunities to realize extra profits. Willingly, they change known equipment in order not to be obliged to be subjected to the whims of the patent holders. Unceasingly, they modify details in the hope of obtaining some advantages that are yet unsuspected. On the other hand, men who are interested in maintaining the past strive to discourage the capitalists by frantically calling attention to the practical difficulties encountered in changes. Transcending the infinitely varied competition manifested among the many productive methods, technical superiorities end up by becoming obvious to everyone. Today it is rare for much time to elapse before the value of a new method is recognized; the natural law incorporated into the triumphant industrial process is judged before the tribunal of economics.

IV

After having recognized the services rendered to art by the medieval *Cité esthétique* and to science by today's *Cité savante,* we are led by legitimate induction to wonder if prosperous peoples perhaps need the aid of a moral group (*Cité morale*) in order to maintain their good customs. The philosophers have not deigned to concern themselves with this question, believing that they have done enough in discoursing on the principle of the sovereign good, in formulating beautiful abstract precepts or in writing pathetic exhortations to virtue. Le Play had the great merit of examining some of the concrete conditions of ethics in the course of the travels he undertook across Europe to keep up with all the processes of metallurgy. He asked those men versed in the practices of various societies about the means by which order was established in their respective countries. His monographs focussed on the *Cités morales,* which were then in the process of disappearing, swept away by the forces of capitalist economics. Later Paul de Rousiers described an American *Cité morale,* which he believed was destined to furnish the model for the natural aristocracies that, in his opinion, the new times would require.[75]

According to this sagacious observer, the evils caused to the United States by politicians[76] are largely compensated by the intelligent activity of a "group of individuals playing an elevated and disinterested role, dedicating to the public good a significant portion of the advantages that they obtained," who have achieved exceptional positions in the economic life of the country as a result of severe selectivity. "The distinctive character of this American aristocracy is the solicitude it shows in raising to its level, the social elements capable of rising."[77] Its members establish strong educational institutions.[78] They exercise and develop "the sense of their social responsibility" on the boards of trustees which are "an effective school of aristocratic government, because one learns in them to manage considerable public interests without remuneration."[79]

Le Play believed that he could teach the heads of industry a social science which would enable them to exercise the functions of "social authorities" as easily as he taught the science of metallurgy to future mining engineers.[80] Being devoid of philosophic spirit, he did not suspect that moral groups (*Cités morales*) are the products of long historical development. His failure was as complete as that of the art lovers who wanted to produce an aesthetic elite in the world of work by means of schools of design.

Paul de Rousiers seems to have believed that Le Play's ideas failed solely because the thought of this reformer was focused on archaic models which had become irreconcilable with the capitalist way of life.

According to this author, Europe should learn from America[81] which institutions can direct the rejuvenation that today is indispensable for the old countries "under penalty of irreversible decline and prompt disappearance." He wanted our masters of finance to form "an alert and active aristocracy," making its power serve "not the suppression but the advancement" of citizens "who struggle unsuccessfully."[82] As unphilosophic as Le Play, de Rousiers did not think of asking if the American *Cité morale* that he admired so enthusiastically did not owe its prosperity to conditions which could sooner or later disappear even in the United States.

First of all, we should note the truly extraordinary passion of a nation of bustling speculators in wanting stubbornly to remain faithful to the traditions of 1777 [*sic*]. In stating that the Yankees have little taste for what are called on the old continent "advanced ideas," many Europeans have accused America of being a routinist country.[83] United States citizens evidently imagine that by unceasingly invoking the teachings bequeathed by the Founding Fathers, they are helping to assure their country an effective means of confronting future storms comparable to those that their forefathers successfully surmounted thanks to the superiority of their public law.[84]

I ascribe to the old "covenant" mentality the associations that Americans form every time that a common peril appears—associations whose action is so practiced, prompt and vigorous.[85] Thus committees of honorable men have many times quelled, by *lynching*, crimes before which official justice remained powerless.[86] In-depth inquiries conducted by men who are respected but who lack any legal mandate have served to rouse popular indignation against municipal magistrates misappropriating public funds.[87] In 1896 an insuperable barrier was erected against the instincts of the masses in order to save "sane money."[88]

The strength of the *Cité morale* still rests on the economic bases that Paul de Rousiers studied so well. Rich men from older Eastern states exercise a very intelligent patronage on settlement in the West, restraining the immigrants and imposing the spirit of the New World on them to the extent that the latter are receptive to it.[89] They had good success with the Germans from the Saxon plains and especially with the Scandinavians, who seemed to have preserved much of the old qualities of their race.[90] On the other hand, almost all the Irish rebel against this adaptation, live in the great metropolises in preference to the country, and join in politico-criminal associations which allow those who are popularly elected to commit frightful acts of piracy.[91]

The ideological, political and economic causes that have contributed to giving the American *Cité morale* the authority it enjoys do not belong, finally, to the area of the universal conditions of capitalism. They cannot be transplanted to our country by propagating a suitable social science. They depend so completely on traditions that we are led to wonder if perhaps they will not resist innovating forces in America.

Not so long ago here, there was a bourgeois intellectual aristocracy which constituted a *Cité morale* profoundly different from the one in America. Its members were thrifty men, having little taste for industrial struggles and greatly concerned with the security of their children.[92] According to the opinion of the French middle classes, the most incontestable principle of natural right should be the obligation imposed on the public authorities to give suitably lucrative posts to the young people with good university educations. Fed with the idealist rhetoric that our schools received from the Jesuits, they could not find strong enough words to condemn governments which favored material interests too much, by opening up opportunities to speculators.[93] Full of enthusiasm for Plutarch's heroes, they bitterly condemned kings for the luxury which surrounded them. Taking the romance of ancient democracies that they learned in school as history, they regarded the republican regime as the only one compatible with reason.[94] Therefore wise statesmen, according to middle-class opinion, should have prepared for this happy future by inundating the people with instruction so that the people would be able to choose their leaders soon. To the critics who called their attention to the vices of politicians, they answered that these vices were monarchical remnants that would be swept away by republican progress. The theories of French liberalism were formed in the bosom of this *Cité morale*. Now that it is in full decomposition, these doctrines of which our forefathers were so proud appear to be derived from a very mediocre metaphysics. But the country has not come to the ideas advocated by Le Play, de Rousiers or Taine, ideas that have remained the property of powerless coteries.

These eminent writers would not have wasted their talent as has occurred if, instead of trying to establish schools, they had only given a clear expression to the well-founded aspirations of a *Cité morale* whose authority would have been uncontested. A teaching based on tradition, on the poetry contained in education, and on the conditions of the economic life of powerful groups would have been productive. The intellectualist translation of instinctive forces would have assured to them more glory than their inventions. Unfortunately for them, they were condemned to crying in the wilderness. Their defeat constitutes a counter-proof, which shows very well the importance of *Cités morales* in the history of institutions, customs and ideas.

In avoiding the mention of the *Cité morale* which exists in his country, William James believed perhaps that he would give an appearance of greater generality to his doctrine. He ended by rendering pragmatism abstract, vague and subject to innumerable contradictions. It has been maintained, for example, that his pragmatism led to submitting morality to the tribunal of that type of vulgar opinion dominated by novelists, journalists and politicians. William James seems to have been greatly surprised at the uproar produced by his teaching. He had taken the precaution of asserting that the truth is not one of those questions which can be decided by a majority of voters. According to him, all pragmatists ought to agree on the following points: that "in the long run it is useless to resist experience's pressure; that the more of it a man has, the better his position with respect to the truth; that some men, having had more experience, are therefore better authorities than others; that some are also wiser by nature and better able to interpret the experience they have had; that it is one part of such wisdom to discuss and follow the opinion of our betters; and that the more systematically and thoroughly such comparison and weighing of opinions is pursued, the truer the opinions that survive are likely to be."[95] Very few things in this declaration of principles would have to be changed in order to conclude that the truth is what we accept as the best, on the advice of the *Cité morale*, which has reconciled conflicting opinions.

William James did not believe it necessary to complete his thought because he shared the illusions of democratic optimism with his American readers. He was raised to respect the dogma of popular sovereignty, according to which the best is realized of itself amidst the struggles of political parties. Accustomed, like all his compatriots, to scorning the idea of ruling classes, our philosopher was not disposed to take an interest in the role played by the *Cités morales*. The extraordinary material prosperity of their nation greatly contributes to blurring the Yankees' critical spirit. The ferocious struggles undertaken among groups of speculators have almost always stimulated some progress in production. The experience of the nineteenth century has shown that the United States has fortunately escaped the grave catastrophies which, according to the predictions of sage European statesmen, ought to have followed certain electoral consultations. Living in an environment that was replete with confidence in the "mysterious forces" of history,[96] William James was little disposed to study in its details the process which had caused the success of the moral ideas that he saw respected around him.

V

One of the most fruitful advantages that William James claimed for pragmatism, in comparison to all the other philosophies, consists in the fact that: "Ours is the only articulate attempt in the field to say positively what truth actually *consists of.* Our denouncers have literally nothing to oppose to it as an alternative. For them, when an idea is true, it *is* true, and there the matter terminates, the word 'true' being undefinable. The relation of the true idea to its object, being, as they think, unique, it can be expressed in terms of nothing else, and needs only to be named for anyone to recognize and understand it. Moreover, it is invariable and universal, the same in every single instance of truth, however diverse the ideas, the realities, and the other relations between them may be.

"Our pragmatist view, on the contrary, is that the truth relation is a definitely experienceable relation, and therefore describable as well as namable; that it is not unique in kind, and neither invariable nor universal."[97]

If one wants to be inspired completely by William James's principles, it is proper to proceed as we have done in the sketches of the three *Cités* which have already been examined above; that is, to study groups of activities belonging incontestably to the same type, according to the opinion of men versed in these experiences, that can be compared rather approximately to organisms and each one of which relates very clearly to a discernible period. In countries in which old social structures still exist, account will have to be taken of many secondary *Cités*, in which are preserved practices of corporative agreements whose power is ordinarily more imperious than that of philosophic morals.

Our Occident possesses an immense Christian *Cité* which has served as a model to the associations whose genius has claimed to rise above purely national interests. I do not think it useful to examine its functioning here, because under its Catholic form, which interests Frenchmen almost exclusively, this spiritual organization is hardly suitable for enlightening us on the functioning of pragmatism. According to the leaders of the Roman Catholic hierarchy, its doctrines are independent of the course of history.[98] They have supposedly been imposed by infallible authorities, instead of being the result of quasi-anarchic competition. Thus, the Catholic *Cité* resembles much less the *Cité savante* which creates science through pragmatic procedures than that *Cité* so dear to Auguste Comte which has reached the age of didactic dullness. It is well known that the Positivists are great admirers of Catholic discipline.

We must not pretend to reduce any of these *Cités* to a mechanism whose laws would rigorously rule the important parts of their functioning. We ought to be able to content ourselves with descriptions which, however, almost never succeed in embracing all the realities having serious value in our experience. We think we are happy when we have succeeded in making precise enough, details enabling us to orient ourselves in the midst of phenomena whose arrangement presents a horrifying complexity.[99] All the more, then, will prudent philosophers be careful not to try to establish a general theory which guarantees the presence or absence of truth to their disciples.[100] But among the various sorts of truths which correspond to the various *Cités*, common sense ascertains formal analogies strong enough to justify the use of a general term designating them. We can even think that certain remnants of medieval theology are not too far from William James's conception of truth.

All the young members of a *Cité* have, in the course of their apprenticeship, acquired a more or less complete confidence in the value of what their elders consider to be great works. Thus in its relations with new generations, every group can be regarded as a school where one learns to do what the masters having consummate experience have judged to be worthy of imitation; to arrive at the firm resolution to conform to this teaching is what is commonly called attaining wisdom. Historic accidents which have exercised a profound influence on the intellectual development of the Occident throughout the centuries have been able to operate in such a way as to suggest the pragmatic terminology of truth. Exaggerating some of the most extraordinary concepts of Greek thought, the Middle Age established such narrow relations between mathematical science, theology and moral principles[101] that the Christian tradition reserves the term "wise" to men who want to take the demonstrated truth as their rule of conduct. William James's pragmatism, which is more concerned with religion than any other modern philosophy,[102] consequently deems it natural to think that the apprenticeships provided by the *Cités* considered here belong to the order of the acquisition of truth. By a reversal of ideas—which is not exceptional in the history of ideas—William James, having often read that wisdom consists in respecting truth, has called "truth" that which is recognized as wise in the American *Cité morale*. Thus, truth would be the product of our consciousness controlled by "social authorities" of incontestable dignity.

The Catholic theory of truth has led theologians to attack pragmatism frantically. The masters of supernatural science pretend to be able to demonstrate that a true religion exists; without knowledge of this religion one could not obtain happiness after death; they say that divine bounty has so happily organized our understanding that the resources of secular dialectic are enough to prove incontestably that Catholicism is identical with the True Religion. The reasons given in favor of this proposition are so varied that there are some adapted to every degree of intelligence in such a way that all men of good faith can know what the True Religion is. The clergy believes that it would be severely derelict in its duties if it did not keep a close watch on the sophists who abuse the simplicity of the masses in order to lead them into the path of condemnation. Such people who make their victims lose the heavenly life are a thousand times more detestable than the murderers who do violence only to the terrestrial life. Therefore all the ecclesiastical doctors think that the establishment of the Inquisition is the natural consequence of their theory of truth.[103]

Present-day educated Catholics blush at the persecutions formerly ordered by the Church.[104] They believe that various sincere convictions, sensible and rich in good works, have equal right to the protection of the state; a few people even dare to assert, with Le Play, that Protestant competition protects Catholicism against the resurgence of abuses suffered by the Middle Ages, with the leaders in the hierarchy unable to remedy the evils pointed out by the scholars. Theologians, scandalized to see our contemporaries thus place on an equal footing the Church, which preserves intact the vessel of faith, and the sects that falsify it, denounce the culpable indifference with which the laws of truth are considered today. They believe that all the trouble arises from the fact that the form given to the theory of the true religion has aged a bit; they hope that one day or another a new St. Thomas will appear to give to a rejuvenated Christian metaphysics the position that it deserves in the totality of our knowledge; while waiting, they strive to stop the advance of systems which favor the negators of the true religion. Pragmatism is odious to them because they believe that, in refusing to place the truth above historical activities, it is the crowning of a liberalism which subordinates the truth to the arbitrary wills of individuals.

If theologians were not blind, as they are, due to professional prejudice, they would easily perceive that their doctrine of the true religion has no chance of converting men so long as general opinion remains hostile to the idea of restoring the Inquisition. They would tell themselves that modern philosophy is bound to be inspired largely by the principle of the equality of sects which holds such an important position in our public law. Pragmatism renders the convictions produced by the teaching of their Christian *Cité* independent of the qualities whose existence the old metaphysicians had claimed to establish in a universal way; thus the theologians should be grateful to pragmatism for furnishing a means of justifying the unshakable faith of believers who do not need to have it proven scientifically that they possess true religion.

The leaders of contemporary paganism have made excellent use of the error committed by the theologians who persist in arguing on the infallibility of the Church in the same terms as if our society were not founded on the negation of this privilege. Being themselves anti-pragmatist, they regard it as obvious that hidden reasons, stronger than the

reasonings of clerical dialecticians, lead Catholics to seem to take doubtful apologetics as perfect certainties. At times pagans attribute to
Catholics a fanaticism unamenable to any critical examination; at times
they accuse them of wanting to exploit advantages gained through
piety;[105] at times they depict them as epicureans who see in religion
only a political instrument. Accustomed to attribute to the artifices of
the devil everything annoying that happens to them, theologians avoid
reflecting on the irreligious consequences that their unfortunate metaphysics suggests to men today.

Skeptical explanations of religion, like those just discussed, could not
occur to William James, whose thinking was so deeply imbued in the
Puritan traditions of America. His countrymen find it as natural for a
people to divide into sects as into competing industrial groups. All
Yankees agree that fundamental Christian beliefs were very important
in creating the prosperity of the States. The spectacle confronting James
in his country greatly contributed to his conception of the pragmatic
way of understanding knowledge. Religious convictions appeared to
James to be as worthy of admiration, as legitimate in the face of criticism, and as useful to society as the most established scientific knowledge can be. In Europe it is rather generally admitted that the mind, in
going from mathematics to theology, undergoes a continuous decline,
due to the fact that the proofs, which at the beginning of this transposition were addressed to the universality of refined intelligence, no longer
interest anyone except a rather limited group of ecclesiastics. The true
philosopher, who, free from all preconceived notions, observes things as
they are in reality, sees clearly that in the two extremities of the chain
identical certitudes are encountered.[106]

As different as mathematics and theology may be in their objects of
study, methods and educational tendencies, they both end in the
absolute. In life we do not usually feel the need of having, as in
mathematics and in theology, propositions to which we give unreserved
adherence. But almost always there exists a marked disproportion between the degree of importance that can be attributed to the proofs
and the social value of the conclusions. The psychologist who wants to
concern himself with the theory of knowledge is led by the nature of
his studies, relating usually to collective life, to think that this theory
ought to be ruled rather more by the way in which beliefs are presented
to the mind in the course of its activity, than by the way in which they
are justified. William James, who felt this difference all the more strik-
ingly as he was highly concerned with religious questions where it is
so apparent, necessarily had to direct his thought toward pragmatism,
which views our knowledge in the context of the functioning of the
scholarly, aesthetic, moral, professional and religious *Cités*.

Pragmatism brings considerable help to Christianity in leading us to a much more satisfying idea of tradition than the usual one. Ordinarily enough tradition is spoken of as an object that intelligence can isolate from history to mold as one pleases. Thus, distinguished contemporary writers have often pretended to be capable of rejuvenating expiring traditions, by means of literature, sociological theories or ingenious legislation.[107] So many mistakes have been made in following these ideas, that men of calm judgment today greatly distrust doctrines in which tradition is invoked as a means of proof.

The traditionalists who created such a furor at the beginning of the nineteenth century mixed in their metaphysics the mythology of the golden age, the theology of early revelation, and the fantasies that Rousseau brought into fashion on the subject of the original goodness of our species.[108] They imagined that if they succeeded in tracing the course of history back to the most distant ages, they would discover several summary expressions of the true nature of things. Modern philosophy would be called upon to reshape elementary intuitions to prepare us for a future conforming to the order desired by universal reason. These notions are still found today in schools of socialism which hope to see capitalism end up in a kind of superior *savagery* where communism, sexual freedom and anarchy rule.[109]

A still commonly held error consists in the belief that an opinion could not have been held through many generations if it had not been verified by innumerable experiences. One can cite not a few rules based in magic that scholars have denied but which are followed nonetheless by prudent farmers.[110] Thus, it is not surprising that so many of our contemporaries do their thinking with the aid of proverbs, without suspecting that these formulas owed their success to the literary merits of anecdotes of which they are the conclusion.[111]

The idea of tradition has been brought into great disrepute by the sophisms that narrow-minded conservatives have put forth to demonstrate that their happiness is very advantageous to the state. They have claimed to be the representatives of a tradition formerly personified by men who, occupying situations analogous to theirs, were in their view greatly useful to society. Their adversaries answer that the experience of tradition is invoked wrongly, because if the privileged people of former times had perhaps rendered certain services, these people were paid for their trouble at usurious prices. Such polemics should remain outside philosophical concerns.

For the pragmatist, tradition is an element of the highest order in knowledge, provided that the tradition is genuine—that is, that it is a result of trial and error by competent men. Here are three observations which seem to me particularly worthy of mention: tradition ought to have long since entered into close relations with the life of a glorious *Cité* (scholarly, aesthetic, moral or religious); it ought to have been personified by men of superior talent; it ought to be rich in good results. When tradition is thus well established, the pragmatist does not hesitate to presume in its favor by virtue of which its affirmations have the right to be received until there are solid proofs to the contrary.

Readers who have followed attentively the explanations in this chapter will recognize that only a very imperfect idea of tradition was able to be made before pragmatism produced its doctrine of truth. Tradition has the definitive force of which I am speaking here only if, in the *Cité* under consideration, there is that free competition of enlightened wills that the Americans regard as indispensable for assuring the prosperity of civilized nations. Nine-tenths of the Frenchmen who pretend to use tradition in their political and religious polemics regard as harmful the conditions which legitimize tradition for the pragmatists. According to them, tradition is not nourished by liberty, but instead records the decisions of authority. Thus, pragmatism has nothing to discuss with the reactionary idea of tradition which flourishes in Europe.

In order to speak of pragmatism suitably, one must never separate liberty from reason. The tradition which we credit with influencing the formation of our convictions is the fruit of the free and reasoned efforts of our fathers. Our freedom and our reason shape this material with a view to improving our present conditions of life and to transmitting something useful to our successors if possible.[112]

A CRITIQUE OF *CREATIVE EVOLUTION*[1]

IV *Bergson's origin of matter and intelligence. The old division of labor in production. New productive organization. Return to the Maxwellian ideas. The struggle between* natural nature *and* artificial nature.

At this point we can usefully examine the most suitable pragmatic interpretation that should be given to what Bergson has described under the name of "simultaneous origin of matter and intelligence"; the doctrine put forth in *Evolution créatrice* is often singularly difficult to understand; on the other hand, when we reason along pragmatic lines on the facts which could have suggested to Bergson speculation whose obscurity confuses more than one reader, we arrive at rather simple conceptions. Moreover, I am persuaded that pragmatism allows us to explore completely this question of matter and intelligence provided that it contains no interest from the religious or aesthetic points of view. A comparison of Bergson's very vague formulations with the precise paraphrases which correspond to them in a pragmatic interpretation will clearly show the great value of the new pragmatic method of philosophizing.

Let us begin by pointing out that a large number of metaphysicians have tried to abolish the duality that popular opinion presumes between matter and intelligence. Some metaphysicians have done this by explaining how our ideas about intelligence can arise from laws on matter; others tell us how our knowledge of matter is conditioned by the properties which characterize the primitive nature of intelligence. According to the first group of metaphysicians, the activity of the mind is subject to the same principles as physical movements; by slightly exaggerating the logic of this system, they have sometimes gone so far as to assert that our brain is a kind of illusion-producing machine which brings forth certain epiphenomena that are adapted to the conventions of language. The second group of metaphysicians maintains that the mind overflows onto everything with which it comes into contact; this is a hypothesis that allows us to see in our own life, a voyage of the image which we call our body by way of a set of innumerable other images.[2] In order to obtain a close connection between matter and intelligence without being obliged to resort to the artifices of sleight-of-hand dialecticians, Bergson considerably narrowed the field of study; he considered only a mathematical intelligence applied to the examination of figures that are shaped in solid matter; we are thus led to concern ourselves with experimental physics and *artificial nature*.[3]

We can admit with Bergson that intellectuality and materiality derive from a more extensive form of existence.[4] Indeed we are used to viewing geometric bodies as exceptional representatives of natural types, whose elements are very similar to one another, that we can identify through names good only for uses in everyday life, but which are not capable of being defined in any precise way.[5] In the eyes of producers who are used to the discipline of geometry, the objects which vague popular knowledge focuses on are only outlines which should be replaced by material that is shaped with a view to satisfying the demands of a scientific intelligence.[6] We never succeed in a workshop in realizing exactly the projects desired by mathematicians. That is why we will accept—albeit in a slightly different sense than the one which Bergson seemed to want to give it—his sentence condemning matter to the fate of never completely attaining spatiality.[7] Finally, to the degree that we perfect our experimental tools, we succeed in forming more precise ideas, not only about the laws of nature directly, but again indirectly on everything that controls intelligence. I would thus be disposed to accept—for reasons other than those given by Bergson and in reversing the order of the propositions—the following formulation: "The more consciousness is intellectualized, the more matter is spatialized."[8]

Our modern civilization rests on an economy whose technique is in continual revolution,[9] while the techniques of previous ages were conservative; earlier philosophies which had to satisfy the sentiments of men who enjoyed stable means of production were right in basing themselves mainly on intellectualist principles, because as Bergson says, "Intelligence has as its essential function to bind like to like, and it is only facts that can be repeated that are entirely adaptable to the intellectual qualities."[10] We are greatly indebted to the author of *Evolution créatrice* for having attempted to make our contemporaries understand the necessity of adapting their mode of thinking to the revolutionary conditions of their life. Let us now find out if his doctrines provide us with insights on the conditions of *modern* technology.

First of all, this is how Bergson conceives of the idea of innovation: "Let us concentrate on what we have that is at the same time the most removed from externality and the least penetrated with intellectuality. . . . It is into pure duration that we re-immerse ourselves, a duration in which the past, always moving on, is growing unceasingly from a present that is absolutely new. But at the same time, we feel the mainspring of our will strained to its utmost limit. We must, by a violent contraction of our personality on itself, gather up our past which is escaping from us, in order to push it, compact and undivided, into a present that it will create by entering there."[11] And further on: "It is necessary that, turning back and twisting on itself, the faculty of *seeing* must be made one with the act of willing. This is a painful effort that can be made suddenly, by violating nature, but which cannot be maintained for more than a few moments."[12] Immediately upon no longer feeling the hard whip of the will to power, we quickly abandon the troubled regions of liberty so as to orient ourselves toward the calm regions of mechanism. As Bergson says: "If the relaxation were complete, there would no longer be either memory or will; that is, we never fall into this absolute passivity, any more than we can ever become absolutely free. But at the freest possible point, we get a glimpse of an existence made of a present which is continuously renewed. . . . At the basis of spirituality on the one hand, and of materiality with intellectuality on the other, there are then two opposing processes." The second is produced automatically by the simple interruption of the first.[13] Again he writes: "Intelligence and matter have adapted themselves to each other, in order to come to rest at a common form . . . [and this is] quite naturally, because it is the same inversion of the same movement which creates both the intellectuality of mind and materiality of things simultaneously."[14]

In order to appreciate fully the utility of this theory of relaxation, it is necessary to refer, first of all, to the old system of organization in manufacturing which has provided so many commonplaces in academic as well as popular literature. All physiologists are familiar with the disturbances—offering a certain analogy with those which could be brought on by the psychological "torsion" of which Bergson speaks—which are produced when we experience doubts about the success of undertakings on which we are concentrating our attention. The efforts we make are naturally all the more laborious the more that we attach importance to the success of our effort.[15] The goal of the division of labor was the suppression of doubts which assail the workers at the time when they must change significantly the pattern of using their tools or of arranging their products. Each manipulation was reduced to such a tiny thing that a person no matter how inexperienced could not have the slightest hesitation in choosing the right maneuver. Economists have noted especially that this artifice allowed a significant reduction of minute losses of time whose accumulation ends by being quite appreciable in the course of a day.[16] We should add that by contributing to the reduction of fatigue, it produced for the owner the same surplus-profit that would have been procured from an unpaid increase in the muscular power of the workers.

The less he was subject to emotions, the more easily man could suit his movements to those of a machine; insofar as his activity assumed this aspect, he became more insensitive to the insinuations of liberty; thus by a confirmation of reciprocal influences the automatism of the worker was perfected. The artisans who had preserved the aesthetic feeling for crafts felt a strong repugnance for a system in which all professional dignity disappeared; on their testimony, many writers denounced the danger that manufactures presented for civilization, in transforming free citizens into a class of serfs.[17] If we employ Bergsonian terminology, we ought to say that manufacturing produced such a great relaxation of the will that all spirituality disappeared in the laboring man, and led him through the discipline of the manufacturing process to a condition approaching that of a geometric determinism. Let us note that if Bergson's psychological description is accurate for materiality, it does not imply that intellectuality is produced in the consciousness of the master at the same time that materiality is produced in that of his worker.

This highly celebrated system of the division of labor no longer corresponds to the requirements of modern industry, which calls for qualities of observation, comparison and decision;[18] until recently, these qualities had been accused of being a waste of time. When a worker comes into a factory whose routine he is unfamiliar with, he cannot avoid a surprising timidity which ordinarily disappears rather quickly if he has received a good apprenticeship[19] and if the machinery has been arranged in such a way as to facilitate intelligent supervision. While in the past the worker would have drifted into automatism, he now thinks about the operation of the machines, while recalling the lessons of his professional masters, the instructions of his foreman and his experiences during his working life.[20]

The opinions expressed about the first high-speed machinery clearly show how much the psychology of the worker has changed: sixty years ago these machines inspired such amazement that acute observers wondered if it would not be less exhausting to do any kind of manual labor than to operate them; although their speed has greatly increased since that time, good workers control them without great difficulty, if the builders have installed means of scientific control.[21] The prejudices arising from the old industry are no longer encountered except in those vain and ignorant employers, of whom there are still too many today,[22] who accuse the graduates of technical schools of losing time by thinking instead of surrendering themselves to routine. When they begin work in a factory, these young people can at times hesitate when faced with minor difficulties because they are used to working only with abstractions. When they reach a method of reasoning that is concrete, individual and therefore rapid, they become the true representatives of modern labor.

These considerations lead us to recognize that the schema of the "simultaneous origin of matter and intelligence" proposed by Bergson corresponds to outdated historical conditions. But when a philosopher of his importance constructs a theory, one must always assume that it is based on observations worthy of notice; let us trace then what realities can be found under his rather complex images. Instead of saying, for example, that materiality and intellectuality are two poles of a psychological line, traced by man sometimes in one direction and sometimes in the other, let us speak of the enormous differences between inventors and engineers. Anyone familiar with economic history knows the obstacles that must be overcome in order to introduce procedures that break with accepted usages; while inventors are elated by their ideas, knowledgeable and skillful experts oppose them with very strong objections, drawn from the exact knowledge of the difficulties encountered in production; methods that are readily employed today were perhaps long regarded as illusions of unbalanced minds.[23]

Various details of the process of psychological relaxation are seen in manual labor. I will limit myself to citing several lines borrowed from a book written by a former caster, become railroad engineer: "It was in the days of our youth that we felt most deeply the intimate joy of work. The great variety of the trade [of caster] stimulates the imagination and manual dexterity; moreover, the fatigue of the body, when it is not excessive and when daily rest dispels it regularly,[24] is not without sweetness. It is accompanied by an indefinable voluptuousness, as if the muscles, formerly made taut by action, found in fatigue a desired relief, a deeper peace, truly complete. The quietude which follows is unique to manual labor, for the nervous and cerebral expenditure being slight, restorative sleep comes readily. It is not the same for intellectual labor.[25] The obsession of ideas exhausts and enervates. The inventor scarcely experiences rest. The night brings dreams of finished designs before his fitfully sleeping brain. No, the fatigue due to purely intellectual labor does not naturally contain the sensual pleasure proper to muscular fatigue."[26]

The connection which exists, according to Bergson, between the intellectuality of the mind and the materiality of things can be regarded as a vague translation of the principle of Maxwellian physics,[27] provided that one understands by materiality the appearance of geometric forms that the operation of our industrial mechanics tries to attain. In this new way of thinking, consideration is no longer given to what scholars and philosophers since the Renaissance have called matter.[28] One no longer believes in studying substances, but instead actions exerted by purely geometric volumes. This science contributes to making Bergson's proposed separation between the living and the inert especially obvious,[29] because a physiologist will never consent to admit that it makes good sense to disembowel an animal in order to identify it with a kinematic combination.[30]

We still should call attention to a corollary that Bergson gave to his theory of relaxation: "The order which reigns [in the concrete reality which fills the extension of our knowledge] and which is manifested by the laws of nature, is an order which must be born of itself when the inverse order is suppressed; a relaxation of the will would produce this suppression precisely. Lastly, the direction which this reality takes here suggests to us now a thing *unmaking itself;* this, undoubtedly, is one of the basic aspects of materiality. What conclusion from this can be derived except that the process by which a thing *makes itself* is directed in a contrary sense to that of physical processes, and that it is as a result by its very definition immaterial. Our vision of the material world is that of a falling weight; no image drawn from matter properly defined will give us the idea of the weight which is rising."[31] Abandoning the sequence of metaphysical doctrines on which Bergson bases this remark, we can now ask if the pragmatist cannot be associated with a philosophy of modern action as we have done already.

In the ages in which production was quite underdeveloped, men were rather disposed to regard themselves as modest collaborators with the earth, the generous custodian of living things. Their work aimed at leading the earth to reserve for a few tribes of primates a large part of the wealth that its fertility spreads at random for all the species of animals.[32] At that stage industry could be compared to a division of a great river brought about by riverside dwellers in order to lead a small stream of water to the village fountain.

The creation of an *artificial nature,* which appears during the feverish era of capitalism, assumes that men have become capable of imposing new directions on the movements of things. In order to obtain hydraulic power, we prevent water from descending through valleys where it had been flowing for centuries; thanks to our steam generators we force gases to undergo pressure, while it is in their nature to be indefinitely diffused. In our exploitation of mines and our metallurgy, in our numerous electrical mechanisms or those of thermal chemistry, we destroy the compounds of cosmic mineralogy.

Nature does not let itself be reduced to the role of servant of humanity without protesting. Passive resistance warns us that we will never be able completely to subject phenomena to mathematical laws, that is to say, to our intelligence. We must destroy an enormous mass of accumulated forces in order to arrive at creating the new forces organized for our benefit.[33] Nature never ceases working, with a crafty slowness, for the ruination of all our works. We buy the power of commanding in *artificial nature* by incessant labor; matter imposes its own laws when the mind withdraws. The true doctrine is that which juxtaposes *natural nature* and *artificial nature.*

Notes

INTRODUCTION

1. *The Illusions of Progress* (Berkeley and Los Angeles: University of California Press, 1969).
2. See, for example, J. L. Talmon, "The Legacy of Georges Sorel," in *Encounter,* Feb. 1970; and Sir Isaiah Berlin, "Georges Sorel," in the *Times Literary Supplement* (London), Dec. 31, 1971. Sorel had, of course, received some earlier critical attention from American scholars, especially in James Meisel, *The Genesis of Georges Sorel* (Ann Arbor: University of Michigan Press, 1953); Richard Humphrey, *Georges Sorel, Prophet without Honor: A Study in Anti-Intellectualism* (Cambridge, Mass.: Harvard University Press, 1951); and Irving Louis Horowitz, *Radicalism and the Revolt Against Reason* (New York: Humanities Press, 1961). But even the best study, that by Horowitz, has not gotten the attention it deserves. Sorel's "coming into his own" here is shown by his treatment in journals such as *Encounter*. Continental treatments of Sorel, of course, are numerous.
3. *Times Literary Supplement* (London), May 14, 1970.
4. Loc. cit.
5. *Réflexions sur la violence* (Paris: Rivière, 6th ed. revised, 1925), pp. 358–60 and n. 2, p. 359. (For a translation, see this volume, below, pp. 214, 335, n. 7 (the second note).
6. "The Legacy of Georges Sorel," p. 58.
7. Paris: Rivière, 2nd ed., 1926, pp. 21, 22n., 29.
8. Paris: Rivière, 1932, p. 194.
9. According to one learned student of totalitarianism, the chief characteristics of totalitarian regimes are ideology and terror. Sorel is against both doctrinaire ideology and terror, as we shall see. See Hannah Arendt, *The Origins of Totalitarianism* (New York and Cleveland: World, 1958), Part III.
10. Ernst Nolte, *Three Faces of Fascism* (New York: Holt, 1966), p. 153, citing Mussolini, *Works,* II, 126; III, 271; IV, 153, respectively. One student of Sorel's connection with Fascism speaks of a more complicated

relationship. Though Jack Roth maintains that what in Italy is called "Sorelismo both directly and indirectly figured significantly in the origins of Fascism," he is careful to distinguish between "Sorelismo," "an organized and vulgarized Italian transformation of the prewar Sorelian movement," and Sorel's original ideas. He further notes that other groups may have arrived at Fascism by routes other than Sorelismo and concludes that Sorel played a somewhat "biblical" role in the formation of Fascism—a role not wholly dissimilar to that played by Marx in Communist debates. Thus there was a Sorelian opposition to Fascism as well as a group of men calling themselves Sorelians who supported it, and any side supporting any position ended by quoting Sorel. As Roth says, "Sorel could be for Libya or against it, for intervention or against it" ("The Roots of Italian Fascism," *Journal of Modern History,* March 1967, p. 30). It should finally be noted that all of these discussions center primarily on Sorel's relationship with the Fascist movement prior to its taking power. This early movement was more diverse and decentralized (hence more amenable to Sorelianism) than after its capture of the state machinery. For a discussion of this point, see Edward R. Tannenbaum, "The Goals of Italian Fascism," *The American Historical Review,* LXXIV, 4 (April 1969), p. 1183. The author says that Fascist syndicalism was a "perversion" of Sorelian revolutionary syndicalism "from any point of view" (p. 1192).

11. *American Sociological Review,* Vol. XXXVI, No. 1, Feb. 1971, pp. 133–34.
12. *Notre Maître Georges Sorel* (Paris: Grasset, 1953), Ch. 1.
13. In his Introduction to a new edition of T. E. Hulme's translation of *Reflections on Violence* (New York: Collier-Macmillan, 1963), p. 19. Cf. below, p. 288, wherein Sorel juxtaposes the engineers to inventors and inclines toward the latter.
14. *Notre Maître Georges Sorel,* pp. 41–42.
15. Ibid., p. 43.
16. Ibid., p. vii.
17. Georges Sorel, "Essai sur la philosophie de Proudhon," *Revue Philosophique,* XXXIII, XXXIV (1892).
18. See Sorel's "Confessions," republished in *Matériaux d'une théorie du prolétariat* (Paris: Rivière, 1919), p. 250, under the title "Mes raisons du syndicalisme." The work first appeared in *Divenire Sociale* of Rome, Mar.–May 1910.
19. See below, pp. 156–57.
20. *Matériaux d'une théorie du prolétariat,* p. 263.
21. Reproduced in the *Matériaux,* pp. 79–133, and additions, pp. 134–67; the main section of this work is translated in this volume.
22. Georges Sorel, *La Révolution dreyfusienne* (Paris: Rivière, 1909).
23. *Matériaux,* p. 263.
24. Paris: Schleicher, 1902.
25. *Matériaux,* p. 268.
26. *Notre Maître Georges Sorel,* p. 61.

27. Ibid., p. 65.
28. Ibid., p. 76.
29. "Le Mystère de la charité de Jeanne d'Arc, de Charles Peguy," April 14, 1910.
30. "Quelques prétentions juives," *L'Indépendance*, May–June 1912. Sorel says little that is anti-Semitic beyond this one article in which he accuses the Jews of "adopting absurd doctrines," adding that "No one would dream of regarding the Jews as enemies if they consented to live as simple citizens" (p. 332). But Sorel defends anti-Semitism as a tactic in "Urbain Gohier," *L'Independance*, Jan. 1912. Earlier he had taken a harsh view of anti-Semitism. Cf. "Essai sur l'église et l'état," *Cahiers de la Quinzaine*, 1901, p. 540.
31. *Lettres à Paul de la Salle* (Paris: Grasset, 1947), p. 126.
32. *Réflexions*, p. 454.
33. *Matériaux*, p. 3.
34. *Réflexions*, p. 9.
35. Ibid., p. 12.
36. *Les Illusions du progrès* (Paris: Rivière, 5th ed., 1947), p. 95 (American ed., p. 48).
37. Ibid., p. 9 (American ed., p. xlv).
38. *Le Procès de Socrate* (Paris: Alcan, 1889), pp. 47–48.
39. *Les Illusions du progrès*, pp. 22–25 (American ed., pp. 5–7).
40. Ibid., pp. 38–42.
41. *La Réforme intellectuelle et morale* (Paris: Michel-Lévy, 1871), p. 94.
42. *Feuilles détachées* (Paris: C. Levy, 1892), p. 4, quoted in *Réflexions*, pp. 346–47.
43. *Feuilles détachées*, pp. 17–18; *Réflexions*, p. 352.
44. Renan, *Histoire du peuple d'Israël* (Paris: C. Lévy, 1887–93), V, 420; cited in *Réflexions*, p. 348.
45. Sorel, *Système historique de Renan* (Paris: G. Jacques, 1905), p. 65.
46. "La crise du socialisme," *Revue Politique et Parlementaire*, Dec. 1898.
47. *L'Idée générale de la révolution au XIXᵉ siècle* (Paris: A. Lacroix, 1867), p. 225. See also Berth, *Du "Capital" aux "Réflexions sur la violence*," p. 120 (n. 8, above). The literature on Proudhon in English is growing. For a competent biography, see George Woodcock, *Pierre-Joseph Proudhon* (London: Routledge & Kegan Paul, 1956); for a study of his philosophy, see Alan Ritter, *The Political Thought of Pierre-Joseph Proudhon* (Princeton: Princeton University Press, 1969). A brief anthology of this prolific writer can be found in a collection of excerpted segments in English translation, *Selected Writings of Pierre-Joseph Proudhon*, edited by Stewart Edwards and translated by Elizabeth Fraser (New York: Doubleday, 1969). A recent essay is William H. Harbold's "Justice in the Thought of Pierre-Joseph Proudhon," *Western Political Quarterly*, Vol. XXII, No. 4, Dec. 1969, p. 723. For comment on Proudhon by Sorel's chief disciple, see the first chapter of Berth's *Du "Capital" aux "Réflexions sur la violence."*

48. *Théorie de la propriété* (Paris: A. Lacroix, 2nd ed., 1866), p. 131. *Selected Writings*, p. 133.

49. *Philosophie de misère* (Paris: A. Lacroix, 1875), I, p. 285.

50. Sorel, "Essai sur la philosophie de Proudhon," p. 633.

51. *Système des contradictions économiques* (Paris: A. Lacroix, 3rd ed., 1867), Ch. XI, sec. 2. Cf. *La Pornocratie ou les femmes dans les temps modernes* (Paris: A. Lacroix, 1875), p. 5.

52. *De la justice dans la révolution et dans l'église* (Paris: A. Lacroix, 1868–70), IV, pp. 276–79. Also see *Selected Writings*, pp. 254–56, and Berth, p. 162.

53. Berth, p. 130, citing *De la justice dans la révolution et dans l'église*, II, p. 348.

54. *La Guerre et la paix* (Paris: A. Lacroix, 1869), pp. 71–72; *Selected Writings*, p. 207.

55. For a discussion of the role that "balance" plays in Proudhon's notion of justice, see *De la justice dans la révolution et dans l'église*, pp. 60–61, and *De la capacité politique des classes ouvrières* (Paris: A. Lacroix, 1873), pp. 124–26; Sorel, "Essai sur Proudhon," p. 42.

56. *La Guerre et la paix*, p. 31, cited in *Selected Writings*, p. 203.

57. *La Guerre et la paix*, p. 54, *Selected Writings*, p. 204.

58. *Les Illusions du progrès*, p. 307 (American ed., p. 170).

59. "Essai sur Proudhon," p. 47.

60. *Réflexions sur la violence*, p. 24 (see below, p. 197).

61. Ibid., pp. 26–27 (see below, p. 198), citing Pascal, *Pensées*, Fragment 298 of the Brunschwig ed.

62. Ibid., p. 26, citing Pascal, Fragment 294.

63. *Le Procès de Socrate*, p. 302.

64. *Réflexions sur la violence*, pp. 35–36, citing Renan, *Histoire du peuple d'Israël*, IV, 269 (see below, p. 201).

65. Ibid. Cf. below, pp. 103, 157 where Sorel does ask for more just laws.

66. "The Ethics of Socialism," (see below, p. 103).

67. For the distinction between force (state repression) and violence (rebellion against that state), see *Réflexions sur la violence*, pp. 256–57, Ch. V, iv.

68. *Le Procès de Socrate*, pp. 375–84.

69. Ibid., p. 168.

70. Ibid., pp. 87–97, 151. Here Sorel relies chiefly on Xenophon's *Symposium*, VIII, 32.

71. *Le Procès de Socrate*, p. 172 (see below, pp. 62–3).

72. "Essai sur Proudhon," p. 44, citing Proudhon, *La Guerre et la paix*, I, 71.

73. *Le procès de Socrate*, p. 169; *Matériaux*, pp. 70, 92 (see below, pp. 77, 303–4, n. 23).

74. *Le procès de Socrate*, p. 179 (see below, pp. 64–5).

75. Ibid., pp. 238–39, citing *Memorabilia*, III, ix, 10.

76. *Le procès de Socrate*, p. 203 (see below, p. 66).

77. Ibid., p. 179 (see below, p. 65).

78. Ibid., pp. 286–87.
79. Ibid., p. 199 (see below, p. 65).
80. Ibid., pp. 282–83.
81. Ibid., p. 287.
82. Ibid., p. 204 (see below, p. 66).
83. Ibid., p. 205 (see below, p. 67). Sorel maintains that the only freedom left in Socrates' ideal world is the freedom of the philosopher to search for the good.
84. Ibid., p. 212 (see below, p. 69).
85. Xenophon, *Cyropaedia,* I, iii, 16, 17.
86. Ibid., I, vi, 37–38. For a general discussion of the similarities between Xenophon and Sorel, see Neal Wood, "Some Reflections on Sorel and Machiavelli," *Political Science Quarterly,* March 1968. I am indebted to Professor Wood for many of the criticisms in the following paragraph.
87. *De l'utilité du pragmatisme,* p. 427 (see below, p. 369, n. 33). Robert C. Tucker says that "the fundamental passion of the founders of Marxism was not a passion for justice." They opposed the notion that "socialism was principally a matter of distribution." Instead, he argues, they defined it as concerned with "the dehumanization of man" (*The Marxian Revolutionary Idea,* New York: Norton, 1969, pp. 36 and 48). Tucker notes that even Marx's directive "From each according to his ability, to each according to his needs" is followed by a condemnation of equal right and fair distribution as "obsolete verbal rubbish" (see the *Critique of the Gotha Program,* Part I, p. 3, and Tucker, p. 48). Rightly arguing that Marx criticizes distributive themes of outmoded forms of justice because they emphasize consumption rather than production, and consequently are biased in favor of accommodation within the existing order, Tucker rather curiously restricts his own concept of justice to "a rightful balance in a situation where two or more . . . are in conflict" (p. 51). But by defining justice as Proudhon would, it is easy to demonstrate Marx's hostility to the general notion. It is certainly true that Marx condemns consumer justice, in his essay *Free Trade,* maintaining (as Sorel did later) that "the most favorable condition for the worker is the growth of capital." But if we broaden the definition of justice to include the production process, could we not say with Marx, "Any distribution whatever of the means of consumption is only a consequence of the conditions of production themselves"? (*Critique of the Gotha Program,* Part I, p. 3 last paragraph). Does this mean only that Marx condemns *eternal* justice and *abstract* ideas? Certainly Marx was more concerned with justice than Sorel. He argued that "besides purely physical limitations, the expansion of the working day encounters moral ones. The laborer needs time for satisfying his intellectual and social wants, the extent and number of which are conditioned by the general state of social advancement" (*Capital* [Moscow: Foreign Languages Publishing House, 1966], p. 232). Is this statement devoid of a sense of justice, or does it express it in historically relative terms? Furthermore, is the concept of justice antithetical to the idea of alienation or does Marx

combine the two ideas? Whereas Tucker sees only one side of Marx, Sorel sees two sides which are threatening to conflict with one another. By dispensing altogether with the theory of surplus value, the danger of misinterpreting Marx as a theorist of abstract justice may be assuaged.

88. "On Bernstein and Kautsky," below, pp. 150–53.
89. "Sur la théorie marxiste de la valeur," *Le Journal des Economistes*, May 1897, p. 215.
90. "Les aspects juridiques du socialisme," *Revue Socialiste*, Nov. 1900, p. 411.
91. See below, p. 151.
92. *Réflexions sur la violence*, p. 46 (see below, p. 205).
93. "The Ethics of Socialism" (see below, p. 107).
94. "Is there a Utopia in Marxism?" (see below, p. 144). Cf. p. 171.
95. *Les Illusions du progrès*, pp. 348, 373 (American edition, pp. 193, 207).
96. *Capital* (Modern Library edition of Vol. I, New York, N.D.), p. 837.
97. "On Bernstein and Kautsky," below, p. 164.
98. "Necessity and Fatalism in Marxism," below, p. 122.
99. Ibid., below, p. 121.
100. "Idées socialistes et faits économiques au XIXᵉ siècle," *Revue Socialiste*, May 1902, p. 520.
101. In *The Poverty of Historicism* (New York: Harper, 1957).
102. *Réflexions sur la violence*, p. 407.
103. *Les Illusions du progrès*, p. 49 (see below, p. 185).
104. See Engel's introduction to the *Poverty of Philosophy* (Moscow: Foreign Language Publishing House, N.D.), p. 12. Sorel cites this passage of Engels in his introduction to the French translation of E. R. A. Seligman's *The Economic Interpretation of History*, tr. Henri-Emile Barrault, *L'Interprétation économique de l'histoire* (Paris: Rivière, 1911), p. xxviii (cf. note 87, above).
105. Preface to Seligman, pp. xxxvii–xxxviii.
106. Preface to Serverio Merlino, *Formes et essence du socialisme* (Paris: Ghio, 1898), pp. ix–xi.
107. Preface to Seligman, pp. xv–xvi.
108. "Is there a Utopia in Marxism?" see below, p. 141. Cf. *La Ruine du monde antique* (Paris: Rivière, 2nd ed., 1925), p. 311.
109. See "Etude sur Vico," *Devenir Social*, Oct.–Dec. 1896.
110. *Réflexions sur la violence*, p. 378 (see below, p. 222).
111. Ibid., p. 372 (see below, p. 219).
112. Ibid., pp. 211, 217.
113. Ibid., pp. 41–42, citing Bergson, *Données immédiates de la conscience* (Paris: Alcan, 1889), pp. 175–76, 181 (see below, pp. 204, 208–12).
114. Ibid., p. 217.
115. Ibid., p. 180 (see below, p. 208).
116. Ibid., p. 180 (see below, p. 210).
117. Ibid., p. 217.
118. "Quelques objections au matérialisme économique," *Humanité Nouvelle*, June 1899, p. 659.

119. *Réflexions sur la violence,* p. 196.
120. Ibid., p. 177 (see below, p. 209).
121. Ibid., p. 46 (see below, p. 205).
122. Ibid., p. 136.
123. Preface to Serverio Merlino, pp. xli–xlii.
124. "Sur la théorie marxiste de la valeur," *Journal des Economistes,* May 1897, pp. 600, 611.
125. See Karl Marx and Frederick Engels, tr. F. Pascal, *The German Ideology* (New York: International Publishers, 1947), p. 14. "We set out from real, active men, and on the basis of their real life processes we demonstrate the development of ideological reflexes and echoes of this life process, which is empirically verifiable and bound to material premises. Morality, religion, metaphysics, all the rest of ideology and their corresponding forms of consciousness thus no longer retain a semblance of independence. They have no history, no development."
126. In a letter to Mehring, Engels says: "Ideology is a process accomplished by the so-called thinker consciously, it is true, but with a false consciousness. The real motive forces impelling him remain unknown to him; else it would simply not be an ideological process" (July 14, 1893). In the *Selected Correspondence* of Marx and Engels (Moscow: Foreign Languages Publishing House, 1953), p. 541.
127. *Matériaux d'une théorie du prolétariat,* p. 337.
128. See Karl Marx, *The Grundrisse,* ed. David McLellan (London: Macmillan, 1971), pp. 44–46.
129. *Réflexions sur la violence,* p. 220.
130. "La crise de la pensée catholique," *Revue de Métaphysique et de Morale,* Sept. 1901.
131. *Histoire du peuple d'Israël,* Vol. V, pp. 420–21, cited in *Le Système historique de Renan,* p. 69.
132. *Le Système historique,* pp. 457–59.
133. Ibid., p. 37.
134. Ibid., p. 73.
135. The idea of the general strike myth came in part from Victor Griffuelles, for whose book *Les Objectifs de nos luttes de classe,* co-authored by L. Niel, Sorel wrote a preface (Paris, 1909). Sorel considered the theoretical justification to be helped by the ideas of Bergson.
136. See especially "L'Evolution créatrice," *Le Mouvement Socialiste,* Oct., Nov., Dec. 1907. This review essay was republished in somewhat changed form in *De l'utilité du pragmatisme* (Paris: Rivière, 1921), Ch. V. Part IV of this essay is translated below, pp. 284–90.
137. Henri Bergson, *L'Evolution créatrice* (Paris: Alcan, 1907); tr. Arthur Mitchell as *Creative Evolution* (New York: Modern Library, 1944), pp. 339–40. All references will be to the translation.
138. Ibid., p. 343.
139. Ibid., pp. 141–42.
140. Ibid., p. 215.
141. Ibid., pp. 215, 217.

142. Ibid., p. 218.
143. Ibid., pp. 194–95.
144. Ibid., p. 245.
145. Ibid., p. 256.
146. Ibid., p. 211.
147. Ibid., p. 219.
148. Ibid., pp. 220–21.
149. Ibid., pp. 153–54; cf. p. 210.
150. *De l'utilité du pragmatisme* (Paris: Rivière, 2nd ed., 1928), p. 396.
151. Ibid., p. 419 (see below, p. 287).
152. Ibid., pp. 419–20, citing Reuleaux, *Cinématique*, pp. 555–56. (See the statement by Reuleaux, below, p. 368, n. 18, relative to the disappearance of the radical division of labor.)
153. Ibid., pp. 426–27. The amount of exhaustion in modern industry is not overtaxing, according to Sorel. On the contrary, he sees in it an almost sexual satisfaction and again stresses the close link between labor and sexual love.
154. Ibid., p. 358, n. (see below, p. 366, n. 1).
155. Ibid., p. 378.
156. Ibid., pp. 390–91.
157. Ibid., p. 428.
158. Ibid., citing *L'Evolution créatrice*, pp. 253–54.
159. Ibid., p. 16.
160. Ibid., p. 4.
161. Ibid., p. 71.
162. Ibid., p. 76.
163. *Réflexions sur la violence*, p. 177 (see below, pp. 209–10).
164. Ibid., p. 202.
165. Ibid., p. 179 (see below, p. 210).
166. Ibid., p. 220.
167. See Shlomo Avineri, *The Political and Social Thought of Karl Marx* (Cambridge: Cambridge University Press, 1968), pp. 74–75. "Whereas pragmatism starts with the premise that man adapts himself to a given, pre-existing environment, Marx views man as shaping his world." Similarly Marx views the world as rational precisely because it is shaped by us, whereas James regards it as chaotic. For a detailed examination of this problem, see Nathan Rotenstreich, *Basic Problems of Marx's Philosophy* (Indianapolis: Bobbs-Merrill, 1965). I think Sorel argues consistently, as does Marx, that man knows only what he makes; but he diverges from Marx on the grounds that what we make is not always understood rationally. Sorel also denies the inevitability of the increasing historical congruity between what we make and our *rational* consciousness of it. This is the basis of his attack on Marx's Hegelianism. Sorel replaces this historicism with an artistic understanding of the world which receives its impetus from labor.
168. It should be noted that Sorel was interested far more in the soviets as independent workers' councils than in the Soviet Union. That he was

a statist would be an overstatement. The closest he comes to being this is in his admiration for the *polis* in his early writings; but the *polis* is not the modern state.

169. For a discussion of the Black Muslims as a moral reform movement, see C. Eric Lincoln, *The Black Muslims in America* (Boston: Beacon, 1963).

170. *Matériaux,* pp. 301–2.

Chapter 1

FROM *THE TRIAL OF SOCRATES*

1. [*Le Procès de Socrate* (Paris: Alcan, 1889). This excerpt is from pages 172–79 and 198–216.—ED.]

2. Ernst Curtius, *Histoire grecque* (Paris: Leroux, 1883–84), translated from the German by A. Bouché-Leclercq, Vol. II, p. 460.

3. "The good in politics is justice, in other terms, the general utility. We commonly think that justice is a sort of equality, and here the popular opinion is, up to a certain point, in agreement with the philosophic principles by which we have treated morality. There is agreement, moreover, on the nature of justice, on those to whom it is applied, and it is agreed that equality should necessarily rule between equals; it remains to be seen how equality and inequality are applied—difficult questions which constitute political philosophy" (*Politics,* Book III, chap. VII, sect. 1).

4. Alfred Fouillée, *Philosophie de Socrate* (Paris: Ladrange, 1874), Vol. II, p. 389.

5. The conservatives, in combatting the new teaching, worked for the maintenance of equality and sound democracy.

6. Aristophanes, *Acharnians,* v. 679, and all of the end of the Parabasis. The choir says (v. 691–95): "The clepsydra kills the old man with white hair, who in the heat of the fray was so often covered with a glorious sweat and whose courage saved the motherland at Marathon."

7. In Plato's *Gorgias,* the Sophist explains that his art may be used to persuade judges, senates, or the people. It is very clearly avowed that the sole purpose of rhetoric is persuasion (sect. VII). To persuade without a moral end is to prostitute knowledge, logic, and eloquence.

8. [Here and in the following paragraphs Sorel is paraphrasing Socratic beliefs.—ED.]

9. Xenophon, *Memorabilia,* Book III, chap. VII.

10. On this point Socrates has not the least hesitation: "For kings and leaders, he said that it is not those who carry a scepter, nor those who have been chosen by chance by the crowd, or whom fate has favored, or who have usurped power, either by violence or ruse, but those who know how to rule. . . . If one objects that a tyrant may choose not to follow the good advice given to him, he says: 'And how is he free not to choose

to follow it, since punishment is always at hand . . ? For, in such a case, if one refuses to follow good advice, one makes mistakes and these mistakes entail punishment'" (*Memorabilia,* Book III, chap. IX, sect. 10).

11. Curtius, after having summed up the teaching of the Sophists, says: "with this outburst of egoism, no constitution, and above all no republican constitution, could exist . . . Thus the greatest service that a Greek could give to his country . . . was to combat Sophistic thought, which compromised the people's most precious possessions . . . and to replace this exclusive education of the intelligence . . . by investigation to reveal the foundations of moral life. That is what Socrates did." (Curtius, Vol. IV, p. 123).

We believe that from the political point of view Socrates' influence was almost as bad as that of the Sophists. The Socratics were submerged in the theory of the absolute; they did not recognize the importance of historical law; this made them revolutionaries.

12. Proudhon said of Condorcet: "The only man who kept sight of equality in '93 was made an outlaw, captured by the tribunal police (of Robespierre), and was forced to poison himself." (*De la justice dans le révolution et dans l'église* (Paris: Garnier frères, 1858), 3rd study, sect. XLI). Proudhon judged Robespierre the same way as did Taine, who has so well proved to us that the great theoretician of the Convention was a perfect cad.

13. At this period the infamous cult of Cotys flourished in Athens. Eupolis wrote the comedy (Curtius, Vol. III, p. 319) against the participants in these orgies. This brings to mind Juvenal's lines about the sodomist debaucheries of the Romans of his time: "Solis ara deae maribus patet. 'Ite, profanae,' clamatur, 'nullo gemit hic tibicina cornu,' talia secreta coluerunt orgia taeda Cecropiam soliti Baptae lassare Cotyton" (*Satire* II, v. 89).

Curtius said, "On the outside Athens was powerful, but on the inside the strength of the republic, which rested on civic virtue and patriotism, was in full decline" (p. 323).

14. Curtius, Vol. III, p. 322.

15. Ibid., Vol. V, p. 202.

16. Renan says: "The Roman Empire, in demoting nobility . . . increased, on the other hand, the advantages of wealth. Far from establishing effective equality among the citizens, the Roman Empire, in opening wide the doors of the Roman city, created a deep division between the *honestiores* (notables, the rich) and the *humiliores* or *tenuiores* (the poor). The proclamation of political equality for all introduced inequality into the law" (*Marc-Aurèle et la fin du monde antique* (Paris, C. Lévy, 1882), p. 598).

17. Curtius, Vol. II, p. 98.

18. *Gorgias,* sect. LXVII. *Oedipus at Colonus* was played only two years before the death of Socrates. Tragedy was thus still in its heroic period.

19. *Philosophie de Socrate,* Vol. II, p. 401.

20. *Banquet,* chap. III, sect. 5.
21. Ibid., chap. IV, sect. 6.
22. A work of this kind, being no longer definitive, no longer has value according to Socratic theories.

Chapter 2

THE SOCIALIST FUTURE OF THE SYNDICATES

1. [This work first appeared in *Humanité nouvelle*, March and April, 1898, was reprinted in various editions and included in *Matériaux d'une théorie du prolétariat* (Paris: Marcel Rivière, 1919)—ED.]
2. Antonio Labriola, *Essais sur la conception matérialiste de l'histoire* (Paris: Giard et Brière, 1897), French translation, p. 37. The first of the two essays which make up the volume is particularly important because its text had been submitted to Engels; it extends from p. 21 to p. 117 in the first edition, which I quote here.
3. In a letter of 1875, published only in 1891 by Engels.
4. *Critica Sociale,* July 16, 1877, p. 215, col. 1. This review was regarded at that time as a very reliable mouthpiece of socialist doctrine.
5. It would be very useful to add here a few explanations in order to clarify the meaning of this idea. I take them from the preface which I wrote in July 1898 to a book by Saverio Merlino: *Formes et essence du socialisme* (Paris: Giard et Brière, 1898). "What is essential in Marx's theory is the conception of a *social mechanism formed by the classes,* which serves to transform modern society from top to bottom, under the influence of ideas and passions which dominate today" (p. v). "By the sole fact of the introduction of a social mechanism, Marx avoids all the purely intellectualist sociology and *separates himself from the utopians.* There cannot be any usable mechanisms in science unless there are stable formations, largely escaping the manipulations of intelligence, forming solid parts of the system. There must be unconsciousness, blindness and instinct in society for these parts to resist a certain length of time with their forms and their laws of observed development" (pp. viii–ix). "We see only men grouped in classes, acting under the influence of "observable feelings." Daily we can verify the movement of phenomena, ask how conditions are transformed, and correct our ideas about the future as the facts become more numerous" (p. vii).
6. Preface to the first edition of the French translation of the *Essais* of Antonio Labriola already quoted (see note 1, above). On the preceding page I said: "The problem of the modern future—considered from the materialist point of view—rests on three questions: one, has the proletariat acquired a clear awareness of its existence as an indivisible class?

Two, does it have enough strength to do battle against the other classes? Three, is it in any condition to overturn, along with the capitalist organization, the whole system of traditional ideology?" This preface was not reproduced in the following edition, Antonio Labriola having decided that I was not a sure enough companion for an orthodox socialist.

7. K. Marx and F. Engels, *Manifeste communiste* (Paris: G. Bellais), trans. by Charles Andler, Vol. I, p. 39. In all revolutions there have been two elements: a *conquest of power,* which gives advantages to a minority, and a *capture of legal process*; according to Marx the first element will disappear in the proletarian revolution; it is for this reason that Marxists have so often said that the state will no longer exist.

8. Marx, *Capital,* French translation, p. 327, col. 1 (Modern Library ed., p. 809).

9. E. Durkheim, *Le Suicide: étude de sociologie* (Paris: F. Alcan, 1897), p. 439.

10. Jean Jaurès, *Socialisme et paysans* (Paris: La Petite République), pp. 118–19. This propaganda pamphlet reproduces Jaurès's three speeches on the agricultural crisis. It will be seen that the orator gives all his declarations as belonging to the accepted doctrine of the Socialist Party. Collectivism goes by the board in this sketch of "property of tomorrow." Paul Deschanel, answering the socialist orator on July 10, 1897, accused him of calling socialization a re-establishment of eminent domain.

11. Professor Espinas said to Andler, in supporting his lovely thesis on state socialism in Germany: "But these are old things which masquerade under new names!"

12. Tocqueville, *L'Ancien Régime et la révolution* (Paris: Michel-Lévy Frères, 1866), p. 241. A curious experiment in philosophical economy was carried out by King Ferdinand IV of Naples in the model manufacturing concern of Santo-Lucio. Thinkers of the period thought that finally the problem would be resolved of knowing if men are always destined to be enemies or if there is a means of making them friends and therefore happy (Benedetto Croce, *Studii storici sulla rivoluzione napoletana del 1799,* [Rome: E. Loescher, 1897], p. 18).

13. Georges Weill, *L'Ecole Saint-Simonienne* (Paris: F. Alcan, 1896), pp. 191–92, 199.

14. Georges Platon, "Le socialisme en Grèce" in the *Devenir Social,* Oct. 1895, p. 669. Cf. G. Sorel, *Réflexions sur la violence* (Paris: M. Rivière, 1910), pp. 250–56.

15. Generally socialist theoreticians have believed that their doctrines depend much less on the customs of workers' organizations than the physical sciences depend on industrial technique.

16. The explanations given by Antonio Labriola are immensely obscure. "Scientific socialism . . . has understood [the state] because it does not rise up against it in a unilateral and subjective way as did (more than once in other times) cynics, stoics, epicureans of all kinds, utopians, visionary ascetics, and finally our contemporary anarchists of every

sort. . . . Scientific socialism has proposed showing how the state rises continually of itself against itself in creating the conditions of its own ruin by means of its own indispensable institutions; for example: a huge system of taxes, militarism, universal suffrage, the development of education, etc. . . . With the disappearance of proletarians and the conditions which make possible the proletariat will disappear all dependence of man on man under whatever form of hierarchy" (*Essais sur la conception matérialiste de l'histoire,* pp. 227–28). But could not that which Labriola claims should lead to the downfall of the state by introducing the proletarian revolution, on the contrary, contribute to making worker agitation end in a bureaucratic, militarist democracy, one which is favorable to financiers?

17. "Large mechanized industry achieves separation between manual work and the intellectual powers of production, which it transforms into the power of capital over work. The skillfulness of the worker appears weak before the prodigies of science, enormous natural forces, the greatness of social work, all incorporated into the mechanical system, which constitutes the power of the master" (*Capital,* French translation, p. 183 [Modern Library ed., p. 462]).

18. That is what explains the revival of Saint-Simonism in our universities. Jaurès, in a speech of January 25, 1897, on sugar, bid the government to use the talents of young bourgeois who lacked money, by transforming them into industrial bureaucrats. This certainly is an echo of Saint-Simonism.

19. Until now, great scholars have almost all been modest people, having no need for large salaries or rich appointments. The interests of knowledge are not always identical with the interests of scholars and the intellectual parasites who surround them.

20. Marx, *Capital,* French translation, p. 84, col. 2 (Modern Library ed., p. 220).

21. In his *Critique of the Gotha Program,* Marx thus defined the rules to be followed after the revolution abolishing capitalism: "The worker's right is proportional to the work done; equality consists here in the use of a uniform yardstick, work. . . . *This very equal right* is an inequal right for inequal work. It ignores distinctions of class because all men are workers by the same right; but it tacitly recognizes as natural privileges the inequalities of individual gifts, consequently, abilities in production. Thus it is an inequal right, like all rights" (*Revue d'Economie Politique,* Sept.–Oct. 1894, p. 757).

22. Marx, *Capital,* French translation, p. 143, col. 2 (Modern Library ed., p. 357).

23. This is why often industrialists prefer as a director a former worker rather than a technician who came out of the schools. The Greeks were already well acquainted with this principle; they said that obedience was the school of command. Elsewhere I have pointed out the influence that the military system seems to have had on ancient ideas of equality.

Le Procès de Socrate (Paris: F. Alcan, 1889) [see chap. 1, above—Ed.].

24. Paul de Rousiers, *Le Trade-unionisme en Angleterre* (Paris: A. Colin, 1897), p. 42.

25. Karl Kautsky, "Le socialisme et les carrières libérales," in *Le Devenir Social,* May 1895, p. 107. The term "liberal career" does not exactly translate the German term *intelligenz*: by this word the Germans mean the professions that have a certain character of artistic or literary culture. Thus Kautsky more recently tells us that social democracy has gained for its cause sculptors, employees in commerce and musicians (*Le Marxisme et son critique Bernstein* [Paris: P.-V. Stock, 1900], p. 250).

26. G. Ferrero, *L'Europa giovane* (Milan: Fratelli Treves, 1897), pp. 65–72.

27. Kautsky, "Le socialisme et les carrières libérales," loc. cit., p. 108. It is, moreover, especially because of salaries that the question of the relationship of the *intelligentsia* with the Socialist Party has been discussed in Germany.

28. In the part of the book which had been submitted to Engels, Antonio Labriola writes these excellent sentences: "Critical communism does not manufacture revolutions . . . It is not a training school in which the chief of staff of the leaders of the proletariat is formed; but it is solely the consciousness of this revolution, and above all, the consciousness of its difficulties" (*Essais sur la conception màtérialiste de l'histoire,* pp. 70–71). "The mass of the proletariat no longer holds to the commands of a few leaders, any more than it regulates its movements on the prescriptions of captains who could raise another government on the ruins of the old . . . It knows, or is beginning to understand, that the 'dictatorship of the proletariat' which will have as its job the socialization of the means of production, cannot be the result of a mass led by a few" (p. 77). But, in order for the leaders to conform to these principles, there must be some mechanism capable of limiting their ambitions. "It is a constant principle," says Laboulaye, "that every time you give power to a man he will draw all that he can from it" (*Histoire des Etats-Unis* [Paris: A. Durand, 1877], Vol. III, p. 305).

29. The example of Lassalle is not fortuitous; thus I ignore it.

30. Marx and Engels, *Manifeste communiste,* Vol. I, p. 37.

31. Kautsky, "Le socialisme et les carrières libérales," loc. cit., p. 115.

32. Ibid., p. 113.

33. Yves Guyot believes that production would function in better conditions than those of today if industrialists would entrust the execution of work to corporations of workers, who would exercise more effective discipline over their members than the employers' discipline. This system has excellent results in the composition of Parisian newspapers (*Les Conflicts du travail et leur solution,* pp. 279–82).

34. [Sorel, who uses the English term "lock-out," means here that the workers will expel many of the managers from the productive process— the reverse of the normal meaning.—*Ed.*]

35. Kautsky, "Le socialisme . . . ," loc cit., p. 114.

36. Marx and Engels, *Manifeste communiste,* p. 60. By "reactionary" we should understand that this socialism seeks to hinder industrial progress.
37. Sismondi, cited by Marx, preface to *Le Dix-huitième brumaire de Louis Bonaparte* (Lille: Impr. ouvrière, 1891), French translation [*The Eighteenth Brumaire of Louis Bonaparte*]. We must also add that the intellectual proletarians rebel at any spirit of solidarity; they see only their *personal and immediate* interest and sacrifice the general interest to it; they bring disorder everywhere by their intrigues and whenever they can, they fight among themselves. Like Caesar, each one of them aspires to be the first in a small group.
38. The intellectuals assimilate the attitudes corresponding to the class struggle, what one of them calls "creative hatred." The ferocious jealousy of the poor intellectual, who hopes to push the rich speculator to the guillotine, is a bad sentiment containing nothing socialist.
39. The above text, written in 1900, was inspired by an article I published in the *Devenir Social* for Jan. 1896; today I would have some reservations on the theses that I presented in this article.
40. On the power of denominations, consult Gustave le Bon, *Psychologie des foules* (Paris: F. Alcan, 1895), pp. 94–96 [*The Crowd*].
41. What is said here about the capitalist can be applied to any other leader who does not belong to the body of workers.
42. Marx, *Capital,* French translation, p. 144, col. 1 (Modern Library ed., p. 364).
43. Marx, *Misère de la philosophie* (Paris: Giard et Brière, 1896), p. 241 (*Poverty of Philosophy*).
44. This is from the point of view of abstract law, which alone is considered by professors, lawyers and judges in their arguments. The function of these arguments is to apply to questions discussed in the courtrooms a logic which can satisfy subtle minds; but the philosophical jurist is aware that quantity can have a decisive value for the determination of quality (cf. Marx, *Capital,* French translation, p. 133, col. 2; Modern Library ed., pp. 337–38).
45. The ideas that I put forth in 1898 are related to a juridical theory which I have sketched in *Science Sociale* (in Nov. 1900, pp. 433–36). The workers believe that they possess a right to work in the factory where they are employed.
46. This is what the Supreme Court of Appeals has decided many times.
47. One wonders if Jules Guesde was really thinking of achieving a proposal for the regulation of strikes; in the *Socialiste* of Dec. 2, 1900, an extract of an article by Parvus appeared which reduced Jules Guesde's proposal to a display intended to agitate people.
48. Office du Travail, *Statistique des grèves et des recours à la conciliation et à l'arbitrage pendant l'année,* 1894, p. 164.
49. Paul de Rousiers, *Le Trade-unionisme en Angleterre,* p. 193.
50. Ibid., pp. 11, 67, and 333–37.
51. Ibid., pp. 246, 322.
52. It has often been said that the proletariat has before it a "reactionary

mass"; against this opinion I quoted in 1848 an article that Turati had just published in the *Critica Sociale* of September 16; I added: "In the hypothesis of the division into two opposing camps, the emancipation of the proletariat would depend on the conquest of power by political revolutionaries; but this hypothesis being false, the emancipation and education of the working classes can be realized by the workers themselves." The difficulty which the conception of the dichotomy of society would seem to present will not appear great to people who have read the last pages of the *Reflections on Violence*. They will see there how proletarian activity can at times conform to this dichotomous idea, and at times be mixed with bourgeois life. (*Réflexions sur la violence*, pp. 428–32.)

53. Paul de Rousiers, *Le Trade-unionisme en Angleterre*, p. 26.
54. Ibid., pp. 154 and 300.
55. Ibid., p. 41.
56. Ibid., p. 93.
57. Ibid., pp. 132 and 272.
58. Ibid., pp. 44, 51, 67, 94, 334. Paul de Rousiers's opinion seems debatable to me now. We must distinguish between two classes of enterprise: in those which have an unlimited field of action practically speaking (such as the textile mills of Lancashire), the work is open to anyone; in those whose expansion is generally limited (building), measures of guild protectionism seem destined to be maintained. Paul de Rousiers's inquiry has pointed up a very narrow guild spirit in the shipbuilding workers (pp. 248–51).
59. Ibid., p. 62.
60. This measure was adapted on the proposal of Tom Man and Ben Tillet (ibid., p. 168). The leaders of this group seem to have been wrong in believing that they would maintain solidarity by constant agitation; they experienced serious failures (pp. 171–73). From 1890 to 1895 the number of dockers included in the two unions of London and Liverpool fell from 90,000 to 25,000 (pp. 161–62).
61. Mutualism is obviously conducive to upholding this instinctive life, without which the social mechanism could not have stabilty, as I have indicated in note 5 above.
62. One of Paul de Rousiers's collaborators was quite impressed by the rules followed by mechanics. Their union is divided into branches, each of which administers its own finances; but the central committee requires that credit always be given in equal proportion to the number of members. That is why from time to time it institutes a levy on the funds of rich branches to endow poor ones. "Such is the spirit of solidarity and, let us say also, the clear idea of their true interests that each feels instinctively: that the strength of the group depends on this mutual assistance" (ibid., p. 268).
63. *Critica Sociale*, Sept. 1, 1897, p. 262.
64. This is one of the most important laws of the history of social trans-

formations, one which is nearer to Marx's materialist conception. Old judicial relationships, before disappearing, regulate new life patterns for a long time.

65. Thorold Rogers makes the following observation: "He does not perceive that only people who enjoy a relative well-being can allow themselves to show their discontent, and that its expression is rare whenever despair and misery reign." *Work and Wages in England since the Eighteenth Century* (*Travail et salaires en Angleterre depuis le XIIIᵉ siècle* [Paris: Guillaumin, 1897], French translation by E. Castelol, p. 359).

66. Radicals and bourgeois socialists do not seem to be very fond of co-operatives. In a paper distributed by André Lefebvre's Electoral Committee in 1896 (*Journal de Neuilly-Boulogne*, Dec. 27) we read the following declarations of this socialist candidate—supported by the socialist group of the Chamber and a millionaire son of Zion—: "The candidate declares that he is not an advocate of cooperation, because it is often fatal to the cooperators themselves and only profits big bosses. The first result of cooperation has always been very quickly to provoke the lowering of salaries." The president of the grocery syndicate upheld André Lefebvre in the following terms: "Since the socialists are the only ones who want to take up our cause, it is up to us . . . to go immediately and frankly to them. Vote for citizen Lefebvre. . . . In him you will have a worthy representative, a faithful agent and a devoted defender."

67. Georges d'Avenel, *Le Mécanisme de la vie moderne*, Vol. I, p. 211.

68. The matron could not even contract *concubinage* [under Roman law, a kind of inferior marriage] with a slave. In Marcus Aurelius' time it was decided that a *Clarissime* [title of honor in ancient Rome—Ed.] woman would lose her title by marrying a man of inferior rank to her own. Calixtus allowed Christian women of dignified mein "to take for a husband either a slave, or a free man in any station, and to consider him as a legitimate husband even when, according to the law, they cannot be legally married" (Paul Allard, *Les Esclaves chrétiens* [Paris: Didier, 1876], 3rd ed., pp. 288–94).

69. De Rousiers, *Le Trade-unionisme en Angleterre*, p. 193.

70. Ibid., p. 93. This skillful observer says that in England one thinks about liberty according to "a rule of common sense which could be translated thus: the honest and capable man must not be hindered in his action by the incompetence of others. It follows that if the negligence, laziness, incompetence or ill-will of inferior or dishonest men creates an obstacle to this action, it is considered legitimate to strike at their liberty" (p. 95). It is evident that Paul de Rousiers implicity likens trade unions to "social authorities" which are at times obliged to disturb some individuals in order to assure conditions of general prosperity.

71. In 1898 I did not yet understand the true function of so-called democratic institutions in the old Swiss cantons of which Rousseau so often thought instinctively (that is what prevented so many readers from understanding his theories, whose real bases remain hidden). "Social

authorities" play a preponderant role in these theories. There is a very similar system of government in Berber villages; everything is decided in a general meeting, but only the notables give their opinion.

72. Sometimes the government of the organized party is cruelly laid bare, as happened for the Guelfs of Florence and our Jacobins during the period of revolutionary government.

73. "Do we see on a man's card that he is a deputy? Immediately, we are forewarned against him; we assume that he must be a failure, run aground there for lack of succeeding in his chosen career. And sometimes this is unjust. . . . Politicians and men of letters, the former occupied in exploiting us and the latter in amusing us, live equally outside of the nation" (R. Doumic, *Débats*, Sept. 21, 1897).

74. In part probably because of the numerous articles in which Jules Guesde formerly declared that his party did not seek so much to achieve reforms (in the manner of the "possibilist" party) as to show the workers that there is an absolute contradiction between their aspirations and bourgeois legislation. According to Malon, Jules Guesde had a lot of trouble in making Marx accept the article of the program of 1880 relating to the establishment of a minimum salary (*Revue Socialiste*, Jan. 1887, p. 54). This article was obviously conducive to agitation.

75. The syndicates appear here as being very like "social authorities" which exercise control over the normal conditions of work.

76. This is just what has been attempted in Paris.

77. And which can be harmful due to the intrusion of politicians.

78. When there is a railway accident, the strengthening of control and the naming of new officials is quickly demanded; control does not cease deteriorating, in proportion as it is reinforced and reorganized.

79. It seems to me that Durkheim has made his investigation into suicide in order to furnish scientific arguments to writers who denounce the abasement of present-day habits. Indeed, usually it is accepted as obvious that the multiplication of suicides is a very sure indication of grave moral troubles: it is well not to take such a connection too seriously. Durkheim has been very justly reproached for having abused statistics when, for example, he thinks that he has found in them evidence suitable for showing legislators the drawbacks of too easily obtainable divorce and the inadequacy of the education of girls (*Le Suicide: étude de sociologie*, pp. 442–44). Economic causes seem to Durkheim insufficient to explain the rapid aggravation of what he calls suicidal tendencies. "It is certain," he says, "that for all levels of the social hierarchy, the average well-being has increased, although this increase has perhaps not always taken place in the most equitable proportions. The malaise from which we suffer does not come, then, from the increase of the objective causes of our suffering; it testifies not to a greater economic misery, but to an alarming moral poverty" (p. 445).

80. According to G. de Molinari, this moral culture has remained below what is needed for the present industrial regime (*Science et religion* [Paris: Guillaumin, 1894], pp. 188–94).

81. Durkheim, *Le Suicide,* p. 445.
82. Molinari, *Science et religion,* p. 94. He says: "It is religion which, in the infancy of humanity, raised the edifice of morality; it is religion which upholds it and can alone uphold it." He hopes that Catholicism will accept the essential ideas of modern progress that it had condemned at the time of Pius IX (pp. 207–8).
83. Durkheim, *Le Suicide,* p. 431. The author has followed perhaps too faithfully the opinion just given by Théodule Ribot in *Psychologie des sentiments* (Paris: F. Alcan, 1896). According to this professor of the Collège de France, "religion is tending to become a religious philosophy" by losing its effective values and by leaving its faithful to give to its rites a symbolic meaning, which puts them on the same level as metaphors (pp. 307–10, 313–14). In this period Catholicism seemed quite lured by innate forces to undergo this decomposition, which liberal Protestantism had realized completely; but it would be bold today to assert that Catholics tend no longer to believe in the virtue of the sacraments.
84. Durkheim, *Le Suicide,* p. 428.
85. Ibid., p. 439.
86. Ibid., p. 435.
87. Ibid., pp. 222–32 and *passim.* The facts brought out by Durkheim require a more psychological and consequently more profound interpretation than his. In very serious crises of will, the individual needs to feel that he is upheld by a force which inspires respect around him: he can receive effective aid from "social authorities"; he can equally receive it from a group in which there exists a powerful *esprit de corps.* Thus we arrive at recognizing, like Durkheim, the good influence of professional associations, but we are better able to determine the causes of this good influence.
88. By this quality of constant tension of the will, the syndicates strongly approximate "social authorities," which do not fulfill well their censorial functions unless they are dominated by a passionate sentiment of the duties imposed by tradition. When this psychological state degenerates, they are transformed into an oligarchy against which the men whom they were supposed to protect revolt.
89. De Rousiers, *Le Trade-unionisme en Angleterre,* p. 189.
90. Ibid., p. 239.
91. Already quoted speech by Vandervelde.
92. The working girl, almost always in workshops, is very naturally included in unions and can find in them a protection that bourgeois society is unable to give her. One of the things that most astonished the Romans of the decline was the life of the German barbarians, who abhorred houses of prostitution. There are socialist municipalities. Have they suppressed the policing of morals and prostitution? I don't believe so. Along the same lines, what have those municipal officials done who are devoted to religious interests and always have the word "morality" on their tongues?

93. It is obvious that, in the various kinds of activity that we have reviewed, the unions play the roles that Le Play attributed to "social authorities."
94. Marx and Engels, *Le Manifeste communiste*, Vol. I, p. 38.
95. Since 1900 experience has taught me that intellectuals almost never accept such a role, unless they have the idea of utilizing the workers' organizations to facilitate their own political career. More than one syndicalist lawyer has become a deputy and aspires to become a minister.

Chapter 3

THE ETHICS OF SOCIALISM

1. Lecture given at the *Collège libre des sciences sociales*, Feb. 20, 1898. [Reprinted in the *Revue de Métaphysique et de Morale*, May, 1899—ED.]
2. Saverio Merlino, *Formes et essences du socialisme* (Paris: Giard et Brière, 1885), p. 4. [The maxim might be reversed as regards Sorel but it appears to mean here that economic practice is more important than doctrine.—ED.]
3. *Rivista Internazionale di Scienze Sociale e Discipline Ausiliarie*, Rome, Jan. 1899.
4. See below, pp. 145–46.
5. [Rudolph Stammler (1856–1938), German philosopher, applied neo-Kantianism to law and stressed a pure, universal theory of law.—ED.]
6. If one attempted to deduce law from economics, one would be committing an error similar to those so frequently committed by scholars who claim to be deducing the natural sciences from theorems on force, matter and evolution; they do not see that they have introduced rediscovered cosmological hypotheses in the course of their studies. These hypotheses have been made more precise; but their nature has not been changed as a consequence of their passage through applications.
7. This opinion has been expressed notably by Croce and H. Cunow.
8. [Jacques Flach (1846–1919) was a comparative legal scholar at the Collège de France, author of *Les Origines de l'ancienne France*, 1886.—ED.]
9. I think that I was the first to propose this interpretation, full of the Marxist spirit, in *Sozialistische Monatshefte* (Sept. 1898); in this article I indicated also the necessity of completing what is ordinarily called "historical materialism" by systems in which developments of religion and the public life would be placed.
10. It is this "justice" that Proudhon wanted to consider the essential element of law [i.e., justice derived from family life. See the introduction, above, pp. 17–22.—ED.]
11. The theater and the novel have used this difference extensively.

12. [Achille Loria (1857–1943) was an Italian economist who regarded the abolition of rent and the diffusion of property as solutions to the problem of capitalist exploitation.—ED.]

13. *Capital,* French translation, p. 129, col. 1 (Modern Library ed., p. 297).

14. Ibid., p. 101, col. 1 (Modern Library ed., p. 259).

15. Often reforms that will act as a revolutionary ferment later are passed along with practical reforms desired by the majority.

16. Good will can intervene in order to render opposition less noticeable in circumstances when conditions are not too tragic. The necessity of tempering the rigidity of laws by good will had been recognized by the ancients.

17. *Histoire du peuple d'Israël* (Paris: C. Lévy, 1887–93), Vol. III, p. 251.

18. Ibid., Vol. V, p. 421.

19. In Germany a lot is said about "returning to Kant"; that is a good sign.

20. Le Play had the honor of having recognized the prime influence of familial sentiments on the general direction of societies; the structure of the family can determine whether we have misoneist societies or disturbed and agitated societies having no concern for the future. Progressive socities hold the middle ground; Le Play claimed to be defining this middle ground exactly.

21. Woman is the great educator of the human race, less perhaps of the child than of the man; love transforms man and disciplines his instincts; it is woman who raises our moral standard; therefore respect for womankind is a very essential element of the march toward socialism. Now is the time to recall a courageous speech by Vandervelde to Belgian socialists. "How many of you would be justly outraged if you were grossly mistreated, bullied and brutalized by an overseer, and how many of you make your wives and children submit to the rude treatment that you would not stand for from your boss!" (Destrée and Vandervelde, *Le Socialisme en Belgique* (Paris: Giard et Brière, 1898), p. 252.

22. In order to be thorough, we should have examined the middle stage, which is interposed between the system of desires, protests and hopes of which I have spoken and the mission of the proletariat. This middle stage has been almost exclusively considered by anarchists and neglected by socialists. From the point of view of education, it is necessary to consider man in the presence of himself and to study his moral formation; socialists have too often believed that the environment acts in an automatic way and, as I said earlier, they have been concerned hardly at all with the conditions necessary to perfect moral sentiments. There is a serious gap in the socialist ethic.

23. An excess of logical zeal is among the causes of the opposition that theorists have for so long made to institutions; no institution is simple; imperfections and contradictions are always found in them. It cannot be otherwise, since in an institution law and morality must coexist and thereby manifest their contradictions.

24. The kingdom of heaven is given to the one who gives a glass of water in Jesus' name.

25. *Histoire du peuple d'Israël*, Vol. III, p. 252.
26. This is one of the central ideas of Merlino's book cited earlier.
27. *Socialisme et liberté* (Paris: Giard et Brière, 1898), p. 193.
28. [The Allemanists were followers of Jean Allemane (1843–1935), an advocate of direct action by trade unions and of rejecting political methods. In 1890 Allemane established the *Parti Ouvrier Socialiste Révolutionnaire* by leading a schism against a group of socialists, advocates of immediate reform, who called themselves "Possibilists."—ED.]

Chapter 4

FROM CRITICAL ESSAYS ON MARXISM

Necessity and Fatalism in Marxism

1. [This essay was first published in *La Riforma Sociale*, Milan, Aug. 1898. It was republished as Ch. II of *Saggi di critica del Marxismo* (Palermo: Sandron, 1902).—ED.]
2. Sombart, *Le Socialisme et le mouvement social au XIXᵉ siècle* (Paris: Giard et Brière, 1898), p. 189 of the French translation); see also what Andler says with regard to the essays of Professor Antonio Labriola (*Revue de Métaphysique et de Morale*, Sept. 1897, p. 657).
3. Ibid., pp. 93, 110, etc.
4. B. Croce, *Per l'interpretazione e la critica di alcuni concetti del Marxismo* (p. 21). A very important reflection.
5. Italian translation, p. 19.
6. P. 170.
7. Karl Marx, *Poverty of Philosophy*, p. 242.
8. Marx, *Class Struggles in France from 1848 to 1850*, p. 10 of the Italian ed.
9. *Revue Socialiste*, March 15, 1898, p. 330.
10. *Manifesto*, p. 16 of the Italian ed.
11. *Class Struggles in France*, p. 24.
12. For example, in Italy the workers buy a pamphlet by G. Stern on Karl Marx's theory of value explained to the people, in which pamphlet the iron law is pointed out as a consequence of the theory of value.
13. This seems to be the opinion of Mr. Tarati (see, for example, *Critica Sociale*, Sept. 16, 1897, p. 281, col. I).
14. *Class Struggles in France*, pp. 5, 7, 127.
15. It is precisely in this way that Engels, too, seems to understand the thought of Marx. He says that they were reproached for this prudence: "We were castigated as betrayers of the revolution" (*Class Struggles in France*, p. 7).
16. *Capital*; French translation, p. 350, col. 2. I cite the French edition

although rather frequently it is inexact (Modern Library ed., pp. 836–37).

17. Proudhon, *Les Confessions d'un révolutionnaire* (Paris: Garnier Frères, 1851).

18. [Giovanni Battista Vico (1668–1744) tried to correlate legal and political institutions with changes in mental outlook (using Roman law and institutions as his example). He divided history into instinctive (or religious), abstract and legal stages. See Sorel's study "Etude sur Vico," *Devenir Social*, Sept.-Dec. 1896.—ED.]

19. We can say that science refers rather to the *species* than to the *individual*.

20. For example, what do the words "slavery," "servitude" and "hireling" mean? Nothing, or almost nothing for the scientist. They are expressions each of which has an infinity of values according to the periods to which they refer. It is never necessary to separate them from the corresponding historical circumstances when one is discussing institutions.

21. It is for this reason that the scientist, absorbed in his speculations, the memory of which is not regulated by common associations, sometimes appears to be a madman to the imbeciles.

22. [Marx's reciprocal dependence (a term he does not use) consists in his depiction of the relationship between the economic *base* (*Grundlage*) of society and the legal-cultural superstructure which arises to correspond to that base. Thus the capitalist epoch has its own set of laws, ideologies, etc. These in turn react back on the economic base.—ED.]

23. Principles, ideas, categories, *Poverty of Philosophy*, pp. 152, 159.

24. Ibid., p. 151.

25. The mathematicians are the last to notice this sophism, because they use the term "function" regardless of the circumstances. When Euclid says that, given certain things, certain other things are given as well, he means only to say that he knows a geometric process for tracing the figures with the "givens" of the problem.

26. Science is like the legendary notice of the barber which sets forth the announcement: *Tomorrow he will shave* [himself] *for nothing.*

27. See p. 657 of the article previously cited.

28. *Poverty of Philosophy*, p. 242.

29. "Wirthschaft v. Recht nach d. Materialist Geschichtauffassung," pp. 338–45. Cited by Andler in the *Revue de Métaphysique et de Morale*, Sept. 1897, p. 653.

30. *Poverty of Philosophy*, p. 106.

31. *Poverty of Philosophy*, p. 91.

32. Contradictions abound in Engels's books; and Benedetto Croce has revealed some of the most curious of them in his biographical essay (see n. 4 above). [Rudolf Stammler (1856–1938), German philosopher and jurist. He applied neo-Kantianism to law and stressed a pure and universal theory of law.—ED.]

33. There would not be anything but some *mixtures*. It is to be observed that this economic anarchy about which Bastiat has described in the

Harmonies économiques, does not differ, metaphysically, from that anarchy of the will which, in the City of J. J. Rousseau, produces the infallible general will—when there are no "combinations."

34. Croce thinks that *pure economics* would have to be employed to complete the Marxist theories (see *Per l'interpretazione*, etc., pp. 14–19).

35. "Ludwig Feuerbach and the End of Classical German Philosophy" was published in French in *Ere Nouvelle*, May 1894, p. 14.

36. "Chance is not a specter created by us to conceal our ignorance from ourselves, nor an idea relative to the variable and always imperfect state of our consciousness" (Cournot, *Considérations sur la marche des idées et des événements dans les temps modernes* (Paris: Hachette, 1872), Vol. I, p. 1).

37. It appears that the essential traits of this picture of the future society belong to Marx and Engels in common. But this last aspect developed completely in Engels's *Socialism from Utopia to Science* (see Croce, biographical essay cited, p. 32).

38. *Revue Philosophique*, Dec. 1897, p. 648.

39. *Capital*, col. 1, p. 208.

40. Article cited (p. 657). In the German text the word "necessary" is substituted for the word "natural," but in the thought of Marx the two terms are equivalent, both corresponding to the idea of a development which is not willed, not foreseen, but coercive with regard to individuals.

41. In general, law has a character quite a bit less necessary than economy; sometimes, also, as in the case of English workmen's legislation, the character of liberty is considerably more marked. Flach has observed that private law is easier to define precisely and more constantly than public law, because it depends less upon historical circumstances (Course in the Collège de France, March 2, 1898).

42. [This means that economic laws like actuarial statistics are true only on average and that individual actions cannot always be explained according to such laws; all physical phenomena, on the other hand, obey some law.—ED.]

43. *Poverty of Philosophy*, p. 159.

44. Sombart, p. 141.

45. Ibid., p. 140.

46. If the concentration of wealth, the depopulation of farmland, and the industrial supremacy of certain countries have been extremely important phenomena in the past, there is reason to believe they will be less important in the future.

47. Plekhanoff, *Anarchisme et socialisme* (Paris: *Galeries de l'Odéon*, 1896–97), French translation, p. 4.

48. We must recognize that almost all the socialists admit these hypotheses as unquestionable postulates; although no one furnishes any justification for them.

49. *Poverty of Philosophy*, p. 159.

50. Ibid., p. 151.

51. *Poverty of Philosophy*, p. 169.

52. It seems useful to me to point out a little-known passage of Marx (*Poverty of Philosophy*, p. 152) in which he says that "there is a continuous movement of *increase* in productive forces, of *destruction* in social relationships, and of *formation* in ideas." It is necessary, I believe, to understand by this that the traditional social relationships *dissolve* by a necessary process (blind and unconscious). As for the new relationships, they form by means of new ideas. This law applies also to phenomena. The bourgeoisie unconsciously deprives itself of authority. Every day the proletariat consciously increases in influence.

53. Cournot, *Considérations*, Vol. I, p. 240; Vol. II, pp. 240, 395.

54. Ibid., Vol. II, p. 117.

55. A letter of Oct. 27, 1890, published by the *Leipziger Volkszeitung* on Dec. 25, 1895, and in French translation in *Devenir Social*, March 1895, p. 235.

56. One may read, with regard to the dispute of Engels against Dühring concerning *force,* the judicious observation of Benedetto Croce (*Per l'Interpretazione*, p. 25).

57. *Capital*, French translation, p. 336, col. 1 (Modern Library ed., p. 824).

58. See also ibid., p. 327, col. 1, concerning this subject (Modern Library ed., p. 824).

59. Ibid., p. 336, col. 1 (Modern Library ed., p. 823).

60. See also *Poverty of Philosophy*, pp. 189–90.

61. *Capital*, p. 315, col. 2. The French translation is rather incorrect and seems to say that the movement was identical everywhere. (Modern Library ed., p. 779.)

62. Ibid., p. 188, col. 2, and p. 206, col. 2 (Modern Library ed., pp. 467–68, 521–22).

63. Regarding this subject, see what Prof. Franz Reuleaux says about the indirect syntheses. *Cinématique*, French translation (Paris: F. Savy, 1877), p. 566.

64. Some excellent advice and some rather useful "suggestions" will be found in the *Saggi sul materialismo storico* (Rome: Loescher, 1896) of Antonio Labriola.

65. Actually, many seem disposed to reduce historical materialism to such a small thing that it would no longer even be worth discussing: Marx would be simply one among so many writers who have pointed out the importance of economic considerations. But it would be necessary instead to call attention once again to what is original in his work.

Is There a Utopia in Marxism?

1. [This essay was first published in *Revue de Métaphysique et de Morale*, March 1899 and republished in Italian as Chap. 5 of *Saggi di critica del marxismo*. This translation is from the original French version.— ED.]

2. Merlino later combined this booklet, *L'utopia colletivista e la crisi del*

socialismo scientifico and his earlier work, *Pro e contro il socialismo* into a work published in French: *Formes et essence du socialisme* (Paris: Giard et Brière, 1898).

3. He does not seem to have studied Spencer. He believed that Germany had produced no notable thinker since Feuerbach! Cherkesoff was wrong to maintain that Engels knowingly distorted science in his writings; Cherkesoff's pamphlet (*Pages d'histoire socialiste*), published by the *Temps Nouveaux* in Paris, is worth consulting, however.

4. G. Sombart, *Le Socialisme et le mouvement social au XIXe siècle*, French translation (Paris: Giard et Brière, 1898), pp. 108–10.

5. It was in order to criticize the absolutist theory of the physiocrats that Necker and other authors of the eighteenth century "inveighed" against property.

6. The Platonic city is aristocratic for other reasons: it is based on the customs, aspirations and ideas which were fashionable in aristocratic societies.

7. Anthime Corbon, *Le Secret du peuple de Paris* (Paris: Pagnerre, 1863), p. 106. This author, who was involved in the workers' movement before 1848, says that Fourierism "made no impression on the minds of the people."

8. Cf. Chiappelli, *Il socialismo e il pensiero moderno* (Firenze: Le Monnier, 1897).

9. Hubert Lagardelle, *La Question agraire et le socialisme* (Paris: Giard et Brière, 1898).

10. Charles Fourier, *Le Nouveau Monde industriel et sociétaire* (Paris: Bossange, 1829–30), p. 446.

11. [The term phalanx (in French, "phalanstère") originally meant a Greek military formation. It is used by Fourier to refer to his utopian communities.—ED.]

12. [Fourier named three "distributive passions": the *butterfly,* which is the need for variety and periodic change; the *cabalist,* which is the penchant for intrigue; the *composite,* which is the desire for pleasures. See Jonathan Beecher and Richard Bienvenue (editors), *The Utopian Vision of Charles Fourier* (Boston: Beacon Press, 1971), p. 419.—ED.]

13. A curious lapse of memory in the Marxists, since the master had placed so much importance on technological questions.

14. Very important observation made by Merlino.

15. Georgy Plekhanoff, *Anarchisme et socialisme*, French translation (Paris: Galéries de l'Odéon, 1896–97), p. 3.

16. Ibid., p. 9.

17. Van Kol, *Socialisme et liberté* (Paris: Giard et Brière, 1898), p. 103.

18. Ibid., p. 194.

19. Van Kol, in spite of this observation, also shows a veritable furor against anarchists and he talks of destroying them as a "painful task" in the case when they would inhibit the *tactics* of Social Democracy (ibid., p. 192).

20. *Jeunesse Socialiste,* Feb. 1895, p. 98.
21. Van Kol hopes that the "pride" of the Teutons of Tacitus will be recaptured (*Socialisme et liberté,* p. 154). It is possible that the "Teutonic idea" has had a certain influence on Social Democratic tenets.
22. Sombart, *Le Socialisme et le mouvement social au XIXe siècle,* p. 109.
23. *Devenir Social,* May 1897, p. 388.
24. Article quoted, p. 394.
25. According to the admirers of the savage, it has not even varied substantially since prehistoric times.
26. *Per la interpretazione e la critica di alcuni concette del marxismo,* p. 24 (Vol. XXVII of the Proceedings of the *Accademia pontaniana*). This very important statement was translated in the *Devenir Social,* Feb. and March 1898.
27. That is what I have called the "laws of succession" in a study on Vico. *Devenir Social,* Nov. 1896, p. 911.
28. *Socialiste,* Oct. 16, 1898.
29. Italian trans., p. 19.
30. French re-edition, p. 168.
31. *Le Nouveau Monde industriel et sociétaire,* p. 46.
32. Merlino, *Formes et essence du socialisme,* p. 272.
33. Fourier has greatly benefited from reading the *Fable des abeilles* (London: J. Nourse, 1750) and its *acorrelaris* [*The Fable of the Bees*]. He borrowed from Mandeville his fundamental idea on the utility of practice condemned by moralists and on the social interdependence which renders the vices of some interdependent with the prosperity of a great country.
34. Cf. *Année Sociologique,* 1896–97, p. 301 (according to R. Hildebrand).
35. Destrée and Vandervelde, *Le Socialisme en Belgique* (Paris: Giard et Brière, 1898), p. 283.
36. [An ideal community conceived of by Rabelais in *Gargantua* where all forms of earthly pleasure are cultivated.—ED.]
37. *Politics,* Book II, chap. 1, #4.
38. J. Guesde in the French Chamber of Deputies, June 24, 1896, and Anseele in the Belgian Chamber, April 30, 1898.
39. *Capital,* French translation, p. 31, col. 2 (Modern Library ed., p. 92).
40. The reader will do well to refer to #436-440 of Hegel's *Phenomenology of the Mind* in order to understand the origin of this theory, just as he should refer to #431-435 in order to understand clearly the theory of the proletariat.
41. Marx's error seems more excusable by the fact that in his time Max Müller had reduced the study of religions to a study of literary forms derived from figures of speech and engendering contradictions. Thus, they could be considered as veils hiding the relations of men with nature.
42. Van Kol, *Socialisme et liberté,* p. 236.
43. Ibid., p. 254.

44. Ibid., p. 246.
45. Cf. *Capital,* French translation, p. 205, col. 1 (Modern Library ed., p. 517).
46. *Le Socialisme en Belgique,* p. 417.
47. *Devenir Social,* April 1897, p. 344. Cited by Vandervelde, *Revue Socialiste,* March 1898, p. 329.
48. *Socialisme et liberté,* p. 247. However, Guesde is an enthusiastic partisan of "social cuisine" (*Le Socialisme au jour le jour* [Paris: Giard et Brière, 1899], p. 378).
49. It is thus that they strive to solve the agrarian problem and promise the peasants to leave them their land.

Polemics for the Interpretation of Marxism: Bernstein and Kautsky

1. Eduard Bernstein, *Socialisme théorique et socialdémocratie pratique* (Paris: P.-V. Stock, 1900), translated into French by Alexendre Cohen. Karl Kautsky, *Le Marxisme et son critique Bernstein: Anti-critique* (Paris: P.-V. Stock, 1900), translated into French by M. Martin-Leray. [This essay was first published in *Revue Internationale de Sociologie,* April, May, 1900 and republished as Chap. IX of *Saggi di critica del marxismo.*—ED.]
2. This monthly review appeared from 1895 to 1898, Giard et Brière, publishers, Paris.
3. This book was translated into French by the author with certain modifications under the title *Formes et essence du socialisme* (Paris: Giard et Brière, 1898).
4. In July 1898 the *Revue Internationale de Sociologie* published an important article by Professor Mazaryck, "The Scientific and Philosophical Crisis in Contemporary Marxism," but Bernstein's ideas were not completely known at that time.
5. In articles and interviews on the Dreyfus affair, Liebknecht has shown that he has the unfortunate habit of speaking about things which he does not understand in the least (cf. *Cahiers de la Quinzaine* of Charles Péguy, Dec. 5, 1900).
6. I read in a book which has no scientific pretensions, but which is one of the authoritative sources, this interview with the Socialist Kaiser: "We are Hegelians; this is why we jump with fury when the chancellor accuses us of continuing the work of Lassalle. . . . Compare the Hegelians and the Kantians! It is enough to make your hair stand on end" (Jacques Saint-Cère, *L'Allemagne telle qu'elle est* (Paris: Ollendorf, 1886), p. 60).
7. *Devenir Social,* April 1897, p. 290.
8. "Bernstein trouble les esprits" in Kautsky, p. 336.
9. "Today, Bernstein and Schulze-Gavernitz warmly embrace him," says Kautsky (p. 94).
10. *Socialisme Utopique et socialisme scientifique,* p. 22.
11. Bernstein, p. 72.

12. Ibid., p. 75.

13. Kautsky does not appear to know the works of Pantaleoni and Pareto on pure economics.

14. Benedetto Croce, *Materialismo storico* . . . (Palermo: Sandron), p. 52, n.2.

15. It would be very necessary to probe the meaning of the concept of value in this case; it seems to me that the *quantum of value* measures social utility here.

16. Thus, two day-laborers, each paid five francs per day, add as much supplementary social utility with their pickaxes as one mechanic paid ten francs to run a highly perfected machine. All this is very obscure and no one wants to clarify it.

17. Cf. Vandervelde, "Livre III du *Capital* de Marx," in the *Annales de l'Institut des Sciences Sociales* (Brussels, April 1897), pp. 90, 99.

18. Kautsky, p. xxix.

19. If the employers reduce the working day from 12 to 10 hours, although daily production does not change, and if in both cases it requires half the day to pay the costs, the net product of the boss formerly represented six hours and is now diminished by an hour (*Critica Sociale*, Aug. 16, 1897, p. 248). This interpretation of the net product is based on a note in *Capital*, p. 93, col. 2 (Modern Library ed., p. 241, n.2). Marx appeared to believe that the progress of machines necessarily makes a loss of profits for the employer, and he thus explained why the latter tried to lengthen the working day (*Capital*, French translation, p. 176, col. 2; Modern Library ed., pp. 444–45).

20. For example, see *Capital*, French translation, pp. 30–31 (Modern Library ed., p. 89).

21. Marx appears to regard it as incorrect (*Capital*, French translation, p. 230, col. 2; Modern Library ed., p. 570).

22. See the protest made concerning some bakers who succeeded in selling bread below the market price (underselling masters) thanks to "the unpaid labour of the men" (*Capital*, French translation, p. 108, col. 1; Modern Library ed., p. 276).

23. Marx quotes this passage of an official report: "The worker now knows when the time that he has sold ends, and when that which still belongs to him begins (*Capital*, French translation, p. 130, col. 2, n.4; Modern Library ed., p. 330, n.).

24. Menger, *Le Droit au produit intégral du travail* (Paris: Giard et Brière, 1900), pp. 75–79.

25. See an article that I published in the *Rivista di Storia e di Filosofia del Diritto*, Aug. 1899, under the title "Le idee giuridiche nel Marxismo." The article is reprinted in *Saggi di critica del marxismo*.

26. *Mouvement Socialiste*, March 1, 1900, pp. 260, 262–63.

27. *Socialiste*, July 31, 1898, col. 4.

28. Ibid., Nov. 27, 1898, col. 4.

29. A good example of this type of propaganda is found in a famous pamphlet by J. Stern ("K. Marx's Theory of Value Explained to the People"),

whose conclusions are: "wages always tend toward the lowest level compatible with the maintenance of life, while the working day becomes as long as possible. Salaried work is servile work: besides the social work necessary to his own needs, the worker must work many hours more to produce solely to the advantage of capital." None of this is a conclusion which can be drawn from the theory of value, but the ill-informed reader believes it is.

30. Croce, *Materialismo storico*, p. 115.
31. Kautsky, pp. 21, 23, 26.
32. Proudhon, *La Révolution sociale démontrée par le coup d'état du 2 décembre* (Paris: Garnier Frères, 1852). This comparison will not fail to astonish Kautsky who reproaches Bernstein vigorously (and several times) for citing Proudhon! Everyone knows that it was from French socialist literature that Marx took the term "class," which he used sometimes in the rather vague meaning that it has in France and sometimes in a special sense.
33. E. Ferri, *Socialisme et science positive* (Paris: Giard et Brière, 1897), p. 152.
34. *Das Kapital*, 4th German ed., p. 143, n. 5.
35. The first two essays are collected under the title *Essais sur la conception matérialiste de l'histoire* (Paris: Giard et Brière, 1897); the third carries the title *Le Socialisme et la philosophie* (Paris: Giard et Brière, 1899). In the first of these volumes, Labriola said: "One must not imitate the teacher who, from the shore, teaches swimming by means of the definition of swimming," and he promised studies made according to Marxist principles; unfortunately he did not keep his promise.
36. Labriola, *Le Socialisme et la philosophie*, p. 72.
37. Ibid., pp. 159, 162–66.
38. Kautsky, p. 20.
39. He would have done well to tell us in what work Marx and Engels demonstrated this. Kautsky does not know the lovely book by Lacombe, *De l'histoire considérée comme science* (Paris: Hachette, 1894), which appeared in 1894 and in which these questions are treated in such a remarkable way; the French author only became acquainted with Marx's work after having written his book.
40. Kautsky, p. 18.
41. Lafargue, *Recherches sur l'origine de l'idée de justice* (Paris: Giard et Brière, 1900, p. 79). This pamphlet first appeared in the *Neue Zeit* edited by Kautsky. In the *Devenir Social* we can read two whimsical articles by Lafargue, one on Campanella (1895), another on "The Myth of the Immaculate Conception" (1898). The author does not know the meaning of the term "immaculate conception"! The extraordinary account of Campanella, which contains such bizarre theories concerning Jewish mysticism, was inserted into the history of socialism edited by Kautsky, who thus assumed responsibility for the "new manner" of writing history.
42. Kautsky, p. 26.
43. Bernstein, p. 15.

44. *Mouvement Socialiste,* March 1, 1900, p. 264.
45. Kautsky, p. 27.
46. Bernstein, p. 8.
47. Bernstein, p. 9.
48. *Mouvement Socialiste,* March 1, 1900, p. 273.
49. This passage concerns the dialectic, which is covered in the next paragraph; but it refers to predestination, which permits quoting it here.
50. Bernstein, p. 18.
51. Kautsky, p. 303.
52. Jaurès, *Mouvement Socialiste,* March 1, 1900.
53. Kautsky, p. 293.
54. Among so many examples that I could cite, I will choose an article by Lafargue in *Socialiste* of February 25, 1900, in which I read that "justice, liberty, motherland and other divinities of the *Capitalist ideology*"(!) are "ethical and metaphysical whores" that one must "undress in public in order to expose their scrawniness and ugliness to all eyes."
55. Bernstein, p. 18.
56. Kautsky, p. 41.
57. Bernstein, p. 18.
58. It is not useless to recall an opinion of Cournot here: "The more that societies age, the more they are stripped of the qualities which belong to them by virtue of being living organisms, in order to come close to the kind of structure, and lend themselves to the mode of improvement, comprised in machinery. It follows that some very absurd theories for the explanation of the past can become serious when they are concerned with tendencies of the future" (*Considérations sur la marche des idées et des événements dans les temps modernes* [Paris: Hachette, 1872], Vol. II, p. 216).

    Here we must distinguish between Marx and Social Democracy. Several paradoxical phrases of *Capital* that he omitted in the definitive German edition have often been cited against him. Thus, on p. 31 (col. 2) of the French edition, we read: "the religious world is only the reflection of the real world"; and on p. 318 (col. 2): "Protestantism is essentially a bourgeois religion." These two statements were unfortunate. [The Modern Library ed., p. 91, contains both assertions and is based on the fourth German edition.—ED.]
59. Bernstein, p. 17.
60. Kautsky, p. 35.
61. Thus, he said that the peasant who produces as much as he needs "completely dominates the mode of production (?) as much as the latter depends on social factors." And is not the savage freer still?
62. Under this label, the Germans confuse very different categories: artistic workers, employees of commerce, artistic professionals, functionaries and men practicing the liberal professions. With his unfortunate habit of mixing up everything, Kautsky never makes the necessary distinctions.
63. Kautsky, pp. 39–40, 242–54, 330–32.
64. Kautsky, p. 252.

65. Kautsky, p. 39.
66. Kautsky, pp. 248, 331.
67. Kautsky, p. 250.
68. Marx, *L'Alliance de la démocratie socialiste et l'association internationale des travailleurs*, p. 48. Reading this pamphlet makes one think of the actions of the contemporary Social Democracy. *De te fabula narratur.*
69. *Mouvement Socialiste*, March 1, 1900, p. 271.
70. Under the condition of taking the word "social" in a meaning that it does not have in the language of politics; the meaning of this word is too often played upon.
71. Why stop halfway and not go all the way to the placing in common of the means of possession as with Lafargue (*Le Communisme et l'évolution économique* [Lille: G. Delory, 1892], p. 8)? Why not call for the disappearance of all differences and reduce society to that perfect unity which exists only in the individual? (cf. Aristotle, *Politics*, II, Chap. 1, sect. 4).
72. Labriola, *Le Socialisme et la Philosophie*, pp. 225 ff.
73. For Engels, idealism means belief (first) in the existence of a soul separated from the body; (second) in the immortality of the soul; (third) in one God.
74. Marx calls these two things the "acquisitions of the capitalist era" (*Errungschaft der kapitalistischen Aera*); the term *Errungschaft* borrowed from legal language should be noted. It is very clear here that Marx understood that socialism respects the material basis of the capitalist economy and does not wish to reorganize the world as the utopians did; it ought to develop and improve the capitalist inheritance.
75. Kautsky, p. 50. Marx supposedly used Hegelian devices only to explain and not to prove.
76. *Devenir Social*, Oct. 1897, p. 874.
77. Bernstein, p. 37.
78. Kautsky, p. 68.
79. Bernstein, p. 39.
80. Bernstein, pp. 40–44.
81. Bernstein, p. 49.
82. Kautsky, pp. 42–61.
83. Cf. what I have said in my preface to the work of Merlino, *Formes et essence du socialisme* (Paris: Giard et Brière, 1898), p. xli.
84. Bernstein, p. 44.
85. Bernstein, pp. 44 and 62. [By which is meant that the dialectic contains a "hidden reason" and is thus "progressive." This progressive development is often violent. Hence violence is creative—i.e., progressive.—ED.]
86. Sombart, *Le Socialisme et le mouvement social au XIXᵉ siècle* (Paris: Giard et Brière, 1898), p. 108.
87. Bernstein, p. 54.
88. The term *Knechtschaft* is opposed in Hegelian terminology to *Herrschaft*. Thus it is too strong to translate as "slavery." On p. 681 (4th German ed.) the terms *Knechtschaft* and *Knechtung* apply as much to the feudal regime as to the capitalist regime; there is a change in the

form of subordination (*Formwechsel dieser Knechtung*) and a shifting of the exploitation (*Verwandlung der Exploitation*).

89. It is very easy to understand that Marx is thinking here of the formation of the property of landlords.

90. *Capital,* French translation, p. 285, col. 1 (Modern Library ed., p. 709).

91. Kautsky, who cites the second text (p. 235), does not seem to perceive this profound difference.

92. *Manifeste du parti communiste* (Paris: Giard et Brière, 1897), p. 25.

93. *Capital,* French translation, p. 127 (Modern Library ed., p. 323). Bernstein has seen this difficulty clearly (p. 283).

94. [The first phrase from the *Communist Manifesto* is an historical analysis of the fall of the feudal orders: "They had to be eliminated; they are eliminated." The second phrase from *Capital* relates to the present capitalist order: "It must be destroyed, it is destroyed."—ED.]

95. The German word *Exploitation* is not isolated in *Capital,* but here it is presented in a completely unique way; indeed, at the head of the chapter following capitalist property is written "Privateigenthum, beruht auf der *Ausbeutung* fremder Arbeit," and here "Privateigenthum beruht auf *Exploitation* fremder Arbeit." [*Ausbeutung* also means "exploitation" and the two phrases both mean: Private property depends on the exploitation of foreign labor.—ED.]

96. Pecqueur's formulation is found in *Théorie nouvelle d'économie politique et sociale* (Paris: Capelle, 1842), p. 435. [Constantin Pecqueur, 1801–87, anticipated Marx's views on the class basis of society and on the labor theory of value; but he based his theories on Christian ethics.—ED.]

97. I have put forth this opinion in the preface to Colajanni's book *Socialisme* (Paris: Giard et Brière, 1900).

98. Bernstein, p. 287.

99. Bernstein, pp. 50–52, 61, 152.

100. Kautsky, p. 54. [Babouvism refers to the extremist "conspiracy of equals" of Gracchus Babeuf, 1760–97, whose violent Jacobism was "inherited" by Auguste Blanqui (1805–81).—ED.]

101. Kautsky, pp. 85–98, 280–89. We should note here that Kautsky, for the convenience of his proof, cites (on p. 287) only what suits him from the program of the Guesdist party. For we read there: *"This collective appropriation can result only from collective action";* and in the explanations given by Guesde and Lafargue on the program, we read: "Only a revolution can permit to the producing class. . . ."

102. Since Kautsky appeals to the ideas in the Guesdist program, let us remember that according to Guesde, forty-eight hours would not pass without having produced decisive results (Speech to the Chamber of Deputies, June 15, 1896).

103. The dictatorship of the proletariat means the *dictatorship of the orators of the clubs,* according to Bernstein (p. 298). See also p. 226. See what G. Platon has written on this subject in his articles on "Socialism in Greece" (*Devenir Social,* Oct. 1895, p. 669).

104. Kautsky, pp. 221, 254.

105. On the contrary, Lafargue maintains that Lassalle in his concept of the *iron law of wages* did not represent all the horrors of proletarian life; there is no limit to increasing oppression (*Socialiste*, Jan. 29, 1899, p. 2, col. 4).

106. Kautsky, p. 227.

107. [Sorel wrote this 32 years prior to the discovery of Marx's 1844 *Economic and Philosophical Manuscripts*. In these, one can easily discern that Marx's concern for alienation (*Entfremdung*) went far beyond mere physical misery and was concerned with the deadening qualities of the work process itself. The question that is still debated is whether this early notion of alienation is a holdover from early idealistic concerns, or whether it is found to be projected into the heart of Marx's mature work itself. The bulk of Sorel's writing bespeaks of the joys and struggles rather than the horrors of work—of the fulfillment to be found on the struggle against nature on the workshop floor. In this, his emphasis on proletarian creativity, even under the aegis of capitalism, differs from Marx—or at least the "early" Marx. For a provocative argument in favor of the primacy of Marx's concern with alienation see Robert Tucker, *Philosophy and Myth in Karl Marx* (Cambridge: Cambridge University Press, 1961); for an opposing view, see Lewis Feuer, *Marx and the Intellectuals* (New York: Anchor, 1971); and Sidney Hook's foreword to the University of Michigan edition of *From Hegel to Marx* (Ann Arbor: 1963). For Sorel's rather romantic view of labour, see the excerpts from the "Critique of *Creative Evolution*" below.—ED.]

108. Kautsky, p. 231. The French edition no longer speaks of the proof drawn from the lowering of the birth rate: the error in reasoning was all too obvious.

109. Kautsky, p. 219.

110. E. Milhaud, "Le troisième Congrès des Syndicats allemands," *Revue Socialiste*, July 1899, pp. 16–28, 31.

111. Kautsky, p. 229.

112. *Musée social*, circular of Oct. 15, 1897.

113. *Museé social*, circular of Feb. 1899, p. 83.

114. *Socialiste*, Oct. 9, 1878, col. 4. Pecqueur compared "monogamy with its perpetual civil minority for the wife" to the situation of the proletarians; promiscuity was for him equivalent to slavery and polygamy to servitude (*Théorie nouvelle*, p. 317). It is impossible for me to understand what Guesde means. If man has the responsibility of supporting the household, woman cannot be compared to the proletarian, whom Guesde regards as supporting his boss through his labor.

115. Kautsky, pp. 233, 260.

116. Kautsky reproaches capitalist society for not having "created more forms of the household in order to replace the present-day ménage founded on a couple" (p. 233). Does he want to revert to polygamy or to housekeeping by groups, of which Lewis Henry Morgan thought he had found the vestiges in the redskins? In *Capital* we find this strange sentence with regard to the dissolution of the family by the factory: "In

history, as in nature, corruption is the laboratory of life," French translation (p. 212, col. 1). This paradox is missing from the fourth German
edition. It is regrettable that socialist writers so often have bizarre ideas
on sexual relations in regard to *Le Calvaire* by Octave Mirbeau (Paris:
P. Ollendorf, 1887), Guesde said that the worker ought to rejoice in
seeing the luxurious carriages of courtesans go by. "These Venuses take
vengeance on your behalf . . . when they wring you dry of the last bit
of your gold and of your bones . . . they are the workers' revenge . . .
What then are 'these lovers of justice' doing except disarming the capitalist class? They accomplish an eminently salubrious work. We shout
to them: 'Carry on, priestesses of social decay' " (*Le Socialisme au jour
le jour* [Paris: Giard et Brière, 1898], p. 474). Guesde writes in the
preface that he has edited this collection of articles for the education of
socialists: truly a beautiful education!

117. Pecqueur, *Des intérêts du commerce, de l'industrie, de l'agriculture et
de la civilisation en général sous l'influence des applications de la vapeur*
(dissertation given a prize by the *Académie des Sciences Morales et
Politiques*, 1839).

118. Considerations of class relations are often analyzed as if there existed
only mechanical industries and not external commerce. Many profits
creating gigantic fortunes have come out of commercial exploitation of
new countries, as Pecqueur had written in 1838. Moreover, in many
countries the countryside, like colonies, has been exploited for the benefit of the towns.

119. [Franz Reuleaux, 1829–1905, was a mechanical engineer and professor
at the Industrial Academy of Berlin. He is the author of the *Kinematics
of Machinery*, English translation by A. B. W. Kennedy, London: Macmillan, 1876.—ED.]

120. Le Play, *La Réforme sociale en France* (Tours: A. Mame et Fils, 1887),
Vol. II, pp. 150–54. Le Play states that under the regime of collective
manufacture, work is less assured than under that of the *mechanical
factory*; "the boss of the former is more of a trader than a manufacturer.
He is not inclined, as is the proprietor of a factory, to maintain in operation a considerable working stock which becomes ruinous when it is not
productive."

121. Kautsky, p. 126.

122. Kautsky, p. 132.

123. Kautsky, p. 133. But then, why do the socialists make such an effort to
win the countryside?

124. Kautsky, p. 147.

125. Kautsky, p. 145.

126. On the true role of rural cooperatives, see what I have written in *Science
Sociale* (Sept. 1899) under the title "Les divers types de sociétés co-
opératives" ["Various types of cooperative societies"].

127. Kautsky, pp. 150, 282–84.

128. Bernstein, pp. 134–40. Kautsky does not make any distinction between
restricting production and regulating it; these things are distinct enough,

however; he does not appear to know the fine book by Paul de Rousiers, *Les Industries monopolisées aux Etats-Unis* (Paris: Colin, 1900).

129. Kautsky, p. 161. It is regrettable that the author has no knowledge of the work of Pareto on the distribution of revenue.

130. Kautsky does not appear to have intended to speak of it: "we have no statistics on stockholders," he said on p. 196.

131. Kautsky, p. 243.

132. Kautsky, p. 247.

133. Kautsky, p. 257.

134. *Capital,* p. 230, col. 1.

135. Bernstein, p. 123. Bernstein shows us that Marx's thought wavered greatly.

136. Kautsky, p. 274.

137. Here again we can contrast to his statements some very explicit declarations of the French Marxists; Guesde and Lafargue in their commentary on the program say, "This *inevitable revolution* will . . . spring forth from international political complications and the *fatal perturbations* which are brought on by the industrial development of Europe and agricultural competition of America and Australia." The revolution and great crises are indeed proclaimed to be inevitable here.

138. Kautsky, p. 272.

139. Pecqueur, *Théorie nouvelle,* p. xii.

140. Kautsky, p. 306.

141. Kautsky, p. 308.

142. Bernstein, p. 288.

143. In the preface to the *Class Struggles in France,* Engels emphasizes the novelty of this formulation used by Marx in 1850. It was only new in the communist milieu from which came the *Manifesto.* Besides, we know that Pecqueur used and abused the term "socialization."

144. On this point Pecqueur enters into great detail and proposes systems of cooperation and election. Marx always assumes that industry will involve a technological division of labor; he is very frugal with details on his idea of the future; on p. 31, col. 2, he speaks of the product of men freely associated (*frei vergesselschafteten Menschen*) and of a process of production placed under their reasoned control (*unter deren bewuster planmassiger Kontrole*): this takes us a long way from the true fraternal communism that many people still dream about. (See *Capital,* Modern Library ed., p. 90.)

145. Pecqueur, *Théorie nouvelle,* p. 699ff. See on pp. 613–16 the objections that he makes to the communist precept: "*to each according to his needs.*"

146. Van Overbergh, *Les Caractères généraux du socialisme scientifique d'après le manifeste communiste,* p. 37.

147. For example, we read on p. 30: "By liberty, one means liberty of commerce"; already in Pecqueur (*Théorie nouvelle,* p. 432) we find "the proprietors call liberty the right of competition." Marx had exaggerated the previous idea.

148. Bernstein, p. 250.
149. Bernstein, p. 255.
150. Bernstein, p. 244. This condemnation of the militia system constitutes an act of great courage, because Social Democracy has made an *indisputable dogma* out of the militia system; it is true that the Social Democracy understands nothing about the military question.
151. Bernstein, p. 257. The London Congress of 1896 demanded that the minimum age be made 16 years, and that up to 18 years a system of half-time be adopted. Bernstein does not even mention this resolution. Undoubtedly, he does not take it seriously.
152. Kautsky, p. 203.
153. Kautsky, p. 205.
154. Kautsky, p. 207.
155. Kautsky, p. 215.
156. Bernstein, p. 151.
157. Kautsky takes refuge in sentimental demonstrations on the "virtues" of the people. And then there is an *elite* (p. 359) in the proletariat; thus business will be directed by the *politicians* who direct the party! What will the workers have gained by changing *masters*? Industry will be very badly directed and not very progressive; the workers will be the first victims of the ignorance of the political chieftains.
158. Kautsky, pp. 334–35.
159. I confess that I do not understand this very well.
160. Undoubtedly by creating national workshops modeled on those of 1848.
161. Bernstein, p. 226.
162. Bernstein, p. 47. Proudhon continues by a comparison between this tyranny and that of Nero. Jacques Saint-Cère also believed that frightening events would ensue if a revolution took place in Germany (Bernstein, p. 69).
163. Cf. Vilfredo Pareto, *Cours d'économie politique* (Lausanne: Rouge, 1896), Vol. I, p. 414.
164. Kautsky, pp. 315–22.
165. Bernstein, p. 318.
166. Kautsky, p. 318.
167. This is why Bernstein says that his opinions on democracy will not be admitted by "those who are incapable of imagining the realization of socialism without acts of violence."
168. This idea could be based on a passage in the *Manifesto* in which Marx said that the communists have their eyes fixed on Germany; in 1847 a revolution was expected in Prussia; Marx never predicted the February movement and the working-class character of the Parisian revolution. In general his predictions were unfortunate (cf. several examples that I have given in the *Rivista Popolare di Politica, Littere e Scienze Sociale* of April 30, 1900). In any case, there is no basis for thinking that Marx intended to affirm an historical law in this passage, which obviously concerns a special historical accident in 1847.
169. Kautsky, p. 305.

170. The meaning of the term "class" has always remained quite vague in Marxist terminology; it has several meanings that must be separated. I have called attention to this point in the preface to *Socialisme* by M. Colajanni. The notion of class in Marx is almost always strongly imbued with Hegelian ideas on *estates* (Hegel, *Philosophy of Right*, p. 203 ff.).
171. Jaurès, who proclaims himself a partisan of Kautsky, nevertheless abounds in Bernstein's interpretations on all practical questions (cf. *Mouvement Socialiste*, March 15, 1900, pp. 357, 367).

Chapter 5

FROM THE ILLUSIONS OF PROGRESS

1. [*Les Illusions du progrès* was first published in *Mouvement Socialiste*, July–Dec. 1906. This translation is made from the fifth edition of the book (Paris: Rivière, 1947), pp. 1, 29–64, and is reprinted from the complete version translated by John and Charlotte Stanley, *The Illusions of Progress*, Berkeley and Los Angeles: University of California Press, 1969, 1972, pp. 1, 9–29.—ED.]
2. Brunetière, *Etudes critiques*, 5th ser., pp. 162–63. Brunetière calls even this morality a completely lay morality.
3. Ibid., pp. 217–24.
4. In a word, the moral reforms of Jansenism were not the consequence of its theology; rather, its theology was the consequence of its moral reforms. This appears to me to be Renan's opinion (*Saint Paul*, p. 486; *Nouvelles études d'histoire religieuse* ["New Studies in Religious History"], pp. 472–73). One can understand the importance of this transposition from the point of view of historical materialism.
5. Brunetière, *Etudes critiques*, 5th ser., p. 210. The king compelled her, however, to live in a convent from 1702 to 1713.
6. Ibid., pp. 210–11. Dubos indicates that the moral changes had been going on for about ten years. The consumption of brandy had quadrupled, and the passion for gambling had become extraordinary.
7. H. Rigault, *Histoire de la querelle des anciens et des modernes*, pp. 259–60.
8. Brunetière, *Etudes critiques*, 6th ser., pp. 202–3. He thinks that "from his ecclesiastical education, Bossuet retained a basic timidity, inexperience, and even clumsiness throughout his life."
9. Brunetière, *Etudes critiques*, 5th ser., pp. 157–58, 180–81.
10. On the role of these three concepts, see my *Le Système historique de Renan* (Paris: Rivière, 1906), pp. 57–61.
11. It is helpful to observe that the need for an apology was all the more obvious as signs of economic decline were being felt in the same period in which Perrault wrote *Parallèles* ["Parallels"]. The price of land began

to decline, and this decline continued well beyond the reign of Louis XIV (D'Avenel, *Histoire économique de la propriété, des salaires, des denrées, et de tous les prix en générale depuis l'an 1200 jusqu'en l'an 1800* ["Economic History of Property, Salaries, Commodities, and All General Prices from 1200 to 1800"], I, 387–88).

12. Brunetière, *Etudes critiques,* 5th ser., pp. 139–40.
13. It is possible that the idea of acceleration, after having gone from politics to physics, forthwith turned around, so the theory of the accelerated fall of bodies contributed to the refinement of the idea of progress. We can observe an analogous phenomenon concerning the hypotheses of evolution; they arose out of the philosophy of history, but they did not make an impression on historians in an imperative way until they took an excursion through the biological sciences.
14. Brunetière, *Etudes critiques,* 4th ser., p. 122.
15. Brunetière, *Etudes critiques,* 5th ser., p. 225.
16. Ibid., p. 46.
17. Sainte-Beuve, *Port-Royal,* V, 367. Brunetière, *Etudes critiques,* 5th ser., p. 47. In his second letter, Bossuet seems to think Descartes followed the Church fathers on many points. Brunetière believes this judgment to be fairly accurate (p. 49).
18. Brunetière, *Etudes critiques,* 4th ser., pp. 144–49.
19. Philosophy (*la philosophie*) means physics (*la physique*); this meaning still exists in England.
20. Sainte-Beuve, *Port-Royal,* III, 414.
21. J. Reinach, *Diderot,* p. 170.
22. Sainte-Beuve, op. cit., p. 412.
23. Brunetière, *Etudes critiques,* 5th ser., p. 147.
24. At least twice, Newton proclaimed the incompetence of the Cartesian mechanisms in science: "Virium causas et sedes physicas jam non expendo"; "Rationem harum gravitatis proprietarum nondum potui deducere et hypotheses non fingo." He did not dare, however, to deny entirely the interest that considerations about such causes presented. We find proof of this in a letter to Boyle and in another to Bentley (Stallo, *La Matière et la physique moderne* ["Matter and Modern Physics"], pp. 31, 34, 35). It was his successors who, provided with an excellent instrument and no longer seeing any interest in Cartesian philosophy, completely freed themselves from it. Côtes was the first to make such a radical declaration, and Euler in his letter of October 18, 1760 ("à une princesse d'Allemagne" ["To a German Princess"]) still protests against this oversimplification.
25. Brunetière, *Evolution des genres,* p. 172.
26. Hypolite Taine, *Ancien Régime,* p. 262; cf. p. 242.
27. Letter of May 21, 1687, in Sainte-Beuve, *Port-Royal,* V, 368.
28. Brunetière, *Etudes critiques,* 4th ser., p. 129.
29. Ibid., pp. 125, 131.
30. Renan, *Feuilles detachées* ("Isolated Pages"), p. 370.
31. Sainte-Beuve, *Port-Royal,* III, 422.

32. Taine observed that the men of the eighteenth century "claim in vain to be followers of Bacon and to reject innate ideas. With another point of departure than the Cartesians, they tread the same path and, like Cartesians, they abandon experience after a little dabbling in it" (*Ancien Régime*, pp. 262–63).

33. Renan wrote several significant lines on this matter: "We would reach a stage of Babylon in our own time, if the scientific charlatans, upheld by the newspapers and by the men of society, invaded the faculties, the Institute and the *Collège de France*. In France, there are certain needs above the whims of these society gentlemen, such as manufacturing explosives, artillery, and the industries dependent on science. All of these will maintain true science. In Babylon, the dabblers won out" (*Histoire du peuple d'Israël* ["History of the People of Israel"], III, 179–80). The seventeenth and eighteenth centuries did not have scientific industries.

34. There could be more than one comparison made between Pascal and Bergson.

35. Turgot (Daire Collection), II, 598.

36. Marquis Jean-Antoine-Nicolas Caritat de Condorcet, *Tableau historique des progrès de l'esprit humain* ["Outlines of an Historical View of the Progress of the Human Mind"], 9th epoch.

37. Ibid., 10th epoch.

38. Ibid., 10th epoch. Taine thought the French language, in becoming impoverished, had become very suitable for saying clearly those things that it could express (*Ancien Régime*, p. 247). This impoverished French became the universal language of the upper classes in Europe, and it was probably this universality of abstract speech that made Condorcet think it would be easy to create a cosmopolitan scientific language. It is evident that a language is all the more apt to be accepted by diverse peoples when it is less proximate to the common things of life. Contrary to Taine's view, I believe the French language lacked clarity in the eighteenth century. It is only with specific terms—the only ones capable of evoking images—that we can express our thoughts accurately without deceiving our readers and ourselves.

39. Condorcet, *Tableau historique*, 9th epoch. Note Condorcet's spite against Buffon, whom he fails to list here.

40. Condorcet, *Rapport et projet de décret sur l'organisation générale de l'instruction publique* ["Report and Proposal on the General Organization of Public Education"], preface by Compayré, p. xviii.

41. Ibid., p. 25.

42. Ibid., p. 29.

43. Condorcet's reasons are not satisfactory. It is indeed very rare that the true motives behind questions of this kind are stressed. He claims that the "ancients" are full of errors and that eloquence is a danger for those living under a parliamentary regime, although excellent for those who govern themselves directly in general assemblies. Representatives should

not succumb to their personal sentiments but should obey only their reason, lest they betray their duties (Condorcet, *Rapport*, pp. 27–28).

44. Dupont de Nemours produced a table of this type under the title, *Abrégé des principes de l'économie politique* ["Sketch of the Principles of Political Economy"]; (*Les Physiocrates* [Daire Collection], pp. 367–85). This example does not give us a very lofty opinion of what can be learned from the procedure Condorcet admired so naïvely.

45. Condorcet, *Tableau historique*, 10th epoch.

46. Taine, *Ancien Régime*, pp. 258–59.

47. Ibid., p. 261.

48. In order to judge Diderot fairly, he should not be compared to Montesquieu, Buffon or Rousseau, but to the great concoctors of modern articles. Brunetière said, "He wrote on all subjects indiscriminately, with the same aplomb, without guide rules or choice, order, standards, and at full speed" (*Evolution des genres*, p. 153).

49. We read in the *Petit Parisien* of March 22, 1910, that "it is not ridiculous to assume in these matters that we are approaching some important discoveries."

50. It is valuable to recall here a perfectly justified evaluation of the "great man" by Gabriel Deville in 1896: "He made the future of all the pedantic terms and forbidding words that, with any luck, one usually only comes across once in a decade. He discovered America several times with an always new, vainglorious satisfaction, and he sprinkled the whole with extraordinary Latin. The result was the confection of a socialism good at the very most for freemasons and spiritualists" (*Principes socialistes* ["Socialist Principles"], p. xxv).

51. Renan, *Marc-Aurèle*, p. 641.

52. Educated Catholics know only the theology which they can find in the seventeenth-century literary works, and, in their eyes, this philosophy does not at all seem unworthy of modern man.

Chapter 6

FROM REFLECTIONS ON VIOLENCE

Introduction: Letter to Daniel Halévy

1. [*Reflections* was first published in the *Mouvement Socialiste*, Jan.–June 1906. The first four sections herein were added to the 1908 edition published by Marcel Rivière, Paris, in the form of an open letter to Daniel Halévy.—ED.]

2. "Sadness, which is put forth as a *presentiment* in all the masterpieces of Greek art despite the life with which they seem to overflow, [shows]

that individuals of genius, even in this period, were able to penetrate
the illusions of life to which the spirit of their time was abandoning
itself without feeling the need to control them" (Hartmann, *Philosophie
de l'inconscient*, Vol. II, p. 436). I call attention to the notion that sees
an historical anticipation in the spirit of the great Hellenes. There are
few doctrines more important for the understanding of history than that
of anticipations, which Newman utilized in his research on the history
of dogmas.

3. Hartmann, ibid., p. 462.

4. The moans that we heard from the so-called desperate people at the
   beginning of the nineteenth century owed their success partly to their
   similarities in form with true pessimist literature.

5. Taine, *Le Régime moderne*, Vol. II, pp. 121–22.

6. The comic Athenian poets several times portrayed a land of milk and
   honey where no one had to work any more (Alfred Croiset and Maurice
   Croiset, *Histoire de la littérature grecque* [Paris: Fontemoing, 1896–99],
   Vol. III, pp. 472–74).

7. Hartmann, *L'Inconscient*, p. 492. "Contempt for the world, associated
   with a transcendent life of the spirit, was professed in India by the
   esoteric teaching of Buddhism. But this teaching was accessible only
   to a limited circle of celibate initiates. The outside world had only taken
   a few external forms from it, and its influence was manifested only
   under the extreme forms of life of hermits and penitents" (p. 439).

8. Batiffol, *Etudes d'histoire et de théologie positive*, second series, p. 162.

9. Hartmann, *La Religion de l'avenir*, pp. 27, 21. "At this time began the
   conflict between the pagan love for life and the contempt, the flight
   from the world characteristic of Christianity" (Hartmann, ibid., p. 126).
   This pagan notion is found in liberal Protestantism, and that is why
   Hartman rightly regards it as irreligious. But the men of the sixteenth
   century saw things in a different light.

10. If socialism perishes, it will obviously be in the same way—for fear of
    its own barbarism.

11. [Sorel says in this section that the terms *force* and *violence* are often
    confused. Sometimes they refer to acts of authority and sometimes to
    rebellion. "The term *violence* should be used solely for acts of rebellion
    . . . therefore, the object of force is to impose a particular social system
    of minority rule, while violence aims at the destruction of that order"
    Réflexions, pp. 256–57.—ED.]

12. It seems to me that the publishers of 1670 must have been startled at
    the Calvinism of Pascal; I am amazed that Sainte-Beuve confines him-
    self to saying that "there was in Pascal's Christianity something which
    was beyond them . . . that Pascal had a greater need of being a Chris-
    tian than they did" (*Port-Royal*, Vol. III, p. 383).

13. I am unable to find the idea of international arbitration in Pascal's frag-
    ment no. 296 in which several people have "discovered" it. Pascal simply
    notes there the absurdity of the custom whereby every belligerent of
    his time condemns the conduct of his adversary in the name of the law.

14. In *Introduction à l'économie moderne* (Paris: Jacques, 1902). I have given to the word *myth* a more general meaning which closely depends on the strict meaning used here. [This part of the essay is an introduction added to the original version; hence the use of the past tense.—ED.]

15. Paul Bureau, *La Crise morale des temps nouveaux*, p. 213. The author, who is a professor at the *Institut Catholique* in Paris, adds, "The recommendation can only provoke hilarity today. We are obliged to believe that the author's strange prescription was accepted then by a large number of his coreligionists, when we recall the staggering success of the writings of Leo Taxil after his so-called conversion."

16. These dreams seem to have had as their main object calming Renan's anxieties on the subject of the beyond. (Cf. an article by Hulst in the *Correspondant* of Oct. 25, 1892, pp. 210, 224–25.)

17. Renan, *Histoire du peuple d'Israël*, Vol. IV, p. 191.

18. Ibid., IV, p. 267.

19. Ibid., IV, pp. 199–200.

20 Ibid., III, pp. 458–59.

21. Ibid., IV, p. 267 (*Jeremiah*, verse 58, chapter 51). [The full Biblical text reads: "Thus says the lord of hosts / the broad wall of Babylon shall be leveled to the ground / and her high gates shall be burned with fire / The peoples labor for nought / and the nations weary themselves only for the fire, and they shall be weary."—ED.]

22. Ibid., V, pp. 105–6.

23. Renan, *Nouvelles Etudes d'histoire religieuse*, p. vii. Previously he said of persecutions: "One dies for *opinions* and not for *certitudes*, for what one believes and not for what one knows. When beliefs are in question, the great sign and the most effective proof is to die for them" (*L'Eglise chrétienne*, p. 317). This hypothesis assumes that martyrdom is a kind of trial by ordeal which was partly true in the Roman period because of special circumstances (G. Sorel, *Le Système historique de Renan*, p. 335).

24. Renan, *Histoire du peuple d'Israël*, Vol. III, p. 497.

25. The Constitution of Virginia is dated June 1776. The American constitutions were known in Europe through two French translations (1778 and 1789). Kant published his *Foundations of the Metaphysics of Morals* in 1785 and the *Critique of Practical Reason* in 1788. It could be said that the utilitarian system of the ancients has analogies with economics, the system of theologians with law and that of Kant with the political theory of nascent democracy (Cf. Jellinek, *La Déclaration des droits de l'homme et du citoyen* [Paris: Fontemoing, 1902], pp. 18–25, 49–50, 89).

26. Henri Bergson, *Données immédiates de la conscience* (Paris: F. Alcan, 1896), pp. 175–76. In this philosophy one distinguishes between "duration" which flows, in which our personality manifests itself; and mathematical "time" according to whose measurement science arranges accomplished facts.

27. Ibid., p. 181.

28. Edouard Le Roy, *Dogme et critique*, p. 239.
29. We easily see the bridge that introduced the sophism, *The Universe lived by us*; it can be the real world in which we live or the world invented for action.
30. Renan, *Histoire du peuple d'Israël*, Vol. IV, p. 329.
31. "Consent," says Cardinal Newman, "as powerful as it may be, associated with the most vivid images, is not then necessarily effective. Strictly speaking, it is not imagination that creates action; it is hope or the fear, the love or the hatred, the desires, passions and impulses of the ego, the 'I.' Imagination has no other role than to put these moving forces into action, and it succeeds by giving us powerful enough objects to stimulate them" (John Henry Newman, *Grammaire de l'assentiment* [Paris: Bloud, 1907], p. 82 [*An Essay in Aid of a Grammar of Assent*]). We see that the illustrious thinker is very close to the theory of myths. Moreover, it would be impossible to read Newman without being struck by the similarities between his thinking and Bergson's; those who are fond of relating the history of ideas to ethnic traditions will not fail to observe that Newman is descended from Jews.
32. The Greek philosophers who wanted to be able to discuss morality without being obliged to accept the practices that historical forces had introduced to Athens are evidently in this category.
33. Renan, *Histoire du people d'Israël*, Vol. III, p. 497.
34. It is extremely important to note the analogies between the condition of the revolutionary spirit and that which corresponds to the *morality of the producers;* I have indicated remarkable similarities at the end of my study, but many have yet to be pointed out.

The Proletarian Strike

1. The nature of these writings does not require long elaborations on this subject. But I think that one could make a still more complete application of Bergson's ideas to the theory of the general strike. In Bergsonian philosophy, movement is regarded as an undivided whole, which leads us exactly to the catastrophic conception of socialism.
2. Jean Bourdeau, *L'Evolution du socialisme* (Paris: F. Alcan, 1901), p. 232.
3. This is seen, for example, in the efforts of the trade-unions to obtain from the laws escape from the civil responsibility of their acts.
4. Tarde could not understand Sidney Webb's reputation; he considered him a dabbler.
5. Albert Métin, *Le Socialisme en Angleterre* (Paris: F. Alcan, 1897), p. 210. This writer received a "diploma of socialism" from the government. On July 26, 1904, the French commissioner-general of the St. Louis exposition said, "M. Métin is animated by the best democratic spirit. He is an excellent republican; he is *even a socialist* that workers'

organizations should receive as a friend" (*Association ouvrière*, July 30, 1904). An amusing study could be made on those persons who possess such diplomas—given to them either by the government, the *Musée social*, or by the "well-informed press."

6. Marx's errors are numerous and at times enormous (cf. Georges Sorel, *Saggi di critica del marxismo* [Palermo: Sandron, 1902], pp. 51–57).

7. It has often been noted that the English and American sectarians, whose religious exaltation was sustained by apocalyptic myths, were no less often very practical men.

8. This doctrine is presently very important in the German exegesis; it was introduced into France by the Abbé Loisy.

9. See above, pp. 204–7.

10. I have tried to show how a devotion that has continued to be extremely important in Catholic life superseded this vanished social myth. This evolution from the social to the individual seems to me entirely natural in a religion (*Le Système historique de Renan*, pp. 374–82).

11. I well believe that all of Spencer's evolutionism should be explained, moreover, by the most vulgar transferral of psychology to physics.

12. This is another application of Bergsonian theses.

13. This is perfect knowledge of Bergsonian philosophy.

The Morality of the Producers

1. Nietzsche, *La Généalogie de la morale* (Paris: Société du "Mercure de France," 1900) [*Genealogy of Morals*], pp. 57–59.

2. Ibid., p. 43.

3. Ibid., pp. 78–80.

4. Paul de Rousiers observes that in all of America one finds approximately the same social circumstances, the same men at the head of large enterprises; but "the merits and shortcomings of these extraordinary people stand out most clearly in the regions of the West; . . . *there is found the key to the whole social system*" (*La Vie américaine: Ranches, fermes et usines* [Paris: Firmin-Didot, 1899], pp. 8–9, cf. 261).

5. Paul de Rousiers, *La Vie américaine: L'éducation et la société* (Paris: Firmin-Didot, 1899), p. 325.

6. Rousiers, *La Vie américaine: Ranches, fermes et usines*, pp. 303–5.

7. J. Bourdeau, *Les Maîtres de la pensée contemporaine*, p. 145. The author tells us, moreover, that "Jaurès greatly astonished the Genevans in revealing to them that Nietzsche's hero, the 'superman,' is none other than the proletariat" (p. 139). I have been unable to obtain any information concerning this lecture by Jaurès: let us hope that he will publish it one day for our amusement.

8. We must always keep in mind that the Jew of the Middle Ages, who had become so resigned, resembles the Christian much more than his own ancestors.

9. Proudhon, *De la justice dans la révolution et dans l'église,* Vol. IV, p. 99. We know that theologians do not much like the curious to consult their writings on *conjugal duty* and on the legitimate way to fulfill it.

10. Proudhon, *Justice,* p. 212.

11. Proudhon, *Œuvres* (Paris: A. Lacroix, 1868), Vol. XX, p. 169. This is taken from his defense, presented at the Court of Paris, after his sentence to three years in prison for the book on justice. It is worth observing that Proudhon was accused of attacking marriage! This affair is one of the disgraces that dishonored the Church under Napoleon III.

12. Aristotle, *Politics,* Book I, chap. XI, 23.

13. Ibid., chap. V, 11.

14. Xenophon, who in all things represents an earlier conception of Greek life than the time in which he lived, is concerned with the manner of training a good overseer for the farm (*Oekonomikus,* 12–14). Marx observes that Xenophon speaks of the division of labor in the workshop and that seems to indicate a bourgeois instinct in him (*Capital,* Vol. I, p. 159, col. 1 [Modern Library ed., p. 402]); I believe that that characterizes an observer who understands the importance of production, an importance of which Plato is completely unaware. In the *Memorabilia* (Book II, 7), Socrates advises a citizen who is responsible for a number of relatives to organize a workshop with them. J. Flach assumes that this was an innovation (Lesson of April 19, 1907); it seems rather that it constituted a return to earlier customs. Historians of philosophy appear to have been very hostile to Xenophon because he is too much of an "old-fashioned Greek"; Plato suits them better because he is more "aristocratic" and consequently more detached from economics.

15. Aristotle, *Politics,* Book I, chap. V, 9 & 11.

16. Karl Kautsky, *La Révolution sociale* (Paris: M. Rivière, n.d.), p. 153.

17. One even wonders if the ideal of relatively honest and enlightened democrats is not at the present time perhaps the discipline of the capitalist workroom. The reinforcement of power attributed to mayors and governors in the United States appears to be a sign of this tendency.

18. This situation is also complicated by a collection of adventures which have been manufactured in imitation of real adventures and which have an obvious connection with those that would make *The Three Musketeers* popular.

19. In a pamphlet that caused some furor, General Donop denounced the ridiculous effects of contemporary discipline, which gives officers "habits of servility." Like Bugeaud and Dragomiroff, he would like every participant in battle to know the leaders' plans in the most exact detail; he finds it absurd that acts of war are frowned on and proscribed, since they call into play and put to the test the noblest faculties of man, under the most difficult and tragic circumstances; that is, "thought and the human soul in the fullness of all the power that God, the God of the armies, has given to them for the defense and the triumph of noble causes" (Raoul-Marie Donop, *Commandement et obéissance,* pp. 14–

19, 37). This general was one of the most eminent leaders of our cavalry; this arm seems to have preserved a feeling about man much superior to that of the others.

20. Jaurès, *Etudes socialistes* (Paris: P. Ollendorff, 1902), pp. 117–18.

21. [*Humanité* was the organ of the French Socialist party. The battle of Fleurus was fought in 1794 and was a victory for the revolutionaries.— ED.]

22. When we speak of the educational value of art, we often forget that practices of modern artists, based on the imitation of a jovial aristocracy, are in no way necessary, and derive from a tradition that has been fatal to many fine talents. Lafargue seems to believe that the Parisian jeweler must dress elegantly, eat oysters and run after women in order to "continue producing the artistic quality of his workmanship" (*Journal des Economistes*, Sept. 1884, p. 386). He gives no reasons to support this paradox; moreover, it could be pointed out that Marx's son-in-law (Lafargue) is always obsessed by aristocratic preoccupations.

23. See in Ruskin's *Seven Lamps of Architecture* the chapter entitled "The Lamp of Truth."

24. It must not be forgotten that there are two ways of arguing about art; Nietzsche accuses Kant of having "like all philosophers meditated on art and the beautiful as a *spectator* instead of relating to the aesthetic problem by relying on the experience of the artist, the creator" (*Généalogie de la morale*, p. 175). At the time of the utopians, aesthetics was purely a game for amateurs, who did not fail to go into ecstasies over the skill with which the artist knew how to deceive his public.

25. Marx, *Capital*, Vol. III, first part, p. 375.

26. Bureau has devoted a chapter of his book on the *Contrat du travail* (Paris: F. Alcan, 1902) to explaining the reasons which justify the boycott of workers who do not follow their companions into strikes; he believes that these people deserve their fate because their professional and moral value is notoriously inferior. That seems to me insufficient to account for reasons to explain these violent acts in the eyes of the working masses. The author takes a much too intellectualist point of view.

27. Lafaille, *Mémoires sur les campagnes de Catalogne de 1808 à 1814*, p. 336.

28. The charlatanism of the Saint-Simonians was as distasteful as Murat's; moreover, the history of this school is unintelligible when it is not seen in the light of Napoleonic models.

29. General Donop lays great stress on the inadequacy of Napoleon's lieutenants, who passively obeyed orders which they did not try to understand, and which were carried out under the close supervision of the master (*Commandement et obéissance*, pp. 28–29, 32–34). In such an army all merit was theoretically equalized and constituted standards of recompense, but in practice errors of evaluation were numerous.

30. Viollet-le-Duc, *Dictionnaire raisonné de l'architecture française, du XIe au XVIe siècle* (Paris: B. Bance, 1859), Vol. IV, pp. 42–43. This does

not contradict what is said in the article on the architect; we learn there that the builders often inscribed their names in the cathedrals (Vol. I, pp. 109–11); from this it was concluded that these works were not anonymous (Brehier, *Les Eglises gothiques*, p. 17), but what did these few inscriptions say to people of the town? They could only have interested artists who came later to work in the same building and who knew the traditions of the schools.

31. Renan, *Histoire du peuple d'Israël*, Vol. IV, p. 191. Renan seems to have likened glory to immortality a little hastily; he was a victim of figures of speech.

Chapter 7

FROM MATERIALS FOR A THEORY OF THE PROLETARIAT

Introduction

1. In the *Voce* (Florence) Feb. 9, 1911. This interview was reproduced in 1914 in the volume: *Cultura e vita morale: Intermezzi polemici* (Bari: Laterza, 1914), pp. 169–79.
2. Benedetto Croce, ibid., pp. 173–76. Croce says: "Syndicalism was a new form of Marx's great dream, which was dreamed a second time by Georges Sorel" (p. 176). "Socialism found its last refuge in syndicalism; in this very form, it died" (p. 178).
3. Croce observes that socialist literature can now be studied in a more impartial way than previously. Since socialism is dead, the books of its experts are no longer party manifestos which provoke anger (ibid., p. 174).
4. G. Sorel, *Réflexions sur la violence*, 3rd French edition (Paris: M. Rivière, 1913), p. 407. [American edition, p. 259—ED.]
5. A notable example of symbols that have indefinable ties to reality is given us by the famous theory of the separation of powers. It was put forth by Blackstone, Paley and Montesquieu, based on English constitutional customs. But in the eighteenth century the king still enjoyed a considerable authority in the parlements, and the towns made their influence felt on the administration; tribunals were not limited to applying the law. Americans considered the separation of powers essential, but they did not apply it rigorously. Whenever the full realization of the independence of power has been attempted, dominance has been given to one or another of them. Laboulaye, from whom I borrow these observations, says that the principle has never existed in an exact way (Edouard de Laboulaye, *Histoire des Etats-Unis* (Paris: Charpentier, 1877), Vol. III, pp. 289–93).
6. Renan, *Histoire du peuple d'Israël*, vol. IV, p. 199. We know that for

all the Greek authors the intelligent search for happiness plays a fundamental role. The Greek always calculates the best stance to take. That is why he has always considered bad conduct to be the result of ignorance.

7. Renan, ibid., vol. V, p. 126. Renan believes that because the sentiment of glory "usually so uncharacteristic of the Jews," is evident in the author of the first book of Maccabees, he must have been influenced by Greek culture, which culture was readily accepted at the court of the Asmonean princes (pp. 122, 125–27). This work was not admitted to the Jewish canon law; it was consecrated by the Christians who gave to their martyrs all the glory they could muster. We must not omit comparing the Book of Acts to the accounts by the Greek historians of the period of the decline when we want to make a serious criticism of them. The Christian conquest remains unintelligible if an important role is not given to the sentiment of glory.

8. The morality of Aristotle corresponds well to this state of mind.

9. Renan says that Alexander seemed to the ancients like a reincarnation of Dionysus (ibid., vol. IV, p. 200).

10. The Bonapartists were agreed in regarding Béranger as the appropriate epic poet to express their idea of Napoleon. The latter would thus be only an Achilles for lackey patriots. One must turn to the philosophy of Hegel to find an echo of this drama that is worthy of events. The *Weltgericht,* which Hegel places between the theory of the state and art, seems to me to be a professional transposition of the Greek aesthetic of glory. We should note that Renan in his schematic exposition of these aesthetics, writes: "In inventing history, Greece invented judgment of the world" (ibid., p. 199). One could not hope for a more Hegelian formula. The *Weltgeist* which, according to Hegel is "always present in history, the tribunal of the world," passes from one nation to another, following the results of wars, which seem to measure moral and physical strength (P. Roques: *Hegel, sa vie et ses œuvres* [Paris: F. Alcan, 1912], p. 256). Napoleon was a "formidable incarnation of the *Weltgeist*" (p. 259). Leipzig and Waterloo brought the *Weltgeist* to Prussia (pp. 257, 265).

11. William James also attaches much more practical value to this idea of the witness than to that of a heavenly reward: the first has the affirmation of the mystics, the second is not based on any experience (cf. G. Sorel, *La religione d'oggi* [Lanciano: R. Carabba, 1910], pp. 51–52). Renan's thought wavers more than once. It is useful to point out here that St. Paul expected a very imminent appearance of the Christ-judge; later, Christianity carried this forward to an indefinite future, and it no longer plays a great role in piety. The idea of a God-witness is upheld very strongly by the Eucharist cult, which could be defined as a sacramental experience of Christ; the dogma of the true presence attracts to Catholicism those Protestants who have remained faithful to Lutheran ideas, but who are shocked by the lack of respect professed for the Eucharist by the majority of pastors.

12. This pantheist formula is unfortunate: if virtuous man appeals to a divine conscience against fatality, it is because he judges God as distinct from the universe.

13. Renan, *Feuilles détachées,* pp. 433–34.

14. I think that I should call attention here to what I wrote in "Vues sur les problèmes de la philosophie": "An historical development can only be a theoretical axis traced in the midst of many attempts (of which most come to naught) that sometimes help movement, and sometimes hinder it; and amongst which there are paths of communication, bringing foreign contributions. It would be impossible to enter into descriptions of all these details; history eliminates everything which seems unimportant to explain development, and it groups the other directions according to their affinities, in order to superimpose a schema of development onto real actions" (*Revue de Métaphysique et de Morale,* Jan. 1911, p. 74). "What is truly fundamental in every future is the state of passionate tension which is seen in the soul" (p. 76).

15. Renan, *Histoire du peuple d'Israël,* vol. IV, p. 346.

16. "The Book of Daniel is truly the seed of Christianity" (Renan, ibid., p. 359); "That is the historian who was Bossuet's master, who in turn was our master" (p. 346).

17. Renan is undoubtedly right in thinking that the Christian philosophy of history is not of Greek origin. But should we not seek some of its sources in Roman thought? Rome had the idea of its dominating role and this idea was effective. In our time it is taught in Italy that if this first Rome (of the Caesars) imposed on Europe the unity of a civilization based on force, and if the second Rome (that of the popes) imposed on a large part of the world a unity based on dogma, the third Rome will create the unity of a rational civilization voluntarily embraced by humanity. This theory does not seem to have been as efficacious as its inventors had hoped.

18. Cf. the preceding section on the uses of that philosopher's *diremption* without well-defined ideas on the value of the method.

19. Hardly anything but pathetic analogies can be invoked in its favor. What is more legitimate, says public opinion, than to transfer into the future the attractions of historical development by which human nature has been affirmed for centuries? More learned people believe that sociologists have the right to imitate physicists, who calculate phenomena outside of the experimental domain by means of empirical formulas. The abstractions which serve the sociologist to replace the characteristic qualities of institutions, customs or ideas, would be equivalent to the mathematical formulas which the physicist superimposes on the material qualities whose importance has been revealed by practice. But physicists use this procedure with extreme caution.

20. Tocqueville has often been accused of having spread this idea of the inevitable triumph of democracy. In *Democracy in America,* he advised conservative statesmen not to try to fight against the will of Providence that desires this end. Present-day bourgeois acclaim as saviors of order,

the politicians who work to destroy slowly old social organization. The *Action Française* seeks to persuade educated youth that the democratic idea is in decline; if it succeeded in its goal, Charles Maurras would take his place among the men who deserve to be called *masters of the hour* since his doctrine would have inspired a change in the orientation of current thought. But is he not himself imbued with the democratic spirit? The modern authors whom he admires above all (Stendhal, Balzac) possess none of that aristocratic distinction which to our fathers was the sign of good literature. (On this aristocratic character of our literature cf. Renan, *Feuilles détachées*, pp. 237, 267).

21. In the advanced democracies there can be observed in the proletariat a deep feeling of the duty of passive obedience, a superstitious use of slogans and a blind faith in egalitarian promises; French democracy could be compared to a New Islam in its incessant desire to march into battle in order to propagate its benefits.

22. Jealousy is one of the most effective powers of democracy (cf. G. Sorel, *Réflexions sur la violence*, pp. 243–44).

23. Bendetto Croce writes: "The rejection of utopian socialism . . . signifies in reality the absolute rejection of the idea of equality," nevertheless egalitarian utopia "is still the understanding of socialism of many self-proclaimed 'modern scientists.'" Marxism, in boasting of having passed from utopia to science, used a metaphor whose profound interpretation is: "This transition is nothing else than the passage from the abstract idea to concrete history, the abandonment of equality, which is an arithmetic and geometric concept, for a biological concept, and for life, which is inequality and asymmetry. From this results the class struggle, the aristocracy of the producers (very different from the proletariat in rags, or beggars) which triumphs over the bourgeoisie and transforms the social organization, increasing control of man over the blind forces of nature, predominance of technology, etc." (*Cultura e vita morale*, pp. 170–71).

24. Taine believed that the peasants had been drawn to irreligion by the example of urban workers (*Le Régime moderne* [Paris: Hachette, 1910–12], Vol. II, pp. 150–51; cf. p. 147); but I believe that in the country anti-clericalism has more profound roots than in the cities.

25. This term emphasizes the analogy which exists between such a sociology and the zoology of fairy tales.

26. They followed the example of the Saint-Simonians, who had already used, with great profit, Hegelian *monsters* at the time when Cousin was introducing Hegelian dregs into France (his 1828 course on the *Introduction to the History of Philosophy*).

27. Marx said in the preface to the second edition of *Capital* that at that time Hegel was treated as a dead letter.

28. In P. Roques's book, *Hegel, sa vie et ses œuvres*, I find this fact which seems to me to be typical: "Boris d'Yxkull, an Estonian baron, very recently still an officer in the Russian army, told with a curious sincerity how he was attracted to Hegel: he understood practically nothing of

the course, but he was drawn by this very obscurity and especially by Hegel's profound seriousness" (p. 170). Many sociologists have preferred to declare that *Capital* is a prodigious landmark rather than to criticize it; Werner Sombart seems to me to belong to this group of simpletons.

29. Kautsky and his friends defend Marx and Engels's most debatable thesis with as much energy as the ancient Greeks defended the sacred walls that assured the liberty of their cities, according to the religious beliefs of the time.

30. William James, *Le Pragmatisme* (Paris: Flammarion, 1911), ch. 1.

31. It is useful to cite here several lines of an interview with Benedetto Croce, published in *Voce*, Nov. 24, 1910: "The Masonic mentality in the eighteenth century called itself encyclopedism and Jacobinism. Italy had a sad experience of its effects at the end of that century at the time of the French invasion and the Italo-French Republics. . . . One could say that the whole *risorgimento* developed as a reaction against French, Jacobin and Masonic rule. The very idea of Italian unity was launched as a password of the opposition aroused by the universal fraternity of the French, whose prosaic reality was manifested by pillaging, destruction and the oppression of the generals and commissioners of the French armies. In literature, in philosophy, in politics, the nineteenth century was characterized, in Italy as elsewhere, by *anti-francesimo*. It seems impossible that at the beginning of the twentieth century in imitation of France, we are again importing into our country an evil from which we had suffered over a century ago and of which we were cured after a violent crisis. . . . If we must suffer from a new invasion of French abstractionism, we will rid ourselves from this epidemic just as we have freed ourselves from the cholera of this year" (*Cultura e vita morale,* pp. 164, 168).

32. William James, *Le Pragmatisme,* pp. 29–30, 37–38.

33. It conforms to the pragmatic spirit to take full account of the milieu in which a doctrine flourishes when one wishes to have a clear idea of it, instead of defining it in scholastic terms.

34. Cf. *Timaeus*, 53b. When Tertullian states that the soul is naturally inclined to accept Christian dogma, it seems that he transposes into psychology an idea of Platonic physics. Commentators of Tertullian have not sufficiently noted that this "naturally Christian soul" is the soul of a Roman who has read the Greek philosophers; there is a sort of silhouette of Christianity in such a man.

35. It has often been found surprising that Aristotle also composed a plan for the perfect city (Alfred and Maurice Croiset, *Histoire de la littérature grecque,* Vol. IV, p. 729); this fact shows the irresistible force of aesthetic ideas in the Greeks; it is thus one of the phenomena which should be brought clearly to light.

36. The first utopias were simple literary compositions, intended to charm Platonic humanists. It has often been pointed out that Thomas More, who died a martyr, wanted nothing of an anti-Catholic nature to enter

into customs. He did not intend to anticipate the future, but to paint a natural pre-Christian society, still very ripe to accept Christianity. It is consequently due to a degeneration of humanism that these idylls were interpreted as projects of social reform.

37. "Every question in our day," says Renan, "necessarily degenerates into an historical debate. Every exposition of principle becomes a course in history. Each one of us is what he is by virtue of his system of history" (*Essais de morale et de critique*, p. 83).

38. A criticism inspired by pragmatism easily points up the extreme difference between the two groups of postulates.

39. This sophism constitutes the soul of what Taine calls the classical mind; this expression is not very felicitous for it concerns an academic mentality and not the mentaltiy of the great authors of classical literature. Taine's analysis is imperfect, because he himself was saturated with academic illusions.

40. On the contrary, these psychological motives form the principal matter of the arguments for the defense in the *court of assises*. It has often been pointed out that rarely does a lawyer succeed both at criminal and at civil law; the principles of argumentation are too different.

41. This literature has become one of the most powerful arms of diplomacy, since printing has provided the means of interesting everyone in a large country in the news as easily as if it were the case of an ancient city whose inhabitants were going to stroll on the *agora* every day. It even seems that it is easier to form the opinion of a modern nation, thanks to the press, than it was to obtain the allegiance of a Greek assembly harangued by skillful orators. In the declaration of July 4, 1776, the Americans said, "When in the course of human events it becomes necessary for one people to dissolve the political bands which have connected them with another, and to assume among the powers of the earth, the separate and equal station to which the Laws of Nature and of Nature's God entitle them, a decent respect to the opinions of mankind requires that they should declare the causes which impel them to the separation." On December 20, 1860, the state of South Carolina, in separating from the Union, said that it "owed to itself, to the other states, and to other nations of the world to declare the immediate causes which led it to this act" (Laboulaye, *Histoire des Etats-Unis*, Vol. II, p. 321 and Vol. III, p. 46).

42. This truth has often been misunderstood because many writers have believed that the state could only be given a solid base by affirming that juridical life runs from the individual to the nation. This is how the theories of the social contract were formed. In *La Guerre et la paix* Proudhon has outlined a theory in which private right derives from war (Book II, chap. XI). It seems to me that a philosophy which proposes to explain the law and not to legitimize it should ascribe two poles to it: war and economics. In the family the two traits seem about equally strong, so that the family may be regarded as the common meeting ground of the two principles of law.

43. Laboulaye says that the American revolution was "a trial" (*Histoire des Etats-Unis,* Vol. II, p. 10); in France in the eighteenth century there was also a large *trial* literature, but it is further from true judicial literature than America's.

44. That is the result of the conclusions reached by André Lichtenberger in *Le Socialisme au XVIIIᵉ siècle* (Paris: F. Alcan, 1895).

45. Babeuf maintained in his Vendôme trial that he had wanted only to form "a society of democrats whose goal was to lead public opinion toward republican principles vigorously to combat the manoeuvres of royalism against the established government" (Adrielle, *Histore de Gracchus Babeuf,* Vol. I, p. 399). He dismissed as philosophic or philanthropic dreams the revolutionary projects that were found in his seized papers (pp. 402, 410, cf. p. 301). His eulogist believes that there was much truth in his rationalizations.

46. This consideration was paramount to the men of the eighteenth century, who measured the degree of civilization by the ease enjoyed by the ruling classes.

47. Cf. Georges Sorel, *Les Illusions du progrès,* 2nd ed., pp. 114–20 (American ed., pp. 59–62).

48. By "juridical progress" I mean a tendency to impose the respect for property on the state.

49. Cf. Georges Sorel, *Réflexions sur la violence,* pp. 402–7.

50. This idea is in some way taken from the providentialism of theologians. In the opinion of the rationalists, the psychology of the men of 1793 appeared too weak to be able to find in it sufficient reasons for the great transformations which occurred during the Revolution.

51. Conservative ministers almost always have great weaknesses in days of crisis. Ministers brought to power on the plebeian wave defend their positions with a new energy.

52. Vilfredo Pareto made an excellent criticism of the "liberal utopia" of which Bastiat was the noisiest representative: he showed that the doctrine of "the harmony of legitimate interests" is very feeble (*Les Systèmes socialistes* (Paris: Giard, n.d.), Vol. II, pp. 45–69).

53. This theory has often been put forth by partisans of free trade, so that it helped to illuminate the state-Church-production trilogy, which should be considered for an understanding of modern society. Note that Cavour was very influenced by ideas proposed by the economists who defended free trade.

54. Cf. the conclusion of my book *Insegnamenti sociale della economia contemporanea,* whose French text appeared in *Mouvement Socialist,* July 1905.

55. My book, *Réflexions sur la violence,* is devoted to the examination of some of these conditions.

56. They avoid seeking to probe the psychological, ideological and juridical questions posed by transformation of the proletarian mass into a developed class. Rationalism greatly pleases them because it is content with superficial solutions.

57. Marxism, having taken on the allure of a utopia, cannot oppose very strongly the renaissance of utopias which has been seen in recent years.

58. Paraphrasing Hegel's *Philosophy of History*, P. Roques wrote: "Reason is not powerless to the point of remaining a simple ideal and existing only outside of reality (who knows where) in the head of a few men; it is the infinite Substance of all finite reality. Anaxagoras affirmed that the intelligence, *noûs*, not chance, makes the world move. . . . We agree, however, that it seems absurd to affirm that history manifests the progress of reason. Indeed, the wellsprings of human activity are need, passion and self-interest—almost never the desire for good. Selfishness and brutality are much more frequent in man than the respect for law, which is acquired only by a long discipline. . . . Thus we will not deny that the world historical figures are especially selfish and violent individuals, and it must be said that nothing great happens in the world without passion. . . . But interests and passion are basically only means by which men realize the spirit unconsciously" (*Hegel, sa vie et ses œuvres*, pp. 271–72).

59. In the preface written in 1859 for the *Critique of Political Economy*, the times which precede the fall of the capitalist regime are thus qualified.

60. Karl Marx, *Le manifeste du parti communiste*, trans. Charles Andler (Paris: Bellais, 1901), Part II, pp. 135, 160.

61. Andler says, "Later they attached minimum importance to this transitional program. It is easily apparent that the communists of 1847, who imposed this program on them, were artisans close to socialist democracy [that of Ledru-Rollin and Louis Blanc, cf. p. 135] by their ideas and by their petit-bourgeois condition" (*Le Manifeste*, pp. 160–61).

62. Ibid., pp. 132, 134, 136, 139.

63. Translation by Georges Platon in *Revue d'Economie Politique*, Sept—Oct. 1894, p. 758.

64. Cf. what I have written in the preface to *La Douleur physique* of Georges Castex (Paris: Jacques, 1905).

65. New ways of conceiving social renovations begin to appear in the Renaissance. A rich life was then desired. Feminism has proposed a fuller dream of luxury and licentiousness than did any other utopia. It is this characteristic which principally explains its success. It is suitable to point out that many social democrats still admire Fourier.

66. In the first edition of *Le Programme du parti ouvrier* (Paris: Oriel, 1883), Jules Guesde and Paul Lafargue said, in describing the Abbey of Thélème, that Rabelais was "a clairvoyant [who] prophesied the communist society toward which we are headed and in which the superabundance of products will permit free consumption" (p. 36).

67. It is remarkable that in 1883 Jules Guesde and Paul Lafargue denounced this method as bordering on the absurd. They believed that needs are too elastic to serve as a foundation for a reasoned distribution of things (*Le Programme*, pp. 17–18).

68. It seems to me very difficult to know exactly what Marx meant in that

part of the *Communist Manifesto* which concerns the family. Andler's commentary does not overcome the difficulties (*Le manifeste*, pp. 150–53). I believe that Marx, thinking of the old German families, was above all struck by the decline of the conservative force of moral traditions brought on by the disappearance of stable homes in the modern working economy.

69. At the beginning of Book V, Polemarchus says that the rules to be adopted for sexual relations dominate the whole communist question. This observation is very profound.

70. Marx, *Capital*, French trans., Vol. I, p. 133, col. 2 (Modern Library ed., pp. 337–38).

71. At the beginning of Book IV, Adeimantus tells Socrates that the guardians of the city will not be happy because, not having any money, they will not be able to receive guests, to travel or to frequent courtesans. Socrates answers that a good education will lead them to be happy; and moreover, it is not a question of the happiness of a few men, but the happiness of the state. One could compare these warriors to monks who, according to the Catholic belief, by their practice of the Christian life protect the regions where they are established. Thus, there is an essential difference between the communism of the *Republic* and those versions to be observed in certain uncivilized peoples. The most famous of these communisms was that of the Arioï, priests and actors, who formed a sort of Freemasonry in Tahiti; they were maintained by the villages in which they lived and had wives in common (Elisée Reclus, *Nouvelle Géographie universelle* [Paris: Hachette, 1876–94], Vol. XIV, pp. 918–19); cf. an institution of bachelors buying girls for their common use in the Palau Isles (p. 592).

72. In Books II and III, Plato speaks almost like a precursor of Msgr. Gaume, who, in the middle of the nineteenth century, declaimed against the canker worm of pagan literature. He points out the venom of the old Greek poems which badly understood the role of the gods, man's fate after death and virtue. Tragedy and comedy should be forbidden, because these imitative arts can give rise to troublesome tendencies of the soul in citizens incited by the theater to imitate characters scorned by philosophy. Only admirable beings must be represented.

73. It is obvious that the emancipation of the proletariat, of which Marx speaks, should be carried out by men who take a serious part in production, since it should be the achievement of the workers themselves and not that of politicians. In reality, Social Democracy has indeed subjected the workers to politicians; but here I am speaking of the philosophical theory.

74. I even believe that more than once Plato directed the arrow of irony, which he wielded with a superior skill, against those who would be tempted to take communist fantasies for legislative programs.

75. Vilfredo Pareto, *Les Systèmes socialistes*, Vol. II, p. 7.

76. Plato refers expressly to Pythagorean opinions on astronomy and music;

the one is related to harmonies of sight and the other to harmonies of the ear (*Republic,* Book VIII, 530d). In the two cases observation can furnish results only very inferior to what is required by reason. Astronomers, who are content with empiricism, resemble the geometricians who, by examining drawings executed by a very skillful artist, hoped to discover what are in truth the relationships of equal to equal, double or any other proportion (529e). Musicians are as ridiculous as these observers of the sky when they torture the chords of their instruments to succeed in making an experimental study of the numbers which characterize the intervals, without rising to the problem of examining what are and are not the consonant numbers, and the origin of these properties (531b–c). This "superior science" is the mystic arithmetic of the Pythagoreans.

77. Aristotle takes the pluralist side against Plato: "Naturally, the city is very diverse; but if it pretends to have unity, from a city it becomes a family, from a family an individual; for the family has much more unity than the city and the individual much more still than the family" (*Politics,* Book II, chaps. ii, iv). Proudhon writes: "One does not conceive why in *Icaria* there would exist more than one man, or one couple. . . . What good is this interminable repetition of marionettes, molded and dressed in the same way? In order to produce the progressive and provident existence, nature . . . which, in repeating itself, never does the same thing twice, gives birth to millions of billions of diverse individuals. . . . Communism imposes limits on this variety of nature" (Proudhon, *Contradictions économiques,* chap. xii, sect. 9).

78. At the end of Book IX, Glaucon says that the Platonic Republic exists only in the discourses of philosophers and not on the earth. Socrates responds that there probably exists at least a model in the heavens that can be consulted, in order to learn to regulate one's conduct well (592a–b).

79. In the book that he wrote to refute Dühring, Engels likened his communist ideal with social monism in a way which leaves no room for difficulty of interpretation. In the future society there will no longer be this anarchy of wills which makes economic phenomena similar to natural phenomena, regulated by necessity; no more particular causes coming to interfere, no more chance, all is subjected to reason alone. (*Philosophie, économie politique, socialisme* [Paris: Giard et Brière, 1911], pp. 364–65); the world is reduced to one man: to Engels.

80. After the Congress of St. Etienne in 1882 there was a schism in the French Socialist party. The *possibilistes,* whose ideas served as a prelude to the politics adopted today by socialist parliamentarians, reproached the *Guesdistes* for not being revolutionary enough and revived communist slogans in order to "maximize" the claims of the proletariat (Jules Guesde and Paul Lafargue, *Programme,* pp. 17 and 18).

81. I have expressed doubts on the communism of Marx.

82. Bendetto Croce, *Cultura e vita morale,* p. 178.

83. Did the defeat of Germany mark the end of the feudal aristocracy of old Prussia or that of the liberal bourgeoisie? I would be tempted to think that the second hypothesis is more probable than the first.

The Organization of Democracy

1. I have published two reviews of this book in the *Divenire Sociale* (of Rome) of Nov. 16, 1906, and in the *Mouvement Socialiste* of the same month. Here, I am giving a third rendition more studied than the previous ones. [This version appeared in *Matériaux d'une théorie du prolétariat*, pp. 365–95—ED.]
2. This doubt is motivated by the following passage found on pp. 182–83 of Prins's book: "The masses who are eager for happiness, well-being, and justice do not themselves have the means to attain their goal. They need leaders. The most egalitarian socialists will not deny this fact. Without leaders, and often even *very authoritarian* leaders who have formed and led it, the Socialist party would be nothing. And if the Socialist party has sects, it is because it has leaders of sects."
3. It is this Bonapartist spirit which has caused the success of the *Action Française;* many men who care little for principles of traditional royalty have been happy to see the vices of democratic government attacked with gusto; it could very well be that Maurras's propanganda was after all more useful to Prince Victor than to the Duc d'Orléans. (I was told that this opinion had been expressed by the Comte de Sabran Pontèves a little while before his death.) During these first ten years of the Second Empire, the French bourgeoisie judged that Napoleon III was governing according to its reactionary needs. It was necessary for the Italian expedition to disrupt the alliance of the clergy and the dictator for liberal opinion to become aroused. At the time when the men of Napoleon's coup of December 2, 1850 seemed ready to be converted to parliamentarism, Proudhon summarized in the following lines the criticisms that can be made against the system called *Juste-Milieu:* "A political system, invented on purpose for the triumph of verbose mediocrity, of deceitful pedantry, of subsidized journalism, using puffery and blackmail; where compromises with conscience, vulgarity of ambitions, poverty of ideas as well as commonplace oratory and academic verbosity are a sure means of success; where contradiction and inconsistency, the lack of honesty and courage, masquerading as prudence and moderation, are perpetually the order of the day; such a system defies refutation; it suffices to describe it. To analyze it would be to enhance it and whatever the critic says would give a false idea of it" (*Contradictions politiques* [Paris: Librarie Internationale, 1870], pp. 222–23). This system is the one that has been imposed on us by democracy since 1871.
4. On p. 191 he adds to these examples that of England: "The secret of the vitality of the old English parliamentary regime was the formation

of a special political class which had learned to administer the country by first administering the county."

5. Prins regrets that, in Belgium, national education is not placed above party quarrels and regulated by specialists (p. 177).

6. The French experience does not conform to this thesis; in many of our provinces the elections to commercial tribunals are often subordinated to party quarrels; they would become entirely political if these tribunals had to nominate delegates for senatorial elections.

7. Taken as a whole the result of Prins's plans is that no one is allowed to vote in two curias.

8. There is, however, a great difference between Proudhon and the Belgian writer; Prins submerges all plurality in one body, while Proudhon is always thinking of the preservation of a federalist multiplicity.

9. In the *Contradictions politiques*, Proudhon examines rather extensively this Constitution of 1793 which has often been regarded as the model of ultra-democracy. "In democracy, in which the sovereign is a collectivity, something quasi-metaphysical . . . , whose representatives are subordinated to each other and all together to a higher representation, called the National Assembly or legislative body, the people, considered as sovereign, is a fiction, a myth; and all the ceremonies by which you make it exercise its elective sovereignty are only the ceremonies of its abdication" (p. 199). And as democracy makes a great show of theories of rights (*droits*), one can say that it "lies to itself" (p. 170).

10. *Ibid.*, pp. 190–91. According to Proudhon, "The essentially empirical forms of government with which mankind has experimented until now can be considered as . . . distortions of the true system which every nation seeks to discover" (pp. 102–3). "Electoral synthesis [which is the true system of popular representation] should comprise, not only in theory but in practice, all systems produced: it should admit simultaneously, as electoral base, not only population, but territory, property, capital, industries; natural, regional, and communal groups. It should take into account inequalities of fortune and intelligence and exclude no category" (p. 189).

11. *Ibid.*, pp. 188–89.

12. "Opposing the absolute to the absolute . . . and considering as real and legitimate only the relation of antagonistic terms, [collective reason] reaches synthetic ideas, very different, often even inverse from the conclusions of the individual 'I.'" (*De la justice dans la révolution et dans l'église* [Paris: Garnier, 1858], Vol. III, p. 101). It is due to freedom that man can thus raise himself above the covetousness of his nature (pp. 217–18).

13. "'Men, citizens, workers,' this collective reason which is truly practical and juridical tells us:

each remain what you are; preserve and develop your personalities; defend your interests; produce your thoughts; argue among yourselves, but always retain the respect that intelligent and independent individuals always owe each other . . . ; respect only the decisions of your common reason, whose judgments cannot be yours, freed as it is from that individual sovereignty without which you would only be shadows."

(Proudhon, ibid., Vol. III, p. 102).

14. The text reads: "to fight against one man"; but it is obviously incorrect.
15. Proudhon, *Justice*, Vol. III, p. 119. The Marxists and the majority of socialists do not seem to have taken this distinction into account—a distinction which appeared obvious to Proudhon's juridical mind.
16. The text reads: "preserved to this word," which makes no sense.
17. Proudhon, *Justice*, Vol. II, p. 116.
18. Ibid., pp. 120–21. On p. 114, Proudhon points out that the term "sovereignty" is not without its dangers: "Whatever the power of the collective body is, it does not constitute a sovereignty in the view of the citizen; that would be almost like saying that a machine in which 100,000 spindles are turning is the sovereign of the 100,000 spinners which it represents . . . between power and the individual there is only law; all sovereignty is repugnant, it is the denial of justice, it is religion."
19. Ibid., p. 128.
20. Proudhon hoped that what he called "agrico-industrial federation" would replace what contemporary socialists were denouncing under the name of "financial-industrial federation," which exploits the collective forces for its own profit (*Du principe fédératif* [Paris: A. Lacroix, 1868], First Part, Chap. XI).
21. Proudhon, *Justice*, Vol. V, p. 179. The five conditions posed by Proudhon divide into three classes: economy, political institutions and military organizations. Proudhon attached a fundamental importance to the economy even more than did Marx; that is why he is even more precise than his rival in his ideas on the economic order. Marxists believe generally that the first question to be resolved is that of government; in this they greatly resemble the democrats of 1848 (cf. Proudhon, *Du principe fédératif*, First Part, Chap. XI). After having put forth his theory of the republic, Proudhon points out that all of the old parties rejected it (in 1860): "The only element that is accepted, and then with great reservations, is the condition concerning political guarantees, which, by themselves, in an unorganized society can only add to the instability of the state and always hold the door open to usurpation and despotism." These guarantees constitute the most abstract part of the system and hence offer great advantages to destructive dialecticians.
22. In spite of certain precepts which have often been interpreted too literally, Proudhon did not confuse "governments of pure abstraction, simplistically unrealizable, like pure monarchies or democracies, and mixed governments or real governments." (*Du principe fédératif*, First Part, Chap. V).
23. Proudhon, *Justice*, Vol. III, pp. 131–32. In his *Correspondance* (Paris: A. Lacroix, 1875), Proudhon often speaks of the Comte de Paris's

chances of replacing Napoleon III; he thought that Louis Philippe's grandson would give France the peace and freedom needed by the socialists in order to spread their doctrines in the country which they intended to regenerate.

24. Proudhon, *Justice*, Vol. II, p. 29.

25. Like many authors whom the public at large knows solely by several reputedly shocking tenets, Proudhon was diffident, and expressed the basis of his thought rather rarely; he wrote on March 4, 1862, to one of his most intimate correspondents that he judged it dangerous from the point of view of the propagation of his ideas to abandon the word "democracy" which is taken by the public "almost as synonomous with republic"; the reader might have been indignant at a change in terminology (*Correspondance*, Vol. XII, p. 7).

26. Proudhon, *Contradictions politiques*, pp. 81–82. At the end of this section there is an apologue singularly injurious to French democracy.

27. Proudhon, *Correspondance*, Vol. XII, p. 7.

28. Proudhon, *Du principe fédératif*, First Part, Chap. VIII.

29. Proudhon, *Correspondance*, Vol. XIV, pp. 218–19. Cf. *La Guerre et la paix* (Paris: A Lacroix, 1869), Book IV, Chap. X. In this last text it is exactly a matter of twelve independent regions which would have as capitals: Rouen, Lille, Metz, Strasbourg, Dijon, Clérmont, Orléans, Lyon, Marseilles, Toulouse, Bordeaux and Nantes; and he advocates the destruction of the centers of collective life in Paris, which would be equivalent to the suppressing of Paris in Proudhon's view.

30. In 1902 Waldeck-Rousseau had 339 government deputies elected, while the opposition obtained 251 seats; the difference between the number of popular votes was only 200,000 out of 10 million electors (Joseph Reinach, *Histoire de l'affaire Dreyfus* [Paris: Stock, 1894–1908], Vol. VI, p. 188). Chance played such a big role in this national consultation that the Vatican thought that it had the right to hope for a Catholic majority (*Libre Parole*, Nov. 18, 1906). The Chamber of Deputies voted anti-clerical laws of great significance, which would have passed with great difficulty if proportional representation had made the Chamber reflect the electoral body. Joseph Reinach finds this legislation excellent; the democratic ideal consists undoubtedly in giving satisfaction to his passions.

31. German Social Democracy has widely distributed the translation of an anti-clerical book by Yves Guyot (*Etudes sur les doctrines sociales du christianisme* [Paris: E. Flammarion, 1881]), but they thought it fair to distribute booklets as well teaching that "Christianity and Socialism are but one" (*Mouvement Socaliste*, May 1, 1903, pp. 71–72).

32. What happened in Germany at the end of 1918 shows that in 1914 I had judged matters rather well.

33. It would be well to wish that in serious matters a simple majority would not be sufficient; the laws that modify our codes, which establish protective rights or which touch on moral interests (religion, welfare, popular education) should in my opinion be voted by two-thirds of the

deputies; but democracy will never consent to attenuate its dictatorship.

34. By enormously increasing the importance of the committees which choose the candidates.

35. It is suitable to recall here a well-known passage from Polybius: "The principal superiority of the Romans over other people appears to me to consist in their idea of the divinity. . . . Among them devotion has taken on such developments and penetrated so deeply into private life—as in public affairs—that nothing further can be imagined. . . . Entrust a sum of money to a Greek charged with the management of public funds, and even with ten contracts . . . and twenty witnesses he would probably go back on his word. The Romans, even those who have a great sum of money in their power, either during their magistrature or in embassies, need only take an oath in order to remain honorable. Finally, while elsewhere it is rare to find a man who abstains from dipping into the state treasury and who is innocent of all fraud, for the Romans it is rare to find a citizen guilty of this crime" (*Histoire générale*, Book VI, p. 56). Greeks contemporary to Polybius believed that the old national religions were not very serious; therefore the historian believed that he was obliged to say that religious precepts would be useless in a city composed solely of wise men; but he declares that it is useful to frighten the mass of people with religious terrors.

36. Adolphe Prins believes that in very early Greece the popular assembly did not vote (p. 22); in Algeria all village decisions must be unanimous; when the parties cannot reach agreement, there is often recourse to arbitration (A. Hanoteau and A. Letourneux, *La Kabylie et les coutumes kabyles* [Paris: Impr. nationale, 1872–73], Vol. II, pp. 22, 32). The institution of the tribunes of the people in Rome is probably connected to the principle of unanimity; seated at the door of the Senate, they correspond to the plebeians in the Kabyle villages who remain in the public square while the notables discuss in a room. They stopped the Senate by declaring that unanimity was not possible; protected by a sacred immunity, they did not have to fear the violence of the party which proposed the measure they prevented. In primitive civilizations, violence indeed serves to overcome many hindrances. (Cf. Emile Masqueray, *Formation des cités chez les populations sédentaire de l'Algérie* [Paris: E. Leroux, 1886], p. 207.)

37. In such comparisons the differences between economies must be taken into account. After the Peloponnesian wars, Attic society was completely urban in spirit; previously the Athenians preferred country life to that of the city (Alfred Croiset, *Les Démocraties antiques* [Paris: Flammarion, 1909], p. 171). Aristophanes and Xenophon are good witnesses of the old rural Attica.

38. Socrates was a victim of this phenomenon.

39. Cf. Pierre Defourny, *Aristote. Théorie économique et politique sociale* in the *Annales de l'Institut Supérieur de Philosophie de Louvain*, Vol.

III (1914). Aristotle was very opposed to the economics of enrichment; his ideal was the autonomy of the old cities, which were almost entirely self-sufficient; he believed that it could be useful to make laws to prevent the concentration of land; he strongly admired the mutual aid which has always existed in rural districts remaining faithful to traditions. He systematically neglected the essential characteristics in the life of Mediterranean metropoles.

40. In the perfect city, Aristotle divides men into classes according to their age.

41. It is very important to notice that Proudhon's republic is a society of producers and that Aristotle's ideal city is a tribe of noblemen whose lands are tended by serfs; such an ideal did not prepare the Greek philosopher to study rural democracies thoroughly.

42. Proudhon said that Virgil's *Georgics* are "the masterpiece of antiquity and perhaps of all poetic humanity, a poem which by itself alone would justify the teaching of Latin in the schools"; he greatly admired the art with which Virgil knew how to introduce so much philosophy into the rustic tableaux of the *Bucolics* (*Justice*, Vol. III, p. 370).

43. We know that Proudhon was an assiduous reader of the Bible, which is so well adapted to rural democracies. In his last days, Heinrich Heine enthusiastically celebrated the Biblical virtues, which he thought he had rediscovered in Scotland, in the Scandinavian countries and in certain parts of northern Germany (*De l'Allemagne*, Vol. II, p. 314).

44. Proudhon, *Justice*, Vol. II, p. 133.

45. Letter of Dec. 25, 1860, to Huet, a Catholic philosopher who sought to revive Gallicanism [the doctrine of an autonomous French church—ED.] (*Correspondance*, Vol. X, p. 258).

46. Proudhon, *Justice*, Vol. IV, pp. 355–56.

47. Ibid., Vol. VI, pp. 343–44. He was very preoccupied with the influence which "spiritualism" seemed to be having (Vol. V, pp. 323–24, Vol. VI, pp. 57–58). His text also alludes to modern Catholicism of which he often spoke scornfully (cf. for example what he says in *La Révolution sociale démontrée par le coup d'état* [Paris: A. Lacroix, 1868], chap. VI), about the cults of St. Philmère, and of the sacred heart of Mary, about the brotherhood of Notre-Dame des Victoires and the miraculous cures of the Abbé of Hohenlohe.

48. In order for collective reason to be able to express itself, discussions must be directed by competent men, and Proudhon believes that they need to be organized to be able to fulfill their function. That is why he writes: "If our academies had retained the spirit of their origins, if they had the least idea of their mission, nothing would be easier for them than to assume this high jurisdiction over the works of the intelligence" which separates "what derives from legitimate reason" in books from the products of individual absolutism (*Justice*, Vol. III, pp. 119–20). The minority which sees the truth must seek to have it recognized by the "ignorant, impassioned majority," make it "feel the depth, the necessity,

and the supremacy" of the law, and lead it "to freely subject itself to it" (Vol. VI, pp. 332–33). That is what the "social authorities" did, somehow or other.

49. *Ibid.*, pp. 285–92. These passages are taken from a note intended to prove that it is wrong to base the theory of the immortality of the soul on the insufficiency of human justice; but the observations that I quote here have a value independent of the author's aim.

50. *Débats* of Jan. 3, 1913. On Oct. 25, 1861, Proudhon said to Beslay (a future member of the Commune): "I want, as much as I am able, to serve the people and my country . . . I live by my work and desire nothing more. If I am right, I want to be right, that is the only glory of which I dream" (Proudhon, *Correspondance*, Vol. XI, p. 247).

In Germany the idea of having a Chamber elected by universal suffrage controlled by a Senate of producers (workers and peasants) is gaining ground every day; this constitution of power is indeed in the spirit of Proudhon's doctrine; the practice of this system could inspire, in our neighbors, a reform of socialist studies.

Chapter 8

FROM THE UTILITY OF PRAGMATISM

On the Origin of Truth

1. Henri Bergson, *Evolution créatrice* (Paris: F. Alcan, 1907), pp. 385–86. (Translated by Arthur Mitchell as *Creative Evolution* (New York: Modern Library, 1944), pp. 387–88.)

2. Renan thought that better to understand the Greek spirit we should refer to the pastoral poetry of Theocritus. "Greece always thrived on this unimportant genre of delicate and amiable poetry, one of the most typical of its literature, the mirror of its own life. This race is always twenty years old" (*Saint Paul*, p. 204).

3. It was believed that the difficulties inherent in integral calculus would in the long run be surmountable (Emile Picard, *La Science moderne et son état actuel* (Paris: Flammarion, 1905), p. 20).

4. The eighteenth-century scholars were greatly concerned with nautical astronomy, the stability of ships and hydrodynamics. Cf. a famous report by Fourier on the works of Jacobi (Emile Picard, *ibid.*, pp. 28, 82; cf. below, p. 361, n. 65).

5. Let us not forget that Kant compared himself to Copernicus's changing the system of the world.

6. *Evolution créatrice*, p. 386 [English ed., p. 388].

7. Horace, *Art poétique*, vv. 191–92.

8. In 1794 Legendre published the elementary geometry text which has

served as a basis of teaching here for a century. Numerous authors strived to simplify further its proofs. It is only recently that new methods based on the consideration of translation of geometric figures have been introduced into classes (*Bulletin de la Société Française de Philosophie,* June 1907). This new geometry seems to have arisen from the practice of descriptive geometry.

9. The story of Auguste Comte shows with what facility a good professor of mathematics, imbued with the spirit of the eighteenth century, could take himself for one of those masters whose authority could not be questioned with impunity. "The intellect," says Vilfredo Pareto, "is declared a disturber; Comte's disciples assert with their master that there should be no freedom of opinion in social science, that this freedom is anarchic, that we must believe what competent people decide. . . . How could we make a choice without falling into the 'negative criticism' of which positivism accuses liberalism? Protestantism is condemned precisely for having wanted to make a choice of this kind" (*Les Systèmes socialistes,* Vol. II, pp. 205–6). Auguste Comte, in his capacity as professor of mathematics, decides at every turn what is normal and irrevocable (p. 211). He believed that Oriental potentates had preserved a belief in the mission of all government; that is, to "promote the good and resist the bad"; on December 20, 1852, he wrote to the Czar to encourage him to take in hand the positivist reform of the world; in 1853 he believed that Turkey was no less admirable than Russia (pp. 212–13).

10. Auguste Comte saw only aberrations of the metaphysical spirit in the hypotheses proposed by physicists of his time to renew mathematical knowledge of nature; fortunately, no scholar listened to him!

11. Without this tactic, they would risk seeming like dead wood one day.

12. This study ought to be made starting from what Eugène Viollet-le-Duc wrote in his *Dictionnaire raisonné de l'architecture française du XIᵉ au XVIᵉ siècle* (Paris: B. Bance, 1854–68). Particularly useful is the article "Sculpture," in Vol. VIII, whose importance is much greater than we can expect from the title. I know that Viollet-le-Duc is often accused of recklessness, but his enemies have too often lacked common sense. I will confine myself to a single example. Seeing that the clergy of his time did not find medieval sculpture sufficiently edifying, he ventured to write that this art reveals the birth of the spirit of doubt (Vol. VIII, p. 143). Emile Mâle disputes the validity of this assertion; he claims that "In the whole cathedral, one feels certainty of faith and not a shred of doubt" (*L'Art religieux du XIIIᵉ siècle en France* [Paris: E. Leroux, 1898], p. 499). It would be quite impossible to justify such a thesis. In support of Viollet-le-Duc's opinion, we can point out the analogies that exist between the thirteenth century and the Renaissance. The artists of this second period were also emancipated more than once. We cannot indicate any reasonable presumption in favor of Emile Mâle's pronouncement.

13. Cf. Viollet-le-Duc, *Dictionnaire raisonné,* Vol. VIII, p. 231.

14. In ꞏChampagne the sexpartite vault was allowed only exceptionally. In

Bourgogne its use was beginning just when it was being abandoned in the Paris area (Auguste Choisy, *Histoire de l'architecture* (Paris: Gauthier-Villars, 1899), Vol. II, pp. 426 and 435–37).

15. The sexpartite vault is probably of Norman origin; indeed, we find an archaic form of this type at the Abbey of La Trinité at Caen: a groined arch on the square plan, recut into two ribs by a pediment supported by an intermediate lining (Choisy, Vol. II, p. 287). It is possible that for aesthetic motives, which we will discuss later on, the sexpartite system was adopted originally in order to double the number of bays in an edifice which was at first intended to be covered by vaults on a square plan. (Cf. Ruprich-Robert, *L'Architecture normande aux XIe et XIIe siècles en Normandie et en Angleterre* [Paris: Librarie des Imprimeries Réunies, n.d.], Vol. I, p. 138.) See below, pp. 266, 358, n. 34.

16. In the gallery in Bourges, the purpose for the rib is to hide the groin, since it follows the line of intersection to the double curvature of the molding and of the openings (Choisy, *Histoire de l'architecture,* Vol. II, p. 290). The preservation of an archaic remnant is not at all paradoxical at Bourges.

17. It is in this way that modern theorists explain Gothic structure based on fifteenth-century monuments. These monuments were constructed under the influence of ideas arising from long practice illuminated at its beginnings by concerns very remote from those of the fifteenth century. This distinction is very clear for the pragmatic philosopher.

18. This conception of the flying buttress is obviously the one found at Pointigny (Choisy, Vol. II, p. 303). I think it is also found in cathedrals which have two levels of flying buttresses. It could well derive from the relieving arches that the Byzantines often placed at the base of their towers (Choisy, *L'Art de bâtir chez les Byzantins* [Paris: Librarie de la Société Anonyme de Publications Périodiques, 1883], p. 112). If this hypothesis is exact, it shows what a distance there is between a work and the idea that suggested it.

19. Viollet-le-Duc, Vol. VIII, p. 230.

20. Viollet-le-Duc thinks that these corporations had an entirely republican organization where a person's opinion had only a purely moral authority, due to long experience, genius, or simple personal merit (p. 231). The ancients called such republics "aristocratic."

21. "The Auvergne, Normandy and above all the Rhine region were Romanesque provinces in the high Gothic period" (Choisy, *Histoire de l'architecture,* Vol. II, p. 293).

22. Viollet-le-Duc notes that it would have been easier to return to antiquity than to go to the Gothic style (p. 231).

23. That the Gothics had closely studied the ancient sculptures is shown by examining a number of bases of columns. These pieces, lending themselves less to fantasy than the capitals, are particularly suitable for studying traditions. (Cf., in the *Dictionnaire* of Viollet-le-Duc, the profiles given on pp. 144–47 of Volume II.) I think that the sculptures at Reims reveal antique influences in a particularly striking way. To me, their interest appears above all to come from this curious mixture.

24. Decorative art becomes most impoverished when inspired by calligraphic fantasies. This is one of the reasons why the "modern style" is condemned to complete failure. Its motifs seem more in place in the embellishments of manuscripts than in architecture.

25. The first Gothic artisans, being inspired by sap-filled plants, adopted a model which was perfectly suitable to the heaviness of the stone then used in building. "Men of taste" much prefer to this early ornamental art, the art which would later be inspired by delicate vegetation. It seems probable that this development is due to the desire to compete in virtuosity with the wood carvers. For many of our contemporaries, the true Gothic is the one that produces the "stone lace"—that is, that decadent art which no longer respects the conditions of the material.

26. Viollet-le-Duc, Vol. VIII, p. 223. He said that Gothic sculpture seems to contribute to the solidarity of the work. Such an effect is practically never noticed in either Roman or modern art. The statues placed in the angles of Gothic edifices always give the effect of guaranteeing the perfect rigidity of angles.

27. Viollet-le-Duc, Vol. VIII, pp. 137–40, 147, 153 and 164.

28. Ibid., Vol. I, p. 158. The method which consists in going back in time is excellent for the study of institutions and indispensable for understanding Christian origins.

29. Viollet-le-Duc considers three triangles; the isosceles rectangle of which the hypotenuse is placed on the ground; a triangle that he calls "Egyptian"; and the equilateral triangle. If we take 8 as the base, the elevations are 4, 5, 6, 93 (or approximately 7). The "Egyptian" triangle is very approximately the one obtained by cutting on a vertical diagonal plane, the Pyramid of Cheops whose profile is equilateral.

30. Choisy, *Histoire de l'architecture,* Vol. I, pp. 52–56, 392–95; Vol. II, pp. 406–7. I think that the consideration of these geometric traces helps to explain the very enigmatic passage of the *Timaeus,* in which Plato said that the demiurge used the regular dodecahedron to establish the plan of the world (55c). This solid is formed of regular pentagons and in order to construct these figures, it is necessary to know how to divide a line into mean and extreme ratios (the Pythagorean "gilded section"). The two segments are in the approximate ratios of 8 to 5; thus we obtain the "Egyptian" triangle of which Viollet-le-Duc so often speaks.

31. It seems very likely to me that the builders used aesthetic triangles in order to control the stability of their vaults. They were bolder than they would have been, certainly, if they had made mechanical calculations. Modern theories of vaults have made our engineers extremely timid.

32. Viollet-le-Duc, Vol. VIII, pp. 263–67. That is especially true of what is seen from afar.

33. The palaces of the Place de la Concorde, built by Gabriel, have twelve columns. I think that The Bourse is the first buliding that surpasses the prescribed number of columns. In the gallery of the Louvre in which there are exits to the Tuileries, there would have been more than eleven divisions if the architect had not cut it into two sections by a monumental entrance-way. In reconstructing the gallery between the exits

and the *pavillon de Flore*, Lefuel did not try to respect the ancient rules [of twelve columns in a façade]; his work is devoid of any quality of good composition.

34. I am speaking only of the aisle placed to the west of the transept. At Bourges, there is no transept and the nave contains thirteen bays; but this edifice is not inspired by a deep expression of Gothic art, as Viollet-le-Duc reveals. At Laon there are a dozen bays, but the first, which corresponds to a gallery, could have been regarded as not entering into account. Ruskin thought that the largest convenient plan is that at Amiens where there are seven bays (*The Seven Lamps of Architecture*, Fr. trans., p. 197). A group of three to four bays is very poor; it is possible that the Normans adopted the sexpartite vault to correct projects such as S. Ambrogio in Milan.

35. Auguste Choisy notes that the stairs were not built in such a way as to permit easy access of the faithful to the upper aisles (*Histoire de l'architecture*, Vol. II, pp. 210, 431).

36. Refer to the gallery joining the Louvre to the gates along the Seine.

37. The Gothic style ended by doing away with the triforium; good authors say that this is logical, but it made a cold composition, scanty and, one could even say, miserable, as always happens when the height of an edifice includes only two sections. The translucent triforium retained its originality because the light crossed two stained glass windows with different designs, producing surprising effects.

38. Emile Mâle, pp. 65–67.

39. Choisy, *Histoire de l'architecture*, Vol. I, p. 413.

40. Unquestionably, in the twelfth century, architects built their vaults as low as composition allowed. Later, they often exaggerated heights in order to obtain those surprising effects that have always been sought in periods of decline of an art.

41. The study of many Gothic bases provides a decisive argument against this comparison. They often give a very clear impression of inert matter strongly compressed by the column; if the "vegetal theory" were true, the bases ought to give the impression of living elements which thrust branches toward the sky and which are swelled by living sap.

42. Viollet-le-Duc, Vol. III, p. 286.

43. The bell-turrets that were often added at the bases of the spires further increased the resemblance of the latter to a flame.

44. The belief in emanations was no less important in medieval Christianity than in Egyptian magic. The lamp oil that burned before the tomb of a martyr and the linen that had been near his body possessed the same miraculous virtues as authentic relics. By means of emanations, the wood of the true cross could be multiplied indefinitely. Pilgrims had the means of creating Holy Burial Shrouds, relics of the Manger or vestments of the Virgin, by placing unhallowed objects in the places designated by tradition as the Sepulchre of Christ, the stable where He was born or the room where His mother had slept.

45. Choisy, *Histoire de l'architecture*, Vol. II, p. 236. In the ninth century

the Greeks stopped building low cupolas as they had done at St. Sophia, and instead started to raise them on drums; it has been assumed that this new disposition was for the purpose of increasing illumination (pp. 54–55); but churches decorated with gold-based mosaic did not gain by being well illuminated (pp. 64–65).

46. This explains why certain images are icons rather than statues conceived according to the spirit of secular art.

47. Because of this enigmatic character, a number of hypotheses have been made to explain by symbolism the construction of the rose windows.

48. I think that we also ought to see magical weapons in the hooks that proliferate on the outside of Gothic cathedrals; these ornaments which hold the snow are inconsistent with the normal usages of Gothic construction, always concerned with purifying the stone work.

49. This façade has perhaps a more Roman character than any of the great works of the Renaissance. It differs greatly from all the other Gothic compositions. At Reims particularly, the arrangement is much less effective than at Paris because the symbolism is less clear.

50. If not realizing the protective spirits, the architect of Notre Dame gave proof to a profound feeling for the power of art. He did not dilute the idea of these fantastic beings suggested by the great height given to the gallery.

51. It has often been noted that the Roman churches contain many statues which seem to resemble Italian acrobats more than saints. (Cf. Athanase Coquerel Fils, *Des Beaux Arts en Italie* [Paris: J. Cherbuliez], p. 37.) These attitudes did not shock the cultivated seventeenth-century Romans in the slightest.

52. Processions particularly inspire the purveyors to the clergy. Pious people find that the art in the shops of the Saint-Sulpice district corresponds very well to their sentiments; for religious imagery to be reformed, a change in daily worship is necessary. Nothing points to the likelihood of such a change.

53. Brunetière cited a letter in which Diderot explained that he admired nature because it stimulated concupiscence (*Discours de combat* [Paris: Perrin, 1900–1903], First series, p. 68).

54. "After the naturally good man, it was very necessary to invent the naturally aesthetic man. And we are told that uncultivated man is more receptive before a great work and less embarrassed by critical ideas. . . . Perhaps many uncultured men would find the nymphs of the modern salons more beautiful [than the nymphs of Jean Gonjon]. It could be that savages are capable of a stronger admiration, but nothing guarantees a more judicious one" (Lucien Jean, *Parmi les Hommes* [Paris: *Mercure de France*, 1910], p. 262). Lucien Jean was a true proletarian, who knew by personal experience how difficult the formation of aesthetic feeling is.

55. Do not forget that magical marvels were regarded until very recently as being among the best-established facts.

56. Similar phenomena have been observed in the history of institutions:

laws of very great social importance were originally brought about through parliamentary intrigues which everyone hastened to forget.

57. We too often forget this in considering the trial of Galileo. The desire to maintain Peripatetic physics had more importance than considerations of positive theology—at least in the trial of 1616. The advisers to the Holy Office declared the heliocentric doctrine philosophically absurd and false (E. Vacandard, *Etudes de critique et d'histoire religieuse* [Paris: V. Lecoffre, 1909], First series, 2nd ed., pp. 310, 390). Bellarmine thought, moreover, that Aristotle's secular science was all the more certain because it agreed with the "inborn science" of Solomon (p. 308). He was persuaded that the Church would never be obliged to abandon the Church Fathers' scriptural interpretations, written in geocentric style, because, in his opinion, the new theory would never be proved (pp. 307, 347). The Abbé Vacandard is astonished that the cardinal believed that the testimony of the senses was enough to justify the traditional beliefs (p. 307). We should recall here that in Aristotle's system, the doctrine of the divine is founded on the physical properties of a sky in which stars circulate that are composed of an element that is foreign to the earth. The scholastics regarded the theory of the prime mover as the best proof of God's existence that could be given. To admit that God made the world and man in such a way that man would be the victim of appearances when he tried to raise himself from the knowledge of visible things to the knowledge of the perfect Being—this would have placed in doubt the beneficence of God for His creatures. Thus, Bellarmine was reasoning almost like Descartes on the subject of Divine Truth, but in a way that is more satisfying to reason, because he limited the certainty of the exterior world to the certainty of a sky which in no way resembles the Earth.

58. Cardinal Bellarmine thought that in the heliocentric system astronomers had found a convenient way to make their calculations and that they had no need to concern themselves with reality (Vacandard, *Etudes de critique*, p. 305). Newton's disciplines, in creating celestial mechanics with the help of infinitesimal analysis, raised this system far above the level of a mathematical hypothesis. The method proposed by Tycho-Brahé was equal to that of Copernicus from the perspective of the geometric representation of planetary movements (Paul Tannery, *Recherches sur l'histoire de l'astronomie ancienne* [Paris: Gauthier-Villars, 1893], p. 101), but it did not ally itself to the admirable celestial mechanics introduced by Newton; it thus had to disappear.

59. We might say that these principles are obtained by sifting the methods of explanation sanctioned by centuries-old experience; pedagogy has reversed the true order of ideas; philosophy discovers it not by an analysis of operations of the mind, but by history.

60. The ancients did *not* have the same ideas on the postulates as our intellectualist philosophers. The *aitêmata* were, for them, propositions entirely similar to those which are the object of theorems. (Cf. Aristotle, *Posterior Analytics*, Book I, Chap. X, 8.) It was not regarded as appro-

priate to submit assertions which belonged to the domain of the conventional wisdom of enlightened society to proofs dictated by logicians. The Peripatetic theories often have as their bases distinctions sanctioned by language. In the *Dialogues,* Plato viewed the opinions that his friends were accustomed to using without embarrassment as beyond discussion. Today we would say that, for the Greeks, the geometric postulates had a pragmatic truth.

61. To explain the possibility of several equally logical geometries, mathematicians have proposed viewing the postulates as disguised definitions. This theory would have greatly surprised Archimedes, who took the following proposition as a postulate: A balanced scale on which are suspended equal weights leans to the side which has the longest arm.

62. In his treatise, *On the Equilibrium of Planes,* Archimedes devoted long explanations to proposition 9 of Book II. His commentator Eutocius wanted to improve his proof. He made it longer, but did not succeed in making it clearer. Several lines of algebra were enough for the translator Peyrard to establish this theorem that antiquity drowned in the morass of dialectics (Archimedes, *Œuvres complètes,* Peyrard translation, pp. xxi, xlv, and 507).

63. Michel Chasles thought that we owe "the immense progress that modern men have made in geometry to the relaxation of the rigor of the ancients" (*Aperçu historique sur l'origine et le developpement des méthodes en géométrie* [Paris: Gauthier-Villars, 1875], p. 359).

64. Ibid.

65. I completely accept the philosophy of science of Laplace, Fourier and Poisson, which holds that mathematical analysis is only an instrument intended to facilitate the research of physicists. In a report presented to the Academy of Sciences on the work of Jacobi, Fourier says, "One would hope that those who are best able to perfect the science of calculation will direct their work toward these worthy applications [of mathematical physics] so necessary to the progress of human intelligence" (Emile Picard, *La Science moderne et son état actuel,* p. 83). In a letter to Legendre, Jacobi protested against this view that holds the principal aim of mathematics to be "public utility and the explanation of natural phenomena"; according to him, "the unique aim of science is to honor the human spirit and thus a question of numbers is just as valuable as a question on the system of the world" (p. 28).

66. Today scholars can be found to recognize in Greek geometry something of this genius of a people eternally devoted to the carefree quality of youth, a genius that Renan had pointed out as that of the ancient Hellenes (Gaston Milhaud, *Etudes sur la pensée scientifique chez les Grecs et chez les modernes* [Paris: Société française d'imprimerie et de librairie], p. 70; cf. Renan, *Saint Paul,* p. 204).

67. Joseph Bertrand, *D'Alembert* (Paris: Hachette, 1889), p. 56.

68. D'Alembert's book, since rendered obsolete by Lagrange's *Mécanique analytique,* was a great event in the history of science.

69. Poinsot [French mathematician (1777–1859)] was famous for the vir-

tuosity with which he avoided difficult questions; according to Joseph Bertrand [French mathematician (1822–1900)], the students of the *Ecole polytechnique* emerged from his courses with the idea that "integral calculus is amusing and easy." Poinsot thought that "profound and subtle discussions" should be reserved for lovers of dialectics (Joseph Bertrand, *Eloges académiques* [Paris: Hachette], New series, p. 113). He therefore obviously gave the future engineers the instruction which best suited their profession; those among them who wanted to become mathematicians would have the leisure to amuse themselves in resolving the difficulties that their first teacher had neglected. His successor, Cauchy, claimed, on the contrary, "to predict, discover and do away with all difficulties." Poinsot thought that Cauchy, with his "exaggerated rigor," might repel the young men (p. 17). Cauchy took the academic viewpoint while Poinsot had the pragmatic perspective of the eighteenth-century military academies, from which the tradition of the *Ecole polytechnique* arises.

70. Claude Bernard, *Introduction à l'étude de la médecine expérimentale* (Paris: F. Levé, 3d ed., 1900), p. 310, cf. p. 305. [Trans. by Henry Green into English as *Introduction to the Study of Experimental Medicine* (New York: Dover, 1957).]

71. Ibid., p. 70.

72. One could no longer say, with Wundt, that the occulists want to make us believe that the world is subject to the caprices of hysterical women (*Hypnotismé et suggestion*, Fr. Trans., p. 67).

73. "Experimental ideas," says Claude Bernard, "are very often born of chance and on the occurrence of a lucky observation. One ranges in the realm of science and pursues what chance puts before one's eyes" (Bernard, p. 266). Frequently it is in failing in a first experiment that new facts which produce new and fruitful experiments are discovered (p. 272). In order to obtain ideas, Claude Bernard recommended unplanned experiments, "experiments for seeing," that he compared to paths by means of which a hunter succeeds in driving out the game (p. 275).

74. Gustave Le Bon, *Les Opinions et les croyances* (Paris: Flammarion, 1911), pp. 274–75. Foreigners discovered nothing.

75. Paul de Rousiers, *La Vie américaine: l'éducation et la société* (Paris: Firmin-Didot, 1899), pp. 145, 160–62. The author tells us that Americans do not like it said that they have ruling classes (*La Vie américaine: ranches, fermes et usines*, p. 121). The term *Cité morale* is more suitable, I think, than the term "natural aristocracy" to designate the group about which Paul de Rousiers is writing, because the word "aristocracy" is often understood in a way that is very different from the one given in this book.

76. The politicians "damage everything they touch, but they touch only very little," says Paul de Rousiers (*La Vie américaine: l'éducation et la société*, p. 162).

77. Ibid., pp. 145–46. "The American is concerned much more with helping

those with ability to climb than with preventing the incompetent from dying of hunger; the first task interests him; as for the second, it is accomplished for conscience's sake but without enthusiasm" (p. 149).

78. Ibid., pp. 153–54.

79. Ibid., p. 159. "It is necessary for the trustees to have a true devotion to the public good in order to accomplish their task [which consists in utilizing the highly endowed universities for the public good] They must also have eminent qualities joined to a high personal station. In a word, they must be superior men."

80. Le Play should have found this undertaking all the more rational as he had always brought to the forefront the technical studies of his profession and the investigations on working conditions. A pragmatist certainly would not commit such an error. [Frederic Le Play, 1806–82, French engineer-economist-traditionalist and conservative.—ED.]

81. "The Americans are not behind the Europeans," says Paul de Rousiers. "It is not they who are coming to us, but rather we who are going to them. The social transformation which took place amidst American society is being prepared visibly elsewhere" (p. 161).

82. Ibid., pp. 161–62.

83. Cf. Chevrillon, *Nouvelles Etudes anglaises* (Paris: Hachette, 1901), pp. 191–92.

84. Here we find one of those intellectualist illusions that are commonplace among men who lack philosophical perspective. They think that formulas engender history.

85. Rousiers, p. 179.

86. Paul de Rousiers thinks that "most of the time in towns where it occurs, lynching is guarded by serious guarantees"; that it is applied to "criminals of undoubtable guilt" and that the vigilance committee is superior to "a jury selected by chance." These committees inspire more confidence than the public powers because they do not allow themselves to be corrupted (p. 220).

87. This is especially true of the "Committee of Seventy" in New York (Rousiers, pp. 192, 223).

88. Eminent Democrats then supported McKinley, the "sane money" candirate, against Bryan, the candidate of the free minting of money. Archbishop Ireland made a "declaration in favor of 'sane money' despite his Democratic attachments and to the great scandal of certain of his friends, lower class Irishmen and indebted farmers of the West" who saw in depreciated paper money "the money of poor men" (Rousiers, pp. 206–7). There was then a "great patriotic surge" that the older Americans compared to the movement against slavery (p. 209).

89. Paul de Rousiers, *La Vie américaine: ranches, fermes et usines*, pp. 111, 112, 119–22, 261, 264).

90. "They are the steadiest elements of the population—those who give a little material stability to a people in constant motion. . . . These people left their homeland with the predetermined idea of creating an independent domain for themselves. They have come to *conquer land*, like

the medieval Normans and, once their goal is attained, they ask only to live and to die on the soil that they have acquired and cultivated by their labor" (ibid., p. 126; cf. pp. 123–26, 146–47).

91. "My readers will note," said Paul de Rousiers, "that I have been able to acquaint them with many farms, factories and banks without speaking much of the Irish. However, there are many of them in the workshops, but as workers, rarely as employers. On the contrary, I cannot touch on public life without mentioning the important position that they hold in it. . . . Everyone has heard about the Tammany Ring, famous for its members' extraordinary misappropriation of funds. The origin of the Tammany Ring is found in an Irish association. . . . Its power has always developed in proportion to the progress of immigration— above all Irish immigration" (*La Vie américaine: l'éducation et la société*, pp. 188–89). He believes that the Irish are capable of forming strong "leagues of incompetents" by dint of their traditions of clans and of secret societies (pp. 187–88). [Tammany was a force in New York politics even before large-scale Irish immigration.—ED.]

92. "In the United States I have often seen," says Paul de Rousiers, "Frenchmen deeply shocked at what they called the selfishness of American fathers. To them it is revolting for a rich man to allow his son to earn his own living; that his father does not set him up. It is true that this is repugnant to our practices, but this is the whole meaning of the American upbringing" (pp. 9–10).

93. The Revolution of 1848 was called the "Revolution of Contempt" by the republican men of letters of that time who condemned the July Monarchy for its sympathies for nascent capitalism.

94. This is why university examination questions have for us an importance completely different from that in countries in which the colleges must prepare their students either for erudition or for business. Many of the old republicans have discovered that the Republic committed a great imprudence in abrogating the old classical curricula.

95. William James, *The Meaning of Truth* (New York: Longmans Green, 1910), Ch. XIII, pp. 269–70.

96. General Walker, director of the Massachusetts Institute of Technology, said to Paul de Rousiers, "I consider [the trusts] absolutely pernicious. They constitute a veritable tyranny, and America will rid herself of them as she knows how to rid herself of all tyrannies. By what means this will take place I do not know, but I have confidence in the enormous force of public opinion in this country" (*Les Industries monopolisées aux Etats-Unis* [Paris: A. Colin, 1898], p. 5). There is something of a magical superstitution in such confidence.

97. William James, *The Meaning of Truth*, pp. 234–35. According to William James, the relation of truth occupies a place in an order of the mind in which one comes upon not only degrees of possibility but again the inapplicability or falseness of ideas.

98. In a study on the nature of the coercive power of the Church, the Abbé Vacandard presents the following argument as most tenable: "There is

no basis for applying to all centuries a theological system that was suitable only to the Middle Ages. If Benedict XIV, Pius VI and Pius IX tried to maintain it, it is because they were unable to accept the idea that the Middle Ages was ever ended. They thus prolonged it by an uninterrupted series of claims, but their efforts have not been able to halt the course of things. The right of the Church to constrain violators of its laws by material force and the theological system of which this right was a part are no longer anything but a relic of the past" (*Etudes de critique et d'histoire religeuse,* 2nd series, 2nd edition, p. 237). In an appendix to his book, this author has presented the vehement protests that his study has provoked on the part of conservative theologians.

99. It has often been observed that this complexity appears all the greater as the observer sees things closer up.

100. "The anti-pragmatist," says William James, "is guilty of the further confusion of imagining that, in undertaking to give him an account of what truth formally means, we are assuming at the same time to provide a warrant for it, trying to define the occasions when he can be sure of materially possessing it" (*The Meaning of Truth,* pp. 195–96).

101. Writers who amused themselves at the expense of the casuists have generally failed to observe that psuedo-mathematical theory ought to lead to the creation of a sort of applied mechanics, intended to evaluate the differences which exist between criminal acts and certain kinds of moral transgressions.

102. Hence the result that pragmatism changed its perspective in passing from William James's hands to those who did not have his Christian concerns; the atheistic Italian pragmatists have ended up in strange paradoxes.

103. "As for the Church, if it appeared severe and at times harsh in the repression of heresy . . . it is because it believed that it stood alone in possession of the truth, and the truth necessary to the eternal safety of its children" (*Quelques Remarques sur l'Orpheus,* pp. 70–72).

104. At the beginning of his book on the Inquisition, the Abbé Vacandard expresses himself thus: "There are hardly any apologists— if at all— who feel a real pride in encountering in the history of the Catholic Church the annals of the Inquisition. The most intrepid attempt to defend this institution against the attacks of modern liberalism only with a certain diffidence. And hardly have they given the first blows to their adversaries when they dodge the question. In vain do they try to show that the detractors of the Inquisition, Protestant or rationalist, have similar misdeeds to their account. . . . Thus a false maneuver intended to outwit criticism seems implicitly to recognize that the Church's cause is untenable."

105. Speaking of the organization of the *Nethinim* or lay brothers who surrounded the second temple in Jerusalem, Renan wrote: "The perspective of an existence of idlers, living off the altar, proved more attractive to them than a life of work in Babylon. A religious foundation is solid only when it assures leisure to a whole class of men. Islam is defended above

all by the Wakoufs and the foundations who support the sloth of the *softas*. Jansenism exists no longer except at Utrecht, because there only one has a Prebend for being Jansenist" (*Histoire du peuple d'Israël,* Vol. III, p. 517). We know that Renan very often spoke of Jerusalem while thinking of Catholic Rome (cf. particularly with regard to this comparison, *Saint Paul,* p. 116).

106. The identity of these two psychological states is undoubtedly one of the reasons which explains why some illustrious mathematicians accept the teachings of Catholic theology with such extreme ease. Naturalists who are not familiar with certitude are more rebellious against dogmas.

107. It is by means of such artifices that certain contemporary journalists imagine that they can lead France to the monarchical faith. They forget that royalty differs above all from tyrannies (such as Bonapartism) by its respect for tradition. The royalist tradition can be engendered only by the *activity of its social authorities*. It is curious that the propagandists of the royalist party admire the government of Louis XIV which Le Play regarded as having been very harmful. It should be noted that French gentlemen very rarely have the qualities that allow them to fulfill the role of *social authorities* and consequently of helping the prosperity of a monarchical country.

108. In his book, *La Jeunesse de Lamennais,* Christian Marechal showed that Lamennais's thought operated on a foundation produced by a reading of Rousseau.

109. Many socialist writers are dedicated to showing that the primitive peoples must have lived under a regime characterized by these three principles which a cruel civilization abolished for centuries.

110. For example, rules relating to lunar influences on the value of wood owing to the time of cutting, on the germination of seeds, and on meteorology.

111. When one considers proverbs from this point of view, it is no longer surprising that they contradict one another so often. The moralists who have criticized the classic fables have not reflected that they are literary pieces appropriate for children in which the moral is very perceptible.

112. It is hardly necessary to call attention to the fact that in the development of capitalist industry, the characteristics that I have enumerated are encountered.

A *Critique of* Creative Evolution

1. Very shortly after the appearance of *Evolution créatrice,* I wrote a study on Bergson's ideas for *Mouvement Socialiste,* 1907. I did not always reach satisfactory conclusions because at that time I did not dream that the use of pragmatism was possible in this critique; Bergson, who had read my articles with benevolent interest, urged me to take them up again so as to give them a definitive form, thinking that they could be read profitably by scholars and philosophers. [This translation is from *De l'utilité du pragmatisme,* pp. 411–27.—ED.]

2. At the beginning of *Matière et mémoire*, Bergson seems to accept fully this last point of view, which was regarded in France at the time when he was attending the *École Normale Supérieure* as the one most worthy of the highest circles of education. There remain rather numerous vestiges of idealism in *Evolution créatrice*, although a doctrine which analyses generation had to be rather realist in outlook; these idealist remnants produce a certain confusion.

3. Bergson, *Evolution créatrice*, p. 166. I recall here that for Bergson we are all geometricians because we are naturally artisans (pp. 48–49). [Sorel distinguishes between the "natural nature" of non-man-made phenomena and the "artificial nature" of man-made phenomena including tools and laboratory experiments.—ED.]

4. Ibid., p. 207.

5. Visual similarities are united to analogies sanctified by language in order to maintain the tenacious prejudice which sees in *artificial nature* a simple perfection of *natural nature*. One can ask whether Bergson was the victim of an illusion of this kind when he wrote: "Prior to the emergence of the discipline of geometry there was a natural geometry whose clarity and obviousness surpass those of other deductions" (*Evolution créatrice*, p. 230).

6. Compare these words of Bergson: "As matter is shaped by intelligence, as there is an obvious agreement between them, the one cannot be engendered without bringing about the other. An identical process must have fashioned matter and the intellect simultaneously from a substance that contained both" (ibid., p. 217).

7. Ibid., p. 220. I am not quite sure I understand what Bergson meant in the theory which is summed up in this sentence; it seems to me that he believed that the images always encroach upon one another, as takes place in the phenomena of irradiation; it will not be difficult for the reader to recognize that I understand spatiality here as conformity to geometry which we assume to be realizable in our experimental devices.

In this respect it is suitable to note that men endowed with strong intuition, like Bergson, often give formulations whose value is entirely independent of the considerations that they develop with the intention of justifying them; their genius has discovered a reality which is hidden from ordinary men and the defects of their scholarship should not prevent us from accepting their discoveries.

8. Ibid., p. 206. Obviously reasoning here according to the data of vision, Bergson has difficulty in separating an object from everything surrounding it. He regards spatial individuation as an artifice of intelligence; intelligence, obliged for practical reasons to make matter act on other matter, sacrifices reality to the needs of artisans. It is suitable here to refer to what was said in the preceding footnote on the meaning of the word "spatiality" and on the value of Bergsonian intuitions.

9. The creators of social utopias hope that progress will soon do away with this anarchy.

10. *Evolution créatrice*, p. 218 .

11. Ibid., p. 218.

12. Ibid., p. 258.

13. Ibid., p. 219.

14. Ibid., p. 225.

15. An Italian colonel wrote to Mosso: "In examinations to give proof of literacy, a requirement for discharge, I have often seen very robust soldiers with pen in hand and large drops of perspiration falling on the paper. I saw one faint during the examination; after he recovered he requested another one, but at first sight of the paper and book he grew pale and fainted again" (Angelo Mosso, *La Fatigue intellectuelle et physique*, trans. into French by P. Langlois [Paris: F. Alcan, 1908], p. 77).

16. Marx compares the lost time to *pores* that are restrained by the division of labor (*Capital*, French trans., p. 148, col. 2 [Modern Library ed., p. 385]).

17. "'We are whole nations of serfs,' wrote Adam Smith's tutor, Ferguson, 'and we have no more free citizens'" (Marx, *Capital*, French trans., p. 154, col. 1 [Modern Library ed., p. 389]).

18. Forty years ago Reuleaux wrote: "In the most advanced modern factories it is generally the custom to interchange among themselves the workers who operate the different machines so as to break the monotony of the work, which otherwise would become intolerable, and to permit, moreover, a worker to familiarize himself successively with a series of machines; thus his labor is utilized under *conditions entirely different from those imposed by the principle of the division of labor*. We think it is worth drawing attention to this new method of work, which is becoming more pervasive every day" (*Cinématique*, pp. 555–56). It is clear that the montony of work is only insupportable for the worker whose reason rebels against the currents that induce routine and finally automatism.

19. One of the goals of apprenticeship should be to dispel the hesitations deriving from the feeling of impotence of the man who feels inferior to his task. Employers do not always fully realize the stress brought on by the obligation to abandon a routine; only an intelligent apprenticeship, begun early, can give the mass of men confidence in their capacities to adapt to a varied number of tasks.

20. Cf. Marx, *Capital*, French trans., p. 183, col. 1. (Modern Library ed., p. 462).

21. Many of our machines are provided with control mechanisms that great physicists would have been happy to have in their laboratories a century ago.

22. The stupidity of big French employers is one of the sadder economic phenomena of our time.

23. Inventors strongly resemble the artists whom the academicians willingly regard as crazy.

24. Physiologists have tried in vain to determine the conditions of this regeneration of forces. In 1890 Napias maintained that, according to the experiments of Pittenkofer and of Voit, a man laboring for nine hours and resting for fifteen would exceed the limits of his strength because

he would have burned more oxygen than he would have taken in by breathing (*Association française pour l'avancement des sciences, Congrès de Limoges,* Vol. I, p. 344). This theory is no longer accepted by anyone.

25. That is why so many men feel the need of abandoning themselves to manual labor in order to make intellectual preoccupations disappear; the muscular fatigue which results from it is enough to bring on the quietude of which our author speaks. It has often been remarked that the manual laborer sings while refined instrumental music bores him. Song is far more suitable than instrumental music for calming the spirit. Finally, it seems to me that a slight muscular fatigue is favorable to the accomplishment of the sexual functions; one cannot say as much for cerebral fatigue.

26. A. Roguenant, *Patrons et ouvriers* (Paris: J. Gabalda, 1907), pp. 27–28.

27. [By which is meant the construction of mechanisms to experiment—ED.]

28. Ibid., p. 306.

29. Bergson, *Evolution créatrice,* p. 216.

30. It is possible that this is one of the reasons for which Aristotle was so hostile to the theories of Plato's *Timaeus.*

31. *Evolution créatrice,* p. 266.

32. That is why magical incantations (such as the *indigitamenta* of the Latins) constituted an essential element of rural labor.

33. This consideration has considerable social importance: the more scientific that production becomes, the better we understand that our destiny is to labor without a truce and thus to annihilate the dreams of paradisiacal happiness that the old socialists had taken as legitimate anticipations. Everything allows for the assumption that labor will always be intensifying. We can again note that this pessimism tends to reinforce the feeling of reality because we will never take for illusions, the sensations engenered by strongly disciplined labor.

A Sorel Bibliography

This list includes all books and articles written by Sorel that are known to the editor. It excludes most book reviews and short notices. In cases in which a book includes former articles I have listed the book except for the *Saggi di critica del marxismo* in which the original French title has also been included. The publication place of books is Paris unless stated otherwise. An asterisk before the title indicates that the work has been included at least in part in this volume.

Books:

Contribution à l'étude profane de la Bible, Auguste Ghio, 1889.

* *Le Procès de Socrate,* Felix Alcan, 1889.

D'Aristote à Marx, Rivière, 1935 (originally published in *Ere Nouvelle* in 1894 under the title "L'Ancienne et la nouvelle métaphysique").

La Ruine du monde antique, Rivière, 1901, 1922, 1933 (originally published in large part in *Ere Nouvelle,* October 1894).

Essai sur l'église et l'état, Jacques, 1902.

* *Saggi di critica del marxismo,* Palermo, Sandron, 1902.

Introduction à l'économie moderne, Jacques, 1902.

Le Système historique de Renan, Jacques, 1905.

Insegnamenti sociale della economia contemporanea, Palermo, Sandron, 1906.

* *Réflexions sur la violence,* Rivière, 1908, and six subsequent editions (translated into English by T. E. Hulme under the title *Reflections on Violence,* New York and London, Macmillan, 1950).

* *Les Illusions du progrès,* Rivière, 1908, and four subsequent editions (translated into English by John and Charlotte Stanley under the title *The Illusions of Progress,* Berkeley and Los Angeles: University of California, 1969).

La Révolution dreyfusienne, Rivière, 1909, 1911.

La Décomposition du marxisme, Rivière, 1908 (translated in English as the *Decomposition of Marxism,* published as an appendix to Irving Louis Horowitz, *Radicalism and the Revolt Against Reason,* New York, Humanities Press, 1963).

* *Matériaux d'une théorie du prolétariat,* Rivière, 1919, 1921.

* *De l'utilité du pragmatisme,* Rivière, 1921, 1928.

Propos de Georges Sorel, ed. Jean Variot, Gallimard, 1935.
Lettres à Paul Delesalle, ed, André Prudhommeaux, Grasset, 1947.

Articles and Prefaces to Books by Year:
1886 "Sur les applications de la psychophysique," *Revue Philosophique* XXII.
1887 "Le calcul des probabilités et l'expérience," *Revue Philosophique* XXIII.
1888 "La cause en physique," *Revue Philosophique* XXIV.
1889 "Socialismo e rivoluzione," *Rivista Popolare di Politica* IV.
1890 "Alcune provisioni storiche di Marx," *Rivista Popolare di Politica* VI;
"Le elizioni municipali di Parigi," *Rivista Popolare di Politica* VI;
"Contributions psycho-physiques à l'étude esthétique. Notes et discussions," *Revue Philosophique* XXIX–XXX.
1891 "Les Girondins du Roussillon," *Bulletin de la Société Agricole, Scientifique et Littéraire des Pyrénées Orientales,* Perpignan;
"Sur la géométrie non-euclidienne. Notes et discussions," *Revue Philosophique* XXX.
1892 "Essai sur la philosophie de Proudhon," *Revue Philosophique* XXXIII, XXXIV;
"François Ducruix—Contribution à la psychologie des Maratistes," *Bulletin de la Société Agricole, Scientifique et Littéraire des Pyrénées Orientales,* Perpignan;
"Fondement scientifique de l'atomisme," *Annales de Philosophie Chrétienne*;
"La physique de Descartes," *Annales de Philosophie Chrétienne.*
1893 "Le crime politique d'après M. Lombroso," *La Revue Scientifique* LI;
"La bonne marche des locomotives à grande allure," *La Revue Scientifique* LI;
"La position du problème de M. Lombroso," *La Revue Scientifique* LI;
"La femme criminelle," *La Revue Scientifique* LII;
"Science et socialisme," *Revue Philosophique* XXXV;
"Deux nouveaux sophismes sur le temps," *Annales de Philosophie Chrétienne*;
"Une faute de crime politique," *Archivio di Psichiatria e scienze penali* XIV, p. 452.
1894 "Le mouvement de la voie des chemins de fer," *La Revue Scientifique* LIII (May 24);
"La psychologie du Juge," *Archivio di Psichiatria e scienze penali* XV.
1895 "Les théories pénales de MM Durkheim et Tarde," *Archivio di Psichiatria e scienze penali* XVI;
"Les théories de M. Durkheim," *Le Devenir Social,* April–May;
"La métaphysique évolutioniste de M. Brunetière," *Le Devenir Social,* Sept. (signed "B");
"L'église et le travail manuel," *Le Devenir Social,* Sept. (signed "B");
"La superstition socialiste," *Le Devenir Social,* Nov.;

"L'évolution moderne de l'architecture," _La Revue Scientifique_ 4th series, Vol. III.

1896 "Etudes d'économie rurale," _Le Devenir Social_, Jan.–Feb. (signed "F");

"La science dans l'éducation," _Le Devenir Social_, Feb.–May;

"Progrès et développement," _Le Devenir Social_, March (signed "B");

"L'idéalisme de M. Brunetière," _Le Devenir Social_, June (signed "David");

"Les sentiments sociaux," _Le Devenir Social_, Aug.–Sept. (signed "X");

"Economie sociale catholique," _Le Devenir Social_, Oct. (signed "B");

"La dépression économique," _Le Devenir Social_, Nov. (signed "F");

"Etude sur Vico," _Le Devenir Social_, Oct.–Dec.

1897 "Preface" to _Essais sur la conception matérialiste de l'histoire_ by Antonio Labriola, French trans., Giard et Brière; (partial translation appears in Labriola, _Socialism and Philosophy_, Chicago, Kerr, 1911).

"La science de la population," _Le Devenir Social_, Feb.;

"Contre une critique anarchiste," _Le Devenir Social_, May (signed "H");

"Sur la théorie marxiste de la valeur," _Le Journal des Economistes_, May;

"La loi des revenus," _Le Devenir Social_, July;

"Sociologie de la suggestion," _Le Devenir Social_, Aug.–Sept. (signed "X");

"Pro e contro il socialismo," _Le Devenir Social_, Oct.;

"Der Ursprung des Staatssozialismus in Deutschland," _Sozialistische Monatshefte_, Nov.;

"Die Entwicklung des Kapitalismus," _Sozialistische Monatshefte_, Oct.;

1898 "Preface" to Serverio Merlino, _Formes et essence du socialisme_, Giard et Brière;

* "L'avenir socialiste des syndicats," _L'Humanité Nouvelle_, March–May (reproduced as Chapter I of _Matériaux d'une thoérie du prolétariat_);

"Betrachtungen uber die materialistische Geschichtsauffassung," _Sozialistische Monatshefte_, July–Sept. (Chap. I of _Saggi di critica_);

"Ein sozialistischer Staat," _Sozialistische Menatshefte_, Jan.;

"Der amerikanische Kapitalismus," _Sozialistische Monatshefte_, Dec.;

* "La necessità e il fatalismo del marxismo," _La Riforma Sociale_, Milan, Aug. (Chapter II of _Saggi di critica del marxismo_);

"La crise du socialisme," _La Revue Politique et Parlementaire_, Dec.;

"Il giuri e la crisi del diritto penale," _Scuola Positiva nella Giurisprudenza Penale, Dec._

1899 "Il socialismo e la teoria delle razze," _Rivista Critica del Socialismo_, July (Chap. III of _Saggi di critica del marxismo_);

"La scissione socialista in Francia," _Rivista Critica del Socialismo_, Oct., Rome.

"Il vangelo, la Chiesa e il socialismo," *Rivista Critica del Socialismo,* April, May (final chapter of *La Ruine du monde antique*);

"Dove va il marxismo?" *Rivista Critica del Socialismo,* Jan.;

"Dommatismo e pratica," *Rivista Critica del Socialismo,* Mar.;

"Socialismo e democrazia," *Rivista Critica del Socialismo;*

° "L'éthique du socialisme," *La Revue de Métaphysique et de Morale,* May;

° "Y-a-t-il de l'utopie dans le Marxisme?" *La Revue de Métaphysique et de Morale,* March (Chap. V of *Saggi di critica del marxismo*);

"Marxismo e scienza sociale," *Rivista Italiana di Sociologia,* Jan. (Chap. VI of *Saggi di critica del marxismo*);

"Morale et socialisme," *Le Mouvement Socialiste,* March;

"L'evoluzione del socialismo in Francia," *Riforma Sociale,* June;

"Le spirito pubblico Francia," *Rivista Popolare di Politica,* Vol. V;

"Les divers types des sociétés cooperatives," *La Science Sociale,* Sept.;

"Quelques objections au matérialisme économique," *Humanité Nouvelle,* June–July (reprinted in *Saggi di critica del marxismo,* Chap. IV);

"Le idee giuridiche del marxismo," *Rivista di Storia Filosofia del Diritto,* Aug. 8 (reprinted in *Saggi di critica,* Chap. VII).

1900 "Uber die kapitalistische Konzentration," *Sozialistische Monatshefte,* Feb.–Mar., IV;

° "Les polémiques pour l'interpretation du marxisme," *La Revue Internationale de Sociologie,* April–May (reprinted in *Saggi di critica del marxismo,* Chap. IX);

"Costruzione del sistema della storia seconda Marx," *Riforma Sociale,* June (Chap. VIII of *Saggi di critica del marxismo*);

"Les dissensions de la social-démocratie allemande à propos des écrits de M. Bernstein," *La Revue Politique et Parlementaire,* July;

"Le système des mathématiques," *Revue de Métaphysique et de Morale,* July;

"Les aspects juridiques du socialisme," *Revue Socialiste,* XXXII, Oct.–Nov.;

"L'économie sociale à l'exposition," *Le Mouvement Socialiste,* Nov.;

"Les facteurs moraux de l'évolution," *Questions de morale* (book);

"La science et la morale," *Questions de morale.*

1901 "Conseils du travail et paix sociale," *Le Mouvement Socialiste,* Jan.;

"Les grèves de Montceau," *Pages Libres,* March;

"La valeur sociale de l'art," *Revue de Métaphysique et de Morale;*

"Economie et agriculture," *Revue Socialiste,* March–April;

"Proudhon," *Pages Libres,* 4 May;

"Quelques mots sur Proudhon," *Cahiers de la Quinzaine* #130 of the second series, June;

"Pour Proudhon," *Pages Libres,* June 8;

"La propriété foncière en Belgique," *Le Mouvement Socialiste,* Oct.

1902 "Jean Coste," *Cahiers de la Quinzaine,* Feb.;

"Idées socialistes et faits économiques au XIXe siècle," *Revue Socialiste*, March–May;

"Storia e scienzia sociale," *Rivista Italiana di Sociologia*, March–June;

"Le matérialisme historique," *Bulletin de la Société Française de Philosophie*, May;

"Soziale Ideen und Organisation der Arbeit," *Sozialistische Monatshefte*, June;

"Les syndicats industriels et leur signification," *Revue Socialiste*, July–Aug.;

"La crise de la pensée catolique," *Revue de Métaphysique et de Morale*, Sept.;

"Preface" to Fernand Pelloutier, *L'Histoire des bourses du travail*, Schleicher.

1903 "Qu'est-ce qu'un syndicat?" *Pages Libres*, March;

"Sur divers aspects de la mécanique," *Revue de Métaphysique et de Morale*, Nov.;

"A propos de l'anticlericalisme," *Etudes Socialistes*;

"Le compagnonnage," *Etudes Socialistes*;

"Léon XIII," *Etudes Socialistes*;

"Nouveaux réquisitoires de M. Brunetière," *Etudes Socialistes*;

"Observations sur le Régime des chemins de fer," *Etudes Socialistes*.

1904 "Due anni di anticlericalismo in Francia," *Rivista Popolare di Politica*, Vol. X;

"La morte di Waldeck-Rousseau," *Rivista Popolare di Politica*, Vol. X.

1905 "Conclusions aux 'Enseignements sociaux de l'économie moderne,' " *Le Mouvement Socialiste*, July;

"Lo sciopero generale," *Divenire Sociale*, Dec.;

"Le syndicalisme révolutionaire," *Le Mouvement Socialiste*, Nov.;

"La restaurazione giacobina in Francia," *Rivista Popolare di Politica*, Vol. XI;

"Preface" to Georges Castex, *La Douleur Physique*, Jacques.

1906 "Il tramonto del partito socialista internationale," *Divenire Sociale*, Jan.;

"Le déclin du parti socialiste international," *Le Mouvement Socialiste*, Feb.;

"Le elezioni in Francia," *Divenire Sociale*, April;

"Le idee di uguaglianza," *Divenire Sociale*, April;

"La storia ebraica e il materialismo storico," *Divenire Sociale*, May;

"L'unita dei riformisti e dei 'rivoluzionari' tradizionali," *Divenire Sociale*, Aug.;

"A proposito del Congresso di Roma," *Divenire Sociale*, Oct.;

"Roberto Owen," *Divenire Sociale*, Nov.;

"Cattolizi contra la Chiesa," *Divenire Sociale*, Dec.;

"L'industria urbana," *Rivista Popolare di Politica*, XII;

"Grandeur et décadence de Rome," *Le Mouvement Socialiste*, July (and Feb. 1907).

1907 "Le prétendu socialisme juridique," *Le Mouvement Socialiste*, April;
     "Les cahiers de jeunesse de Renan," *Le Mouvement Socialiste*, May;
     "Jean-Jacques Rousseau," *Le Mouvement Socialiste*, June;
     "La crise morale et religieuse," *Le Mouvement Socialiste*, July;
     "L'évolution créatrice," *Le Mouvement Socialiste*, Oct., Nov., Dec.;
     "L'idéa di libertà," *Divenire Sociale*, III, June;
     "La démocratie," *Le Bulletin de la Société Française de Philosophie*,
     March;
     "Le pragmatisme," *Bulletin de la Société Française de Philosophie*,
     April.

1908 "Morale e socialismo," *Divenire Sociale*, May;
     "La decadenza parlementare," *Divenire Sociale*, May;
     "La politique américane," *Le Mouvement Socialiste*, June;
     "Les intellectuels à Athènes," *Le Mouvement Socialiste*, Sept.;
     "Le modernisme dans la religion et dans le socialisme," *Revue
     Critique des Livres et des Idées*.

1909 "La religion d'aujourd'hui," *Revue de Métaphysique et de Morale*,
     May;
     "La disfatta dei 'muffles'," *Divenire Sociale*, July;
     "La Russia e Clemenceau," *Divenire Sociale*, Aug.;
     "Il dolori dell'eria presente," *Divenire Sociale*, Oct.;
     "La maturita del movimento sindicale," *Divenire Sociale*, Dec.;
     "Gli intelletuali contro gli operari," *Divenire Sociale*, Dec.;
     "La leçon du malheur," *L'Almanach de la révolution*;
     "Preface" to Victor Griffuelhes and L. Niel, *Les Objectifs de nos luttes
     de classe*.

1910 "Preface," Arturo Labriola, *Karl Marx: L'économiste, le socialiste*,
     Rivière;
     "Le mystère de la *Charité de Jeanne d'Arc*, de Péguy," *Action Fran-
     çaise*, April;
     "Lettre à Lanzillo sur 'La Cité française,'" *Giornale d'Italia*, Nov.;
     "Vues sur les problèmes de la philosophie," *Revue de Métaphysique
     et de Morale* XVIII (and XIX, 1911).

1911 "Le monument Jules Ferry," *L'Indépendance*, March;
     "L'abandon de la revanche," *L'Indépendance*, April;
     "Lyripipi sorbonici moralisationes," *L'Indépendance*, April;
     "Les responsabilités de 1870," *L'Indépendance*, July;
     "L'otage de Paul Claudel," *L'Indépendance*, July;
     "Sur la magie moderne," *L'Indépendance*, Sept.;
     "Si les dogmes évoluent," *L'Indépendance*, Sept.;
     "Une critique des sociologues," *L'Indépendance*, Oct.;
     "A la mémoire de Cournot," *L'Indépendance*, Oct.;
     "Trois problèmes," *L'Indépendance*, Dec.;
     "Psychologie politique," *Bulletin de la Semaine*;
     "Le democrazia antiche," *Rassegna Contemporanea*, Nov.;
     "Preface" to E. R. A. Seligman, *L'Interprétation économique de l'his-
     toire*, Rivière (originally published in English as *The Economic*

Interpretation of History; Sorel wrote the preface to the French translation only).

1912 "Urban Gohier," *L'Indépendance*, Jan.;
      "La rivolta ideale," *L'Indépendance*, April;
      "Quelques prétentions juives," *L'Indépendance*, May–June;
      "Aux temps dreyfusiens," *L'Indépendance*, Oct.

1913 "Preface" to an Italian translation of Ernest Renan, *La Réforme intellectuelle et morale* (in *La Critica* in 1931).

1914 "Preface" to Edouard Berth, *Les Méfaits des intellectuels*, Rivière.

1915 "Preface" to Missiroli Mario, *Il papa in guerra*, Bologna.

1919 "Charles Péguy," *La Ronda* I, April;
      "Perche si processa il Kaiser," *Resto del Carlino*, Sept.;
      "Proudhon," *La Ronda*, Sept.;
      "Respublica litteratorum," *Les Lettres*, Oct.

1920 "Gambetta et Madame Adam," *La Ronda*, May 5;
      "Cristianesimo greco e Europa moderna," *La Ronda*, Aug. 8–9;
      "La Correspondenza di Thiers," *La Ronda*, Dec. 12;
      "La Chine," *La Revue Communiste*, July 5;
      "Le travail dans la Grèce antique," *La Revue Communiste*, Nov. 7;
      "Le Bolchévisme en Egypte," *La Revue Communiste*, Sept. 7;
      "Irlande et Egypte," *Il Tempo*, Dec. 7.

1921 "Lénine d'après Gorki," *La Revue Communiste*, Jan. 11;
      "Le Génie du Rhin, *La Revue Communiste*, April 14;
      "La neutralita Belga in teora e in practica," *La Ronda*, July 6;
      "Proudhon e la rinascita del socialismo," *La Ronda*, Nov. 11–20.

1922 "Jeremy Bentham et l'indépendance de l'Egypte," *Revue Le Mercure de France*, April (with L. Auriant).

1927 "Lettres de Georges Sorel à Benedetto Croce, 1895–1922," *La Critica* XXV–XXVII.

1928 "Ultima meditazione," *Nuova Antologia*, Rome.

1929 "Lettere di Georges Sorel à Roberto Michels, 1905–1917," *Nuovi studi di diritto economia e politica*, Feb.

1931 (See listing for 1913.)

1934 "Lettres de Georges Sorel à Hubert Lagardelle," *L'Homme réel*, Feb.–March.

      The editor has often referred to Paul Delesalle, "Bibliographie Sorelienne," *International Journal of Social History*, March 1938.

Index

Education, 11, 62-64, 78, 80, 91, 105-6, 140, 157, 187-91, 221 ff, 277, 306 n. 52, 311 nn. 21-22, 362 n. 69
Edwards, Stewart, 293 n. 47
Egoism, 18-19, 195
Einaudi, Luigi, 146
Empiricism, 74, 112, 114, 116, 121, 234; in political science, 254-55, 258
Encyclopedists, 189, 331 n. 48
Engagement, 5, 98
Engels, Frederick, 96, 101, 120-21, 127, 129-30, 136, 141, 144-45, 147, 149, 151, 153, 155, 159, 161, 169-71, 233, 296 n. 104, 297 nn. 125-126, 313 n. 32, 314 n. 37, 316 n. 3, 322 n. 73, 326 n. 143, 347 n. 79
Enlightenment, 15, 185-90
Entente cordiale, 12, 246
Epic (social poetry), 23-24, 26, 40-47, 63, 69
Epicurus, 185
Equality, 17, 25-26, 29, 63-70, 75-79, 88, 103, 109, 300 n. 16, 303 n. 21, 341 n. 23
Ere Nouvelle, 8
Erfurt Congress, 72
Ethics (*see* Morals)
Eucharist, 196, 339 n. 11
Euclid (*see also* Geometry), 260, 271-72, 313 n. 25
Euripides, 69
Evolution (*see* Life)
Excellence, 25, 26, 29, 57-58, 224, 363 nn. 77-79
Exchange, mode of, 119
Experience, 41, 53, 55, 81, 135, 140, 168, 189, 194, 209, 278; integral, 53-54, 55
Exploitation, 162-5, 323 n. 95, 324 n. 105, 325 n. 118

F

Fabian society, 149
Faguet, 107
Family life (the household), 19-20, 25, 26, 86, 97-98, 103, 146, 150, 166, 171, 173-74, 188, 215-16, 307 n. 68, 311 nn. 20-21, 324 nn. 114 and 116, 343 n. 42, 346 n. 68
Fascism, 2-4, 11, 43-44, 291-92 n. 10 (*see also* Monarchism)
Fatalism (*see also* History), 101, 111-29
Fénelon, 177
Ferdinand IV, king of Naples, 302 n. 12
Fernandes, Raymon, 3

Ferri, Enrico, 154
Feudalism, 112-13, 264
Feuer, Lewis, 324 n. 107
Fichte, 258
Flach, 97, 314 n. 41
Fleurus, 221
Fontenelle, 179, 180, 185, 187
Force (*see also* Violence): as state repression, 23, 24, 43-44, 127, 161, 170, 174, 198-99, 294 n. 67; forcing history, 50, 127-28; as *Realpolitik*, 99; as "Justice," 23, 198-99, 306 n. 52, 315 n. 56, 332 n. 11; distinguished from violence, 43-44
Force, Mlle de la, 177
Fourier, Charles, 132-34, 137, 138, 142-44, 223, 316 nn. 7 and 10-12, 317 n. 33, 345 n. 65, 361 n. 65
France: intellectual elite in, 5, 58; Revolution, 9-10, 28, 43, 44, 66-67, 73, 100, 126, 164, 194, 200, 210, 224, 237; Empire, 23-24, 41, 162, 220, 224-25, 246; Second Empire, 6, 21, 113-14, 238, 348 n. 3; origin of the Idea of Progress in, 176-91; in 1848, 101, 327 n. 160; war with Prussia (1870), 7
Franciscans, 16, 17, 28
Freedom, 4, 18, 23, 28, 50, 52, 88, 121, 139, 143, 204, 246, 250-51, 326 n. 147
Free market economy, 18-19, 35, 99, 120, 124-25, 127, 166, 206, 239, 295 n. 87, 313 n. 33, 326 n. 147
Free thinkers, 180, 183
French Workers' Party, 88
Future, vision of, 209-10 (*see also* Utopia)

G

Galileo, 179, 202, 360 n. 57
General Confederation of Labor (France), 10-11
General Strike of May 1906, 10 (*see also* Myth)
Genesis, Book of, 255
Geoffrin, Mme, 189
Geometry, 271-72, 285, 313 n. 25, 354 n. 8, 357 nn. 29 and 30, 361 nn. 60-66, 367 n. 5
German Social Democratic Party (*see also* Social democracy; Socialism), 73, 77, 106, 127, 132, 141, 148-75, 348 n. 83, 351 n. 31
God, 180-81, 191, 199, 229-30, 258-60, 360 n. 57

contradictions, 5, 13; general strike myth, 39-47; Lenin, 59; Marxist reconstruction, 30-39; myth and ideology, 36-38, 45; morality, 24; pragmatism, 55-60; definition of virtue, 26; works referred to: *L'Avenir socialiste des syndicats*, 9, 60; Preface to Colajanni, *Socialisme*, 323 n. 97, 328 n. 170; "Confessions," 7; *Contribution à l'étude profane de la Bible*, 7, 8; "Les divers types de sociétés cooperatives," 325 n. 126; Preface to Castex, *La Douleur Physique*, 345 n. 64; *Les Illusions du progrès*, 1, 2, 10, 33-37, 45, 234, 291 n. 1; *Insegnamenti sociale della economia contemporanea*, 344 n. 54; *Introduction à l'économie moderne*, 333 n. 14; *Matériaux d'une théorie du prolétariat*, 2, 7, 13, 60-61, 292 nn. 18, 20, 23, and 25; Preface to Merlino, *Formes et essences du socialisme*, 322 n. 83; *Procès de Socrate*, 7, 24-30, 303-4 n. 23; *Réflexions sur la violence*, 1, 2, 3, 10, 14, 23-24, 39-45, 57, 59, 192, 228, 291 n. 5, 302 n. 14; *La religione d'oggi*, 339 n. 11; *Saggi di critica del marxismo*, 2, 33-39, 335 n. 6, 310 n. 9, 319 n. 25; *Système historique de Renan*, 10, 328 n. 11, 333 n. 23, 335 n. 10; *De l'utilité du pragmatisme*, 2, 14, 53-58; "Vues sur les problèmes de la philosophie," 340 n. 14
Soviets, 12, 298 n. 168
Space, spatiality, 41, 48, 51, 285-86, 367 nn. 3, 7, and 8
Spencer, Herbert, 186, 316 n. 3
Spinoza, 258
Spontaneity, 220
Stammler, Rudolph, 96, 119
Standard work day, 99, 341 n. 20
State, 4, 23, 32-33, 37-38, 44, 74-75, 77, 80, 84, 93, 127, 144-45, 149, 170, 185-86, 221, 302 n. 7; ideology of, 199-200
Steam generation, 122
Strike breakers, 82
Strikes (*see also,* Myth of general strike), 86-87, 128, 305 n. 47
Subjectivism, 55-57
Sublime, the, 216, 223
Success, cult of, 64, 68-69, 213-14
Suicide, 91, 308 n. 49
Supernatural, 46
Supply and demand (*see* Free Market economy)
Surplus labor, 150

Surplus value, 32, 150-53, 169, 296 n. 87, 319 nn. 19 and 22-23
Switzerland, 251, 254
Symbolism, 41, 135, 228-31, 266-67; undermined by rationalism, 235-37
Sympathy, 194
Syndicalism, 9, 10, 11, 14, 40-46, 71-93; as *cité* (or social authority), 87-91, 102, 170, 200, 217, 256

T

Taine, 66, 189, 195, 277, 300 n. 12, 330 n. 38, 341 n. 24, 343 n. 39
Talamo, S., 95
Talmon, J. L., 3, 4
Tammany Hall, 364 n. 91
Tannenbaum, E. R., 292 n. 10
Technocrats, 6
Technology, 34, 35, 38, 52-53, 122, 128, 158, 167-68, 222, 274, 285-90, 316 n. 13, 321 n. 58
Telegraph, 122, 273
Teleology, end, 33, 106-9, 171
Temperance, 27
Terror, 40, 164-65, 255, 291
Theocritus, 354 n. 2
Theology, 40-47, 184, 281-83
Theory (*see also* Philosophy), 27-28
Thesius, temple, 266
Third Estate, 10, 78
Thirty Years' War, 99
Thomas, St., 281
Thrasybulus, 67
Time, 48
Tocqueville, Alexis de, 75, 302 n. 12, 340 n. 20
Totalitarianism, 3-5
Trades Unions, English (*see also* Great Britain), 82-84, 86-87, 108, 163, 208-9, 218, 306 nn. 58, 60, and 62, 334 n. 3
Tradition, 23, 172-73, 188, 198, 232, 254, 265-84
Tragedy, 300 n. 18
Tucker, Robert C., 295 n. 87, 324 n. 107
Turgot, 186
Tyranny: despotism, 100, 250, 327 n. 162, 348 n. 3, 351 n. 33; and democracy, 251; and royalism, 366 n. 107

U

Ultramontainism, 239
Uniformity (in Marx), 147, 151-52, 243